History of
PEEBLES
1850 - 1990

J. L. Brown and I. C. Lawson

This comprehensive work on the Royal Burgh of Peebles is both a fascinating social and local history.

Early nineteenth-century commentators described Peebles as a 'finished town' imbued with an 'air of decayed royalty' but the coming of the railways brought dynamic changes to the burgh. For once its beautiful valleys had opened up, the town soon attracted the interest of entrepreneurs from the Border woollen trade eager to exploit the abundant water-supply in the area. Peebles flourished as the Thorburn and Ballantyne Mills, with their reputation for fine cloths and tweeds, became the 'chief arteries' for a new economy and an expanded township.

Now, the railways have gone and only a much-reduced woollen industry remains. However, Peebles has since acquired a reputation for being a major conference centre and attracts a good share of tourist business, justifying the old boast of 'Peebles for Pleesure'.

Exploring the information available from the 1851 census returns and with chapters by some of today's eminent Peebleans – on everything from education to medicine, journalism to the Church – all aspects of the town's colourful past are examined in this volume. It is a fascinating history of the town – quite simply, the definitive local history.

History of
PEEBLES
1850 - 1990

J. L. Brown • I. C. Lawson

MAINSTREAM
PUBLISHING

© The Royal Burgh of Peebles Callants' Club, 1990

First published in Great Britain 1990 by
MAINSTREAM PUBLISHING COMPANY (EDINBURGH) LTD
7 Albany Street
Edinburgh EH1 3UG

ISBN 1 85158 332 7 (cloth)
ISBN 1 85158 333 5 (paper)

British Library Cataloguing in Publication Data
Brown, Joe
  A history of Peebles: 1850-1990.
  1. Scotland. Borders Region. Peebles, 1796-1815
  I. Title II. Lawson, Iain
  941.382

  ISBN 1 85158 332 7
  ISBN 1 85158 333 5 pbk

The publishers gratefully acknowledge the financial assistance
of the Common Good Fund of the Royal Burgh of Peebles.

Cover photographs by R. B. Robb and E. R. Stevenson

Typeset in 11/12 Baskerville by Becee Typesetting Services
Printed in Great Britain by Mackays of Chatham Plc, Kent

Contents

Acknowledgments

I am greatly indebted to I. C. Lawson, J. Gordon Fyfe and E. L. Smith for their ready acceptance to be members of the editorial board and to have had their advice and guidance on the structure and content of the History and to gain from their extensive knowledge about Peebles. Their undoubted enthusiasm has sustained the project and brought it to a successful conclusion. However, with great sadness I record the untimely death in December 1989 of my co-author, Iain Lawson. His passing was a great loss, but his love of Peebles and its history are to be read in his chapters and they are a fitting memorial to a 'worthy' Peeblean and local historian. I also record my warmest thanks to my wife, Mabel Brown; although not an official member of the editorial board, she was always there to give help and encouragement.

I gratefully acknowledge my indebtedness to the distinguished contributors: E. L. Smith, J. Gordon Fyfe, Dr R. B. Wilson, the Revd D. C. MacFarlane, R. Montgomery and E. Laverock; Michael Lister for his bibliography; and R. B. Robb and E. R. Stevenson for advising and providing the photographs. Each one made his contribution for the love of Peebles and not one has been financially reimbursed for the work done in the preparation of this book. Equally, Mrs Rosemary Shaw (Blyth Bridge) has made a valuable contribution by producing typed chapters for Iain Lawson and Ted Smith, tackling the drafts with enthusiasm and asking only to be of assistance to the project.

Miss Sheena Stavert, editor of the *Peeblesshire News*, must also be thanked, as well as the proprietor and staff of the newspaper for allowing ready access to the files of the *Peeblesshire News* and the *Peeblesshire Advertiser*. These two newspapers are indeed the local history books that contain the unabridged story about the social life and events of the town and they are extensively used to tell about the past 140 years.

There are many others who unhesitatingly helped in so many ways: Mrs Rosemary Hannay, curator of the Museum in Peebles; Paul Taylor, librarian; Pieter J. van Dijk, Peebles Hotel Hydropathic Limited; Riddell Graham, Border Tourist Board; George Barbour and the staff at the Scottish Records Office (Edinburgh); Miss Linda Pender, Scottish Courts Administration (Edinburgh); Mike Greenwood and John Hutton, British Railways Property Board (Glasgow); Forbes Alexander (Edinburgh), Ex-Cornet Allan Beveridge, J. D. Birchall, Ian Brown, James Brown, Neil J. Brown, Christopher Buchan, David Clyde, Ian Curry (Edinburgh), Sandy Finlayson, Arthur Foster, Graham H. T. Garvie, Hugh T. Gilmore, Hugh Gilmore, Peter Gilmore, Mrs Evelyn Gordon, Roy Hamilton (Rutherglen), Douglas Harper, Willie Hennigan (Sheffield), David Hoyle, Atholl Innes (Galashiels), John Ker, Ronald Kerr, A. J. Litster, Bill Lynn (Birtley, Newcastle-upon-Tyne), Mrs Joan Pascal, Graham McGrath, John McOwan, Dr J. McPhater, Dr R. S. Miles, James Renwick, Jack Roney, Mr and Mrs Rowe (Leicester), R. Renwick Sanderson, Monty Smith (Glasgow), Robert Swan, D. Hunter Thorburn, George D. Thorburn, Ex-Cornet Turnbull, Douglas W. Veitch, Ex-Provost A. W. Walker and William Watson.

The financial help extended by the Royal Burgh of Peebles Common Good Fund is most gratefully acknowledged. In thanking all the Councillors concerned — in particular the former Provost of Peebles, Councillor A. W. Walker — I pay tribute to their ready understanding and support that enable this History to be published in this the Anniversary year. Their financial help enables the book to be a viable publishing proposition and to keep the price of the book at a reasonable level.

I am proud that the Royal Burgh of Peebles Callants' Club have accepted the invitation to become the holders of the copyright of the *History of Peebles: 1850 – 1990* and that they will repay the Common Good Fund a proportion of its financial subvention from the royalties that they receive in the years ahead.

J.L.B.

Contributors

JOSEPH LAWLER (Joe) BROWN, CBE, TD, BA (Open), FRSA, CBIM

Born in Glasgow 1921 and residing in Peebles from 1921 to 1950, he started his newspaper career with the *Peeblesshire Advertiser* in 1936 as a 'printer's devil' and, after serving as a local 'territorial' with the 8th and 7/9th Battalions The Royal Scots (The Royal Regiment) 1939-46, he held a number of executive posts in the newspaper industry, his last appointment being Chairman and Managing Director of *The Birmingham Post & Mail Ltd.* His directorships included the Press Association (Chairman, 1972) and Reuters Ltd and his other posts included: President of the Newspaper Society, 1976; President of Birmingham Chamber of Industry and Commerce, 1979; Warden of Neidpath, 1983; Callant; Life Member of the Court of the University of Birmingham; Commander, Order of Merit, of the Italian Republic and Deputy Lieutenant of the County of the West Midlands since 1975.

IAIN CAMPBELL LAWSON, BA (Hons) (Open), FSA (Scotland)

Born Glasgow and educated Glasgow High School, on leaving school he served as an officer in Palestine and Korea with The Royal Scots (The Royal Regiment). On leaving the Army he held a number of administrative appointments in Glasgow and Peebles including Administrative Assistant at the Peebles High School. He died in December 1989. Author of *Drives in the Scottish Borders* (1982), he also acted as adviser to Peebles Civic Society for their publication *Peebles Town Walk* — a tour-guide of the royal burgh. He was an acknowledged authority on military history (American and Scottish).

11

EDWARD L. (Ted.) SMITH, BA (Hons), Dip Educ, Bristol

A retired teacher, he was Head of the history department and sometime organiser of adult evening classes, Peebles High School (1946-77). A former member/vice-chairman of March Riding Committee, for nine years he was Editor of the Beltane Programme, as well as being Warden of Neidpath (1969), President Tweeddale Society, member of Callants Club and Guildry Corporation, and Honorary President of the PRFC.

JAMES GORDON FYFE (Lawyer — Writer to the Signet)

Born in 1918 in Peebles, the son of Alexander Fyfe, lawyer, he was educated at George Watsons and Edinburgh University (MA, LLB). He served in the Royal Artillery (1939-46) and then returned to Peebles to join the firm of Blackwood & Smith WS, in 1948. Latterly the Senior Partner, he retired from full-time practice in 1983, though continuing as Consultant until 1988. He was awarded the Territorial Decoration (TD) (1956), appointed a Deputy Lieutenant (1966), and Warden of Neidpath (1970).

Dr ROBIN B. WILSON, MBE, FRCP

Born Peebles in 1908, and educated at Peebles and Glasgow Academy, he was a general medical practitioner in Peebles from 1935 to 1973, when he was awarded the MBE. He was Warden of Neidpath in 1961. He died in May 1990.

The Revd DAVID C. MacFARLANE, MA

Minister of The Old Parish Church of Peebles — its twenty-third since the Reformation — he was educated at the High School of Glasgow and the University of Glasgow before he came to Peebles in 1970. In addition to his considerable professional and pastoral duties in Peebles and surrounding parishes, he has a wide and varied involvement in the whole community and area. A Callant and member of the Guildry Corporation, he was President of the Rotary Club of Peebles in 1974-75, and Warden of Neidpath in 1984.

RAE MONTGOMERY

Born Edinburgh in 1937 and educated at Melrose and St Bees, Cumbria, he is a project manager with British Rail, where he has worked for over thirty-two years, and is interested in the history of the Borders and the railways in Scotland and the North-East of England.

EDWARD LAVEROCK, MA, LLB

Born in Dunlop, Ayrshire, in 1919, he was educated at Hutchesons Grammar School, Glasgow, and the University of Glasgow. Retired as Senior Partner of J. & W. Buchan, Solicitors, in 1986, he was Town Clerk of Peebles (1948-75), Procurator Fiscal of the County of Peebles (1949-76), Joint Manager, Peebles Building Society (1954-79), Honorary Burgess (Freeman) of the Royal Burgh of Peebles (1975), Honorary Sheriff (1983) and Warden of Neidpath (1975).

MICHAEL LISTER, BA, Dip. Lib

Born in Peebles in 1962, he was educated locally and graduated from Stirling University, later training as a librarian in Aberdeen. He has been a lecturer at the Scottish College of Textiles in Galashiels since 1988.

BERT ROBB and ERIC STEVENSON have gathered together an outstanding collection of old photographs, plates and negatives of Peebles and Tweeddale and they have published a selection from their extensive archives: *Glimpses of Old Peebles* (1987) and *Glimpses of Old Innerleithen and Traquair* (1989).

Introduction

When man first came to our valley, historians conjecture. But having entered it, they held fast and to the earliest of our forbears we owe our heritage of a valley, unsurpassed and of those comforting, surrounding, guarding, protecting hills. The past is not the past but a continuing stream. Their spirit is born within us and proudly we, too, hand their trust — our heritage — on to each succeeding generation. Centuries have flitted by — fierce times, fighting times and hard times — but none has ever driven us from our door.

IT IS FITTING that these words, spoken by William Kerr as Warden of Neidpath in 1959, should introduce the *History of Peebles: 1850-1990*. Many of the years the volume will cover were avidly and expertly chronicled, week-by-week, by William (Will) Kerr when he was Editor of the *Peeblesshire News*. He wrote with warmth and affection about Peebles and Peebleans, and in 1959 he looked back to the years of the second half of the nineteenth century and spoke of the 'torch of progress' that had livened up the town, as the valley between Hamilton Hill and Venlaw opened up with the advent of the railway in Peebles and the mills that became the 'chief arteries' for the town's future.

Peebles is now without its railways and Tweedside and Damdale Mills have disappeared. It would have seemed incredible to Peebles men and women of the first half of the twentieth century that this could happen; they could not have imagined life without them. Yet, in 1990, 'Grandmother Venlaw' will not be displeased with the Peebles and the Peebleans she now looks upon.

In commemorating the 850th Anniversary of the granting by King David I of Scotland (1124-1153) of the Charter which made Peebles a Royal Burgh, it is fitting that we record these changes and chronicle how the Royal and Ancient Burgh and its succeeding generations have cherished their heritage. The volume seeks to be a worthy complement to J. Walter Buchan's *A History of Peeblesshire* (1925, 1927).

The *History of Peebles: 1850-1990* is dedicated to the men and women who served during the Second World War and to commemorate the Fallen Sons and Daughters of Peebles and remember them with grateful pride.

March 1990

Part One

1850 – 1900

CHAPTER 1

Industry, Trade and Commerce

IT WAS A significant event in the history of the Royal and Ancient Burgh when, on 4 July 1855, the Peebles railway carried its first passengers to and from Edinburgh on the newly-opened local line which linked into the North British Company's railway system at Eskbank. This connection was supplemented nine years later by the Symington, Biggar and Broughton railway extension to Peebles, providing the town with a railway link to Glasgow via the Caledonian Railway's network. However, the full potential of the 'coming of the railway' to Peebles was not fully realised until the Peebles railway extension to Innerleithen was further developed to provide a connection to Galashiels in June 1866; an event that truly made Peebles the centre of an important railway network that was to play a major role in the development of the burgh.

The *Peeblesshire Advertiser* informed its readers in July 1853 that the Railway Bill had been passed, commenting: 'This is a great era for Peebles, and we anticipate that it is the commencement of a career of prosperity of which we can at present form a very vague conception.' The *History of Peebles: 1850 – 1990* is about these times and the events which followed, from the coming of the railways to their closing nearly a century later. It is the story of the tweed-mills and their near virtual disappearance, in terms of capacity to provide employment, and how the town has fared with the loss of these 'engines of improvement' that our forefathers welcomed when Peebles was described as 'being at its deadest'.

It is clear that the innovation of the railways had an immensely stimulating effect on the whole of the Scottish economy and that was certainly true in terms of 'sparking off' the development and expansion of the burgh of Peebles. In the decades after the coming of the railways, it was no longer a place that could be referred to as 'quieter than the grave'.

PART I: 1850 – 1900

The often quoted Lord Cockburn had something apt to say about most Scottish towns. He was referring to Edinburgh when he suggested it 'was as quiet as the grave, or even as Peebles';[1] Dundee he dismissed as 'the palace of blackguardism'. Certainly the memoirs of William and Robert Chambers support his view that, in the early nineteenth century, Peebles was indeed a very quiet place and had 'little advanced from the conditions in which it had mainly rested for several hundred years'.

It was the county town of one of the four slowest shires in Scotland in terms of population growth during the period 1755 to 1821. At that period, when Scotland's population rose from 1.26 million to just over 1.6 million, a rise of 27 per cent, Peeblesshire only increased by 12.8 per cent, and whilst neighbouring Lanarkshire trebled its population through the development of new industries, Peeblesshire continued to be a shire mainly concerned with farming.[2]

Peebles was at one time an important meeting place for the growers from the east and the dealers from the west, providing a profitable market for the town. That was before the building of good roads across Soutra and the opening of the canals between Edinburgh and Glasgow in the late eighteenth century, however. Once the Forth and Clyde Canal opened in 1790, the farmers in the south began to send their corn to Dalkeith for shipment on the canal. It was 'with oratorical enthusiasm' that the toasts to the trade of the town would urge the need for a good weekly corn market with a 'row of farmers' carts laden with grain lining every side of every market day with plenty of merchants going to buy'. It was naturally assumed, when the railways were first mooted, that Peebles would re-establish itself as a market-place for grain. This was not to be the case, but the failure to achieve a thriving market for grain was more than compensated by the other beneficial opportunities that followed in the wake of the railways.

The River Tweed and its tributary, Peebles Water, better known to many generations as the 'Cuddy', were recognised by the town council as assets in their endeavour to attract the attention of 'manufacturers, capitalists and others' to the possibility of setting up a manufactory in the burgh. The town council was remarkably enterprising at this time. They not only advertised these assets but took steps in 1829 to develop them, constructing a cauld at the lower part of the Minister's Pool to ensure there would be sufficient water to drive the corn-mills. They also showed great initiative in 1828, when they readily gave permission for the burgh's streets to be opened up for gas pipes to be laid, making it possible for a newly-established private gas company to provide lighting for the streets, shops and dwelling-houses.

However, it was the combination of the two rivers, with their facility to provide water-power, and the advent of the railways, with their communication links to markets, that attracted to the town a share of the beneficial inventions of the industrial revolution. These ingenuous inventions, created for the cotton industry by Hargreaves, Arkwright, Crompton and Cartwright, in time became adapted for the carding, spinning and weaving of woollens, bringing about the 'modern' woollen-mill with its machinery driven by water- or steam-power. When these developments were utilised in Peebles with the establishment of the Tweedside and Damdale Mills, the town became renowned for the manufacture of quality woollen cloths and tweeds, rather than its eighteenth-century reputation as a centre for the marketing of grain, increasing the burgh's population from 1,982, in 1851, to 3,495 in 1881 — an increase of 76 per cent in just thirty years.

Peebles was not an early starter in the speculative venture of acquiring a railway system. It only became a railway town some thirty years after George Stephenson's engine, *Locomotive*, had run at a speed of twelve miles per hour on the Stockton to Darlington railway, and twenty-five years after the practicability of steam locomotion had been accepted when the *Rocket* engine reached a speed of nearly twenty-nine miles per hour. Despite the fever of speculation which had swept through Britain after the Liverpool to Manchester railway had made a large profit, there was insufficient local interest during the peak periods of investment between 1835 to 1837 and from 1845 to 1847. There were, however, three unsuccessful attempts made by private enterprise groups to bring the railway to the area. The first, in 1810, was based on a plan prepared from a survey by Thomas Telfer to provide a tram-line for horse-drawn carriages from Glasgow to Berwick via Peebles. The earliest railway in Scotland was based on a similar system which conveyed coal, timber and grain between Kilmarnock and Troon.[3] Another proposal was made in 1836 and led to a more developed plan in 1845/6 which only just failed because of insufficient local financial backing. Renewed efforts were made again just before 1850 when it was discovered that the route for an Edinburgh to Hawick line was going to by-pass the town and that Peebles would be the last county south of the Tay without a railway link.

PART I: 1850 – 1900

The history of the two successful railway ventures are recorded in Chapter 20, and it will suffice to mention that by 1864 there were two Peebles stations connected to a railway network that was in the process of extending into every part of Britain. These lines covered 6,621 miles in 1850 and, as Peebles became linked to the network, it reached 15,537 miles by 1870 and over 23,000 miles by 1910.

The train journey from Peebles to Edinburgh took ninety minutes and there were several daily trains available each way. The number of railway passengers in the first four months after the line was opened was about 40,000.[4] Only seventy years before, in the 1780s, the journey was chiefly made on horseback and 'so insecure was the road on account of highwaymen that usually several persons arranged to ride in company, and in defence almost everyone carried holster-pistols.'[5] It was often the case that men and women walked the distance to Edinburgh and then back to Peebles. This practice continued even after the availability of coach transportation and in the biography of Professor John Veitch it is mentioned that, when he had entered Edinburgh University in 1845, his mother did the journey of 'full twenty miles to Edinburgh on foot on more than one occasion'.

The earliest system of passenger service to Edinburgh was William Wilson's Caravan consisting of a two-wheeled vehicle drawn by a single horse which left Peebles at eight o'clock in the morning and arrived at Edinburgh Grassmarket at six o'clock at night. The nine-to-ten-hour journey was broken 'wi' a drap of kail from Tibby of Howgate'. The 'Caravan' was superseded in about 1806 by the 'Fly', which took half the time, reducing the journey to five hours. It was an old post-chaise which was drawn by two horses and was 'more genteel in appearance . . . green pickit out wi' red, three yellow wheels and a black one'.[6] It also carried mailbags and 'carriers' to take remittances and cheques to the banks in Edinburgh. In 1825 it was replaced by a service of stagecoaches which left the Harrow Inn (now the County Hotel) in the High Street and would stop at the Tron Kirk and the corner of Princes Street in Edinburgh; the journey took just three hours and you could return to Peebles on the same day. The coach carried six passengers and the fare was five shillings (25p). There were connections in Edinburgh to other parts of the country as more than fifty stagecoaches left the city daily; ten were available to Glasgow and six to London.

Pennycook & M'Pherson, as well as Croall & Co., ran services but eventually Croall dominated and they bought up the opposition, although it is reported that Croall then put up the fares and operated only one coach per day and at such an hour that prevented anyone from Peebles using it except at great inconvenience. An appointment in Edinburgh for half an hour on a Wednesday forenoon required the traveller to leave on Tuesday at 4 p.m., staying in Edinburgh all Wednesday and returning to Peebles on the Thursday morning. The presentation of a brace of whips from the inhabitants of Peebles to the coachman, James Stewart, for his 'general good conduct and obliging manner to the passengers under his care', shows that, despite the inconvenient time-table, there was indeed high regard for an essential service that operated right up to the day before the railway line was opened.

The railways were obviously welcomed for the tremendous improvement they made to the convenience of travelling. It became relatively easy for a wider section of the community to travel to distant places and Peebles also gained through having many more visitors.

Perhaps the most immediate benefit that became apparent to the majority of townspeople and tradesmen was the substantially reduced cost of transportation. It was claimed that the charge for carrying a ton of goods from Edinburgh to Peebles by horse-drawn cart was 'greater than would have been the freight by sea or rail from Edinburgh to London . . . coal was so extravagantly dear in the district, as almost to be placed beyond the reach of the humbler classes.' The railway brought about a reduction in the price of coal in Peebles to about half the rate it was previously, with the charge for carrying a ton of goods from Edinburgh reducing from 20s (£1) to 9s 9d (49p). The cost of transporting a truck-load of cattle became as low as 5s (25p) and just 7s (35p) for sheep.[7]

There was no sudden 'take-off' in the development of the town with the coming of the railways but with the advantage of hindsight, we can now readily identify that the major benefit was the impetus it gave to the early signs of enterprise that were already astir in Peebles. Banking was the first commercial activity in a chain of events that contributed to the economic growth of the town. Although there were three banks already established in the town (one bank agency lasting only seventeen years, from 1840 to 1857), the other two national branch-banks that were to become an integral part of modern Peebles, the Bank of Scotland and the Union Bank of Scotland, did not appear until later on.

PART I: 1850 – 1900

The British Linen Co. (later to be known as The British Linen Bank) had taken the lead in the trend of 'branch-banking' and had selected Peebles for one of its twenty-one branches that it had established throughout Scotland by 1830. Peebles, therefore, got its first bank in 1825 when the British Linen Co. opened its branch at Glencorse House in the Northgate. The first agent was John Welsh, WS, of Mossfennan, and he was succeeded by the partners of Stuart & Blackwood, WS, in 1843 which later became Blackwood & Smith, this link being maintained for 120 years. The bank transferred to new premises at 39 High Street in 1887 and remained there until 1965, when it was amalgamated with the Bank of Scotland.[8]

The second branch-bank in the town was established by Walter Thorburn when he became the local agent for the City of Glasgow Bank in 1840, relinquishing this in 1857 when he became the agent for the Bank of Scotland. The City of Glasgow Bank was started up in 1839 but failed in 1878, and this had serious consequences for a number of stockholders in Peebles. A local public meeting was called and a committee appointed to raise subscriptions in aid of a fund for the relief of those affected by this calamity.[9]

The third bank to open up in 1846 was a new type of local savings bank which accepted small deposits and this was an improved facility for local tradesmen and townspeople. Robert Stirling was the Treasurer. It originally operated between ten and eleven o'clock each forenoon at the offices of the British Linen Bank at Glencorse House, taking deposits of not less than one shilling.

The Bank of Scotland (whose first agent was Walter Thorburn, succeeded by his son, Robert Thorburn) was set up in premises on the north side of the High Street in 1857. Ten years afterwards, the Union Bank of Scotland (later called the Commercial Bank of Scotland, before being known as The Royal Bank of Scotland) moved into premises in the centre of the High Street and subsequently removed to the west end. The first agent was John Bathgate and later, in 1881, John Buchan took over (grandfather of John Buchan, the first Lord Tweedsmuir).

These early signs of commercial activity befitted the status of a county town, but the economic roots of expansion lay in the development of its textile industry through the interest taken in Peebles by entrepreneurs from the Galashiels and Hawick woollen trade after the coming of Peebles railways. Earlier, in 1829, Mr James Dickson, the founder of the well-known Galashiels woollen firm of Arthur Dickson & Co., took over the tenancy of the old corn-mills on Peebles Water and set up a 'manufacturing house' which 'finished' locally-woven blue cloth of a common kind and also materials for plaids. James Dickson earned the distinction for Peebles as the first place in Scotland to produce 'fancy trouserings' woven in the shepherd-tartan check and these were hailed as a great success in London.

There had been a local association with the weaving of cloth long before Dickson had set up his 'manufacturing house'. It can be traced back to 1480 when the first waulk-mill was built at the east end of Tweed Green. The waulking (or fulling, as it is now called) thickened or made the woven cloth more firm or compact. The weavers of Peebles were certainly a 'trading craft' since 1563 and the earliest incorporation recorded in the royal burgh. They 'enjoyed the exclusive privilege of manufacturing' within the burgh and no one was allowed to work in the craft as a master till he was a burgess and had been passed as worthy and had sufficient work looms.[10] David Loch, General Inspector of Fisheries in Scotland, noted in 1776 that Peebles had forty looms which were employed in the making of coarse woollen goods. This was the same number of looms that Kelso had, but Galashiels only had thirty whilst Hawick had as many as fifty-six looms employed on 'jobbing' work.[11]

In addition to the weaving of woollens, Peebles produced linen and cotton. In the eighteenth century, cotton manufacturing was introduced into the town by William Chambers, a deacon of the weavers' craft in 1703, and the grandfather of William and Robert Chambers. When cotton was in great demand, William Chambers employed about a hundred looms. Therefore, it is interesting to note that with the development of the modern woollen industry in the nineteenth century, there has been a continuous link with weaving in Peebles from medieval times through to the present time (1990) and with the spinning of yarn up to the time when the Tweedside Mill was destroyed by fire in February 1965.

The first 'modern' woollen-manufacturing mill came into being the year after the opening of the railway, when, in 1856, Thomas Dickson took over the corn-mill at the Tweedside, south of Castlehill. It was rebuilt and developed as a 'factory' with machinery driven by water-power, having acquired the feu for the use of the waterfall. Within two years the Tweedside Mill was acquired by Laing & Irvine, who were woollen merchants in Hawick. William

Irvine told the Duke of Buccleuch that the reason for setting up the mill in Peebles was due to the want of sufficient land in Hawick. He added that the 'warehouse must remain in Hawick as no buyers visit Peebles, where there is nothing to induce them but our own solitary factory'.

The first loom of the Laing & Irvine factory in Peebles was brought into operation in 1860 by John Cumming, who resided in the Old Town, and the first piece of tweed manufactured by power-loom left the mill on the 7 March 1860 and was sold at the shop of Messrs Thorburn & Co. The spinning operation at the Tweedside Mill was carried on by Robert Todd, who was provost from 1870 to 1875.[12]

Laing & Irvine started the Tweedside Mill with six looms and planned that these were to be followed by four more looms and then by two more each week until a total of twenty-six were in operation, employing fifty workers. This was the scheme for the upper flat of the mill and the lower flat was to be developed later. A water-wheel, with a diameter of fifteen feet and a width of twelve feet, was built to supply the power.[13] This local initiative was one of seventy-two such factories that were in operation in Scotland in 1861 when there were eighty-two factories with 1,069 power-looms.[14]

The Tweedside Mill was eventually bought over by Messrs Walter Thorburn & Bros. in 1875, as Laing & Irvine had not been successful and the company became bankrupt. It was Thorburn's second mill, as they had built Damdale Mill in 1869 on the site of the eighteenth-century waulk-mill situated beside Peebles Water. The March Street Mills were established by D. Ballantyne & Co. in 1885 and consisted of a series of single-storeyed buildings that were equipped with electric lighting, as this wonderful, innovative source of power had now been brought into the county for the first time.

Another important local enterprise, connected with the woollen trade, started up in 1860 when Walter Thorburn developed from selling tweed and cloth in his shop in the High Street and established a 'wholesale' tweed business in a warehouse next to the Green Tree Hotel under the name of Thorburn & Co. It later became the firm of Lowe, Donald & Co. The business developed into international markets in 1881 and, in March 1897, opened a magnificent warehouse in Station Road (now Dean Park). As a company for the distribution of woollens, it was a most successful venture, which brought great credit and international recognition to Peebles. It ultimately established subsidiary warehouses in London, Paris, Budapest, Buenos Aires and Canada; and a separate firm of the same name became established in Boston, USA. It was a far-sighted move that showed a belief in the future of Peebles and its potential to develop a worthwhile woollen industry.

Peebles owes much to the enterprise of two families: the Thorburns and the Ballantynes. Walter Thorburn was born in Holylee in 1801 and came to Peebles in 1821. He started in business as a general merchant in a small shop on the south side of the High Street which he sold to Melrose, Menzies & Co. in 1866, six years after he had successfully established the tweed warehouse. He was provost of Peebles from 1836 to 1838.

Two of Walter Thorburn's sons, Michael G. Thorburn (1851 – 1934), later Sir Michael of Glenormiston, and Walter Thorburn (1842 – 1908) later Sir Walter of Kerfield left their father's business to set up the firm of Walter Thorburn and Bros., which established Damdale Mills. Later, in 1903, it became a limited liability company under the name of Walter Thorburn & Bros. Ltd. A third son, Major William Thorburn of Craigerne (1847 – 1926) became head of Lowe, Donald & Co. Robert Thorburn, the eldest son (1841 – 1911) was a solicitor and banker and senior partner in Thorburn & Lyon, the Peebles firm of solicitors.

The Ballantyne family had been associated with textiles since the seventeenth century and their descendants can be traced to William Ballantyne, a Galashiels weaver who was born in 1650. A descendant, Henry Ballantyne (1802 – 65) rented Caerlee Mill, Innerleithen, in 1820 – 9; this was the first woollen-mill built in the Borders. In 1829 he founded the firm of Henry Ballantyne & Sons at Walkerburn. Three of his sons founded the firm of Ballantyne Bros. and built the Waverley Mills at Innerleithen, David Ballantyne (1826 – 1912), the eldest son, establishing D. Ballantyne & Co. at the March Street Mills, Peebles.

Peebles added to its status when it became a town with its own local newspaper which was started in 1845 by Andrew Murray, a publisher and printer of newspapers in Edinburgh. However, the success of the *Peeblesshire Monthly Advertiser and Tweedside Journal* was largely due to Alexander Scott who became the newspaper's 'local agent'. 'Booky' Scott (he was a bookseller) was the one most likely to have foreseen that the town had potential to support its own newspaper, already having two banks, J. Dickson's 'manufacturing house', and, in a short period of time, a railway.

PART I: 1850 – 1900

'Booky' Scott got off to a good start with his first main news report which concerned the launching of a subscription list to raise a fund for the 'Improvements of Peebles'. The report outlined a programme of developments that were aimed to improve the streets, pavements, entrances to the town, water-supply, drains, and the levelling and beautifying of the Tweed Green — at a cost of £1,100. Peebles already had a small printing press which was first brought into the town in the early 1800s by Alexander Elder, a bookseller and stationer in the High Street; it was this business that 'Booky' Scott acquired on the owner's death. However, the town did not have a newspaper printing-press and William Chambers, who was always anxious to further the town's interests, took the initiative with Scott to have a newspaper press installed in Peebles in March 1853.

It was at this time that Robert Stirling took over the business, as the Scott family had decided to emigrate to America. Having taken over as 'local agent', he immediately reversed the roles and became the publisher, appointing Andrew Murray as 'agent' for the newspaper in Scotland's capital city. From March 1853 the *Peeblesshire Monthly Advertiser* became truly a local newspaper: published by Robert Stirling with his editorial office in the shop where Sandy Elder had first installed his folio press in 1814 and had produced the first book printed in Peebles; printed for the first time in premises on the south side of the High Street.

Once the town had its own newspaper printing-press it seemed to encourage the appearance of more local newspapers. There followed another monthly publication, the *Peeblesshire County Newspaper and General Advertiser*. This was not successful and soon became amalgamated with Robert Stirling's newspaper which then became a weekly publication with the title *Peeblesshire Advertiser and County Newspaper*. Later, Allan Smyth started up the *Peeblesshire Herald* but it was only published for a number of weeks during 1878. He then became a partner in the publishing firm of Watson & Smyth and had a long association with the *Peeblesshire Advertiser*. In 1887 J. A. Kerr's *The Peebles Commercial News* appeared as a 'gratis' weekly publication, with the content of its four quarto pages being mainly advertisements, but in due course it developed into a newspaper with the title *Peeblesshire News*. Both the *News* and the *Advertiser* were to exist side-by-side in rivalry for nearly sixty years, faithfully recording events and commenting on the town's affairs. In 1954 the *Advertiser* ceased publication but fortunately the *News* is still being published. (The history of the local press and media is given in Chapter 19.)

The 'oratorical enthusiasm' of the earlier years that predicted that all would be well if Peebles could re-establish itself as a market-place, was quickly put to the test when, three months after the opening of the Peebles to Edinburgh line, a market for grain and other farm produce was held every Tuesday from eleven to four o'clock. It started with great success as almost seventy carts of grain came into the town, quickly bought by buyers from various districts.

In 1860 the market was replaced by the Corn Exchange which was built behind the Old Town Hall in the High Street, but the vision of Peebles as a market-place of old did not materialise. Just as the canal system changed the scheme of things, so did rail transit. The Corn Exchange became obsolete and it was taken over for other purposes. The building exists today, with its bell that many old Peebleans believed came from the Old Tollbooth that stood at the foot of the Briggait and where the town council met in the fifteenth century. It was later referred to as the 'labour bell' and in 1885 was rung at six and ten o'clock in the morning and at two and eight in the evening.

The local monthly newspaper on 1 January 1856, reviewing the impact of the railway on the life of the town during its first six months of operation, reported 'thousands of visitors' had been to the town during the previous five months. The year before, there had been about 250 'strangers' and it was anticipated that there would be about 500 visitors rather than the 'thousands' that had eventually come. It was even boastfully suggested that 'Peebles is becoming every season more fashionable'.

The railway had also opened up a market for the county's timber, the purchasers being mainly from Lanarkshire. There were reports about increased building activity as well, and the local monthly paper had expressed concern that 'house rents were rising considerably', adding that 'there was quite a furore for house accommodation, as land had become more valuable'. It noted, however, that 'coals and minerals were now cheaper'.

'Growth' was the key-word in the years that followed. The success of the local woollen-mills provided more job opportunities and the population was increasing through migration into the town to take up the work, creating a pressing need for more houses to be built. The success of the Damdale Mill is referred to in glowing terms by the Peebles Gutterbluid Club in their records for 1873 as 'the spirited firm of Thorburn & Co.', making advances that 'bid fair to place it on a level with the largest manufacturers in the south of Scotland'.

29

They fully lived up to that expectation by taking over the Tweedside Mill in 1875 and, a few years later in 1881, they enlarged their Damdale Mill and then in 1917 acquired the adjoining small mill known as Damcroft for use as a wool store. The *Peeblesshire Advertiser,* commenting in 1879 said:

> '[The burgh had] made progress during the past year. Whilst other towns suffered from great depression in trade, the commercial character of Peebles has at least been maintained. For a few months there was a lull in the manufacturing industry; but as the cold months set in, trade was again in full swing. Building operations have been carried on in an extensive scale . . . in the neighbourhood of the Old Town a new town has been created.'

Perhaps the most significant building to be erected, and a project that was to have a more lasting impact on the town than the local railways and two of its woollen-mills, was the building of the Peebles Hydropathic Establishment. Originally the plan was to build a 'hydro' round a spring at Innerleithen but the plan was changed and it was built in 1878-80 on the side of Venlaw Hill so that it could provide for 'the reception of visitors and patients'.[15] Involving an investment of upwards of £80,000, it was a tremendous act of confidence in Peebles and demonstrated that it was an up-and-coming town worthy of a venture of this importance.

The Hydropathic Establishment was described rather proudly in the Gutterbluid Club notes as a 'handsome palatial edifice . . . in point of style, position and surroundings', second to none of its kind in the United Kingdom.[16] The original and beautiful building was built with red sandstone from the Corncockle Quarry near Lockerbie but was unfortunately destroyed by fire in 1905. It was replaced by a magnificent Georgian Hydropathic in 1907, being designed by James Miller who was the architect for the Glasgow Exhibition in 1901.

The Peebles Hotel Hydro quickly established an identity for the town as a leading centre for visitors to the Scottish Borders. It has virtually outlived the other major factors that contributed to the growth of Peebles in the nineteenth century. Since the end of the Second World War, the Hydro's enterprise and flair for attracting visitors has inspired the town in its development and enabled it to take advantage of the wealth that can be created by tourists coming to this beautiful town: 'A beauty so elusive, so varied, and so full of sweet surprises that it can win the heart of the most jaded traveller or weary sightseer.'[17]

It was fitting that the foundation stone of the Hydropathic Establishment was laid by Dr William Chambers of Glenormiston, an outstanding and distinguished son of Peebles and the town's greatest benefactor. In his address that Saturday morning on 24 August 1878, he said that Peebles would have the largest and most magnificent of the sixteen hydropathic establishments located throughout the country. He particularly pointed out that the 'tradesmen of Peebles would need to be on their mettle to supply the general wants and keep pace with the demands of the commissariat'.

As a county town in the 1880s, there were available a wide range of suppliers and services that indicated a lively degree of commercial activity. However, in the early years of the nineteenth century there were no shops as we now recognise them; merchants and tradesmen vied for business from their own dwellings, each opening the top half of their front door when ready for customers, each invariably sporting the merchants' sign or that of their trade guild.[18] Robert Stirling's newspaper commented in April 1853:

> We recollect witnessing within the last thirty years the principal streets of Peebles lined with stalls, where shoemakers, coopers and other craftsmen from a distance exhibited and sold their wares. Good roads and easy access to the burgh have rendered it more convenient for the customer to meet his necessities as they arise, and hence traffickers from a distance have given up attending our markets and to replace street trade our shops have increased in accommodation and extent of stock.

A year later, the newspaper was suggesting that the number of shops was altogether absurd and that competition was too great, quoting as an example, that there were nineteen grocers in the High Street. In 1867 the number had reduced to thirteen and seven of these were also spirit dealers.

Slater published a directory in 1867 which contained five and a half pages about Peebles and its neighbouring parishes. Directories compiled in the nineteenth century are generally regarded as a reliable source of information, although it has to be borne in mind that keeping details up-to-date must have presented a very difficult task, as communications were slow and costly. The directory's reference to Peebles started with a quite disparaging comment about the town: 'Although profiting by manufactures or external trade, Peebles takes a station inferior to many towns of less magnitude, and not so happily favoured by situation.' It has to be understood that

31

PART I: 1850 – 1900

Peebles in 1867 was just at the beginning of its period of expansion. Although it had by now two railway stations, four banks and a local newspaper, it has to be remembered that the 'modernised' Tweedside Mill had only come into operation in 1860, and the mills at Damdale and March Street were not yet in existence. Slater correctly recorded, however, that there was some external trade and this was very likely the famous 'fancy trouserings' supplied by J. Dickson's 'manufacturing house'.

The directory shows that Peebles, like most towns in Scotland, had a brewery. In 1867 it was located at Saint Michael's Wynd with Robert and John Potts as the brewers. Almost a century before that William Ker of Kerfield, who was provost of Peebles from 1773 to 1778, erected 'one of the completest breweries and distilleries' and was reputed to have made a new and useful improvement in the art of brewing.[19] The directory shows just one cooper — James Robertson, who had premises in the Old Town — but in 1851 there had been three.

Seven inns were listed in 1867 but specific reference is made to the town having 'four good inns'. The Tontine is specially mentioned and John Smith listed as the licensee of this 'posting-house' in the High Street. Hugh Mitchell is shown as the licensee of the Cross Keys, or Cleikum, in the Northgate, the town's oldest inn, being built about 1653; it was originally the town house of the Williamsons of Cardrona. Marion Ritchie was the worthy landlady at the end of the eighteenth and the beginning of the nineteenth centuries, and is generally regarded as the prototype of 'Meg Dods' in Sir Walter Scott's novel, *St Ronan's Well*. The other inns listed in the directory are: the Tweedbridge (with landlord William Crosbie), whose original building had to be demolished and a new inn built to allow for the widening of the Tweed Bridge in 1899; the Crown (run by Margaret Mathison), in the High Street; the Railway Hotel (with Walter Brydon) in the Old Town; the Commercial (run by Alex Wallace) in the High Street and formerly known as the Harrow Inn and later as the County; and Robert L. Kerr had premises in the Northgate.

Some impression of the local economy in the late 1860s can be gained from the number of outlets supplying the personal needs of a population of about 2,500. Peebles had five bakers (run by Robert Dickson, John Hume, William Martin, Davidson R. Mitchell and James Rutherford), and four butchers ('fleshers') all in the High Street (run by William Dalling, John Keddie, John Laidlaw and John

Little). There were fifteen grocery and sundry suppliers and six of these were in the High Street (Rosina Brydon, Edward Dickson, James Haliburton, James Melrose, Alexander Thomson and Thomson & Tait), three in the Old Town (Elizabeth Fleming, Thomas Hughes and James Whitson) and three in the Northgate (Peter Dalling [also a toy shop], Catherine Leadbetter and Margaret Niven). There was also Elizabeth French's grocery in Bridgend, Charles Grieve's in Biggiesknowe and Robert Lawrie in the Bridgegate.

In addition, there were ten grocers who were also spirit dealers. Six of these outlets were in the High Street: William Borthwick, Robert Innes, James Pairman, Thomas Peden, Jane Thomson and Ann & Isabella Veitch. The others were: Samuell M'Innes, Eastgate; James Small and Isabella Young, both in the Northgate; and Alexander Sheill in the Old Town. Thomas Peden in the High Street was also a wine and spirit merchant too, and also Italian warehouseman. The only greengrocer was Andrew Cosser, in the High Street.

Personal needs like boots and shoes were obtainable from nine suppliers: in the High Street were John Baptie, James Jones, Neil M''ntyre, James Stavert, Robert Stirling, James Whitie and John Whitie; in Elcho Street was George Lumsden; and Alexander Walker in Biggiesknowe. In the High Street there were also four shops supplying linen and woollens: John Stirling, Alexander Thomson, George Veitch and Melrose, Menzies & Co.

Dressmaking and millinery could be purchased from Isabella Bertram and Agnes Ramsay in Elcho Street, M. & H. Hollis and Melrose, Menzies & Co. in the High Street, and Marion Forbes in the Northgate. Peebles' eight tailors were: Archibald Donaldson & Sons, Andrew Green, James Ker, John Paxton, William Scott and Robert Williamson — all of whom had premises in the High Street; Peter Dalling, in the Northgate; and James Hill, in the Old Town.

The town was well-equipped with craftsmen, tradesmen and suppliers to look after the building needs of the town. There were five builders and masons (Alexander Dickson as well as John and Robert Veitch, located in the High Street; James and David Murray, in the Bridgegate; George Wilkie, at Damdale; and William Graham), two slaters (Alexander Henry, in the Old Town, and Robert Russell, at Damdale), and three plumbers and gas fitters (Thomas D. Grieve and John Wilson, both in the Old Town; and John Thomson in the High Street). Grieve, Thomson and John Paterson were also tinsmiths.

There were three painters and glaziers: John Turnbull (founded in 1790, the firm which became known as David Mitchell) and Peter Walker — both in the High Street; Thomas D. Grieve (also plumbers), in the Old Town. The two cabinetmakers/upholsterers were John Ballantyne in Biggiesknowe and John and James Smith, in the High Street, and the six ironmongers were Archibald Blackie, William Moffat, John Paterson, Robert Stirling and John Thomson, all in the High Street; and Thomas D. Grieve in the Old Town.

The town also had a tannery in Greenside and Anderson & Forrest were the tanners and skinners. There were three blacksmiths and farriers (veterinary surgeons), Patrick Ferguson and Charles T. Ker, both located in the Northgate, and Thomas Brydon & Son, Cuddyside, and three saddlers in the High Street: James Symington, William Weatherstone and John Young, as well as the following: three watch- and clockmakers (Charles Tait, High Street; James Edey, Old Town; and Robert Hislop, Bridgegate); James Grosart, a rope-, twine- and netmaker, High Street; John Smith, a cab and carriage owner located at the Tontine Hotel; Thomas Wallace, an engineer and millwright in Damdale; David McCombe an engineer in the Northgate; J. H. Wallace, coachbuilder, Damcroft; Matthew Dyer, a wood merchant, Old Town; Adam Watson, sawmill and implement maker, Old Town; Steam Sawmills in Damdale (James Yellowlees, manager); and two nailmakers, William Moffat and John Paterson, with premises in the High Street. Charles Hogg's coffee shop was located in the Old Town. The other shops were: druggist, George Morrison, High Street; two stationers and booksellers, John Paterson and also Robert Stirling (who had by this time become the owner and publisher of the *Peeblesshire Advertiser*), both in the High Street; printer, William Clark, High Street (the printer of the *Advertiser*); tobacconist and hairdresser, John Hunter, High Street; three china and glass dealers, William Broadly and Mary Dixon, both in the Northgate, and Joanna and Margaret Mormon, High Street. (China could be 'hired' for dinner, supper and marriage parties from William Broadly.)

The town had six nursery and seedsmen: Archibald Blackie, Andrew Cosser, Thomas Gentle & Son, James Pairman and Thomas Spalding & Co., with premises in the High Street; and William Scott in Tweedgreen. There was also an auctioneer, Archibald Gibson Blackie, High Street, and the town had an artist (miniature painter), P. de Castelain who lived in Biggiesknowe.

Slater's Directory lists the woollen manufacturers of the time as

Laing & Irvine, producing tweed at Tweedside; Thorburn & Co., located on the High Street, and also providing tweed; and Robert Todd shown as a yarn spinner, also at Tweedside. The three weavers were: John Hunter, Biggiesknowe, Alexander Laidlaw, Old Town, and Robert Stoddart, High Street, and there was a wool warehouse at West Port owned by Justins Murray.

We need to visualise the High Street of Peebles in 1867. Trading was carried out by five bakers, six grocers, seven grocers and spirit dealers, one greengrocer, four butchers, seven boot- and shoemakers, four linen and woollen merchants, one dressmaker and milliner, six tailors, one clock- and watchmaker, two stationers and booksellers, one cabinetmaker and upholsterer, one glass and china dealer, three saddlers, one druggist, one tobacconist and hairdresser, two nailmakers, two plumbers and gas fitters, five ironmongers, two builders and masons, two painters, six nursery and seedsmen, one printer and bookbinder, one weaver, one rope-maker, one cab and carriage owner, and an auctioneer. It is a formidable array of trade and services all in the main street with thirteen shops or tradesmen's premises in the Northgate, twelve in the Old Town, and twenty-three elsewhere in the burgh. It was, of course, the county's main centre and when this survey was taken of Peebles in 1867 it was in the middle of a decade that was experiencing a substantial increase in population.

Never before had there been growth at such a pace. From 1861 to 1871 the census returns show that the population increased from 2,045 to 2,631; 586 more people had come to live in the town. This rise of 28.6 per cent brought about a 50 per cent increase in the number of houses in Peebles, from 340 to 512.

These ten years contained the dynamics of growth that brought about even more expansion in the remaining decades of the nineteenth century. By 1871 Peebles had two woollen-mills, and their success led, in 1885, to the third mill — Ballantyne's March Street Mills — which attracted many more workers into the town. These mills and the impact of the railways on the fortunes of the town were the factors that enabled Peebles to expand and its population to increase to 5,266 by 1901. The burgh had to extend its boundaries to provide space for 1,123 dwelling-houses; this compared with the 340 houses that comprised the town forty years earlier.

Inevitably, there was an evolving trend of changing customs. Villagers could travel more frequently as road access improved and consequently market and fair days in the county town gradually gave way to shops catering for an increase in the frequency with which people visited the town. With a regular pattern of business evolving, there grew with it a resentment about the holding of 'fair days' as these were now considered to be more concerned with the hiring of labour and were proving to be an interruption, rather than an advantage, to trade. The October Fair in 1878 recorded that attendance was meagre as compared with a few years before, despite the fact that the morning trains on both railways had brought in a considerable number of people. A cattle sale held near to the North British Railway station had apparently attracted a large proportion of the visitors and apparently relieved the usual crush of people on the High Street. Here, there were only a few stands for the sale of toys and sweets, as well as two photographic saloons, one or two 'cheap johns' and a few fruit stalls. On the Tweed Green there were two or three steam-driven merry-go-rounds, a shooting saloon, but nothing in the shape of the shows which used to be a characteristic of earlier years.

By the end of the century there were not so many shops and this was due to the changing needs as new consumer demands became apparent, as well as the effects of competition. Shops solely devoted to confectionery came into vogue, with Kate Watson in the High Street and Matthew Oldham in the Northgate, and Philip De-Meo having a confectioners at 22 High Street and an ice-cream shop at 28 Northgate. Mr William Ker started a dairy in the High Street, there were more chemists and the number of tobacconists shops had increased to four. The demand for coal provided opportunities for seven coal agents in 1899 compared with four in 1867.

A major consumer 'marketing revolution' in the second half of the nineteenth century was undoubtedly the establishment of the 'co-operative movement'. It came into being in Peebles in 1872, when twenty members met to form the Peebles Co-operative Society; each investing one pound to start the business. In the first year the shop takings amounted to £1,264 12s 3d and a dividend of 5 per cent on purchases provided its members with 1s 2d (nearly 6p) for every pound they had spent. Six years later, in 1878, with a membership of 108, they declared a dividend of 2s 9d (nearly 14p).

The first Co-operative Store in the 1870s occupied the future site for the post office in the Northgate which was built about 1901; before that the 'Co-op' moving to the Eastgate and then in 1888 establishing itself at Greenside Place. It soon set up shops in the Old

Town and Elcho Street Brae and in the 1930s had branches in Rosetta Road and the Northgate. The co-operative movement over the years provided groceries, meat, baking, furniture, clothing and footwear for many local families. By 1900, there were 628 members.

There was an intention to take the 'co-operative' idea a stage further when, in October 1899, the Border Counties Co-operative Conference Association met in Galashiels and a proposal was made to establish a co-operative tweed-mill in Peebles. It was suggested that the providers of the capital, labour and consumption would share in the profits. The resolution was passed but the venture did not materialise. The success of the local tweed industry in the years towards the end of the nineteenth century had no doubt encouraged the supporters of the co-operative principle that they should get involved in an expanding and profitable business. The local mills, however, were fully entrenched, and the Thorburns and the Ballantynes too highly experienced in the business of woollen manufacturing for a co-operative mill to have had any chance of success.

The Peebles mills were well established as producers of high quality tweed, and as good, reliable employers by the time the century was drawing to a close. A South of Scotland Chamber of Commerce representative told a Royal Commission on Labour in 1892 that its ninety-five woollen manufacturers had 'fairly regular trade' and that 'work is very plentiful'. Apparently, the producers of tweed for the more expensive market were less concerned about the effect of foreign competition which was proving to be a problem in the other sectors of the textile trade at this time.

Equally important was the fact that the mill workers of the Border counties of Peebles, Selkirk and Roxburgh were well placed in the earnings league-table, as their rates of pay for both men and women were higher than the rest of the United Kingdom in the textile industry. This was confirmed in the Census of Wages for 1906, when the weekly rate for men was 27s 7d (£1.38) whilst in the rest of Scotland it was 23s 11d (£1.20) and in England 26s 10d (£1.34). For the women of Peebles, the rate was 18s 6d (93p) whilst women in the rest of Scotland earned 11s 8d (58p) and in England 13s 10d (69p).

As the county town, Peebles had established and developed a range of professional and medical services from the middle of the nineteenth century, and this aspect of the history of the town is contained in Chapters 13 and 14 below. There were also a great many professional and business agencies providing insurance cover for virtually every contingency. That there was great competition provides further evidence of a lively and busy economic life in the town during the period around 1867: Accidental Death (G. Morrison, High Street); British Guarantee (Stuart & Blackwood, Northgate); Briton Medical & General (life) (A.G. Blackie, High Street); Caledonian (John Stirling, High Street); Crown (life) (John M. Russell, High Street); Economic (life) (John Buchan, High Street); Edinburgh (life) (William Blackwood, Northgate); English & Scottish Law (life) (Robert Stirling); General (John Smith, High Street); Insurance Company of Scotland (Walter Thorburn, High Street); Life Association of Scotland (John Buchan); North British (J. D. Bathgate, High Street); Patriotic (Robert Stirling, Northgate); Phoenix (John Buchan); Plate Glass (G. Morrison); Railway Passengers' (J. D. Bathgate); Rock (life) (G. Morrison); Royal (Walter Hume, High Street); Scottish Equitable (life) (J. D. Bathgate); Scottish Imperial (life) (A. G. Blackie); Scottish Mutual Plate Glass (A. G. Blackie); Scottish Provident (Robert Stevenson, High Street); Standard (life) (Walter Thorburn); Sun (fire) (William Blackwood.)[20]

Before we close this chapter on the development of commerce and trade, mention must be made of a number of local trading enterprises that originated in the second half of the nineteenth century. They have given service to generations of Peebleans and today they still are in business. In the High Street: Veitch's, Ladies' and Gentlemen's Outfitters; William J. Whitie, Booksellers, Stationers and Newsagents; and Scott Brothers, Ironmongers. In the Old Town: the Castle Warehouse, Outfitters and Furnishers. Elcho Street Brae: James Clyde & Sons, Builders & Contractors. Innerleithen Road: L. Grandison & Son, Plasterers. (A fuller reference will be made below to these businesses, and others too, which started before the First World War.)

Footnotes:

1. Ferguson, W., *Scotland: 1689 to the present* (Edinburgh, 1968) p283
2. Pryde, George C., *Scotland from 1603 to the present day* (Edinburgh, 1962) p140
3. Bremner, David, *The Industries of Scotland — their rise, progress and present condition* (Edinburgh, 1869) p81

4. Chambers, W. and R., *Peebles and its Neighbourhood with a run on Peebles Railway* (Edinburgh, 1856) p9
5. Ibid, p5
6. Ibid, p6
7. Ibid, p9
8. Fyfe, J. G., *Country Lawyers* (Private circulation, 1986) p5
9. Buchan, J. Walter (ed), *A History of Peeblesshire* (Glasgow, 1925) Vol II, p158
10. Ibid, Vol III, pp630-34
11. Murray, Norman, *The Scottish Hand Loom Weavers 1790 – 1850 — A Social History* (Edinburgh, 1978) p2
12. Buchan, J. Walter (ed), *A History of Peeblesshire* Vol I, p222
13. *Peeblesshire Advertiser*: 11 February 1860
14. Bremner, David, *The Industries of Scotland: their rise, progress and present conditions* (Edinburgh, 1869) p158
15. Thom, Heather, *The Story of the Peebles Hydro* (private circulation, 1987), p5
16. Peebles Gutterbluid Club Minutes, Extract of Minutes, 1823-83 (1973) p13
17. *The Official Guide to Peebles* (1946 – 7) p9
18. Lawson, I. C., (personal notes)
19. Sinclair, Sir J. (ed), *The Statistical Account of Scotland 1797 – 1799* Vol III, pp869-85
20. Slater's Directory 1867, p1306

CHAPTER 2

The Burgh

WRITING AS A child of his native town, Robert Chambers was to say of Peebles: 'In the early years of this century, Peebles was little advanced from the condition in which it had mainly rested for several hundred years previously.' He said it was a quiet place and that Peebles was a 'finished town', by which he meant that no new houses were ever built within it. Within his own lifetime, however, both William and Robert Chambers were to see vast changes, not only in Peebles, but in Scotland as a whole, as the results of the Agricultural and Industrial Revolutions took effect.[1]

Of the same period William, in more pragmatic vein, was to report that the town consisted of but three main streets, the High Street, Eastgate and Northgate. Lesser streets existed, the Briggait and Biggiesknowe and a straggle of mean, single-storeyed thatched cottages which lay along the Old Town westwards to the Town Well at the top of the Old Town Vennel. The two-storey buildings in the main streets were thatched also and within them the apartments were small and few in number. 'Even of the good kind the houses consisted only of kitchen, parlour and bed chamber closet.' As to furnishings, 'in perhaps no more than two dozen were there any carpets; horn spoons were giving way to pewter; and silver forks were unheard of.' There were no public meeting places and such two or three newspapers which arrived daily or bi-weekly were handed round in clubs.

The transit of goods from Edinburgh was conducted by carriers' carts over roads which had yet to be improved under the provisions of the Toll Road Act of 1790. Of property, as a guide to social and economic status, William Chambers was to say: 'Shortly before the period referred to [1800] there was a tax on clocks and watches.' From the tax returns we glean the following: 'In the town of Peebles

there were but fifteen clocks, nineteen silver and two gold watches';
this in a town of 1,800 inhabitants.

No pavements existed and the main road surface was of impacted
sand and gravel; drains likewise were non-existent, and middens and
piles of refuse were commonplace, although the council made
frequent efforts to keep streets and wynds clear. Burghers were
permitted to lay cobbled ways and such 'causies' did exist mainly at
the 'Crossgait' where stood the Mercat Cross and where markets,
usually on a Tuesday, were held.[2]

Government of the town was still in the hands of the town council,
as it had been since 1469. By the Act of Scottish Parliament, the
constitution provided that the council consist of a provost, two
bailies, a Dean of Guild, a treasurer, eleven councillors and one
deacon: the old council to elect a new one annually. Abuse of the
latter provision was to lead directly to the Burgh Reform Act of 1833
which, combined with the extension of adult suffrage under the
Reform Act of 1832, led to a fairer election of the council. To some
extent at least, the municipal oligarchy of merchants and traders,
often above criticism, ceased to exist. With the introduction of the
£10 property value as a qualification to vote, an electorate of just
ninety-four was created in Peebles where the population was still only
1,800 as enumerated in the census of 1831.

On the whole, Peebles was well served by its town council. In the
years that followed, they were to lead the community in general
improvements to the town and, with a growing population, were to
make constant efforts to introduce industry. In particular, centred in
a wool-producing area with a plenitude of clean water, the town was
ideally placed to attract textile manufacturers, there was already a
thriving hand-loom industry, mainly in the Biggiesknowe, so skills
were available. Ironically, with the introduction of textile machinery
and the consequent building of mills, the hand-loom weaving was to
be the first casualty. The town also derived benefit from the
formation of upland farms as a result of the enclosure and
improvement of land by dyking and draining and, perhaps more
important, the liming of the predominately acid soil. The tenants and
workers from such farms looked to Peebles as an entrepôt for their
produce as well as their needs. Thereby both rural and town economy
grew. Indeed, Peebles in the nineteenth century was regarded as
much more the county town than it was to be in later times. Because
of this pre-eminent position, the neighbouring landlords were much

more inclined to join the townsfolk in voluntary and public subscriptions which, by enhancing the tax revenue, made possible the numerous improvements which were to take place.

The improvements which were to mark the end of Peebles as 'a finished town', to return to Robert Chambers's illuminating phrase, began as early as 1784 with the building of the Parish Church on the Castlehill. Some five years later, the town jail was built, immediately to the north of the church. A new and imposing County Hall (now the Sheriff Courthouse), incorporating the jail and fronting on to the West Port, was completed in 1843. In order to complete the Parish Church, the West Wark or New Wark, a defensible building standing some thirty yards east of the church athwart the High Street, was removed. At the same time the defensive ditch across the West Port, which covered the approach across the causeway over Peebles Water, was infilled and in 1815 the first Cuddy Bridge was completed. Prior to its completion, the main route to and from the Old Town was by Biggiesknowe and the Briggait.

Before the doubling in width of the Tweed Bridge in 1834, which was carried out by local tradesmen and funded, in the main, by public subscription, the town meal-mill on the south side of Castlehill was demolished, although the north wall still survives opposite the entrance to the swimming pool. At the same time, the mill lade, or goyt, was infilled. This ran from the intake on Peebles Water, through the northern arch of the bridge and along the line of the present roadway before it entered the Tweed after serving the waulk-mill at Walkershaugh, and the infilling permitted the removal of much of the Town Wall on the south and permitted building to take place. Here the two burgh schools were built on either side of School Brae; originally single-storeyed, they were doubled in size by the addition of an extra floor in 1862 and 1878 respectively.

The *Peeblesshire Advertiser* of Tuesday, 4 February 1845 led with a story concerned with the planned improvements to the main streets of Peebles and with the subscription lists which had been opened for that purpose. The town council promised £200, Provost Ker, £10, Bailies Stirling and Frazer, £5 each, with the same amount coming from the Dean of Guild. Thereafter were listed the gentlemen of the town and county, William and Robert Chambers leading the list with £50.

The improvements envisaged the lowering and repaving of the principal streets after the system developed by Macadam;

the removal of some projecting buildings; the introduction of a more abundant supply of water; the renewing and repair of the drainage system; and lastly, the levelling and beautifying of Tweed Green. All of this work was carried out within the estimates of £1,100. In addition, the remaining thatched roofs were to vanish to be replaced by Stobo slated ones. Cobbled causeways were constructed at suitable crossing points to enable pedestrians to cross dryshod in inclement weather. At this time the last of the bastel-houses were converted to normal dwellings, the Harrow Inn (now the County) being a good example of this. Another victim of progress was the Mercat Cross which was removed to ease the traffic flow. Fortunately, the thirteenth-century shaft was preserved and the Cross subsequently returned to the High Street after a spell in the quadrangle of the Chambers Institution. This latter building had been largely rebuilt in 1857 thanks to the munificence of William Chambers, with the original Queensberry Lodgings being converted and added to, to create a complex of reading-room, museum and later, a library with a 'grand' hall in the rear, much as we see it today.

Lord Cockburn had said of the Edinburgh Town Council, prior to the 1833 Burgh Reform Act, that it was 'omnipotent, corrupt, and impenetrable'.[3] Whether we can say the same of the Peebles Town Council of the same period is irrelevant. The primary factor of the reform of Peebles Town Council was a willingness to involve itself in the modernisation of the burgh and, in consequence, display a more forward looking attitude to change. Indirectly, the extension of adult suffrage also led to an expansion of the town, particularly to the north and west. The terraced houses of Elcho Street, Cross Street and parts of the Old Town we owe to the £10 property clause of the Burgh Reform Act. This provision was later to cause problems when it became politically expedient to create the so-called 'Faggot Voters'.

A Napoleonic maxim states that in war, communications are all important. This general truth could well be applied to settled and peaceful communities. Indeed, the geographical situation of Peebles illustrates the importance of such a dictum. The road and street improvements which took place in the burgh after 1845 were already mirrored in its links with Edinburgh to the north and also, to some extent, areas to the west. As a consequence of the Turnpike Act of 1790, a toll road had been constructed from Peebles to Leadburn and was in full use by 1806. Thus, access was gained to a network of toll roads via Edinburgh. The *Second Statistical Account* describes the Peebles-Leadburn section as of excellent construction, albeit narrow, the local whinstone being the material used.[4] The opening of this route introduced in time that most elegant of all forms of land travel, the stagecoach. Firstly, as already noted, the journey was carried out by a 'Wilson's caravan', a primitive two-wheeled vehicle drawn by a single horse which took about ten hours to make the journey to Edinburgh including stops. This means of transport was superseded by the 'Fly', a post-chaise in appearance which was drawn by two horses.[5]

The *Second Statistical Account* marks the reluctance of manufacturers to expand the nascent textile industry in Peebles; this the author ascribes to the high cost of coal. With the coming of the railway that cost fell substantially. Other immediate effects of the railway included the opening of a mineral yard at Dovecot, later a sale-ring for sheep and cattle at Dean Park and, when the sale-ring was moved to Cross Road, the housing development of the Dean Park area and the Northgate moved on apace. Similarly, the opening of the Caledonian Railway Station caused the creation of Caledonian Road and, in due course, Edderston Road, Frankscroft and Chambers Terrace.[6]

The High Street, reflecting the increased prosperity of the town through the expansion of textiles and agriculture, renewed itself as buildings became unfit. By the 1870s and 1880s the street had taken on the appearance that we know today. The East Church was built in 1872 and the Leckie Memorial Church followed five years later. Venlaw Court was rebuilt in 1872 as was much of the Northgate between 1872 and 1878. The Parish Church of Peebles was replaced in 1887: a splendid building in the Gothic style with lantern steeple in conscious imitation of St Giles in Edinburgh, a true reflection of civic pride and Victorian self-confidence. The present police station completed the West Port in 1887 and, in the same year, the Caledonian Railway Hotel opened (now Whities'). At the other end of the High Street, two new hotels were opened in 1887, Forresters' Temperance Hotel at 2 Eastgate and, next door, the Waverley Hotel, also devoted to the anti-strong-drink movement, an interesting comment on the social morals of the late-Victorian era.

The Duke of Wellington, who objected to the coming of the railways, said that they would only encourage the lower orders to travel about the country in an idle fashion. In his prescient way he had identified the effect without looking too closely at the cause. Indeed, the railways were to lead directly to what we now choose to call the tourist industry. Undoubtedly it was this change which caused the opening of hotels in places such as Peebles and was to lead directly to such establishments as the Peebles Hotel Hydro being built. Further, the introduction of commercial and railway hotels (there was one in Damdale, the tenemental building on the north side) contributed directly to the retail trade of the town. The railways made it easier for commercial travellers, along with their samples, to visit small towns such as Peebles and during this period Veitch's Corner House (1885) and the Castle Warehouse (1896) came into being.

No one can doubt the part played by the woollen industry in the general growth of Peebles both in terms of population and the overall prosperity of the burgh. It was the engine which propelled the local economy along for a crucial seventy years. The extensions of Peebles to the north all took place during this period, with the building of Crossland Crescent, Gladstone Place, St Andrews Road, Rosetta Road up to and beyond the isolation hospital and the poorhouse (now District Council offices). Wemyss Place, March Street and George Street were all areas largely populated by textile workers.

To the south of the river, Springhill and Bonnington Roads were being developed. Springwood and Chambers Terraces were to follow. Larger villas and country houses were built for the mill-owning families at Springwood, Craigerne and so on. The Loaning was built for Professor Veitch. In the same period (1870 – 1880s) imposing dwellings appeared on Venlaw and out as far as the burgh boundary to the north at Swinton Bank. By 1900, with various extensions to the burgh boundaries and the consequent building activity, Peebles had become more of 'a finished town' than even Robert Chambers could have imagined.

The growth of the town brought with it the inevitable problems. Peebles, by nature of its location on a sand and gravel ridge and enjoying a high water table, had few problems in its early history with water supply. By the middle of the nineteenth century, with a burgeoning population and a heightened awareness of the importance of cleanliness and hygiene, the adequacy of the water supply was in question. From earliest times, the sinking of a vertical shaft when suitably lined with masonry provided a well which then filled with seepage water. Evidence of many of these private wells still exists.

The town council had furnished two wells for the public supply. One in the High Street, St Mungo's Well, had a wellhead on the southern flank of Venlaw where a spring-fed cistern was established. Water was then piped by wooden pipes, later in 1838 supplanted by lead pipes, to the outlet on the High Street. A similar system operated from the Meadow Strand Well, to the west of the town, to an outlet well at the top of the Old Town on the corner of Young Street (now Lindores). By 1867, and under the provisions of the 1867 Police and Improvements Act, a town council decision established a reservoir on the Meldon Burn which then piped water, not only to the two public wells, but also to the new houses which were being built.[7]

On the south side of the river many of the new houses relied on a private water-supply system with a spring-fed system on Morning Hill which was satisfactory until further development in the 1880s rendered it inadequate. Thus, it was in 1883 that an intake on Manor Water was created, with a pumping and filter station at Bonnycraig, and more or less the same system as Peebles now enjoys was set up. Incidentally, the Hotel Hydro, which was built in 1878 and subsequently rebuilt in 1905 – 7, still utilises the wellhead of St Mungo's Well for some of its water requirements.

The other public utility which had a tangible effect on the burgh was the introduction of lighting by gas. A meeting of the burgesses was held on 9 January 1829, with Sir John Hay of Smithfield in the chair. It was then resolved to form a company to be known as the Peebles Gas Company. The management committee included Sir John Hay, Provost Turnbull, John Paterson (later Provost), John Welsh, James Spalding and Alexander Wilkie. The capital of the Gas Company was £700 and the site for the gasworks was west of Castlehill, directly behind the bowling green. The gasworks, or 'guffie', was to serve the town well until 1905 when new premises were constructed at Eshiels.

Originally, coking coal was brought in by cart from the Lanarkshire coalfield. Gas was only made for ten months of the year and the public street lamps were only lit for 119 nights, the cost of lighting each lamp being 14s (70p) per lamp. The cost to domestic consumers was 13s (65p) per 1,000 cubic feet. By 1849, the annual consumption of gas was 736,000 cubic feet, a clear indication of the growth of the town. With the arrival of the railway, trade improved, the town continued to expand as we have seen and the gas consumption rose to 903,000 cubic feet at the reduced rate of 8s 4d (just over 41p) per 1,000 cubic feet.

In 1898, the assets of the Peebles Gas Company were acquired by Peebles Town Council. The following period marks the introduction of gas cookers, grillers, hot plates and other items of cooking equipment, marking a further improvement in the standard of living within the burgh. By 1900, the output of the gas works reached 13.5 million cubic feet and demand was shortly to outstrip production, requiring a greatly-increased plant capacity. Since the original site was constrained from expansion by its situation, the new gasworks were planned and thereafter built. The Eshiels site is still used as storage for natural gas.

At the time of its transfer to the town council, a director of the Peebles Gas Company was William 'Paraffin' Young of Priorsford House. He it was who demonstrated the distillation of oil shale in vertical retorts with the consequent production of paraffin oil and ammonia. His original theories were adapted to the carbonisation of coal to produce illuminating gas. Indeed, his ideas spread far beyond the West Lothian shale-fields and his home in Peebles.[8]

Long before the introduction of coal gas as a relatively safe method of heating and lighting, the hazards of domestic fires and lighting by 'crusie' were considerable — especially in houses which were huddled together and often thatched. Fire is often mentioned in the records of Peebles. As early as 1826 an 'engine of the latest design' was purchased. Manned by volunteers, this was a hand-drawn vehicle which also relied on manpower to drive its pump and utilise the leather hoses and buckets which completed the sum of its equipment. In 1868, as part of the provisions of the General Police and Improvement Act (Scotland), a new horse-drawn fire-engine was purchased by the town council and a regular fire brigade appointed. This, in the main, meant the retaining of eighteen volunteer firemen by paying them a fee for turnouts. This system prevailed until the Second World War brought certain changes, mainly in the removal of control to autonomous bodies. In the case of Peebles, this was to be eventually the Lothian and Borders Fire Brigade. The 1868 fire-engine survived for many years under the northernmost arch of Tweed Bridge, whilst successive engines were housed in the Town House on the High Street, a situation which prevailed until the 1960s when a new fire station was built in Caledonian Road.

Cholera was the spectre that threatened Britain's cities in 1862; no respecter of person, the Prince Consort was to die of it in this year. As the epidemic spread, there was a cholera scare in Peebles although no cases were diagnosed. Nonetheless, the town council prudently appointed a committee to examine the state of the burgh's water supply, sewage disposal and other aspects of public health. In this they were overtaken by events since the provision of the General Police and Improvement (Scotland) Act made such improvements mandatory. Further, the duties of the council became immediately more onerous. No longer were improvements to be determined by the vagaries of public subscription or private investment. In future, matters of public health and housing became the direct responsibility of the council as Police Commissioners; the burgh boundaries were also determined by application to the sheriff under this Act.

With the passing of the Public Health Act of 1867 additional duties devolved on the town council. As a result, the first sanitary inspector for the burgh, a James Grant, was appointed. Likewise, in the same year Dr John Connel was appointed as medical officer. The drainage of the town was again drastically overhauled in 1876/7. In 1891 the various offices of burgh surveyor, sanitary inspector and inspector of roads, buildings, water, etc., were combined in one post, the first incumbent being Samuel Cowan.

The Burgh Police (Scotland) Act of 1892 occasioned the final improvements undertaken by the town within the nineteenth century. In 1895/6 pavements were uniformly constructed throughout the burgh. The 'fleshmarket', which had been built by the burgh in 1652, was finally deemed to be inadequate and, although the fabric of the original building off Dean's Wynd still survives, a completely new slaughterhouse was built at South Parks in 1895. The burgh boundaries were extended in 1896 and the widening of Tweed Bridge considered. The latter was carried out and by 1900 the rebuilt bridge opened. The cost of widening was £8,000 and the new width, 40 feet. The gift to the town of Victoria Park by Sir John Hay of Haystoun, Bart., to mark the Diamond Jubilee of Queen Victoria, occasioned the building of another bridge over the Tweed, that of the suspension bridge at Priorsford. Opened in 1905, it linked Tweed Green with St Ninian's Haugh on the south bank and thence to the new Victoria Park.

Of the dwelling-houses that were built between 1860 and 1900 the bulk were constructed from local greywacke with sandstone facings. Local builders and tradesmen were in the main responsible. The dwelling-houses were extremely well built and, in design, followed the style of the Scottish vernacular, showing an instinctive regard for proportion and appearance. A rule of thumb which locals used for cost in the 1870s and 1880s was 'fifty pound a lum', giving a price-range for anything from a small cottage to a modest villa of £150 to £300. Larger houses on the south side or in Innerleithen Road, for example, would range from £400 upwards.

Given the increasing prosperity, the growth in population and the intellectual and cultural influence from outside agencies, it is hardly surprising that Peebles entered into a forward-looking period. The burgh was well served by a succession of provosts and town councillors who prudently handled the town's affairs to make the best of an expansionary era. By 1900, the town looked forward, full of confidence, to face the challenges of a new century.

Footnotes:

1. Chambers, Robert, *Memoirs* (Edinburgh, 1872), p9, 11
2. Chambers, William, *History of Peeblesshire* (Edinburgh, 1864) pp274-5
3. Cockburn, Henry, *Memorials of His Time* (Chicago, 1974) p87
4. *Second Statistical Account of Peeblesshire* (Edinburgh, 1861) p17
5. Williamson, Alex, *Glimpses of Peebles* (Selkirk, 1895) p104
6. *Second Statistical Account of Peeblesshire* (Edinburgh, 1861) p15
7. Buchan, James Walter (ed), *A History of Peeblesshire* (Glasgow, 1925) Vol II, p154
8. Mackie, D., *Peebles Gas Company* (Unpublished Monograph, 1978)

CHAPTER 3

Social Life

IN THE YEARS just after the middle of the nineteenth century, Sir Thomas Dick Lauder described Peebles as a town with a 'singular air of decayed royalty' hanging over it, that blended with its 'perfect simplicity and rurality'.[1] It is true that Peebles lies in a perfect rural setting in a site chosen by the first settlers of a bygone age; chosen because it was a fertile valley and a meeting place of two rivers that provided natural protection from marauders. As the 'settlement' grew over the centuries and became a town, it did so with a natural simplicity.

It is also true that, Peebles more than any of the other Scottish Border towns, had a right to talk of royalty. A royal poet sung of her Beltane Feast and it was at one time a favourite place of the Scottish monarchy. However, if a century and half after Scotland's royal court had moved to London there was any lingering atmosphere of 'decayed royalty' hanging over the town, it was soon to be buried by the changes which came about in the second half of the nineteenth century.

The dynamics of change were the new work opportunities which became available for the townspeople — slowly at first and then at an accelerated pace as the Thorburns and the Ballantynes developed their woollen-mills. The success of the mills created sufficient jobs to attract crowds of incomers into the town and a great many more houses were built and new districts and streets came into being. Peebles took on an air of enterprise and its pace of life quickened as it became a different place from what it had been in the middle of the eighteenth century. This chapter is about these changes and how they affected the life of the townspeople.

The population was 1,898 when the census was taken in 1841 and there were just eighty-four more people in the town ten years later in

1851 when the census count showed 1,982. An analysis of the 1851 census indicates that the population was 52.3 per cent female and 47.7 per cent male. These figures are derived from a 99.4 per cent sample, taking 1,970 of the inhabitants, as compared with the total population of 1,982: there being 569 males (28.9 per cent), 371 boys under the age of fourteen (18.8 per cent); 710 females (36 per cent) and 320 girls under the age of fourteen (16.2 per cent). (This 99.4 per cent sample will be used throughout the following analysis.)

The fact that the town had more females than males is not particularly significant, as this has proved to be the result of every census taken here. It is of interest, however, that just over one-third of the population were under fourteen years of age, and shows that Peebles had a very young population. This is possibly due to the great number of people who had come into the town, for they were mostly younger men and women looking for work.

The large number of migrants living in the town in 1851 is very impressive because they were settled in Peebles before the coming of the railways. They had made the journey when travel was difficult and more suited to younger rather than older travellers, especially when coming from a long distance. An analysis of the birth-place of each head of household shows the extent of such inwards migration and is a guide to where the newcomers had originated. There were 443 households in the 99.4 per cent sample and this indicated that 39.8 per cent (176 heads) were born in Peebles and 17.8 per cent (seventy-nine heads) were born in others parts of Peeblesshire. Therefore, some 57.6 per cent of the heads of household were born within the 'shire'. However, from farther afield 20 per cent (eighty-nine heads) came from the counties bordering Peeblesshire and about 15.1 per cent (sixty-seven) were born in other parts of Scotland. The remaining 7.2 per cent (thirty-two heads) were born outside of Scotland: nineteen in Ireland, eleven in England, and two in France.

Most of the heads of household who were incomers appeared to be settled in the town and had children who were born in Peebles. The sample showed there were 55.6 per cent (1,096) born in Peebles, 13 per cent (256) born in Peeblesshire, 24.6 per cent (484) born in other parts of Scotland, 2.2 per cent (forty-four) born in England, 3.6 per cent (seventy) born in Ireland and 1 per cent (eighteen) born overseas; the places of birth of two are not shown.

There were boarding schools in Peebles and the census showed that there were eight boarders born in East India, three in Van Diemens

Land (Tasmania) and two in Jamaica. There were three men born in France and there was also one American and one Canadian.

To complete the picture of the town in 1851, it is essential to know what kind of work was available for Peebles folk before the woollen-mills were established. In Peebles, as elsewhere, the demand for hand-loom spinning and weaving of cotton was in decline. Glasgow was becoming the main centre in Scotland and even in that city the cotton workers were troubled by the severity of the cyclic trading conditions, the industry being at its lowest ebb from about 1848 to 1852. The census in 1841 showed that there were only 101 cotton, linen and woollen workers in Peebles and this number had fallen to forty-two when the 1851 census was taken.

Agricultural labouring and domestic jobs were the main source of work in the neighbourhood and most of the weavers had to turn to this kind of employment when they could no longer find hand-loom work to do. However, a detailed analysis of the occupations and status of the population, based on the above sample, provides a great deal of information about the life and work of the town at the middle of the nineteenth century. This is set out in appropriate groups:

auctioneer 1, bank agents/accountants 2, doctors 4, ministers of religion 5, divinity students 2, officers (Navy/Army) 2, rector 1, schoolmasters/schoolmistresses 12, solicitors/writers 6, veterinary surgeon 1: a total of 36

burgh officer 1, farmer 1, governesses 3, manager (gasworks) 1, postmistress 1, sheriff's officer 1, jail keeper 1, matron (jail) 1: total 10

bakers 11, fleshers/butchers 4, grocers/victuallers 22, millers (flour/grain) 4 and tripe dealer 1: total 42

brewers 2, hotel keepers 2, inn-keepers 4, spirit dealers 2, tavern keeper 1: total 11

drapers 6, dressmakers 14, milliners 9, seamstresses 5, tailors 20, shoemakers 31: total 85

booksellers/stationers 2, china dealers 2, clock-/watchmakers 4, druggists 2, hairdresser 1, nursery/seedsmen 4, printer 1, toy merchant 1: total 17

blacksmiths 7, cartwrights 2, ironmongers 2, millwrights 2, nailers 3, ropemaker 1, saddlers 4, tinsmith 1: total: 22.

cabinetmakers 2, glazier 1, housepainters 7, joiners/carpenters 11, masons 22, plasterers 2, plumber 1, slaterers 6: total 52

coopers 3, skinners 3, tanner 1: total 7

hand-loom weavers (cotton/linen) 14, (woollen) 14, manufacturers (cotton/linen) 1, (woollen) 2, stockingmakers (woollen) 9, yarn spinners 2: total 42

clerks 9, coachmen 2, coal dealer 1, coalminer 1, contractors 2, letter carriers/post runners 3, dyke builders 12, lodginghouse keepers 4, mail driver 1, midwives 1, nurses 2, policemen 3, servicemen (Navy/Army) 2, shop assistants 5, traveller (commercial) 1: total 49.

carriers/carters 21, grave digger 1, hawkers 13, agricultural labourers 100, general labourers 18: total 153

cooks 3, cowherd 1, footman 1, gardeners 6, general servants 106, groom 1, hostelers 3, housemaids 3, housekeepers 16, laundry/washerwomen 21, nurserymaids 1, shepherd 1, valet 1: total 164

artist (miniature painter) 1, bird stuffer 1, horse-breaker 1, mole catcher 1, pew opener (St Peter's Church), 1, teacher of dancing 1: total 6

apprentices 45, errand boys/girls 4: total 49

proprietors of land/houses 19, gentlewomen 10: total 29

housewives 256

children under 14 years of age 691

The remaining 249 of the population in the sample extracted from the census enumerator's returns covered annuitants, pensioners (including five Chelsea pensioners and one Greenwich Pensioner), widows and widowers, visitors and those who did not record an occupation; this latter group consisted of many unmarried daughters.

Those in employment (745) comprised 118 labourers (15.8 per cent) and 164 domestic workers (22 per cent); together they are the main category of employment and total 37.8 per cent of the gainfully employed population. Professional and official workers comprised 6.2 per cent, food and drink 7.1 per cent, shops 13.7 per cent, artisans 10.9 per cent, textile workers 5.6 per cent (there was an estimated 12 per cent in 1841), apprentices and errand boys/girls 6.6 per cent and other workers 12.1 per cent.

Two of the men born in France were likely to have been prisoners-of-war in Peebles during the Napoleonic Wars. Augustus H. Gregor, born in 1788 at Dunkirk, married a Peebles woman; they resided in Biggiesknowe, and he was a 'teacher of dancing'. John Malinch, born in 1787, also married a local woman and they lived in the High Street where he was a grocer. However, Phillip de Castelaine, born in

Paris in 1790, came from London in response to an advertisement in *The Times* when the Rev William Bliss, the Episcopal minister, was seeking a tutor for his boys' boarding school. He was an artist and lodged with Miss Crockett in the High Street, later residing at Biggiesknowe in the house where the Chambers brothers were born.

Two other unusual occupations were the 'bird stuffer' — a service provided by James Hall, brother-in-law of Walter Stavert, High Street — and the 'horse-breaker' George Renwick, also in the High Street. Another job of work indicative of these early years was postrunner. James Grosart (born in 1826) was the postrunner between Peebles and Stobo in 1851; he did this job for almost twenty years. However, in Slater's Directory for 1867 he was shown as a rope-, twine- and netmaker, a business he carried on for another twenty years, having a shop in the High Street that was at one time Mungo Park's surgery.

Mr Grosart was also sheriff's officer for upwards of forty years and the town's Inspector of Weights and Measures. He had the distinction of succeeding Alexander Tait ('Poet Tait') in 1861 and became the second 'poet-laureate' of the Peebles Gutterbluid Club. He will be remembered for his renowned book, the *Chronicles of Peebles: Chronicles from Peebles Briggate* (1899). James Grosart died in 1905, a great Peeblean and a gifted narrator of the sayings and doings of the Auld Burgh Toon.

The scarcity of work in the 1850s for the textile workers must have caused considerable concern, the numbers in employment falling from 101 to forty during the ten years to 1851. This was due to the decline in hand-loom weaving, which first affected the cotton industry as it changed to factory production in major industrial centres. The days of the woollen hand-loom workers were also running out and they, too, would need to adapt their skills to operate the power-looms of the mills.

Peebles cotton workers who had been earning only 6s (30p) and sometimes as low as 4s 6d (22½p) per week in 1839, endeavoured to get employment in Galashiels where the hand-loom woollen weavers were earning from 12s (60p) to 17s (85p) per week, but they were barred by the other workers because of their low earning status. Never again would the hand-loom cotton weavers attain the high earnings of the post-Waterloo period.

Wae days for the weavers,
    ay, hard times indeed
For the knights o' the shuttle,
    the heddles, an' reed;
When payment for weavin' o'
    shirtin' stripes fell
Doon, doon to a penny-three-
    farthings per ell.

At tuppence 'twas e'en
    a hard struggle for life,
Where there were a twa-
    three wee weans an' a wife,
Nae ill sitten weaver was
    he, he wad say
When kept up his darg
    o' ten ells day by day.

Auld men used to tell o'
    the grand times they knew,
When they were young
    fellows afore Waterloo,
When they could, wi'
    comfort, twa pounds a week come,
Now they were content wi'
    a fourth o' that sum.

These lines were printed in the *Peeblesshire Advertiser* (30 March 1901), author unknown. An 'ell' is a measurement of cloth equal to 1.25 yards but in times past the Scottish 'ell' was equal to 37.2 inches. A practice adopted by hand-loom weavers in Peebles was the use of a large round glass vessel filled with water as a magnifying glass to assist in counting the threads in the web.[2]

Hand-loom weavers formed a large section of the industrial population of Scotland in the 1840s when there were about 84,560 workers. However, numbers employed dropped drastically to 25,000 by 1850 and to only 10,000 in 1860 and, twenty years later, to a mere 4,000.[3] On the other hand, the national figures for 1858 to 1881 indicated the trebling of persons working in the manufacture of tweed. Both these trends reflected the local situation.

PART I: 1850 – 1900

Local textile workers, living in a town in the centre of a largely agricultural area, were to some extent cushioned against the worst effects of these changing times before the appearance of the woollen-mills. They were able to turn to labouring or domestic work and it was fortunate that the period from 1846 through to 1873 was one of 'general prosperity for Scottish agriculture'.[4]

The opportunity for local textile workers to change over to a form of manufacturing occurred in 1829 when J. Dickson provided the town with what could be described as a 'factory-ised hand-loom shop' — a manufacturing house. For a number of weavers this meant a transference of workplace from their home to a workshop. It was the first stage of a development that heralded far-reaching changes in the years ahead: the mechanised factory.

When power-driven machines for spinning and weaving were installed in these early years, the mills were small and changing over from hand-looms to operating mechanical looms was that much easier. It occurred in Peebles in 1860 when Laing & Irvine implemented their ambitious plan for twenty-six mechanical looms that were to provide jobs for fifty workers. It failed just fifteen years afterwards but by then, Thorburns had built Damdale and were well-placed to take over the bankrupt Tweedside Mill in 1875. Thorburn incorporated it into their manufacturing set-up and, along with Ballantyne's equally successful March Street Mills, they became the major employers in Peebles.

Taking a sample from the 1881 census of every fifth household in Peebles, it provided information from 164 households (19.9 per cent) compared with the town's 824 households. Twenty-nine per cent (forty-eight households contained in the sample) had 106 persons employed in the woollen-mills, comprising forty-eight males and fifty-eight females. Over 16 per cent (twenty-seven) of these households had more than one worker employed in the mills. One household, consisting of nine persons, had five mill-workers; in another household, the father was a tweed weaver, one daughter a woollen winder, another daughter a woollen-yarn winder, one son a tweed weaver and another son a designer. Clearly this was quite a transformation from the situation of thirty years before; a sample comprising a fifth of the households now provided evidence of 106 mill workers and indicated that there were now several hundred woollen workers in Peebles by 1881. This was, of course, due to the Thorburn mills at Damdale and Tweedside; Ballantyne's March Street Mills were still a few years away.

Population, too, had increased over these thirty years from 1851 and at a pace not previously experienced in Peebles. It had risen from 1,982 to 3,495 — an increase of just over 76 per cent. Peebles would continue this trend of expansion throughout the two remaining decades of the nineteenth century and the population would reach 5,266 in 1901. With an increase of 165 per cent in fifty years, there were 3,284 additional people living in the town. It is understandable, therefore, that there was a continuous pressure on living accommodation from the 1850s to the end of the century that was never fully alleviated and more often than not there was acute overcrowding.

Looking at the size of the households contained in the 1851 sample (of 99.4 per cent) taken from the census enumerator's returns, there were forty-eight households comprising one person in each household; seventy-six with two people; seventy-two with three; sixty-one with four; forty-nine with five; forty-five with six; thirty-six with seven; twenty-one with eight; twenty with nine; five with ten; three with eleven; one with twelve; one with thirteen; two with fourteen; one with seventeen; one with eighteen; and one with twenty-four. When these household sizes are 'weighted' it shows the average mean experienced household size to be 6.13 persons per household. It should be remembered that it was common practice for a number of households to live in the same dwelling-house due to the severe shortage of housing, and, because dwellings were constructed with small rooms and low ceilings, it is clear that living conditions for most families must have been appallingly cramped.

Housing was in short supply even before the opening of the first mechanised woollen-mill. The Peebles Railway Co. quickly identified the need to do something and offered an inducement of a 'free ticket' for a term of years to the occupier of each dwelling-house built in the vicinity of the town.

Laing & Irvine, having equipped the Tweedside Mill with machinery costing about £4,000, complained that they were about to start up in 1860 without a single house being erected for the occupation of the workers. They claimed that small houses were not to be had in Peebles. In 1860, editorial comment was pressing for much greater effort to meet the housing shortage: 'The overcrowding of the houses of the working-classes in the town is a scandal.'

According to the census returns, there were 480 households but only 340 dwelling-houses fit for occupation in 1861; therefore, 140 households (29 per cent), ranging from a single person to a family, had to share another household's accommodation.

A local initiative established the Peeblesshire Savings Investment and Building Society in 1859 and this provided facilities for its members to either purchase or build their own house. At a meeting in 1878, it was reported that 1,794 shares were being paid up and nearly a third of these had been held since the formation of the society. It indicated a spirit of independence and thrift.

Just as the woollen factories had brought new life to the town and the townspeople, so did the railways. Its social impact on the town was apparent from 4 July 1855, the first day the *Tweed* brought in its passengers. As if to reinforce its facility to open the people of the town to new experiences, on the second day the train brought Marion Thomson and Janet Brown from Fisherrow and the town heard the cry: 'Caller Haddies . . . Caller Herrin' . . . Wha'll hae my Caller Cod?' They quickly sold out and there was a promise that they would return regularly. In the 1930s their successors were still keeping that promise. 'Jennie the Fishwife' carrying her heavy creel supported by a strap round her forehead, began her round by calling on her regular customers in the Northgate as they were nearest to the station. When the fish had been selected and the price had been bargained, she would clean and prepare them with a marvellous economy of strokes with her sharp gutting-knife.

Back in the nineteenth century, the grocer, George Ferrier, advertised that he expected 'this day by rail a supply of Banffshire powdered butter at 1s 0½d (5p) per pound.' Nicol Dixon advertised that he had made arrangements for the railway to bring coal from the Lothian collieries. Thomas Peden, a merchant in the High Street, advertised 'marmalade oranges'.

Peebles was well-advanced in having its houses and streets lit by gas but at that time, in 1854, the town did not have a furniture shop for household items such as a chair, table or a bed. These had to be obtained from Edinburgh or ordered to be made by a local carpenter. The town did not have a hearse either; that, too, had to be hired from Edinburgh. Then, in May 1859, James Mathison of the Crown Inn advertised the availability in the town of a 'handsome new hearse'. It could be hired with one horse and a plain hearse for 6s (30p) whilst 'with plume', the charge would be increased to 7s 6d (37½p) and, if required with plume and two horses, it would cost 10s 6d (52½p).

The Revd Dr William Dalgleish, Minister of the Parish Church who wrote the section about Peebles in the *Statistical Account of Scotland: 1797-1799*, stated that the inhabitants of Peebles were generally healthy and lived to a very advanced age. He added: 'Lately there have been six men living at the same time within fifty yards of one another in the old town whose ages together amounted to 528 years and several died near 100 years old'.[5]

In 1855 there were 69 deaths: under one year, thirteen; one to twelve years, seventeen; no deaths between twelve and fifty-two, 'except for three unpreventable'; and the remainder between fifty-two to ninety years. That was the year Peeblesshire was listed as the third healthiest county and the year following in 1856 it was listed so again 'with increased salubrity'. In 1857, it was the second healthiest![6]

Peebles had a police force from 1840. A committee appointed to consider the problems arising 'from upwards of 4,000 vagrants who spend a night in Peebles each year', recommended in 1840 that the Peeblesshire Constabulary should be established. It consisted of one superintendent and one constable, stationed in Peebles, and five constables to cover the rest of the county. In the 1851 census, Ninian Notman was the superintendent and Alex Gunn the constable.

Offenders against the law were at one time 'captured by Drummer Wull on the verbal command of the provost'. However, in 1807, there was a constable appointed and paid from the fines received from delinquents apprehended for 'riding their carts through the town or driving loose horses along the streets'. A new appointment in 1828 changed the constable's responsibility to searching for vagrants and beggars in the town and sweeping the streets, with a weekly wage of between 9s and 10s 6d (45-52½p).[7] During the Great Depression of the 1930s, Peebles was still 'attracting' large numbers of vagrants: in 1934, the casualty house recorded the admittance of 2,661 persons; in 1935, 2,729; 1936, 2,267; 1937, 1,897; 1938, 1,648. These yearly totals tell their sad story of those times.

An expanding town with an increased hazard of fire risk from overcrowded houses, led to the setting-up of a regular 'volunteer' fire brigade in 1868. The first hand-drawn fire engine was bought by public subscription in 1826 and it is reported that the town council were the volunteers; the provost was the 'captain' and the bailies were 'deputies'.

Amongst the major events during the years from 1850 to the end of the century was the opening of the Chambers Institution with its library, reading-room, museum and hall. It was handed over in 1859 by Dr William Chambers to the town council to be held in trust for the townspeople and he asked that the Institute should be conducted 'on a broad and universal basis'. Since its opening, the Chambers Institution has been used by generation after generation of townspeople who have praised its inspired facilities and honoured the name of its generous founder.

Dr William Chambers of Glenormiston had acquired the property in 1857 from Dr James Reid who had been provost of Peebles from 1788 to 1803. On the doorway of the then keeper's house, the lintel bears the initials 'J. R.' with the date 1781 — the year Dr Reid had bought the property from the Duke of Queensberry. The house was believed to be have been at one time in the possession of the friars of the Monastery of the Cross Kirk. However, in the seventeenth century it was owned by Sir James Hay, the first Baronet of Smithfield, before passing to the Earls of Morton and eventually to William, Earl of March.

Reviewing the use being made of the various facilities some twenty years after the opening of the Chambers Institution, the annual general meeting held in 1878 noted that there had been 1,500 visitors to the museum during the previous twelve months and this had brought in receipts of £18 15s (£18.75). The reading-room was being well attended, especially by young men in the evening, and the billiards-room was more than self-sustaining.

Most Peebleans were avid readers and the local newspaper gave regular information about the additions to the Chambers Institution library. In January 1860, for example, it reported that two copies of Dickens's *Tales of Two Cities* were available as well as the novel *A Love Lost*, and *Electro-Chemistry* by Charles Chalmers, and that the pamphlets on the table included *The Pope and the Congress*, *How to Mismanage a Bank*, and *Dr Strachan's tract address to the working men of Scotland*.

Dr Chambers claimed that his love of books was in no small degree due to Alexander Elder's circulating library. It had thousands of books and he and his father had been subscribers. In his book, *Memoir of Robert Chambers, with autobiographical reminiscences of William Chambers, LL.D*, he refers to Sandy's library in the High Street, which he said possessed copies of the *Edinburgh Review*, the *Quarterly Review*, the *Scots Magazine* and a few other periodicals. In acknowledging his appreciation of Sandy Elder's library, Dr

Chambers gave 150 volumes to start the Chambers Institution public library which quickly became recognised as 'the library of all'.

There had been a reading-room next to the Town House some time before the days of the Chambers Institution. A few newspapers and magazines were placed on a long table in the centre of the room and Andrew Stavert 'presided' over the reading-room when he had finished delivering the letters round the town. Peebleans were known to be keen readers of newspapers and the writer was told in the 1960s by the head of TV News at the BBC in London that his old newspaper editor had counselled young reporters writing their news reports to have in mind 'the man standing on the Tweed Bridge at Peebles' and to ensure that their news 'facts' were balanced, forthright and intelligently presented.

In order to celebrate the opening of the Chambers Institution, there was a week-long programme of events which began on Monday, 8 August 1859. These were held in the hall of the Institute, which was to become the scene of many distinguished and happy occasions during the remaining years of the nineteenth century.

A grand occasion in the first year was a 'Social Meeting of All Classes in the District', which was held in the hall. Attended by 500 to 600 residents, tea was served at 6.30 p.m. and there was an 'abundance of substantial cake'. The gathering had been suggested by the Misses Hay of Kingsmeadows and John Bathgate took the chair. The programme included a number of 'short-pointed addresses' on various subjects and there was also, 'Scrooge's remarkable conversion from Dickens *Christmas Carol*,' and there were hymns and a duet on the flute and harmonium. Before the evening ended at 11 p.m. the 'company were regaled with oranges'.

In the 1860s, this hall was the venue for a series of Saturday evening readings and popular lectures. Dr Chambers gave the inaugural address: 'An account of the rise and nature of the National Association for the Promotion of Social Science.' Another lecture in the series was 'China and its Commerce'. The local newspaper commented that these lectures, forming almost the only public entertainment which Peebles could boast in 1860, were promoted and ably supported by a few public-spirited persons.

The YMCA also sponsored a remarkably forward-looking programme of lectures in the hall in 1878. There was an address on 'The problems of Flight and the possibilities of Aerial Navigation', which included not only an exhibition but also models which flew over the heads of the audience. Another lecture in the series was 'Darwinism — True or False?; or, the Facts and Fallacies of Natural Selection.' Peebleans were not only avid readers of books and newspapers but they also had an awareness and interest in a changing world.

Another important event in the life of Peebles was the building of the Hydropathic Establishment, which opened in 1880. The townspeople were invited to a special programme that was arranged during the Christmas period of 1884, so that they could see for themselves the magnificent interior of the imposing turreted renaissance building. There was a Christmas evening concert and a fancy-dress ball on New Year's Day; a special 'Tea' at 8.15 p.m. for the townspeople at the usual charge of 3s (15p) for ladies and gentlemen, 1s 6d (7½p) for ladies and 2s (10p) for gentlemen. Children, too, had a special 'Magic Lantern Show' conducted by Jonas Mitchell, the governor of the poorhouse. Sadly, this was the unfortunate building that was destroyed by fire in July 1905 and replaced within two years by another very fine Hydro.

Before entertainment became available in the hall of the Institute, there were other events and venues. For example, there was the appearance of Wombwell's Menagerie for a performance in the town on a Saturday evening in February 1850. Clearly, it was a spectacle that was long remembered in the town.

> It was a stormy day, blowing a hurricane — and the tempest added great interest to the day and citizens believed the old narrow dilapidated Cuddy Bridge was doomed to destruction by the weight of Wombwell's 'great war elephant' and his ponderous vans which were expected to enter the town in procession that day at noon. Every place where standing was possible and shelter obtained was occupied patiently for hours. By-and-by the music van appeared but no musicians, and next the elephant pulling its den and looking distressed and dirty and draggled. The bridge was crossed in safety and the horses were put up at the Crown Inn. One of Wombwell's men had done up the horses by the light of the candle . . .

And the day came to an end with the stable on fire.

Dr Clement Gunn, in *Leaves from the Life of a Country Doctor* recalls that late one Saturday night he was called to the show-ground by the riverside to attend to a patient in one of the caravans.

All was bustle and confusion . . . the camp-fires glowed redly, and the booths, lit by naphtha-flares, were being hastily dismantled for the midnight journey. The lions and tigers, still excited by the rolling of the drums, roared vehemently from their cages; the caravans shook in the darkness with the sound. I found my patient in a large wagon: she was the lion-tamer's wife. She was in agony, and an immediate operation was essential, I lost no time, and having administered chloroform, operated there and then.

The Good Templar's Hall was used by the Ancient Order of Foresters and readings were given on Saturday evenings. That was in 1880 and it was also the year that the Peebles Amateur Dramatic Company made its first appearance with a performance in the Chamber's Institution Hall to raise funds for the Tay Bridge Accident Relief Fund. The programme consisted of Allan Ramsay's pastoral comedy, *The Gentle Shepherd*, and the farce, *Mad as a Hatter*. Mr A. Yule's orchestra played during the evening (A. Yule, violin; E. Bonong, violincello; Mr Stavert, cornet; A. Watson, piccolo).

Perhaps the most unusual event occurred one evening in September 1889 when a large crowd gathered in the High Street to witness Madame Sartis (an American lady) extracting teeth. The lady occupied a very handsome carriage in which her patients were accommodated with a chair, and where she performed all her operations in full view of her large audience. Never before — nor since — has Peebles witnessed such an exhibition.

As Peebles grew and its economic situation steadily improved, so did the number of activities. There emerged a programme of regular seasonal events involving special train excursions such as the Special Constables trip and a whole series of picnics; sporting activities like those of quoiting on Tweed Green and bowling at Walkershaugh; meetings of organisations such as the Band of Hope, Choral Union, Horticultural Society, Boys and Girls Religious Society in the Good Templar's Hall on a Monday evening — all these activities were part of a new and active social life in the last quarter of the nineteenth century. The new way of life embraced the old customs — at least until the time of the First World War when many of these customs, including the Peebles Gutterbluid Club itself, faded into a past age.

PART I: 1850 – 1900

Charles Ker, a renowned secretary of the Peebles Gutterbluid Club, tells of Hogmanay in Peebles:

> Rise up, auld wife, and shake your feathers,
> Dinnae think that we are beggars;
> We're only bairns come out to play,
> Rise up and gie's our Hogmanay.

Old Laird Hamilton was lying over his half shop-door and every bairn who came got a halfpenny. Laird Girdwood, too, had always a good word and a halfpenny. He would give his head a shake and find a halfpenny, saying all the time 'hoots callant de ye think am made of hapines'. Meanwhile Jamie Dickson, the baker, had his own way of making fun with the bairns. When he saw them coming he would run in to his door and await the onslaught and cry from behind his half-door: 'A'm no ready yet!' But in a very short time the board was brought round and each one got his 'snap' — a little cake. And tradesmen, too, called on Hogmanay to present their accounts personally and receive payment along with some appropriate refreshment.

The Peebles Gutterbluid Club was a worthy institution started in 1823 and their dinner was an important event. With their traditional quaichs, mallets and 'muccle snuff horn well supplied with the choicest snuff called Gutterbluid blend', the Club worthies met each year. John Fergusson, senior, in a toast he proposed in 1903 to the Gutterbluids, put into words the spirit that is still embodied in annual gatherings of the Peebles Callants and the Peebles Guildry Corporation which continue to be well supported in the late 1980s. He said:

> It was good to meet each year to refresh themselves, not only with a bite and a 'wee drappie o't', but especially with song and sentiment and old-world cracks which told them how things went on in the good old days and what worthies lived in the days of auld langsyne in the Auld Burgh Toon, which to the Gutterbluids were precious because they brought to them a thousand remembrances of their boyish days and of friends who had passed away like a dream; it kept their hearts warm.[8]

It is good to see that the Peebles Gutterbluid Club was re-formed at a meeting in December 1974. Attended by George Thomson, Drew

64

Fraser, Jimmy Raeburn, Jim Carruthers and Bill Wallace, they took steps to draw up a new constitution for a Gutterbluid Society.

The size and the composition of the population had wrought changes and there was a new atmosphere as well as an improving environment. A timely decision made in 1895 was the transfer from Dean's Wynd of the 'fleshmarket' that was originally built in 1652 as a slaughter-house; its removal from the centre of the town to South Parks at the west end of the Caledonian Road was a much needed improvement. Equally important was the decision to widen Tweed Bridge in 1897, which improved the appearance of the town and greatly facilitated the movement of traffic.

The generous gift to Peebles by Sir John Hay of Haystoun, Bart., of the beautiful Victoria Park to commemorate the Diamond Jubilee of Queen Victoria became a popular place for the family to visit during weekends and summer evenings. Another facility, started in 1898, was the building of a new Drill Hall at Walkershaugh. Costing £2,000, funds for this were principally raised by a 'Grand Bazaar'. It was built as a drilling place with a headquarters and an armoury, and the Volunteer battalions for the First and Second World War mustered there before they left for service. Happily, it is to be remembered as a venue for a wide range of social activities during the years and the scene of many dances, especially the annual 'Nicht Afore the Morn'.

The first Drill Hall was temporarily in the buildings vacated by the United Presbyterian Church (East) at the Gytes and it is interesting to note the evolving use of this site, which reflects the social history of the town. It was the location of the UP Church that was built about 1791 and then became a drill hall. In 1904 the premises, still very much in the style of church buildings, became a motorcar workshop for Laurence Bell's Peebles Motor Company, the firm having originally set up in a workshop near to the old gasworks in 1903. When Thorburn & Co. (Lowe, Donald & Co.) built their new warehouse at Station Road, their former premises next to The Green Tree were taken over in 1905 as the third-stage move by the Peebles Motor Company. The Gytes site was then redeveloped as an indoor swimming baths, and this facility was generously presented to the town by Sir Henry Ballantyne of Monkrigg in 1919. A new swimming pool has been built in more recent times at the former site of the Tweedside Mill and part of the site at the Gytes has returned to being the location of another church, the Peebles Evangelical Church at 17 Tweed Brae.

PART I: 1850 – 1900

Of course there were from time to time cyclic set-backs in the tide of good fortune; for example, in 1879, when the national trade was dull and there was also a very poor harvest, and when there was a prolonged and severe winter, such as 1886, which brought great distress to the building tradesmen and labourers. These occasions would bring the town's beneficial agencies into action and the soup kitchen would be opened up. This first became available in 1817 when Sir John Hay presented a boiler and a recipe for making soup, having calculated that the boiler would be sufficient for 300 'chopins' (nearly 300 quarts).[9]

Despite these 'economic hiccups', the closing years of the century reflected a vibrant, growing town. It was well served by its two stations that linked Peebles with the national rail network. Travelling to other parts of the country — near or far — was now relatively easy and it was a great social advance. There were improved opportunities for employment, even allowing for a greatly increased workforce living in the town, and more people able to travel to work in Peebles from the outlying districts.

The population in 1883, gutterbluids and incomers, keenly supported social and political progress and were to the fore when a demonstration about the Franchise Bill was held on the Tweed Green. The Bill was to extend the franchise by some two million voters and, as this had been opposed by the House of Lords, some 2,000 from the county met to give their support. The Tweedside Mill workers paraded a banner of Stuart tartan with a blue centre which had on the reverse side:

> First we'll have the Franchise Bill
> Then Ye'll know the people's Will.

The Damdale banner proclaimed:

> We weaver chaps frae Damdale Mill
> resolve to hae the Franchise Bill.

There were two 'symbolic' events in the closing years of the century that were, in a way, a reflection of the changed town, keenly aware of its future yet conscious of a proud past.

First, was the decision to revive the ancient custom of Riding the Marches of the Royal and Ancient Burgh of Peebles. An earlier attempt to revive this in 1874 had failed, but it seemed eminently

66

suitable to Ride the Marches in celebration of Queen Victoria's Diamond Jubilee in 1897.

The ancient ceremony was proudly carried out by W. H. Williamson, the burgh's treasurer, who had been chosen to be the first Cornet. He went round the Marches in unique style, seated in a brake accompanied by mounted supporters. Two years later, the ceremonies were enhanced by the inclusion of the coronation ceremony of the Beltane Queen, and the first to be honoured was Margaret Muir.

Two years before that there was also a gesture made that indicated the awakening of the town to its future while at the same time honouring its ancient heritage. It was the initiative taken in 1895 to bring out the ancient Mercat Cross of Peebles from the Quadrangle of the Chambers Institution and place it in a site of great prominence at the east end of the High Street. This involved the removal of the octagonal shaft that dates from before 1320 and setting it on a new pedestal — a task that required the utmost skill and care.

The Mercat Cross originally stood in the market place in the Old Town and it was eventually placed in the Quadrangle of the Chambers Institution in 1807. The 'new' plinth — a magnificent base to hold the shaft proudly aloft in the centre of the new, emerging town — was given to the royal burgh by Colonel William Thorburn of Craigerne. Understandably, in 1965, the plinth had to be redesigned to allow for cars and other traffic to see over and round it.

At the close of the nineteenth century, it seemed entirely appropriate that a member of the family that had done so much to generate the change of economic fortune for Peebles and Peebleans, should make this symbolic gesture to resite the Mercat Cross prominently, showing that Peebles was indeed a market-place, not for grain but for the finest woollens.

Footnotes:

1. Lang, Andrew and John, *Highways and Byways in the Borders* (London, 1929) pp336-7
2. Bathgate, Alex, *Reminiscences*; (reprinted in the *Peeblesshire News*, 1974)
3. Murray, Norman, *The Scottish Handloom Weavers 1790 – 1850: A Social History* (Edinburgh, 1978) p23
4. Pryde, George C., *Scotland from 1603 to the Present Day* (Edinburgh, 1952) p226

PART I: 1850 – 1900

5. Dalgleish, Dr William, *Statistical Account of Scotland 1791-9*, Vol III pp869-85
6. *Peeblesshire Monthly Advertiser*, April 1856
7. Buchan, J. Walter (ed), *A History of Peeblesshire* (Glasgow, 1925) Vol II, pp135-6
8. Peebles Gutterbluid Club Minutes dated 21 February 1902
9. Buchan, J. Walter (ed), *A History of Peeblesshire* (Glasgow, 1925), Vol II, p130

Part Two

1900 – 1950

CHAPTER 4

Industry, Trade and Commerce

THE NEW CENTURY for Peebles started in a most appropriate way, with Walter Thorburn, Member of Parliament for the United Counties of Peebles and Selkirk, being awarded the honour of Knighthood by Queen Victoria in the New Year's Honours List. Later, Henry Ballantyne was similarly honoured when he received the accolade from King Edward VII in 1906. These awards were warmly greeted throughout the town and were regarded as a sign that all would be well for the Thorburn and the Ballantyne Mills in the century that was just beginning.

Peebles was now a town that was better able to respond to uncertainties of the future. There was a new vigour from its greatly increased population and an economic strength that came from the town's very successful woollen-mills. Although these mills would reflect the cyclic ills of world trade in the years ahead and the town would suffer accordingly, nevertheless their contribution to the long-term economic advancement of the townspeople and the town would be immense.

It has been suggested that Peebles without its tweed-mills would be a mere village. If Thorburn's Damdale Mill had failed like its sister mill when it was under the control of Laing & Irvine, then we might well have known whether that was a reasonable assumption to make. However, it leaves out of the reckoning the impact of the railways. These had given a new status to the county's main town and had encouraged commercial enterprise with more branch-banks coming into Peebles to make it an important service and professional centre. Peebles today in the 1990s has no railway and is almost without a tweed industry, with just over one-third remaining in terms of people employed, but, despite these losses, it is far from being a 'village'. Indeed, it is a town proficient at generating wealth through all kinds of enterprise, especially from tourism, and it has developed a supportive business environment that keeps the money it earns circulating in the town.

The years from 1896 to 1913 were generally good for the woollen trade and exports doubled. Apart from some short periods of recession, the mills were busy and there were long hours of work; starting at six o'clock in the morning through to six in the evening with two breaks lasting from 8.15 to nine in the morning and 1.15 to two in the afternoon. That was on weekdays but on Saturdays work was from six in the morning to twelve noon. The 58½-hour week gradually reduced over the years to forty-five hours in the 1960s and to thirty-nine hours in the late 1980s.

Remuneration was satisfactory, said the *Peeblesshire Advertiser* in January 1907. The March Street Mills had a profit-sharing scheme for their employees and it provided a bonus, for those who had worked the full year, of 2¾d (fractionally over 1p) per £1 on wages earned. It was an indication of the concern for the welfare of its employees. This forward-looking policy was further in evidence when a canteen was provided for the workers in 1917, and later on, in 1930, similar provisions were made in the Thorburn mills.

Sir Henry Ballantyne, speaking about trade conditions at the annual social meeting and dance in 1907 — held in the Drill Hall: doors open six o'clock; tea at seven o'clock prompt — said: 'A few years ago, every year was beating the record. During the last two or three years they had been passing through comparatively trying times and at present the results were not so good as they had been accustomed to have.' He added that the price of wool had risen rapidly during the past three years but he forecast that the following six months 'would be busier than ever'.

On the declaration of war in 1914, Peebles quickly became awakened to a changed way of life. The immediate reaction was that all the mills went on half-time that same day, Tuesday, 4 August. Damdale and Tweedside Mills then closed down completely from the Friday of that week, 7 August. Lowe, Donald & Co. had closed on the Wednesday. The March Street Mills issued a statement: 'We fear we may have to close the works from the 7th till the 17th August.' However, by the end of August the local war effort was swinging into action as orders came into the mills for yarn and cloth for army uniforms. A report in the *Peeblesshire Advertiser* in October 1914 confirmed that the mills were very busy with Government orders. It was also anticipated that the work would be plentiful for several months and that there was likely to be a scarcity of labour because many of the mill workers had joined the armed forces. This was borne out when overtime was needed during November to keep pace with the orders for tartan and khaki. There were also problems when the Border mills lost their main source of yarn as the German army advanced into Belgium, capturing the town of Verviers, and the Yorkshire yarn was judged to be inadequate. The Peebles mills found it difficult to handle the khaki contracts as it was 50 per cent 'shoddy'. What export business there was, such as to America, had to allow for a 40 per cent increase in freight and insurance charges.[1]

In the aftermath of the First World War and as the armed forces were demobilised, the woollen industry began to experience periods of 'fluctuation' in orders and this continued for a number of years. Fortunately for the Border mills there was some demand for finer woollens and this helped the local mills up to the middle of the 1920s.

More encouraging and reassuring news came for the employees of the March Street Mills in July 1919, when D. Ballantyne & Co. brought under their control the Caerlee Mills and the Waverley Mills at Innerleithen and formed D. Ballantyne Bros. & Co. Ltd. It was now one of the largest and most successful undertakings in the woollen industry in Scotland. The March Street Mills, which started up in 1885 with forty-five slow-moving looms, had these replaced when 200 Hattersley machines, with an employment capacity of some 500 workers, were installed at the Ballantyne mills in Peebles and Innerleithen. These mills produced woollen cloths, from light-weight worsted (seven ounce) to overcoatings (thirty-five ounce) and ranged from the Harris-type cloths to the softest cashmere fabrics. Damdale and Tweedside, equipped with sixty-two looms, had an employment capacity of 360 workers producing high-grade men's suitings, sports cloths with a limited trade in women's suitings and yarn for the knitting trade.

A survey of the textile industry reported that Peeblesshire in 1921 had 2,098 persons working in the wool textile industry, comprising 1,048 males and 1,050 females. This was 10 per cent of the total employed in woollens throughout Scotland (20,931). Woollen workers in the neighbouring county of Selkirk totalled 4,883 (23.3 per cent).

Sadly for those workers, the woollen industry was beginning to find itself in the trade slump of 1921. The industry was now on a slippery slope moving slowly towards the Great Depression caused by a world slump in trade during the years from 1929 to 1934. The United Kingdom's figures for the industry's unemployment were 23,600 in December 1924 and 22,500 in December 1925 but in June 1926 there were 64,000: as a percentage of the insured persons, 9.1 per cent, 8.8 per cent and 25.1 per cent respectively.[2] By 1931 the total of all unemployed in the United Kingdom was nearly 2.7 million; according to the local newspapers there were 2.1 million men, 422,836 women, 72,489 boys and 55,508 girls.

The decline in the woollen trade was caused by a number of factors. Firstly, the increased cost of producing woollen suiting and overcoatings in early 1925 had reached an index figure of 223, compared with a figure of 100 for 1914. Woollens were now more expensive to buy and there was less money to buy them with because of the decline in real wages as well as an increasing number of people unemployed. These were the factors directly affecting demand in the home market. However, there was, in addition, some diversification of expenditure from clothing to such items as motor cars, motor cycles and wireless sets, as well as the new interest that was being engendered by cinemas and other entertainment.[3] In 1927, H. Dawson & Co., whilst accepting the drop in home demand was due to competing expenditure, suggested that the overseas competition was less of a problem because of the excellence of British woollens. France and Italy had not been able to maintain their exports at the high level of 1925, but Germany, on the other hand, was well on the way to regaining her former position as a textile country.[4]

Work was none too plentiful during 1930/31. 'It was difficult for employers and employed' was the view of the *Peeblesshire Advertiser* and, although there had been a few busy spells, the mills did not operate at anything like full capacity. The March Street Mills had been reduced to a three-day working week in January 1932. The very low levels of stock which were now being held by retailers and wholesalers were causing problems. Lowe, Donald & Co. was a typical example; their export trade was considerably reduced and they, in turn, were unable to purchase from the mills at the level that they had done previously. Thorburn's Damdale Mill was closed down for one week during August of that year, but the Tweedside Mill kept at work. A 'week-on and week-off' arrangement was introduced and, although this was regarded as a temporary measure, the future looked far from bright. 'Extremely difficult for the tweed trade' was the judgment about these years of the early 1930s. The *Peeblesshire Advertiser* believed the pre-1914 prosperity of the Border tweed trade had perhaps been too largely based on foreign orders and that the quality of the product of our local mills was higher than many in this country could afford to buy.

Fortunately, the first half of 1935 turned out to be better than had been anticipated and was considered to be the best six months since 1931. There were still problems in the early months of 1936 and many of the mills were not able to keep their machinery running at full capacity but there was some improvement as the year ended. This was the time D. Ballantyne & Bros. undertook a comprehensive reorganisation and all the carding and spinning machinery was concentrated at the Waverley Mill in Innerleithen and March Street became the centre for the weaving machinery.

Then it happened, just before the Second World War: the mills were again running at full capacity. The Defence Programme had invited competitive quotes for the production of one million yards of Army serge and the Peebles mills were successful in getting part of the order. No doubt the representations that had been made to the then Secretary of State for Defence, Mr Hore Belisha, on behalf of the Tweedside Mills for a share of this work had helped to secure the order.

In retrospect, the wartime economy of the town during the First World War was good and strong. In addition, the county's agriculture was reaping good harvests and that helped the economy in every part of the shire. The hard years came in the 1920s, when the fluctuations of the woollen trade created uncertainty. Then followed acute periods of recession and during these times hopes were raised that, once the latest setback had been overcome, there would be a pattern of regular employment and better days.

The number of the unemployed in Peeblesshire in September 1932 totalled 603; in July 1934 there were 787 and the number had fallen to 472 in July 1935. In Peebles it had fallen over this period from 228 in July 1934 to 196 in July the following year, indicating thirty-two more people at work.[5] In October 1936, the unemployed in Peebles had further reduced to ninety-nine but by October 1937 it was up to 115. This was against a background of about two million unemployed throughout the United Kingdom in the middle of 1935; it had been very near to 2.7 million in 1931.[6] The unemployed were generally from all sectors of trade and industry; in Peebles they were nearly all mill employees out of work.

The local unemployment figures were not as bad as in Lanarkshire where they were as high as 37.6 per cent of the insured workers in the 1920s and 1930s.[7] Traditionally, the Peebles folk were careful and independent but, nevertheless, for those who depended on the mills for their livelihood — and that included a high proportion of the households in the town — these were long and disappointing years of economic hardship. It was a long, bumpy slide into the World Slump and a slow and hard climb out of it.

Fortunately, the town's economy between the years 1919 and 1939 was helped by an enterprising programme of house-building which began almost immediately after the end of the First World War. Twelve two-bedroom houses were built before the war in George Place in 1909 at a cost of £3,400. However, it was in 1919 that the 'march of progressive house-building' was really started when the town ventured upon the first of its 'housing schemes'.

The Housing Acts (Scotland) 1919 and 1932 gave financial scope to Local Authorities to consider housing requirements and made available government grants, which enabled the Peebles Town Council to undertake housing schemes at Eliot's Park, Dalatho, Connor Street, George Terrace, George Place, Rosetta Place, North Place and North Street. Another major investment project was the building of a new sewage works at a cost of £36,000. It was to be completed by the end of 1937 and the contract stipulated that fifty out of the eighty workers had to be local, to help reduce the number of unemployed. Two other major building projects undertaken during these years of Depression were the construction of the Playhouse Cinema in the High Street, which opened in 1932, and the new County Buildings at Rosetta Road, in 1936.

Much earlier in the century, the Hydropathic was re-built. On a summer evening while the guests were at dinner, the Hydro caught fire. This happened on 7 July 1905, the fire spreading rapidly so that, by eight-thirty at night, the whole structure was fully ablaze. The 'new' Hydro was built in less than two years. Numerous friends were invited to the opening on 25 March 1907, with the reassuring invitation: 'it is constructed fireproof throughout!' The new building is Georgian in style and regarded as a very fine replacement.

The Hydro had been greatly missed when it was no longer bringing in business to the town, and local shops had looked forward to this reopening. The town still had a good array of shops and in 1900 there were as many as ten drapers, outfitters and tailors shops: seven in the High Street, the Eastgate had two and there was one in the Old Town. Those still in business and mentioned in Slater's Directory of 1867 included George Veitch, Robert Williamson and Green — all in the High Street.

Another outfitters that became successfully established before the century began was Veitch's Corner House. It was started in 1884 by Robert Veitch and his wife, Helen Binnie Peden, at their house in Gladstone Place, and one year later they moved into newly-built premises at 2 High Street. About 1887 the business extended into the adjoining shops, which had been formerly occupied by J. Laidlaw (butchers) and J. Mason (bootmakers) at 1 and 3 Northgate and twenty-three years later they took over premises at the rear, for a men's department. The upper-floor living-accommodation was also converted for business use at that time.

There have been four generations since 1884 to the present time (1990): Robert Veitch, JP; Robert Bishop Veitch, JP, Hon. Deputy Sheriff; Douglas Weir Veitch and Robert Douglas Veitch. Veitch's must be one of the better-known businesses in the town. It has an imposing building located on a prominent corner site at the east end of the High Street and it has a most distinctive and stylish name-plate. This 'logo' was originally drawn on the back of an envelope by a friend of R. B. Veitch whilst they were serving together during the First World War, and has remained unchanged since then. Its beautiful lettering and stylish design must have appeared in many of the town's photographs since the 1920s.[8]

In 1896 George Anderson established a draper's business in the Old Town that was to grow into a flourishing and successful enterprise known as the Castle Warehouse. His father used a part of the Greenside site for a tannery and skinner's business and these premises, along with his house in the Old Town, were demolished to be replaced by George Anderson's first shop. George Anderson started as an apprentice with Whitie, Tailors and Drapers, High Street and, in addition to developing his business, he took a great interest in local affairs and was provost of Peebles for seven years (1926 – 1933).

In 1915 A. Finlayson went into partnership with George Anderson and in 1933 both Robert and Alex Finlayson, A. Finlayson's sons, took over the business. After the Second World War the premises in the Old Town were developed and expanded in 1953 and again in 1978, with their Northgate furniture, bedding and carpet business being opened in 1964. Branches were established in Penicuik (1969) and in Galashiels (1972 and 1982). Robert Finlayson's sons, Sandy and Ian, joined the business in 1963 and 1970 respectively and became responsible for its running on the deaths of Alex (1970) and Robert (1982).[9]

There were fewer grocery shops in the town in the 1930s — eighteen compared with twenty-five in 1867. The Co-operative Society which had came into existence in 1872 had three grocery shops, the main one at Greenside but with branches at 1 Wemyss Place and 77 Northgate. However, none of the grocery businesses listed in 1867 were still trading under their former name. Changes over the years tended to make the retailing of grocery foods easier to handle and some grocery shops were now being described as 'general stores'. Tinned foods were introduced at about the time of the First World War and in the 1930s packaged foods were becoming available. Brand-names like Heinz, Kelloggs and Ovaltine were generally known. There was some resistance by the older and more traditional townspeople to the use of tinned foods because they were believed to lack the quality and taste of fresh food, were expensive and their use in preference to fresh food was considered lazy.

The availability of fish-shops was a later innovation in Peebles. There were none in 1867 but sixty years later there were four: John Fergusson and J. M. Wood in the Northgate; Allan & Horne, in the Old Town; and Thos Turnbull, in the High Street. There were many more butcher shops in the 1930s when the town had seven compared with four in the 1860s. These were well spread around the town: Crichton and Sinclair in the High Street; M'Kenna in the Eastgate; Walker, in the Northgate; Goldie, in the Old Town; the Co-operative, in Elcho Street Brae; and Harris, in Montgomery Place.

These changes were not only indicative of more consumers in the town but also a change of diet with more fish and meat being consumed; no doubt due to the economic improvement generally experienced over the years despite the effects of unemployment. The growth in the number of confectionery shops was also a sign of changing times and consumer habits. There were certainly three confectionery outlets in 1900 but by 1936 there were twelve: Birrell, Agnes Douglas and the Premier Cafe in the High Street; M. Frame, C. S. Frame and C. Shearer in the Northgate; J. Turnbull in the

78

Eastgate; M. & C. Caldwell in the Bridgegate; R. A. Shearer in Elcho Street Brae; A. W. Craig in Edinburgh Road and T. Kelly and M. Clark in the Old Town.

Another change of consumer requirement was the establishment of fish-and-chip shops (Potato Chip and Fish Merchants). In the early 1900s, Philip De-Meo and Thomas Ford had shops, and in 1937 there were George Hamilton (School Brae), G. Dobson (Old Town), and Andrew Johnstone (Northgate). There was also a horse-drawn fish-and-chip van that went round the main streets on most evenings, stopping to serve customers on demand.

Garages and cycle shops became a well-established section of the town's business activities. First and foremost was the Peebles Motor Company which was started in 1903 by Laurence Bell, with a small shed for a workshop, located at the old gasworks at Greenside. Mr Bell had previously been an engineer and manager to the Gas-Light Company at Innerleithen. He built his own car in 1901, making the car parts right through to the finished body and it was the first car to be made in the Scottish Borders. His reputation was such that he was approached by many car owners to undertake repair work and that encouraged him to set up in business as the Peebles Motor Company. A lot of the business came from Edinburgh, and the Peebles Motor Company decided to establish a branch at the Haymarket in the capital. As the Edinburgh business was so successful, the directors decided to concentrate all their efforts in that city and the Peebles connection came to an end. However, in 1928, the Edinburgh-based Peebles Motor Company was taken over by the Scottish Motor Traction Company (SMT).

Their former showroom and workshop in Peebles was acquired by the Jones Motor Company. Robert Mathison, proprietor of the Green Tree Hotel, then bought the business which now carried the sign: 'Robt. Mathison — The Motor House'. In 1924 he sold the business to the Tweeddale Motor Company. It was James Hopkirk, originally a driver with Harpers Motors and Thomson of Ellerslie, who developed the Tweeddale Motor Company and made it one of the leading businesses in Peebles, acquiring in 1947 James Thomson's Ellerslie Garage.

Another highly successful pioneering venture that brought credit to Peebles was Harper's Motors. Andrew Harper provided the town and the district with its first omnibus service which came into operation in 1923 between Peebles, Innerleithen and Walkerburn.

PART II: 1900 – 1950

The business rapidly expanded and became one of the largest of its kind outside the big combines. Mr Harper gradually increased his fleet to twenty-seven buses by 1932, when he sold the business to the Caledonian Omnibus Company Ltd.

He had started up in business in 1894 at Broxburn in West Lothian as a carrier, and eventually had a number of horses, lorries, carts and a furniture removal van. In 1922, with a four-ton Dennis ex-War Department lorry, Andrew Harper started up a carrying service between Leith and Edinburgh to Peebles, Innerleithen and Walkerburn. The lorry was parked in Station Road overnight until a garage was acquired in Dovecot Road, and by 1923 a Peebles base had been established with three lorries employed. It was at that time the risk was taken to buy the first Harper bus, which was a twenty-seater, built on an ex-War Department Daimler chassis which could carry approximately two tons. In April 1923 Joe Harper, one of the sons, with a sixteen-year-old conductor, Jackie Elder, set off on the first bus run from Peebles to Innerleithen and Walkerburn, having obtained the permission of the local authorities to pick up and set down passengers at recognised places. Harpers Motors also operated an extensive programme of bus tours which were extremely popular in the late 1920s and thirties.[10]

Another local 'omnibus' pioneer was William Ramsay and he provided services to link Peebles, Lyne, Stobo, Drumelzier, Rachan, Broughton, Skirling and Biggar.

The first half of the twentieth century was the age of the car but in the 1930s car ownership in Peebles was still very restricted. Although the cost of a new Austin Seven was about £118 and nearly half the price it was in the 1920s, not many people could afford to have one. There was, however, a steady and growing interest in both new and secondhand cars and also in vans and lorries for the small business. A hire service that could supply vehicles with drivers for all kinds of needs was also a new type of business. James Thomson of Ellerslie was one of the local firms that advertised a wonderful array of vehicles such as 'motor landaulettes, touring cars, charabancs, motor and horse hearses, as well as carriages for hire'.

In addition to selling and hiring vehicles, there was a developing trade in the provision of petrol and oil, tyres and skilled repair and maintenance services. By the 1930s there were six garages in the town: Crossburn Garage, Edinburgh Road; Greenside Motor Co., Greenside; M'Pherson & Smart, Old Town; J. Thomson, Ellerslie

Garage; Tweeddale Motor Co., Innerleithen Road; and T. Wallace & Sons, Station Road. It was also the age of the bicycle. The safety bicycle became available in about 1906, with pneumatic tyres and a rear chain-drive. A new 'bike' at that time cost about £5, so it was a popular means of getting to work and used for leisure at the weekend. In Peebles, the expert cycle dealers were J. M. Wallace, Eastgate; A. A. Wilson, Northgate; and Greenside Garage.

The family of 'Wallace the Engineers' started in Peebles in 1835 when two brothers came from Leadburn to settle in the town. Alex Wallace became the proprietor of the Commercial Hotel in the High Street and Thomas Wallace set up business as an engineer and millwright in Damdale. Thomas Wallace had two sons, J. M. Wallace, who struck out on his own as a successful cycle agent and engineer with a workshop at 19 Eastgate and Thomas W. Wallace, who carried on his father's engineering business. The latter successfully developed this business at the Bridgegate where he was for a time the landlord of the premises that were used by the *Peeblesshire Advertiser*. The newspaper was printed on the first floor above the engineers shop and it had to be strengthened in load-bearing to take the weight of the heavy printing-press. He also acquired the Station Road Garage in the late 1920s from Alexanders who had built the premises.

Both these divisions of the T. W. Wallace business were highly regarded. His engineering knowledge was extensive. He developed, for his own business requirements, a gas combustion engine that was regarded to be in the forefront of knowledge at the time he designed and built it. A Wallace patent also exists for an innovative washing-machine for cleansing sheepskins, which was widely marketed. The idea was developed through observation and taking part in the skinning operations at the Greenside tannery where they used cleaning trestles in the Cuddy. These trestles were called 'cuddies' and it may be that Peebles Water became the 'Cuddy Pool' because of this practice.

Thomas Wallace died in 1949 and the company was divided between the family. Although they no longer have the garage at the corner of the Northgate and Dean Park, the engineering firm continues under William Wallace who is a great-grandson of the founder who started the business in 1835.

The changing community and its needs over a period of seventy years can be interpreted from the different type and number of shops and services that became available in the 1930s compared with the 1860s. In the 1930s there were three furniture dealers (none in 1867); three ironmongers (previously six); eight tobacconists (one before); four chemists (one in the past); four china merchants (three in the 1860s); four boot-and shoemakers (nine previously); six hairdressers (only one before); and two jewellers/watch- and clock-makers (when there were three in the past).

John McOwan acquired in 1913 the business of watchmakers and jewellers at 28 High Street from the widow of John Hislop, grandson of its founder. The watchmaker's business had originally been in Bridgegate but was transferred to the High Street about 1863 by Robert Hislop (John Hislop's father). John McOwan was a native of Crieff and, after training as a watchmaker in his father's shop, he successfully built up his business in Peebles, being succeeded by his two sons after the Second World War, John and Kenneth McOwan, and they have continued the reputation of this long-established business up until 1990.

The vault of this jewellers shop at 28 High Street was used as a prison for a short time. The town council acquired it for this purpose in 1775 at a price of £20. Despite having a double grating, liquor was able to be passed to the prisoners by their friends in the High Street and, having decided it was unsuitable, they sold the vault and the house above it some twenty-three years later for the sum of £220.[11]

The three ironmongers in the 1930s were Scott Brothers and T. Watson Bracewell, both in the High Street; and R. H. Wilson in the Northgate. Twin brothers, Robert Douglas Scott and James Mitchell Scott, came to Peebles in 1891 and set up in business at 50 High Street. It was first known as 'R. D. and J. M. Scott', later changing to Scott Brothers. In 1910 they moved into their present premises at 48 High Street, next door to their original shop, which had been previously occupied by J. Pairman.

Robert Douglas Scott is the present owner, having succeeded his father W. M. Scott and is the third generation to run this very successful business. Today it is the only ironmongers in the town and the business shows great flair and enterprise in providing a wide range of ironmongery and items for the household, kitchen and garden. The business keeps pace with modern demands and it has been a successful pioneer in Sunday trading, which particularly caters for visitors. An equally enterprising ironmonger in 1854 was John Paterson whose business was 'ironmongers and booksellers'.[12]

T. Watson Bracewell came from Canada in 1915 and served as a captain in the Royal Engineers during the First World War. He acquired an existing ironmongers business at 64 High Street in 1921 and, being mechanically-minded, built up a very successful business becoming a specialist in wireless and television.

There were five builders in existence in 1867 and Alexander Dickson, High Street, was one of those firms. In 1898 the firm of Dickson & Clyde was operating from a yard at the Caledonian Station and, when Robert Dickson retired in 1907, the business became James Clyde & Sons. Succeeding generations of the Clyde family have managed this business which has the distinction of having built many of the houses and shops from the time of the town's expansion, which began about the 1860s onwards. David Clyde took over the running of the business in succession to his father, James Clyde.

Their reputation as first-class stone-masons is to be seen in the fine stone work used in the difficult task of widening Tweed Bridge in 1897, almost doubling the width from twenty-one feet to forty feet (from parapet to parapet). Their continuing skill can be seen in the plinth built for the Mercat Cross in 1965.

Thomas Tod & Co., Murray Place, and James Cleghorn, School Brae, were the other two builders and masons in the town along with Clyde in the 1930s. William Tod had his builder's yard at the Old Station in 1898 and an example of Tod's fine masonry was the beautifully-built post office building which once stood on the west side of the Northgate at Usher's Wynd; sadly, it is now demolished. The Peebles builders from the 1880s through to the 1940s have produced many fine houses and shops which have enhanced the appearance of the town. Sadly, this cannot be said about many of the houses and shop fascias that have been built in recent years.

There were two firms of plasterers in the 1930s and they were L. Grandison & Son, Innerleithen Road, and J. & J. Aitken, 12 Rosetta Road. Leonard Grandison, born in Prestonpans, had been a foreman plasterer with Jas. Annan and worked on the building of the British Linen Bank premises in the High Street in the mid-1870s, but in 1886 he set up his own firm in Peebles. The firm of Grandisons quickly gained a reputation for ornamental plaster work and was involved in the rebuilding of the Hydro in 1906 – 7 also working at about that time on the new Council Chambers at the Chambers Institution.

The demand for ornamental work fell off after 1914 but partly

83

revived again after the Second World War, particularly for skilled restoration work. Grandisons have been well to the fore as specialists able to undertake this exacting task and a notable example is their work in restoring the dining-room ceiling at Blair Castle. Through the initiative of Leonard S. Grandison, grandson of the founder, a Museum of Ornamental Plaster Work has been established in Peebles and this is widely recognised as a major contribution in preserving examples of this decorative art and highly skilled craft. It is interesting to record that Grandisons used a 'sand boat' on the River Tweed in the years up to 1939, having permission to extract sand and aggregate from a gravel bed at a point in the river near to Neidpath Castle. Each time the river was in flood, it would replenish the gravel. The sand and gravel was brought down by the barge to the junction with Peebles Water (the 'Cuddy') where it was unloaded.[13]

In the 1930s there were five painter/decorator businesses and these included David Mitchell, which was founded in 1790 and is one of the oldest businesses in the town. It was started by John Turnbull and succeeded by David Mitchell, followed by David Murray and David Wood (nephews) and later by George Murray Thorburn, and now by George and Ian Thorburn. The other firms were: J. Vannan, Eastgate; James Lindsay & Son, Northgate; and Mason Stevenson and A. W. Hamilton, both in the High Street.

There were two booksellers and stationers in the town in 1867 and four in 1936. The oldest business is that of William J. Whitie, 73 High Street, who acquired it from Thomas Davidson in 1889. He was the son of William Whitie, tailor and draper, who was provost of Peebles from 1883 to 1889. William J. Whitie's son, Wilbur, who was Cornet in 1949, succeeded to the business in 1954 and, when he died in 1988, Mrs Whitie continued to run the family business. The Whitie family have a long association with Peebles. In the middle of the nineteenth century, James and John Whitie had a boot and shoe business which originated in the seventeenth century. Their workshops were in the East Port and they had a bootshop in the West Port.[14]

The Kers are another family with roots in the town that go back to the seventeenth century. They had been blacksmiths and farriers (veterinary surgeons) from about that time and from 1870 have had their family home and business at Ker Place in the Northgate. Ker's smiddy was originally situated behind the premises of Thomas H. Ralston & Son, 18 – 20 Northgate (formerly Thomas Baker) and before that on the site where the St Andrew's Church Hall now stands.

It is accepted as authentic by succeeding generations of the family, that the soldiers of King James VI had their swords ground there when they passed through the town. There was an occasion, too, when Lord Darnley, the husband of Mary, Queen of Scots, had his horse shod at the smiddy when he was paying a visit to Neidpath Castle. John Ker, who continues in the family tradition, resides at Ker Place, and is a veterinary surgeon for the Department of Agriculture in Scotland. He confirms that these stories were believed to be true by the family and he has a pair of cuff-links that have been made in the smiddy from the metal of the swords.

The 1851 census shows John Ker's great-great-grandfather, born in 1811, was a blacksmith and nailer at the smiddy in the Northgate, next door to the Cross Keys Inn. It must have been an ideal location for the business with plenty of work from the inn's coaches and horses. The details of the household in 1851 showed that the father — born in 1777 and also a blacksmith — was living with his son who was running the business. John Ker's great-grandfather, James Ker, then aged 14 was an apprentice blacksmith in his father's smiddy; later he went to the Edinburgh Veterinary College in 1862. There he studied and trained under William Dick, who founded the college, and the family still have the great-grandfather's notes from the Dick lectures. John Ker's grandfather (John Ker, 1866-1938) also qualified as a veterinary surgeon; he attended the Royal Edinburgh Veterinary College in 1893. John Ker's father, James Ker, chose not to follow in the footsteps of his forefathers; he became a butcher. John Ker, however, qualified at the Royal (Dick) Veterinary College in 1959 and practised abroad before returning to Peebles in 1982 to take up his present appointment.

Interestingly, James Ker (1836 – 79) devised a formula for the treatment of the disease of sheep and lambs, which he called 'Ker's Specific Alternative Pills'. These were widely marketed and carried the instructions: 'Press it gently past the root of the tongue, when it will go over at once. If any should choke a little in giving them, put them back into the folds, when in a few minutes they will be all right again.' There is a current school of thought that the 'killer disease' of sheep today is 'stress' because they are not handled so intimately.[15]

Peebles had strong farming connections and agricultural labouring was a major occupation for the townspeople before the woollen-mills

85

were established. As the county town, it was the centre of services for the farming community and in 1906 was chosen to stage the Highland and Agricultural Society's Show. This was achieved despite 'pessimistic prognostications' that the show would be a failure. Indeed it proved to be financially more successful than when it was held in other Border towns, and a surplus of £415 was recorded by the Society. It should be added that local people raised £1,489 in aid of the show; evidence that support is always forthcoming in Peebles when the challenge is there — true then and still true today.

A more important and continuous link with the farming community in Tweeddale is the town's very successful auction market. It was first at Dean Park, then relocated on a 1¾-acre site at the corner of Montgomery Place and Cross Road, and was started by John Cairns of Winkston, who took over as local auctioneer following the death of Archibald Gibson Blackie. In 1936 the auction mart was acquired from John Cairns & Sons by Lawrie & Symington Limited of Lanark, and changed in 1938 to a new site with an area of just over 20 acres at South Parks Farm.

A photographic saloon would normally come to the town on Fair Days in the late 1870s. There were three photographic studios established in the town prior to 1900. Mr J. McNaught had studios at 31 High Street and his selection of portraits and wedding photographs in his display-cabinet were always a feature of High Street 'window shopping'. There was also Robertson in March Street, twice a prize-winner in open competition for portraiture in London, and he could provide a large framed portrait, twelve inches by ten inches, for 16s 6d (82½p). Another photographer was E. Watson in the Old Town, who could provide ferrotype portraits costing one shilling (5p).

Early in the 1920s Tom Litster, who was a native of Peebles, turned to photography and he was joined by his brother, John, establishing the firm of Thomas Litster in 1923. (In addition to McNaught and Litster there was also R. L. Webb, photographers, Young Street.) Litster's photographic coverage of the Beltane Festival year by year and their timely and comprehensive display mounted in their windows — at the Northgate from the 1930s and more recently at 61a High Street — quickly became established as a regular part of the festival itself. From the 1930s the photographs produced by Litsters and also by the *Peeblesshire News* have become treasured souvenirs of the various parts played by the family in the Beltane Festival.

The first telephone exchange in Peebles was established by the National Telephone Company and located in Damdale. It opened in 1891 with six subscribers but by 1936 there were nearly 250 local business and professional firms and hotels on the 'phone. Dr C. B. Gunn claimed he was the first to have the telephone installed but, because there were so few subscribers in the very early years, he abandoned the exchange and used a private wire to the chemist 'to whom I telephoned prescriptions . . . the charm of telephonic communication in such circumstances soon palls'. He eventually came back on to the exchange when his 'tête-à-tête' with the chemist was extended to a wider sphere of usefulness'.[16]

The half-century to the end of the Second World War witnessed the innovation and development of the entertainment business. First was the phonograph and this led to the innovation of the 'gramophone'. It was a new business opportunity for many local shops, particularly the sales of records, as there was always a demand for the latest music and entertainment. However, another new entertainment business grew in Peebles from the introduction of Scott's cinematography. James A. Scott was described as 'the country's leading cinematographist'. Starting with the silent films in the Burgh Hall, these were later superseded by the 'talkies' in Scott's Empire Cinema at the Bridgegate and The Playhouse on the High Street. The cinemas became popular places of entertainment for the family and attracted regular patronage with each change of programme. As a local business venture it was very successful, right through to the 1950s.

It was the introduction of the wireless in 1922 that had the greatest impact on the generations before the Second World War. It became the dominant entertainment medium in the home. The first sets were very simple receivers with a crystal ('cat's whisker') and headphones. The use of radio valves and the incorporation of a loudspeaker as part of the set allowed for major improvements in design. By 1936 there were ten dealers in Peebles and they could supply the latest models and arrange installation, attend to repairs and, before the 'mains electric' sets were available, recharge the accumulators. Bracewells at this time were advertising 'His Master's Voice is the best in radio receivers, prices from £7 19s 6d' (£7.97½), while Scott Brothers had 'New seven stage battery sets, 9 guineas' (£9.45).

Peebles was itself 'recharged' by a half-century of growth, despite the hard years of the Depression. At the end of it the mills were still strong; the railways were necessary but the car, buses and lorries had reduced the community's dependence on rail transport. The local economy had been undoubtedly strengthened since the early 1900s — and there was still a belief in the enterprise of the town and its future progress. The loss of our two railway stations, and the disappearance of two of the woollen-mills and a reduction of employment capacity at the March Street Mills, were events that no one could have foreseen halfway through the twentieth century, or believed possible.

Footnotes:

1. Lawson, I. C., personal notes
2. *Survey of Textile Industry (Great Britain); Part III of a Survey of Industries* (1928) pp270, 211
3. Ibid, pp213-4
4. Ibid, p217
5. *Peeblesshire Advertiser*, August 1935
6. *Peeblesshire Advertiser*, November 1937
7. Bulloch, J. P. B. (ed), *Third Statistical Account of Scotland: The Counties of Peebles and Selkirk* (Glasgow, 1964) p87
8. Veitch, Douglas W., personal recollections
9. Finlayson, Sandy, personal recollections
10. Harper, Huge Geddes, (personal reminiscences, 1964) supplied by his son, Andrew Douglas Harper
11. Buchan, J. Walter (ed), *A History of Peeblesshire* (Glasgow, 1925) Vol II, pp105 – 6
12. Scott, R. Douglas, (personal recollections)
13. Grandison, Leonard S., *100 Years On: 1886 – 1986* (printed privately; 1987)

14. Smith, Herbert H., *Recollections of a Tweeddale Laddie* (Selkirk, 1987) p12
15. Ker, John, personal recollections
16. Crockett, Rutherford (ed), *Leaves from the Life of a Country Doctor* (Clement Bryce Gunn, MD, JP) (London, 1935) pp88-9

CHAPTER 5

The Burgh

THE PEEBLES OF 1900 had much to be proud about. It had left behind the crushing poverty of the eighteenth century and in a hundred years had achieved a modest prosperity which extended to the bulk of its citizens. The main industry, textiles, had enjoyed almost forty years of growth and increased trade. The main product, woollen cloth of high quality, enjoyed a world-wide reputation, much of it being marketed through merchants within the town. Other lesser industries flourished and the shops and businesses reflected the needs of a population which, by 1900, had reached 5,266.

The principal streets were well lit and the pavements universally level. The road surfaces, however, were still of whin grit which became reduced to a grey slime after wet weather or snow melt. With the preponderance of horse traffic and the consequent droppings, the resulting admixture can be imagined. Nonetheless, the fellmongers and tanners had gone from Greenside and Tweed Green and the 'stinking stairs' existed in name only.

The High Street, Eastgate and Northgate were as we see them today. Three architectural aberrations had appeared by 1900, the 'Trust', which had been rebuilt in mock-Tudor after the rebuilding of Tweed Bridge, the property at 32 High Street and the Liberal Club (later the Social Club) at 17 Eastgate. These were in a quasi-Tudor style totally out of place in an otherwise noble street.

As we have seen, the vast increase in administrative and legislative activity in the nineteenth century led to a transformation of local government. Although the town council still comprised the same officials and councillors, to them had been added professionals to carry out their advisory and technical needs. In Peebles the extra staff consisted of a town chamberlain, a burgh surveyor and various foremen of trades and superintendents of cemeteries, parks and so on.

Added to the town council, however, were a multiplication of boards at local level, each with a specific function. Thus parochial boards were set up for poor law. In 1872 school boards, elected by ratepayers, were constituted in Peebles. In 1857 boards of lunacy were established at county level. Road Trustees had been appointed under the Turnpike Acts but, under the Roads and Bridges Act of 1878, new Road Trustees were constituted in Peeblesshire whilst, in Peebles, the town council acted as Road Trustees. The toll bridge at Innerleithen still bears a Peeblesshire Roads Trustee plaque.

Peeblesshire, as a county, did not acquire a real organ of government until 1889, when county councils appeared to take over the functions formerly exercised by Commissioners of Supply and those of Road Trustees. County councillors were to be elected triennially, the franchise being widened as the Parliamentary franchise was by the various Reform Acts. The county council had powers to control capital expenditure on public works requiring loans, and also to act as the County Police Committee. From 1889 there were also district committees, consisting of councillors for the various constituencies, plus the parish councils.[1]

It became evident by 1900 that the system which had developed in the nineteenth century had defects. The multiplication of elected bodies inevitably led to a decline in the interest of voters and candidates alike. Indeed, as time went on and apathy grew, difficulty was experienced in persuading the voters to turn out. One glaring flaw in Peeblesshire related to the size of the parishes. They were quite simply too small a unit. If we take education as a case in point this was certainly true; larger units such as counties made it easier to arrange for itinerant teachers for special subjects to be employed. It became easier to deploy teachers within a number of schools and economy of scale could be practised in the laying down of standards and in supply costs. Moreover, it became obvious that secondary education could never be satisfactorily organised on a parochial basis.

Changes were therefore made which set the relationship in education between Peeblesshire and Peebles for some years. Secondary education committees were set up in 1893. In 1908 parishes were permitted to amalgamate for school board purposes. The next logical step by the Act of 1918 made the education authorities coterminous with the county. So Peebles lost direct control of its schools.

Similarly, the 1929 Act dealt with other aspects of administration. By this time there were no less than nine bodies in local government, many of them applicable to Peeblesshire and Peebles. In the terms of the Act, seven of them were abolished. The *ad hoc* bodies disappeared and only the town and county councils were retained. One new body, however, was added; that of district council. This consisted of the county councillors of the district plus members elected at the same time as the county councillors.

The 1929 Act produced, in effect, a two-tier structure, a solution which, in the main, was to serve Peeblesshire and Peebles well until the 1970s. The generally competent body became the county council. The lower tier was formed by the burgh and districts, although the districts had very limited powers. The burgh retained such matters as lighting, cleansing and housing and also the control of such municipal enterprises as cemeteries, parks, the golf course, swimming baths and the gasworks. The county council was enlarged to include delegates from town councils, in this case Peebles and Innerleithen. Such members had powers to vote on matters which the county had responsibility for within the burgh.

There was animosity over the years between the burgh and county, mainly on the much vexed and perennial question of finance, the burgh members holding the somewhat parochial view that the burgh was providing more than its share for the services provided. When we consider that the combined population of Peebles and Innerleithen was generally rather more than 50 per cent of the total population of the shire, they may have been presenting a fallacious argument.[2]

All this was in the future when Provost Henry Ballantyne and his bailies took office in 1898. Under the provisions of the Council (Scotland) Act of 1900, the burgh boundaries were extended. From the east in a clockwise manner they embraced Nether Soonhope, Woodside, Bonnycraig, Morning Hill, Firknowe (in the west), Rosetta and Swinton Bank (in the north). The continuing march of progress was to further extend them after both wars by the acquisition of landward property, an important factor in the development of the burgh.

The South African War (1899 – 1901) which followed hard on the Diamond Jubilee of Queen Victoria had little effect on Peebles. Nonetheless, a number of Peebles men volunteered for service. They were already members of the local Volunteer Battalion of The Royal Scots. Their names are recorded in the Drill Hall. This act of memory we owe to Dr C. B. Gunn, that well-loved local physician. As already mentioned, the town had taken the opportunity offered by the Queen's Jubilee to resuscitate the annual Riding of the Marches and to incorporate this ancient ceremony, one which arguably dates from prehistoric times. This latter, the Beltane, was recast, in an imaginative way, as a children's festival with a Beltane Queen and Court. It required also the active participation of the pupils of the local school; this was to be Kingsland School after it opened in 1900.

The minutes of Peebles Town Council between 1901 and the outbreak of war in 1914 reflected in some respect the mundane business of a settled community where the permanent officials of the council carried through the wishes of the elected councillors in an exemplary manner. There are, however, exceptions to the placid administration and month to month business of the burgh. In January 1901 Queen Victoria died peacefully and the patriotic condolences of the burgesses of Peebles in the name of their council are recorded. So also are the best wishes of the community to Edward VII on his accession to the throne. Indeed, for his Coronation in 1902, Provost Henry Ballantyne saw fit to have a medal struck to commemorate the occasion, one to be given to each child of school age. Later in 1909, the brother of Henry Ballantyne (later Sir Henry of the March Street Mills) had a further medal produced to mark the Beltane Festival of that year when the principals were as follows:

Provost	–	J. A. Ballantyne
Cornet	–	David Ballantyne
Beltane Queen	–	Bessie Ballantyne

This again was given to all the pupils of school age. The last commemorative medal, again its presentation sponsored by Provost J. A. Ballantyne, marks the Coronation of George V and again loyal greetings were conveyed from the burgesses of Peebles.

This period marks the decline and final extinction of the philosophy of Samuel Smiles (1812 – 1904), the religion of 'Self Help', as it affected the growth and development of Peebles. From now on national and local government were increasingly to determine major changes within the burgh. Indeed, the last major work to take place, funded purely by public subscription, was the building of Priorsford Bridge, the work of W. Inglis of Tantah, who designed and supervised the construction in 1905.

PART II: 1900 – 1950

In the same year, the skill and enthusiasm of Peebles Fire Brigade was tested to the full. The fire which destroyed the Hotel Hydropathic was apparently caused by an electrical fault started in the roof space. In consequence, the fire was almost out of control before the fire brigade was in attendance, although they turned out very quickly. In fighting the fire they were hampered by a lack of water-pressure, the sheer size of the Hydro building and the shortage of hoses which would have been required for such a situation. Despite assistance from other brigades, the fire literally burned itself out. All this was duly minuted along with the thanks conveyed to Peebles Fire Brigade for their efforts. Within two years, the Hotel Hydro had been rebuilt albeit in a different architectural style. The present building is substantially the same as the one rebuilt and reopened in 1907.[3]

Provost Peter Dalling had not long been in office when the First World War broke out. Since the council were on summer holiday, no mention is made of this world event until later the same year. First mention, indeed, marks the departure for France of 1/8th Battalion The Royal Scots who left Haddington for overseas service in late October 1914. The battalion, which numbered a company from Peebles and one from Innerleithen/Walkerburn in its ranks, was the first Territorial Army unit from Scotland to be sent for active service in France.

Despite this early response to the outbreak of war, the initial reaction in Peebles was to follow the Government's guidelines, 'business as usual'. However, the settled pattern of the town's economy was disturbed as the textile industry of the Borders, including Peebles, was immediately affected. Some raw materials and markets were cut off, enlistment reduced the labour force, and there was an immediate increase of up to 40 per cent in freight and insurance charges which affected textile exports to the Americas.

In agriculture the drive was to be for production. As in the Napoleonic War a vast Army and Navy had to be supplied and a home population maintained. In response to soaring shipping losses, land was put under the plough which had lain fallow for a hundred years. As elsewhere, both in farming and in industry, recruitment and later conscription forced up wages. More important for the future, governmental bodies increasingly took charge of industry through a network of advisory bodies and governmental boards.[4]

The war reached a conclusion in 1918 and it was the task of

94

Provost James Forrester to lead the community of Peebles into the troubled post-war world. The crowning need of the burgh was now housing, both for the returning servicemen and to replace the ageing housing stock. Little building had taken place in Peebles after the boom years of 1870 – 90. Clearly, the burgh required more land for development of all kinds.

Towards this end, the following acquisitions had already been made: Kingsland, on the north side of the town from Lord Elibank for £1,900 in 1917; Kirklands, purchased from the Earl of Wemyss in 1918 for £3,500; the farm at Jedderfield in the same year, from the same proprietor, for £2,850. In 1919 Hay Lodge Park was also taken over from the Earl of Wemyss together with the haughland on the adjacent south bank for £3,500. Lastly, in 1919, the farm of Eliot's Park adjoining Rosetta Road was acquired for £1,850. There was a certain logic in these acquisitions, not only to fill the needs of housing and general amenity, but because the burgh could claim that they should have fallen heir to these properties when the Reformation removed them from ecclesiastical control. Kingsland, for example, had been acquired by the laird of Blackbarony and as early as 1638 the 'ferme duties' on 'twa aikers' were being paid by the tenant to Dame Margaret Mould, 'Ladie of Blackbaronie'. The Murrays continued to hold the land until its sale to the town in 1917. The town was to use the ground initially as a refuse tip, allotments and, much later, for municipal housing.

The vicar of the Parish Church of Peebles had the patrimonial enjoyment of the lands of Kirkland. In June 1569 Master Thomas Archibald, designated vicar with the consent of the Dean and Chapter of Glasgow, conveyed to John Wightman, Burgess, the said lands. The annual feu duty to the said vicar was £26 15s Scots and sixty-three poultry. After a number of intermediate transactions, the land passed to James Williamson, Burgess of Peebles. By 1634 it had passed to the Earl of Traquair. The feu duties then, by act of the Scots Parliament of 1641, were payable to the King. In 1757 the second Earl of March purchased much of the land, which eventually passed to the Wemyss family. In 1908 the ground was let as a golf course and was purchased by the town council in 1918 for £3,750.

From 1892, when the Peebles Golf Club was founded, until 1908, golf was played on a smaller course at Morning Hill. The golf course was administered by the council and forms one of the finest inland courses in Scotland.

PART II: 1900 – 1950

Eliot's Park lying to the north of the golf course comprised a farmhouse and forty-five acres and was composed partly of the original Kirklands of the burgh and partly by the lands of Acrefield.

The earliest recorded writ is a charter by David II of Scotland in 1365 to William of Gledstones, the family which owned Hundleshope. A descendant was William Ewart Gladstone. Sir John Eliot was a London physician who eventually became the proprietor of lands near the burgh; he then styled himself 'of Peebles'. After 1778 Sir John Eliot bought up the remainder of the lands which had been the original Kirklands; the whole property then became known as Eliot's Park. This property remained in the hands of the Eliot family until 1919 when it was purchased by the town council for £1,850. A section of ground extending to five acres adjoining Rosetta Road was used as the site of the burgh housing scheme in 1919. The remainder of the land remained as a farm until the 1960s.

Arnotshaugh, later the Hay Lodge Park, can be traced back to the eighteenth century when it appears as one of the possessions of the Chapel of St Mary which was built at the west end of the High Street towards the fourteenth century. The land remained as a possession of the chapel, of which the town council of Peebles were patrons, till the Reformation. After 1560 it became burgage property. The ground was then split up into small lots which were only reunited in the eighteenth century. In 1797 this parkland was sold to Lord Armadale for £1,410; thereafter, the property changed hands several times until purchased by Alexander Campbell, merchant of Glasgow, in 1822. It was he who had the present wall built on the Neidpath Road. Many of the older Peebleans still refer to this wall as 'Campbell's Dyke'.

After 1846, when Campbell's heirs sold the lands, they were acquired by the Earl of Wemyss. They remained in the hands of the Wemyss family until purchased by the town council of Peebles in 1919, who thus assumed their earlier ownership for £3,500. The property, together with the haughland on the south side of the river, remains as a public park and an outstanding amenity of the burgh.[5]

Between the First and Second World Wars the park was the scene of the Glasgow University OTC's annual camp. Their engineers section, as part of their training, bridged the river close to the boundary with Neidpath Woods. In consequence, the concept of a permanent footbridge was born. It was not until 1952, however, that, thanks to the generosity of a South African Peeblean, Mr J. S. Fotheringham, a bridge was finally built. An imaginative design for such a structure by Sir Basil Spence had later to be abandoned in favour, for financial reasons, of the more utilitarian structure which was finally built.

The acquisition of the lands aforementioned marks a major step in the development of the burgh, a highlight in the grim days that marked the closing year of the First World War and the uncertain years which were to follow. It was also a remarkable act of faith by the town council of a small burgh in securing as they saw it, the land requirements for the foreseeable future. Not only had they made safe an area of outstanding amenity to the west of the town, but they also laid claim to the area to the north which could be used for housing. The provost, bailies and councillors deserved congratulations for their foresight and acumen, as did their permanent officials. Indeed, we can see the shrewd hand of the town clerk, J. Walter Buchan, and the town chamberlain, Alex Williamson, in the successful return to the burgh of its ancient rights.

In Peebles, as elsewhere, the transition from war to peace was hard, not only in terms of economic and administrative difficulties, but in terms of human and social attitudes. Firstly, we must consider the human toll. On the Peeblesshire War Memorial for the First World War are listed 225 names of young Peebleans who were killed. From a male population in 1914 of 2,257, one in ten of the population failed to return. This was, in military terms, decimation. Few things could be so poignant as the 1900 photograph of an infant class at Halyrude School which indicates by a cross those who did not survive. This shows a higher percentage than even the overall figures: seven killed from a class of thirty-five, a loss of 20 per cent.

Secondly, as in the country as a whole, it took almost two decades to convince Government, national and local, and trade and industry, that the halcyon days of the Edwardian era had gone for ever. The main employers in Peebles, the woollen manufacturers and the tweed warehousemen, had lost markets, some of which would be lost for ever. Fashion, as we know from hindsight, had changed out of all recognition. The 'flappers' of the post-war years required a fraction of the tweed cloth for their outfits compared to their Victorian grandmothers and men's clothing and fashions were less formal and the slow demise of the three-piece suit had already begun. With the increase in motorcar ownership, the need for heavy great- or overcoats also lessened.[6]

In a one-industry economy the other trades and businesses suffered from the slowing of that 'motor of early industrialisation', the textile industry. The building trades were also in serious trouble. No houses had been built in Peebles since 1914 and financial stringency prevented the sort of speculative building which had formed the basis for expansion of the town in the 1880s and 1890s. Yet the politicians promised 'a land fit for heroes'. Houses had to be built, albeit by the local authorities. As early as 1909, Peebles Town Council had plans for slum clearance and improved housing. In 1909 the infamous 'lang close' was rebuilt and transformed into Newby Court on School Brae; at the same time some property in the Northgate and on Cuddyside was improved. But it was in 1919 that, under the provisions of the Housing Act (Scotland) 1919, the town council became the main agent for municipal housing.

Under the terms of the 1919 Act, fifty houses were built at Eliot's Park. Of the drab and uninspiring design which we have come to associate with municipal housing, they nonetheless were well equipped and doubtless offered a vastly improved standard of living to their first tenants. The high cost of the 1919 schemes, £1,200 per house, reflects not only the effect of wartime inflation but also the inexperience of local authority. This inexperience, coupled with the absence of proper advisory staff and consequent cost controls, explains the high cost per unit.

The Act of 1924 owed much to the zeal and vision of John Wheatley, the ablest of the Clydesiders. Also provost of Peebles by this time was George Wilkie, a builder himself and from a family of builders. Doubtless his advice was of value in the application of the 1924 Act here. The following housing schemes resulted: George Terrace, where sixteen houses were built on part of the old Kingsland ground; and a further fifty-six houses, completed between 1924 and 1928, at Dalatho, on ground purchased from the Venlaw Estate at a cost of £1,200 each. These comprised Dalatho Crescent and Edinburgh Road. In consequence, the northern entrance to Peebles has been described as the ugliest aspect presented by any Border town to the visitor from the north (*Third Statistical Account*).

The Housing Act of 1932 shifted the thrust of municipal housing to slum clearance which, although largely a problem of the cities, was not unknown in Peebles. A limited scheme brought Connor Street into existence, building sixteen houses on part of the former Kirklands. The later Act of 1935 concentrated on relief of over-crowding and again the elimination of substandard housing. To this

Act we owe a further thirty-five houses at Connor Street, Connor Place, built at a cost of £450 per unit. To these was added the more extensive scheme of seventy-six houses at £450 each at North Street, North Place, George Terrace and Rosetta Place. Again the ground was readily available due to the prudent foresight of the council when they purchased Kingsland.

The building of 178 houses to the north of the town altered the focus of Peebles quite dramatically. From their inception, the core of the older part gradually eroded. Some substandard buildings were demolished, notably in the Old Town, but, more often, they continued to be let, thus creating problems which only now (1989) are being tackled. Witness the plans ongoing for Cuddyside. The fact that all building ceased in 1939 with the outbreak of war did not permit the planned flow of municipal building and replacement.

Few private houses were built in Peebles in the inter-war period, an indication almost certainly of the trade depression which had such a dramatic effect on Peebles. Carlyle categorised economics as the dismal science. Had he been alive and in Peebles in the 1930s then his conviction would have been fulfilled. Nonetheless, houses were built for private ownership, notably at Edinburgh Road on the east side. Walkershaugh was developed at this time, also a few on the south side of the river at Springwood and Springhill. In the main, however, private builders had a hard time. Work schemes were devised for the unemployed, tradesmen and millworkers both. Many will recollect the improvements made at the Gypsy Glen at this time, on the south bank of the Tweed, west to the viaduct bridge and at the 'Dookits', where a swimming area was created.

The council also developed the Whitestone Kerfield Park at this time, much with the skills of the unemployed. The Gytes, whose name, albeit in corrupted form, commemorates the 'goyt' or 'lade' which ran from Castlehill to Walkershaugh and thence into the Tweed, was also levelled and improved. The town also acquired swimming baths through the generosity of Sir Henry Ballantyne of Minden. These were built on Tweed Brae, opposite the Drill Hall. They proved an outstanding amenity not only for the swimming bath but for the bathing facilities, an important factor in a town where most houses still had no baths.

Further, as part of the public works and an indication of the increase in municipal housing and, in consequence, better sanitation, the sewage and drainage system of the town was improved and an extensive modernisation of the works at Eshiels undertaken. Also worthy of note was the extensive new building at what was then the County and Burgh High School. A whole new block of classrooms and gymnasium was completed in 1936 – 8.

Trade did pick up from about 1935 onwards and by early 1939 the mills were busy again, often on Government contracts (ominous sign). More motorcars were seen on Peebles High Street. Local garages were able to run coach services to the remoter valleys of Peeblesshire. Butchers, bakers and the ubiquitous Co-op were sending out motorvans to the farms and villages, although many of their local deliveries were still by horse-drawn vehicles. Confidence was returning to the town which, like the rest of Scotland, had suffered grievously.

The gathering of the storm clouds of war must have caused many Peebleans to think of twenty years before when the high promise of the Armistice, the 'land fit for heroes', was exposed as a cruel sham by the subsequent Depression. They might well have thought, as Grassic Gibbon was to write in *Sunset Song*: 'They died for a world that is past, these men, but they did not die for this that we seem to inherit.'

The Second World War started again with the Government preaching 'business as usual'. In contrast to the First World War, production was subject to centralised control. In consequence, both the woollen-mills and the farming industry were allocated production targets and allocated resources accordingly. Conscription was introduced, firstly on a partial basis by the Militia Act of 1938 and later was made universal. The mills again lost labour, as did agriculture, but deferments also applied for key workers.

The doubling of the Territorial Army in 1938 saw the resuscitation of the 8th Battalion The Royal Scots who, with the 57th Regiment Royal Artillery, the Peebles frontline TA unit, were embodied for service in 1939. Both units were to distinguish themselves in the course of the next six years. Obviously, with both voluntary service and conscription, many young Peebles men and women served in all three services and travelled worldwide during their time in them.

As we have seen, house-building in Peebles, as elsewhere, ceased in 1939. The business of the town council centred largely on the administration required in support of civil defence, of the auxiliary fire service and of those voluntary organisations who provided

100

facilities for the servicemen and women stationed in or near the town. Later in the war, the Home Guard was to make heavy demands on a workforce which was already working overtime. Nonetheless, it was a 'people's war' and it created a unifying factor in the burgh town. Indeed, many were to regard 1939 – 45 as the years when they were closer to their fellow-townspeople than ever before or since. War, indeed, creates its own equilibrium.

Footnotes:

1. Donaldson, Gordon, *Scotland* (London, 1974) pp144 – 8
2. Ibid, pp149 – 52
3. Peebles Town Council Minutes, 1904 – 5 (unpublished)
4. Harvie, Christopher, *No Gods and Precious Few Heroes* (London, 1981) p13
5. Buchan, Walter (ed), *A History of Peeblesshire* (Glasgow, 1925) Vol II, pp310 – 16
6. Harvie, Christopher, *No Gods and Precious Few Heroes* (London, 1981) p42

CHAPTER 6

Education

DURING THE LAST three decades of the nineteenth century, the population of Peebles had doubled (from 2,631 in 1871, to 5,266 in 1901) and no fewer than five schools were needed to fulfil the requirements of recent legislation. By 1901 children between the ages of five and fourteen were obliged to attend school and fees were no longer compulsory at the several establishments under the aegis of the Board — i.e. Committee — elected by the ratepayers of the parish. The wise members of this Board had already anticipated accommodation needs by enlarging the old Burgh School at the foot of the familiar Brae leading to Tweed Green and building another one which has since been known as Kingsland on the northern periphery of the town — at a cost of £12,000 which was borrowed and repaid in forty years! Furthermore they took over Bonnington Academy as primarily a High School, enlarged Halyrude to take mostly infants and older girls, but closed the little Grammar School on the east corner of the Brae. Unassisted by grants, St Joseph's continued independently for local Catholic children.

Then, on 26 November 1901, Mr Todd, headmaster of the 'First English School', led his charges on the long walk to the new Kingsland where, 'They were housed in excellent premises and teachers/pupils work under the most favourable conditions', according to HM Inspector's report of 1902. Work was often interrupted when illness, or even epidemics, struck; mumps and measles, chickenpox and whooping cough, scarlet fever and diphtheria took their toll at times to the tune of 200 pupils absent out of less than 400, whilst several seem to have been afflicted by nits, lice or other vermin! Holidays, too, were frequent both for national and local events: fair days in March and October as well as 'Beltane Friday' when the 'Queen' was crowned and the Riding of the

Marches took place, plus days off for any royal occasion whether wedding, coronation or funeral! Despite these interruptions, progress continued satisfactorily according to annual inspectors' reports which were important because government grants could be withheld if these august personages from the Scotch Education Department were displeased with the academic standards attained. An oddly cogent criticism of children's counting methods was that they used their fingers! Consequently, in 1905 the infant mistress 'began teaching counting by means of beans!'.

An equally momentous decision was taken three years later when jotters were substituted for slates in Kingsland School — this despite the findings of the School Board's serious discussion of the matter: 'The meeting was inclined to think that slates were better than jotters!' His Majesty's Inspector was quite a bogeyman in the early days of the century when he would personally ensure that no child under fourteen could leave school unless the Labour Certificate exam had been passed. Many pupils took an alternative Merit Certificate exam which was a passport to the High School not always utilised by parents who preferred their offspring to start earning at an early age.

Peebles was fortunate to boast a 'Higher Class' school in that the former Bonnington Park Academy on the south side of the burgh was now in the very capable hands of Mr George Pringle who was Rector from 1888 to 1917 and who was responsible for extending and staffing the school to such acceptable standards that it was recognised as one of only twenty such establishments in Scotland at the turn of the century. There are many elderly people in Peebles and elsewhere who can well remember the old school on the hill where the shell of the original buildings may still be seen and where they received an excellent education which took some of them on to even higher academic erudition. One such was the Rector's son, George Pringle, who was dux in 1906 and became in the course of time HM Senior Chief Inspector of Schools in Scotland. Mr Pringle himself was mainly responsible for the dimensions of the 'new' school (1902) which consisted of a central hall surrounded by some seven class-rooms, another for woodwork and cookery, a couple of labs and the usual staff and cloakrooms.

Of approximately 120 pupils, some came from far away places like Linton whence the train left (Broomlee) at 7.20 a.m. and arrived back at 6.00 p.m. Unlike Lyne, Broughton or Stobo's scholars, who had the daily distinction of missing the first period on the timetable because of their late arrival at the old Caledonian Station, lucky Innerleithen and Walkerburn pupils, envied no doubt by their contemporaries, were allowed to leave school at 3 p.m. to catch the train which took them home by 4 p.m.

Despite these disparate hours of attendance, academic attainments were of a high order and quite a number passed the Senior Leaving Certificate exam (inaugurated in 1888). But it was not all work and no play: rugby and association football, hockey, hares-and-hounds, cricket and athletics were indulged in, although not yet as part of the school timetable! It is interesting to note at the turn of the century that the School Rugby Club was 'affiliated with' the Peebles Rugby Club (whose pitch was a field near Haystoun) and that the school cap-badge was scarlet and white — the Peebles colours.

It was possible, for some years after 1900, for pupils to spend their entire school life at Peebles High School because a Preparatory Department had been started before the end of the nineteenth century to which Miss Russel Green had been appointed 'Governess' in 1897 and continued to hold sway over her young charges until 1935 when she was transferred to Halyrude, only to resign in 1936 and spend the rest of her long life in well-earned retirement — except that she still gave piano lessons to yet another generation of young hopefuls. It was also possible for students to continue their education at evening classes either at the High School or at Kingsland where Pitman's shorthand, woodwork and drawing were only a few of the subjects on offer. For many years the headmaster of the Evening Continuation School was Thomas Heddle — one of a small staff of characters associated with the old Bonnington Park Academy or Peebles Burgh and County High School as the pundits would have it be known officially by the beginning of the century.

Even before Mr Heddle arrived in 1905 to put his stamp on the English Department (which included history and geography in those days), a Mr Mackay had been appointed in 1902 to teach woodwork and art, Mr Mowbray Ritchie in 1903 to establish science as a key subject in the curriculum and, in 1904, Mr Duncan Mackay came from Campbeltown to make his mark in mathematics and occasionally on a hapless pupil. A little later that lad o' pairts, Mr W. G. Russell, started his thirty-eight-year stint as English-cum-geography teacher, a career covering both world wars and welcoming after the first of these a new colleague in the person of that redoubtable teacher/scholar Mr R. A. McClements, a painstaking purposeful physics master, equally at ease with mathematics.

It must be borne in mind that educational policy then, as now, was directed by top civil servants — Sir Henry Craik until 1905, followed by John Struthers, who headed the Scotch (Scottish after 1918) Education Department until 1925 — and that they themselves were subject to Government legislation of which there was no lack throughout these years. The Act of 1901 raised the age at which children might be employed from ten to twelve, allowing school boards to grant exemption from attendance for pupils between twelve and fourteen on certain conditions.

The 1908 Act was more far-reaching: it authorised boards to provide not only accommodation, but apparatus and service for the supply of school meals (not necessarily 'free') and medical examinations of all children whose parents could be prosecuted if their offspring were found to be unclean, underfed or ill-clad unless poverty could be pleaded. In such cases provision was to be made out of the school fund or voluntary aid. The same 1908 Act ensured pension rights for teachers by starting a superannuation fund with contributions by the State, the School Board and the teachers themselves, who also won the right of appeal to the department against arbitrary dismissal by their local employers. The Act also helped higher education by ensuring that grants for poorer potential students enabled them to continue their studies at secondary school and beyond without being a burden on their parents.

Ten years later, a more revolutionary Act was passed abolishing the old School Boards which had striven with some success to establish and maintain a satisfactory system of education since 1873 (locally, Robert Thorburn was chairman for many years: his partner in their legal firm William Lyon, clerk and treasurer) and substituting committees for the management of schools within given areas consisting of members of the local authority, parents and teachers. To the new Peeblesshire Education Committee, as an integral part of the county authority, were thus given rights to raise money by rates or loans, control of expenditure, teachers and their salaries, schools including books for pupils and adults, plus provision for religious instruction. Voluntary religious schools could negotiate entry into the State system, provided that the Church was allowed to vet new staff for beliefs and that former levels of religious instruction were maintained. St Joseph's School thereupon took its place alongside

Halyrude, Kingsland and the High School under the aegis of Peeblesshire Education Authority and received its due share of grants: it was not, it may be noted in passing, allowed to share in the annual choice of the Beltane Queen!

The churches, too, had until 1905 controlled the training of teachers, who had to undergo a five-year apprenticeship as pupil teachers in the old Board schools. In that year the Department of Education took over the colleges of the Church of Scotland and the United Free Church and transferred their management to provincial committees connected with the four university districts. A senior student, or training-college stage was added to the old pupil-teacher type of entrant who had to pass, *inter alia*, the Leaving Certificate examination in a suitable group of subjects. Provision was made for graduates to add a year's professional training to their degrees in order to become secondary school teachers of one or more subjects; primary school headmasters and their male assistants were also usually graduates.

Such a one was Mr Todd, headmaster since 1883 of the old 'English' school which became Kingsland in 1901. He continued in office until the end of the decade having seen his precious new school firmly established and having persuaded His Majesty's Inspector to agree to the system of changing classes half-yearly to accommodate the biannual influx of infants from Halyrude. He lived at a time when the population was increasing rapidly and Halyrude had to be enlarged for the extra intake; as on similar occasions later in the century the Parish Church Hall (alas! no longer there) was used as an annex during modification to Halyrude. Mr Todd also saw the award of the Nelson Shield to the best essay writers (as in the High School) on a naval subject — commemorating, in the first instance, the centenary of the Battle of Trafalgar.

He experienced the effects of both the 1901 and 1908 Acts and bade farewell to many of his best pupils who passed the preliminary exam to the Supplementary Course which gave them free places to the High School. He made good use of the magic lantern and screen which had been provided for the school, and welcomed the beginnings of a library and first-aid equipment which accompanied the medical service for all pupils and probably envied the celestial globe and telescope which had been donated to 'Bonnington Park Academy' by Dr Connel's widow in memory of her husband who had for long been chairman of the Board. Probably Mr Todd had enough on his mind not to notice in July 1904 the plea of the janitor that the windows had not been cleaned since the school was built!

Mr Scott, the new headmaster, took up his duties in January 1911: he was to remain for thirty years linking both world wars. The old District Board had chosen him from an original list of eighty-seven applicants and he was to serve the community well as many old residents of Peebles can verify. His immediate requests were not all that demanding — a unique register, four self-binders, a barometer and a wastepaper basket! These articles would hardly break the bank at a time when coal for heating the schools cost 13s (65p) per ton! Mr Todd's régime had been begun in Queen Victoria's reign, had included the whole of Edward VII's and just managed to include the proclamation of George V in 1910. The latter's Coronation in 1911 was celebrated lavishly in terms of medals, mugs and holidays, a whole week being devoted to its commemoration, but these extra days off school-work did not affect standards, as witness the new headmaster's very favourable Inspector's reports which enabled Kingsland to qualify for a £949 grant which pleased the local School Board administrators.

The outbreak of the First World War in August 1914 is not noted in the log book but, in December, leave of absence was granted to young male members of staff including Mr C. R. Murray 'for the period of the war'. Less than two years later, Second-Lieutenant Murray was killed in action and in 1917 a memorial tablet in his honour was unveiled. Meanwhile, we are told in April 1915 that 'children commenced to sow seeds in the garden', and a little later the School Board took over an allotment for scholars, the older ones being diverted from their indoor studies 'to prepare the ground for potatoes'. By 1917 soup or broth were on offer at midday to children who were taken to see an exhibition of war photographs in Chambers Institution. In May 1918 the headmaster himself was called to Edinburgh for his Army medical and a 'teacher of gardening' is significantly mentioned the same year.

Thus, although there is no mention of Armistice Day (no radio or television then), the First World War did have an impact on personnel and policy: its indirect effect was far more devastating because the appalling influenza epidemic of 1918/19 resulted in five teachers and 250 out of 340 pupils being incapacitated. The net result was the closure of the school for ten days, the death of several children and the thorough disinfecting of Kingsland. Probably due to the war, by 1920 there was no male assistant until the appointment of Mr A. B. Mackenzie in September. Thereafter, educational progress continued unabated throughout the 1920s and Mr Scott was congratulated by the authority on the 'excellency' of HMI's report for 1922. In October of that year the local War Memorial was unveiled by Earl Haig and Peebleans became accustomed to peace in our time. School population increased; we read of seventy-eight new 'wee ones' joining Halyrude's Infants in 1923, necessitating three older classes to be combined and maybe, who knows, leading to the retiral of Miss Dalgleish, Infant Mistress since 1883!

Imperceptibly, perhaps piecemeal, modifications to the old system were becoming apparent: toothbrushes are introduced for junior infants and even the 'baby class' are scheduled for toothbrush drill. Children are allowed to go potato lifting, lantern slides are used to illustrate history and geography, record cards are mentioned, senior classes are taken to Edinburgh on educational excursions and choirs go to Galashiels for music festivals — even 'character training' is undertaken by the headmaster who must have entered the 1930s armed with splendid HMI reports despite their criticism of accommodation at Kingsland which still used the same room for 'benchwork and domestic subjects', and an old storeroom as a science laboratory! Could it be that greater changes were on the way?

To answer that question we must return to the High School where Mr Pringle, who had coped expertly with the exigencies of wartime and had been honoured with an MBE for his work in connection with War Savings, was appointed Organising Secretary of the Educational Institute of Scotland and consequently resigned the rectorship in December 1917. The members of the old School Board of the Parish of Peebles in their wisdom appointed as his successor Mr Mowbray Ritchie who, for fourteen years, had been in charge of the teaching of science — a subject he obviously favoured during the next twenty-odd years as headmaster: a period of change indeed! The original Bonnington Park Academy, enlarged earlier in the century, was to receive further additions after the First World War to accommodate extra staff and pupils who now had to climb stairs to get to their new classrooms. By 1927 (some senior citizens may have a photograph to prove the authenticity of these statistics) there were approximately 200 pupils and a dozen members of staff who taught *inter alia* all the basic subjects of a typical secondary-school curriculum between the wars: traditionalists would remind us that this sound system of senior education, with minor adjustments, lasted for half a century — well into the 1960s.

Recreation was not neglected. The Peeblesshire Schools Athletic Association was established by that redoubtable pair of worthies, W. G. Russell and Duncan Mackay, and Peebles High School earned a reputation, second to none in the Borders, for prowess on the track. Mr Mackay had a particular bent for hockey whilst Mr Russell included most sporting activities in his repertoire with perhaps noticeable leanings towards soccer, a game to the organisation of which he devoted a great deal of his spare time. He also spent many hours reporting details of matches for the local press and papers further afield; his pseudonym appropriately for a schoolmaster was 'Examiner'.

The Special School Management Committee for Peebles High School, which had been established in 1919, included in its personnel Mr Mowbray Ritchie, Rector, and Mr T. Heddle, destined nearly thirty years later to become interim Rector. Meetings were held in the Council Chambers where educational policy was thrashed out until 1936 when the County Buildings became headquarters of all local administration. Important decisions were taken in terms of the rearrangement of both primary and secondary education. Kingsland was becoming overcrowded; its intake from Halyrude increased annually, most remained until they were fourteen and accommodation for advanced division pupils was inadequate. Rather than enlarge the public school, it was decided to build an entirely new extension at Bonnington Park known ever since as the '1936 Block' — although it was but barely finished in 1937 and officially opened only in April 1938! Meanwhile the Preparatory Department at the High School was disbanded and its youngsters dispersed to Halyrude or Kingsland (a few continued their primary education at a nearby private school).

Then it was ordained that all pupils, whether or not they passed their Qualifying Examination, should proceed to the High School at the age of twelve or thereabouts to continue their education, and new courses of study were started to satisfy the requirements of all academic levels. Thus was inaugurated a kind of comprehensive (mixed ability) education, long before the idea was mooted at central Government level nearly thirty years later. It must have been a proud moment for Mr Mowbray Ritchie and his professional colleagues when Sir James Peck, CB, MA, FRSE, Secretary of the Scottish

Education Department, performed the opening ceremony and Captain Thomson, DL, County Convener, proposed the vote of thanks! It's a saddening thought to recall that Mr Ritchie, whose health had suffered a setback in November 1937, survived as Rector only until November 1938 and died in April 1939 — one year after the culmination of his life's work which had begun in 1903 when he first took up duty as science master. His daughter, the late Dr Margaret Ritchie, carried on her father's tradition as chemistry teacher at the High School until 1969, whilst his son, Dr Mowbray Ritchie, did scientific research and became Reader in chemistry at Edinburgh University.

All the changes that had occurred during the late 1930s would not have been possible without a transfer of staff from Kingsland to the High School. For men like A. B. Mackenzie, it must have seemed like a second career to be suddenly transferred from an Advanced Division Primary School to a six-year secondary, with its abundant playing fields and rural surroundings, but he had been at Kingsland since 1920 and he adapted full well to the new order. Very keen on sport, along with Messrs Russell and Mackay, he had been a founder member of the Peeblesshire Schools' Athletic Association and also initiated inter-school football matches. He took over Room 4 in the 1936 Block and remained there for twenty years during which time he acted as treasurer of Peebles High School Magazine and the General Purpose Fund: he was not at all keen to release money for rugby jerseys! Another Kingsland teacher who had moved to the High School in 1937 was Miss Pearson, whose skills in homecraft were thenceforth applied to a wider range of pupils. Long before her retiral in 1966, she became Lady Adviser to many children of parents she had taught a generation before.

Meanwhile at Kingsland itself, Mr Scott continued to merit most favourable reports from HM Inspectors: 'Under its sanely progressive and humane headmaster who is supported by his staff in his efforts to make effective use of all that is best in modern educational development, the excellent tone of the school is well maintained.' Obviously Mr Scott was a sensible and experienced head who could cope with changes imposed by local government and even crises occurring as a result of central government's involvement with foreign powers. Just when he was beginning to feel less worried about being cramped for space — because of the transference of his 'advanced' pupils to the High School — Mr Scott was faced with

110

four new classes of evacuees and four new teachers from Edinburgh: the Second World War had arrived! It took time to sort out the 173 city strangers and their teachers, and practise gas-mask drill but, within weeks, the headmaster of Kingsland was able to report that most problems had been dealt with: 'School working satisfactorily' is the crisp comment in the log book for early December 1939.

Yet, as the older generation remember, this was the 'Phoney War' period, so that in January 1940 Mr Scott notes that '23 per cent of evacuees had not returned'; in fact, the weather was worse than the war! Before the end of the month, attendance at Halyrude was down to 44 per cent and a planned medical inspection had to be postponed. An epidemic of whooping cough followed and the log book simply says that, owing to the absence of teachers and of scholars, work 'has been carried out under difficulties'. One retired lady who returned to teaching was Miss Mary Bonong. Starting as a pupil-teacher in 1888, she had given up officially in July 1938 but came back to help in 1940 and was still 'standing in' for brief periods in 1942. (No *Guinness Book of Records* in those days!)

However, the weather improved out of all recognition later in 1940 and Mr Scott was able to allow classes to be held outdoors from 1 May to the end of June — including even the Beltane Ceremony which was held in the playground of Kingsland. The ensuing summer holiday must have also constituted a record because school did not reopen until 25 September to allow for the completion of air-raid shelters. Before 1941 began, wire-netting protection had been provided for windows, a number of desks and two teachers had been returned to Edinburgh and Mr Scott was nearing the end of his stint as headmaster. But first he had to endure another severe winter, practise taking the children to their air-raid shelters — ' with overcoats' — accommodate another twenty evacuees, and their desks, from Edinburgh and arrange for 316 pupils to take advantage of the 'milk in school' scheme during the summer holidays. Relieved he must have been to write in the log book on 10 July 1941: 'School closed for summer vacation. Mr Scott, Headmaster retired from duty', as he laid down his pen for the last time since January 1911 when he had started as head of Peebles Public School.

Another 'head' who started in January was Mr John Wilson who came from George Heriot's in Edinburgh and entered on his duties as Rector of the High School at the beginning of 1939 so that most of his span of seven years was wartime. Educationally, it is worthy of note that the old Day School Certificate (Higher) candidates (third year secondary) still merited visits from HM Inspectors who frequently examined pupils for the award of the Senior Leaving Certificate in the course of their visits between March and May. The examination for the Day School Certificate (Lower) was taken by those who completed three years secondary education in June, whilst Scripture exams for all classes took place in July! Life could be hard in those halcyon pre-war days! Before he could resume his first full session, Mr Wilson had to face up to wartime conditions and the inevitable concomitants — evacuees, six of their teachers, 150 extra desks and an air-raid warning!

Early in 1940 talks were given by lecturers from Edinburgh College of Agriculture on food production, a School National Savings Association was formed and science teacher, Mr Todd, was sent on a Gas Detection Course at Leeds University. Later he attended an Instructor's Course on Anti-Gas Precautions. In lieu of the normal (i.e. national) Senior Leaving Certificate, a Borders schools' panel of heads and principal teachers was established to set and mark an equivalent examination. Autumn term 1940 was delayed pending the completion of air-raid shelters, eight of which were 'tried out' in November. In December, twenty-five dual desks were returned to Edinburgh which remained the venue for Air-Raid Precaution Courses, and one on food decontamination was attended by Mr McClements. Otherwise 'work proceeded normally' except that gas-masks were worn occasionally.

Near the beginning of 1942, as a wartime measure and with due regard to rationing and food restrictions, it was resolved to utilise the High School cookery-room for the preparation of meals for all Peebles schools. The only snag was snow! Once again wintry conditions prevailed and roads were blocked causing the closure of schools at noon each day, attendance being approximately halved. (Records do not reveal what happened to all that prepared food!) Even as late as March we read that 'only Senior Leaving Certificate pupils were brought in from outlying districts'. Later in the year, recruitment to the Forces was the obvious aim of officers of the Army, RAF and RNVR (Navy, Marines and Fleet Air Arm) and of the ATS and WAAF who visited the High School and brought with them sound films of the Services in action! Until they left school, many senior boys contented themselves with helping to bring in the harvest, holidays were rearranged to coincide with farmers' requirements and school parties were held in the afternoons before Christmas 'in view of war conditions'.

Meanwhile, several male members of staff were 'called to the Colours', others joined the Home Guard or auxiliary organisations, two or three lady teachers returned to Edinburgh and Polish children appeared to multiply — what excellent pupils they proved to be. Soon we read of three days' holiday in celebration of Victory in Europe and, later still, two days' 'deferred VJ holidays'. Happy days were here again and the Polish contingent showed their appreciation of their Peebles hosts by giving a Christmas party for children at their Victoria Park Convalescent Depot. Five months later Mr Wilson resigned as Rector of the High School and reverted to his earlier calling of modern language teacher. Maybe he had become used to girls as well as boys under his care for it was not Heriot's he returned to but Dumfries Academy. There are many former pupils who started their secondary schooling in September 1939 or 1940 and left in 1944 or 1945 followed by National Service who recall with satisfaction and not a little nostalgia their austere yet hopeful High School days where the old men tried to cope with the capriciousness of youth in a changing world. Now in their sixties, the same pupils can look back forty-five years, just as their older mentors had memories of the Boer War at the beginning of the century — when they had launched themselves on their life's work and were destined to take two world wars in their stride.

Peebles emerged from the war virtually unscathed and education had been interrupted only slightly despite evacuees from Edinburgh and elsewhere, Polish soldiers and their families, transport difficulties, the prolonged absence of several staff on war service and the less than perfect 'panel system' for the Senior Leaving Certificate. Afterwards, a new generation took over as teachers and administrators although several of the younger 'Old Guard' remained to consolidate pre-war concepts and values. Gone were those worthies, W. G. Russell, Duncan Mackay and Tommy Heddle, although the latter remained, after the retiral of Mr Wilson, as interim headmaster of the High School until October 1946 when Mr George Rothnie was installed as Rector. Back came D. C. Smith as maths master and David Ritchie as teacher of technical subjects, whilst D. G. Todd and G. L. Boyd held sway for several years as symbols of the old régime. New faces appeared and new posts were created for John Jamieson as the first Director of Education for Peeblesshire, Miss Wills, head of a separate Geography department and E. L. Smith, the first principal teacher of history. The ageless

PART II: 1900 – 1950

Mr McClements, who had presided over the Science Department since 1919, and Miss Campbell, in charge of modern languages since 1925, remained for a while to set their assistants on the right road into the post-war era, whilst the unfortunate pupils faced the worst winter on record in February and March 1947 when several were unable to get to school to sit their 'Highers' on the fateful history examination day.

The Senior Leaving Cetificate continued to be the academic accolade bestowed on a minority of students as it had been for some sixty years but, in those days, 'passes' were awarded only on a group of subjects and the examination was held, madly, in the month of March. Hence, perhaps, the paucity of pupils who gained their 'Highers' — fifteen out of a school population of 340 in 1947. This was the year which saw the implementation of the Wartime Act raising the school-leaving age to fifteen and the High School began to expand: by 1948 there were over 400 on the roll. Four new wooden classrooms were erected to accommodate the overflow and a dining-hall, which had all the appearance of utility huts designed for dormitories, coped with the demand for midday meals in an era of rationing and other post-war shortages. A decent dinner cost a pupil 5d (i.e. about tuppence in modern money) and a majority took advantage of such cheap sustenance.

At Kingsland School meals were made available even in the holidays and the children were encouraged to collect rose-hips in response to the Government's pursuit of the popular vitamin C! The headmaster behind this and many other ploys was James R. Lawrie, MBE, MA, FEIS, who had been introduced to pupils and staff in September 1941 and had therefore completed four years wartime service in charge of Peebles Public School before VJ Day. Quite an enlightened schoolmaster, he favoured outdoor education especially local history, geography, industry, nature rambles and sketching on Tweed Green — all of which helped to give youngsters material for their compositions! Sometimes he accompanied a class and held forth on local lore; in June he might travel with a larger group to far-away Flodden or distant Dunoon, Linlithgow Palace or Border Abbey — all in an acceptable cause. A useful pianist himself, Mr Lawrie tried to inculcate appreciation of music, verse speaking and dancing; he would take the school for an hour's singing in the hall, organise concerts and send children to take part in the annual Borders Festival where they invariably did well.

114

He acted as adviser to producers of BBC programmes for primary schools, served on the National Savings and County Library Committees, reached the higher echelons of the Educational Institute of Scotland and, in the fullness of time, became provost of Peebles. By the 1950s he was indeed an experienced pedagogue — after all, he had been a dominie all his days, was probably a traditionalist by nature but had the prescience to be ahead in educational expertise. Some children outwith the burgh bypassed their little local schools and were accepted by Kingsland. Their parents must have thought it was worth their while.

The new rector at the High School was Mr George Rothnie, a scholar still in his thirties, yet with educational roots that were unmistakably pre-war. He aimed at academic excellence as had been his own goal during student days at Aberdeen where he had obtained a 'double first' in English and history — subjects which he patronised throughout the nineteen years of his rectorship. He believed that all potential secondary pupils should take promotion tests in composition, English, arithmetic and 'intelligence' so that they could be graded academically and allocated appropriate first-year places — two foreign languages, one, or none — each according to attainment in his/her qualifying year! This emphasis on merit meant that two extra periods were packed into timetables for Thursday and Friday, resulting in an abbreviated lunch-hour twice a week: Mr Rothnie exacted high standards of dedication from staff and pupils alike!

Teaching methods remained much as they had been for half a century except that ancillary aids were adopted; sound and film-strip projectors, epidiascope and BBC Schools programmes supplemented the old-fashioned 'talk and chalk' to children seated in serried rows sedulously receiving instruction from forbidding figures in academic gowns! But outwith this rather rigid discipline of learning, there was a deal of interest to be had in various school activities — literary, debating, dramatic and music societies, the latter including choirs and orchestra, as well as a comprehensive range of sports available. Organised games had sunk to a low ebb by the end of the war but by the late 1940s they were restored to their rightful place in the curriculum. Rugby football was restarted and fixtures arranged with other Border schools; soccer, hockey, cricket, tennis, badminton, netball and swimming — all were given their due, whilst in athletics Peebles High School achieved commendable standards, more than holding their own in competition with other junior and senior secondary schools, regionally and nationally.

PART II: 1900 – 1950

Four other factors which helped to inculcate school spirit were a house system, a magazine, a Former Pupils' Association and a school badge. The latter was just one of the historical interests of the Rector, whose researches into earlier days resulted in the registration of a coat of arms for the Burgh and County High School of Peebles. The design of the badge was suggested by the Lord Lyon, King of Arms, and was matriculated in November 1949. Not surprisingly, it incorporated portions of both burgh and county coats of arms plus a torch of learning and a new motto: *Mente et Manu* which, for the benefit of those who did not qualify for inclusion in Mr Rothnie's two-language course, means 'with mind and hand', thus indicating 'the importance of both the academic and the practical sides of education', to quote the Rector's own explanation.

The resuscitation of the school magazine which embodies *esprit de corps* was an even greater inspiration in that it helped the formation of a Former Pupils' Association which linked alumni with the post-war generation. The house system (Craigerne, Kingsmeadows, Neidpath and Venlaw) added an extra dimension to work and play: no longer personal but corporate achievements constituting motivation. Periodic reports on the High School issued by the Scottish Education Department via HM Inspectorate are warm in their appreciation of standards attained and constructive in any criticism proferred: the Rector, who deplored such non-academic diversions as potato lifting in school-time was elated when his principal teachers could claim 100 per cent passes in the Scottish Leaving Certificate.

Meanwhile, those same teachers instructed the 'B' course pupils who often earned their own certificates on completion of three years secondary education. Before they left school, they were addressed by Youth Employment Officers and given appropriate advice by Ministry of Labour and National Service careers officials. In all likelihood their history or geography teachers had taken them round the three mills already, ensured that some of them had familiarised themselves with local farms or even explored a coal mine; in addition, they would have been subjected to the blandishments of visiting services or nursing recruiting officers armed with the glamorised films of their respective callings! To inveigle school leavers to work in the mills, one famous firm staged a fashion parade in the Drill Hall where a clever commentator so captivated the teenagers that the girls all decided to become mannequins and the boys to become compères — presumably to get a closer view of the proceedings!

116

Sources:

Buchan, J. Walter (ed), *A History of Peeblesshire* (Glasgow, 1925) Vol II
Education Authority Minute Books, 1919 – 30
Halyrude Infant School Log Books, 1893 – 1930, 1930 – 58
Kingsland School Log Books, 1905 – 33, 1933 – 50
Mackinnon, James, *The Social and Industrial History of Scotland*
Peebles First English School becoming Kingsland in 1901 Log Book, 1882 – 1905
Peebles High School Committee Minute Book, 1919 – 47
Peebles High School Log Books, to 1950
Peebles High School Magazines, 1899 – 1910, 1947 – 50
Peebles School Board Minute Book, 1873 – 1919
Peebles School Management Committee Minute Book, 1919 – 47
Scotland, James, *The History of Scottish Education,* two Vols
Smout, T. C., *A Century of the Scottish People, 1830 – 1950*

CHAPTER 7

Peebles in Two World Wars

BRITAIN'S DECLARATION OF war came on 4 August 1914, the Peebles holiday weekend. The Peebles Company of the 8th Battalion The Royal Scots, numbering 122 men from the burgh, left for Haddington to join the remainder of their battalion on 5 August. With them went 'F' Company of the same unit from Innerleithen/ Walkerburn, a further number of Peebles men who, as ex-members of the Territorial Army, were able to enlist and join the battalion at Haddington.[1]

The 8th Royal Scots was the first Scottish Territorial unit to cross to France in 1914. The battalion arrived in Le Havre on 5 November 1914 one month after its mobilisation. It was sent initially to 22 Brigade of the 7th Division and was very quickly on active service in the trenches. During 1915, the battalion took part in a number of the battles which took place in the British efforts to breach the German line, notably at Aubers Ridge where it suffered its first casualties. It also suffered severely at Neuve Chapelle and at Festubert where their first Commanding Officer Lieutenant-Colonel Brook was killed. By the end of 1915 the original battalion had suffered the following losses in killed and wounded: thirteen officers and 390 other ranks.[2]

As a unit which had a number of miners within its ranks, recruited as it was from the Lothians as well as Peeblesshire, the 8th Royal Scots became the Pioneer Battalion for the 51st (Highland) Division. This was somewhat of an unenviable task since they remained front-line infantry who were also required to spend much of their time on trench maintenance for other units of the division. The fact, also, that they were part of the famous 51st Highland was to guarantee that the '8th' would invariably be in the hottest part of the line. The battalion saw much service in France during the four years of the war. It is fitting perhaps that the last commanding officer should

118

have been Lieutenant-Colonel William Thorburn, DSO, TD, of Kingsmuir, Peebles, remembered by many in the town with affection as 'Colonel Willie'.[3]

Honours gained by the 8th Royal Scots in the course of the war include one Victoria Cross (won by Corporal W. Angus), nineteen Military Crosses, fifteen Distinguished Conduct Medals and sixty-three Military Medals. One of the most decorated soldiers was a Peebles man, Private J. Lamb, DCM, MM. The battalion's total casualties were 389 killed and 1,280 wounded. Of the killed, sixteen belonged to the original Peebles 'G' Company which left Peebles for Haddington in 1914 and, of this gallant company, only one, William Shortreed, still survives (1989).[4]

'G' Company of the 8th Royal Scots was not the sole contribution made by Peebles to the prosecution of the First World War. A number of regular reservists had departed to return to their regiments in August 1914. In pursuance of the Government's dictum 'business as usual', mill workers had remained at their looms and indeed the changeover by the mills to Government contracts for khaki and other uniform cloth was deemed to be work of national importance. The same could be said for workers in agriculture and on the railways. In consequence, there were few enlistments from Peebles until Lord Kitchener's appeal for 'the first hundred thousand' began to have an impact on voluntary recruitment. In October 1915, as the scale of the conflict became apparent, the Derby Scheme for voluntary service was introduced and from then on a stream of men left to join the Armed Services; by the end of 1915 a roll of 1,764 men had enlisted from Peeblesshire for service.[5]

Conscription was introduced in March 1916 by the Military Service Act of that year. By 1918 it was estimated that a further 1,000 had been conscripted from the burgh for wartime service. The burgh itself was much affected by the war as the struggle intensified. As early as the end of 1914, numbers of territorials were sent to the town for training purposes and, over the following year, the numbers were to increase greatly. Indeed, by 1915 the town had taken on the status of a great military camp. In the main, the units were from the Royal Scots and consisted of the second-line battalions, embodied on the departure of the front-line units for service. The following were represented, together with their later third-line equivalents: the 2/4th, 2/5th, 2/6th, 2/7th, 2/8th and 2/9th Royal Scots. In all some 7,000 men were in training in Peebles by 1915.[6]

119

PART II: 1900 – 1950

The King's Muir and Kingsmeadows, the ancient muster ground of the burgh's levies, was the main camping ground, although Hay Lodge and Morning Hill were also pressed into service as camping grounds. Much was done from local resources to make their time in Peebles easier for the troops in training. A Soldiers' Club was opened in the Quadrangle of the Chambers Institute in March 1915, this under the aegis of the YMCA and later the same year Soldiers' Institutes were also opened at Kingsmeadows and at Hay Lodge Park, again with the assistance of the local populace. Baths for the troops were also furnished by the town, aided by private subscribers. Much was done by local organisations, church guilds and the like, to provide additional comforts for the troops and also those already serving overseas.

In October 1915 the 2/8th Royal Scots, a unit which contained almost as many Peebles men as its front-line, which had been in France since November 1914, left Peebles for further service. By the following month Peebles ceased to be a military camp with the departure of the remaining Royal Scots battalions. Although a unit of the RAMC remained in camp in Peebles and later a battalion of the Argylls was stationed in the town for a brief period, the end of 1915 saw the end of the military presence in the town.[7]

Total war, for such it was, created its own demands. Not only was the manpower of Peebles called into war service but that of the womenfolk also. Amongst them were women who acted as hospital nurses, as members of voluntary aid detachments, and also those who visited and comforted mothers and wives who had men at the front. Work parties from the church and other organisations were involved in the making of hospital garments and surgical dressings for the wounded. In addition, women and children scoured the hills round Peebles for sphagnum moss which, when picked and cleaned, could subsequently be sterilised, placed in muslin bags and used as wound dressings.

The Red Cross had been created in 1864 as a result of the horrific casualties suffered by both combatants at the Battle of Solferino. By 1909, perhaps in the aftermath of the South African War, a branch had been formed in Peeblesshire. A scheme had been organised by the Army Council and the British Red Cross Society by which voluntary aid to the sick and wounded, always forthcoming in time of war, would be so organised in peacetime as to form a valuable supplement to the RAMC particularly that of the Territorial Army.

By 1912 a men's detachment had been raised in Peebles, with Sir Duncan Hay as commandant. Later, a women's detachment was also raised with Lady Erskine of Venlaw as the commandant. In the remaining years before the outbreak of war in 1914 intensive training was carried out, and by its outbreak, the local organisation was fit to be placed on a war footing. The ranks of all detachments were supplemented by willing recruits. Training in nursing was organised by Dr Richards for women recruits and, amongst the men, first-aid and stretcher drill was taught.[8]

Houses in the county and burgh were offered as hospitals and mansions as convalescent homes. Venlaw House became a convalescent hospital for Naval officers. The Peebles poor-house also became a military hospital commanded by Dr C. B. Gunn who was honorary surgeon to the Royal Scots. The Hotel Hydro was requisitioned as a Naval hospital and remained as such for the period of the war.

A Central Red Cross Store was opened at the March Street Mills, with Sir Henry Ballantyne as convener of the stores committee. This directed the purchase of raw material which, when issued to work parties, was eventually returned as finished garments for transmission to the Central Red Cross Stores in Edinburgh. There were also a vast number of garments and articles produced by individuals who knitted and sewed to help the war effort and to comfort the soldiers.

Further, a great deal of money was raised from the burgh in support of the County Red Cross, much of the success of fund-raising being due to the efforts of Mr D. S. Thorburn of The Mount who acted as treasurer throughout the war. In 1915 the Red Cross rented 'Morelands' on Tweed Green and opened it as an auxiliary hospital, the local doctors, Dr Henderson, Dr Marshall and Dr Wilson, successively acting as honorary medical officers. The number of military patients to be treated in the course of the war reached 959. In 1922 as a war memorial, 'Morelands' and the two adjoining houses on Tweed Green were handed over as a local hospital to the community. The War Memorial Hospital remained in use as such until a new medical centre at Hay Lodge was opened in 1983. Regrettably, 'Morelands' was sold to private operators by the Borders Health Board despite it having been a gift to the people of the county and burgh.[9]

Although it is difficult in hindsight to imagine a threat of invasion

121

of the United Kingdom during the First World War, a Home Guard was formed. Lieutenant-Colonel W. Thorburn of Craigerne became the County Commandant and a number of Peebles men, otherwise ineligible for war service, were enlisted. Drill was carried out assiduously; uniformed and armed, the force acted as guards on main railway lines and bridges. Eventually, the Home Guard were to be recognised as an efficient force and were designated as the Volunteer Battalion The Royal Scots.

Another unlikely threat from 1916 onwards, so far as Peebles and Peeblesshire were concerned, was attack from the air. Nonetheless, chains of what were officially styled observer posts were established throughout the county to give warning of the approach of hostile aircraft. Four of such posts were sited in Peeblesshire, the one in Peebles being on the high ground to the north of the town on what was to become the golf course. It was thought that the main threat would be from Zeppelin raids following the course of the Tweed, the target being the war industry based in or near the Clyde basin.

The posts in Peeblesshire were manned by men of No 16 Observer Company, the posts being in telephone communication with the appropriate military department in Edinburgh. In the event, no hostile aircraft ever appeared over Peebles in the course of the war although Zeppelins were sighted on the lower Tweed near Berwick. Significantly, lighting restrictions were enforced in Peebles by February 1916, the blackout being designed to prevent street and other light acting as a guide to hostile aircraft.[10]

As in other wars the people of Peebles played host to incomers seeking refuge. In this case they were Belgians driven from their homes by the German invasion of their country in 1914-15. The first party of twenty-three arrived in Peebles in October 1914 and eventually about forty were billeted in the town. Here they were maintained both by public and private funds, the men being found employment at various trades. The refugees found difficulty in adjusting to life in an alien community but in the main were quiet and well-behaved. Much sympathy was shown by the Peebles citizens to these unfortunates. Concerts were also arranged in aid of the British-Belgian Red Cross, where Belgian artistes performed. By the end of 1915 most of the refugees had departed from Peebles for larger centres where more suitable employment was to be found.[11]

The Armistice of 1918 was greeted in Peebles with quiet relief, rather than the wild celebrations with which it was marked in larger town and cities. Perhaps the grievous losses suffered by the burgh were too close, too immediate and too intimate for a small, close-knit community to contemplate with anything but sadness and relief. For Peebles and indeed the whole of Scotland, the supreme sacrifice had also been a disproportionate one. The Scottish National War Memorial showed by 1920 that 100,000 Scots had died in the First World War; given 10 per cent of the United Kingdom population, then the casualty rate equalled 20 per cent. As we have seen, in the case of Peebles, one in ten of the male population had been killed. Scots Territorials, whose enlistments had achieved 5 per cent of the population, nearly double the United Kingdom average, had been mauled in the indecisive battles of 1915, Loos, Neuve Chapelle, Festubert and the like.[12]

Perhaps because of such casualties and the consequent impact on small towns and rural communities when locally recruited battalions suffered devastating losses, the revived Territorial Army in the post-war period was altered in structure. In Peebles, for example, the 8th Royal Scots was not resuscitated; a Royal Artillery unit was due to take its place. This is not to suggest that artillery units remained unscathed in wartime, but certainly their casualty rates were markedly less than their infantry comrades.

In accordance with the revised concept of the Territorial Army distribution, the unit allocated to Peebles in 1919 was a Royal Artillery Troop in the 57th (Lowland) Medium Regiment RA. For those die-hard Royal Scots, provision was made for them to join one of the two remaining battalions of the Territorial Army, both of which were based in Edinburgh. They were the 4/5th (QE Rifles) The Royal Scots and the 7/9th (Highlanders) Battalion The Royal Scots; it was this latter which the Peebles men joined.

The Peebles Troop RA were based at the Drill Hall in Walkershaugh, their two six-inch howitzers being housed in the adjacent gun shed. Here also they assidiuously practised their gun drill. Their summer camps were generally held on Salisbury Plain where it was possible to fire live ammunition from the howitzers. As Bill Watson (later commissioned as a captain) remembers: 'With good eyesight the six-inch shell could be seen in flight as it left the muzzle of the gun.'[13]

During the Munich Crisis a second-line Artillery unit was authorised to duplicate the 57th (Lowland) Regiment RA. This became the 66th Medium Regiment RA and again a troop was allocated to Peebles. Just before the outbreak of war in 1939, the original troop was divided to form the second-line troop in Peebles. In the former group were Bill Watson, David Murray, and the three Brown brothers, Duncan, Willie and Basil. This front-line unit became eventually part of the 51st Heavy Regiment RA and it was as such that the unit mobilised as a battery of that regiment at Dalkeith.

From Dalkeith, the 51st Heavy were posted to Salisbury Plain where they took over 9.2-inch howitzers of First World War vintage. Three of the four batteries were equipped with 'ante-diluvian siege guns' (Bill Watson remembers!). The 9.2-inch howitzers could be disassembled into three lorry loads; to further complicate matters, ten hours were required to bring the gun into action. The fourth battery in the regiment were equipped with 6-inch mobile guns which were borne on rubber-tyred wheels.

In due time the 51st Regiment joined the British Expeditionary Force in France and continued to train there during the bitter winter of 1939/40. As a heavy regiment of the Royal Artillery, they were designated as Army Troops in support of the British First and Second Corps. Ironically, the port of disembarkation in 1939 was the port of Dunkirk. The regiment took part in the advance to the River Dyle in support of the Belgians. The only battery able to get into action against the advancing German Army was the one with the mobile six-inch guns.

An indication of the general lack of preparation by the British Army for the new mobile tactics of the enemy was the inclusion in a field force of the 9.2-inch howitzers, a gun clearly designed for the reduction of trench-work and consequently useless for mobile warfare. In the debacle of the Flanders Campaign little was left with the collapse of the Allied Armies than the grim retreat of the BEF towards the Channel coast, the destruction of their stores, guns and vehicles and their evacuation from the beaches of Dunkirk. This was the fate of the 51st Heavy Regiment RA. Back in the United Kingdom their future lay in retraining and re-equipment.

In many ways, the second-line artillery unit, formed when the 51st Regiment mobilised in 1939, had a more adventurous war. Formed as a Troop of 288th Medium Battery RA, the new regiment thus formed was to be the 66th (Lowland) Medium Regiment RA. Like its first line, the regiment was formed from Territorial Army units from Peebles, Dalkeith, Edinburgh and East Lothian. Mobilised at Dalkeith, the Peebles Troop joined its battery firstly at John

Watson's College in Edinburgh and then as a regiment at Dreghorn Barracks. In the spring of 1940 the regiment moved to the south of England as part of Southern Command. Initially, the regiment was equipped with 6-inch howitzers; as in the case of its parent unit these were relics of the First World War. Later, more modern equipment appeared in the shape of the 5.5-inch medium gun, a piece of equipment which was to be one of the ordnance successes.

A long period of training followed until in January 1943 the Regiment embarked for Egypt to become part of the 8th Army. The journey was by the long sea voyage, via the Cape of Good Hope and the Suez Canal. By the time of their arrival the 8th Army had defeated the enemy in Tunisia after the long pursuit following El Alamein. The 66th Medium Regiment was then readied for the invasion of Europe itself via Sicily. Despite enemy air-attacks, the regiment landed safely in Sicily and gained the distinction of being the first Medium Regiment to engage the enemy in Europe since 1940.

Like most gunner regiments, the '66th' were in constant action from July, in Sicily, until December 1944, when they were in Italy itself; here they had a month's respite for rest and refitting. In their six months of action they had earned a well-deserved reputation for efficiency. In the course of the Italian Campaign, the regiment was engaged in the following actions in support of the infantry: Catania, the crossing of the Straits of Messina, Reggio, Campobasso, the crossing of the Sangro River, Cassino, Rome, Arezzo, the crossing of the Arno at Florence, the breach of the Gothic Line, Senio, the advance to the River Po and the subsequent pursuit of a beaten army into Austria.

By far the longest and most memorable engagement was the Battle of Cassino. During the night of the final assault on the Monastery of Cassino from 22.00 hours until dawn, each gun of the regiment fired 1,000 rounds. It was at this battle that Battery Sergeant-Major John F. Rennie, one of the original Peebles Territorials, was killed by enemy shell-fire. Amongst those who returned to Peebles having served were James Renwick (whose recollections are included here), Tom Irving, William Greenshields, Chris Smith, Adam Grandison, Bob Shearer, David Miller and Jock Brown. A number of the original members were to serve in other units during the war, notably William Greenshield, Jock Brown and Chris Smith.[14]

The seizure of Czechoslovakia by Hitler had caused the passing of the Militia Act, the first time in Britain's history when conscription in peacetime was resorted to. At the same time, with the certainty that war with Germany was inevitable, the Territorial Army was doubled in size. In consequence, the 8th Battalion The Royal Scots was revived; aided by a cadre of the 7/9th Royal Scots, recruiting for the newly-formed unit was begun. The headquarters company of the new battalion was to be based at Peebles and was to be recruited from Peebles, Innerleithen and Walkerburn. Appropriately enough the Commanding Officer was to be Lieutenant-Colonel J. E. M. Richard, OBE of Kailzie; with his gazetting on 2 August 1939 the battalion officially began its new corporate life.

Lieutenant-Colonel J. E. M. Richard has been described as a man who knew exactly what he wanted and was never afraid to speak his mind. He was also a man of infinite patience, a quality which stood him and the battalion in good stead in the months of uncertainty and improvisation which followed mobilisation. The battalion recruited well; a body of Walkerburn men came forward led by W. H. Ballantyne. Another group, including the whole of St Ronans Silver Band as well as members of the British Legion Pipe Band, enlisted from Innerleithen. Peebles men likewise joined, many of them from the Ex-Servicemen's Pipe Band.[15]

On mobilisation, despite a woeful lack of equipment, the battalion concentrated, as part of the 44th Brigade, 15th Scottish Division, at Earlston and Lauder. The strength of the battalion was made up with the arrival of army-class recruits. Not only did Colonel Richard understand his new 'civilian soldiers' but he was a superb trainer of men. By the time when he relinquished command in 1942, he had created and maintained the basic structure of a well-trained and organised unit, despite the many calls made for drafts to be posted to other units of the regiment. Above all, despite many vicissitudes, he succeeded in preserving the character of the battalion.

The following year, 1943, was spent in extensive training at both division and corps level. A new commanding officer, Lieutenant-Colonel Cameron, was forced to retire due to ill-health, to be succeeded by another regular officer of the Royal Scots, Lieutenant-Colonel Rohan Delacombe. It fell to Colonel Delacombe to 'fine tune' the battalion for its future role which became obvious as a part in the invasion of Europe. By this time also the 15th Division became part of the 8th Corps, the unit in which it was to remain for the landing in Normandy and the subsequent campaign.[16]

In April 1944 the 15th Division concentrated on the south coast in Sussex. By 13 June the 8th Royal Scots were in the Normandy Beachhead and by 24 June they were deployed for their first taste of active service. Their first task involved a divisional attack to the south of Caen, the objective being the Odon River. Operation 'Epsom' as it was coded envisaged an attack on a two-brigade front with 44 Brigade on the right. In consequence, when the division formed up on the start-line, the 8th Royal Scots had taken up the traditional place of the regiment on the 'Right of the Line' of the British Army in Normandy. The weather on 24 June was overcast and dispiriting; nonetheless, as the leading companies crossed the start-line, the pipes played 'Blue Bonnets' for the Royal Scots and the Kings Own Scottish Borderers, 'Cock o' the North' for the Gordons and 'Hieland Laddie' for the Glasgow Highlanders.

In three days of savage fighting, a salient some six miles deep was driven into the German lines. This salient became known as the 'Scottish Corridor'. This success was to cost the 15th Division dear. The '8th' at Odon and at Gaurus were to suffer the following casualties: nineteen officers and 442 other ranks.[17]

On 30 July, after resting and refitting, the 15th Division attacked south of Caumont and it was from here that the supporting armour broke out to the east. The 8th Royal Scots rested again until 23 August when it took part in the race to the River Seine. By 5 September they were over the Somme and *en route* for Belgium.

Gheel was recaptured and the bridgehead over the Meuse-Escaut Canal held. At Aart, however, the Royal Scots encountered severe opposition; again casualties were heavy before the advance could proceed. As the summer went on the division advanced and by October they were at Tilburg. Further advances led to Blerick and from there to the Siegfried Line by February 1945. By the end of March, the 8th Royal Scots had crossed the Rhine at Xanten. On 27 April the battalion crossed the River Elbe and with the river crossing their war was virtually over. A testament to the savage infantry fighting of 1944 – 5 remains in the casualties suffered by the 8th Royal Scots in Europe. These were fifty-four officers and 1,140 other ranks.[18]

In the immediate post-war period in 1947, both the 7/9th Royal Scots and the '8th' were revived. Again a company, this time Support Company, was based at Peebles. Jack Nicholson (later Major), the most decorated Peebles soldier of the Second World War with a DCM and MM returned to the 8th Royal Scots as Company Sergeant-Major. Jack had spent his war marauding in the Mediterranean with the Special Boat Service.

In 1952 with the 1st Royal Scots in Korea, the '8th' were called to carry out public duties both at Edinburgh Castle and at Holyrood. During this year they paraded at Peebles when the Royal Scots received the Freedom of the Royal Burgh of Peebles. On this occasion they and the burgh were honoured by the presence of the Princess Royal as Colonel-in-Chief of The Royal Scots (The Royal Regiment). On parade that day, Major Joe Brown commanded the 7/9th Royal Scots detachment from Edinburgh.

The cutback in the Territorial Army led in the 1960s to the amalgamation of the 7/9th and the 8th Battalions as the '8/9th'; later still, with the formation of the 52nd Lowland Volunteers, the TA ceased to exist as such and the Royal Scots presence reduced to two companies within the new volunteer force. The Colours of both battalions and their drums are still on display in the Regimental Museums in Edinburgh Castle as a tangible reminder of outstanding service in both world wars.

In the Second World War the 'Phoney War' of 1939 was to become, in the apt phrase of Angus Calder, the 'People's War' from 1940 – 45. In the first period the main preoccupation was with the possibility of attack from the air on the civilian population, with all that was implied in the terms of casualties and destruction of property. In Peebles as elsewhere, air-raid precautions, or civil defence as it was to become, had already been organised by the outbreak of war. A local civil defence controller for Peeblesshire, Mr Sime of Darnhall, had been appointed. A network of warden posts had been set up with the concomitant telephone communications. Adam Tillotson was active in Peebles in this respect and liaison was maintained with the police force who were augmented by special constables. In the same way the Peebles Fire Brigade was reinforced by the establishment of the Auxiliary Fire Service whose members were exempted from military service. Eventually, all fire brigades were to operate on a national basis under the aegis of the AFS.

The Observer Corps also was revived and in Peebles William Neilson will be remembered in this connection. As in the First World War, observation posts were manned throughout the country, the one in Peebles being on the golf course.[19]

By 1940, however, the fall of France had accelerated the extent to which the general public were affected by war. The prospect was not only of invasion, but of overwhelming air-attacks on the United Kingdom. Civil defence was intensified. Universal conscription was extended with women being directed either into the Women's services, the Land Army, or, in the case of Peebles, into the tweed-mills. In short, all methods of production were directed towards the war effort. The mills were already involved in war production but shortly engineering concerns such as Wallace were brought into the effort. Agriculture was mobilised and became more intense as the need for home-produced food rose.

On only one occasion in the course of the war were the emergency services in Peebles close to being required to demonstrate their hard-won skills. In March 1941, during a series of devastating air-raids on Clydebank, Greenock and later Belfast, German aircraft jettisoned their loads of incendiary and high-explosive bombs as close to Peebles as Hamilton Hill and northwards towards Eddleston. Fortunately, there were no casualties although the story could have been quite different.

On 14 May 1940, the Home Secretary, Anthony Eden, in the face of an invasion threat, launched the Local Defence Volunteers, later the Home Guard. In Peebles over 100 men volunteered immediately, the first to enlist being George S. Taylor. As a county force, the Peeblesshire Home Guard were organised into companies based on the following: Peebles, Innerleithen/Walkerburn, West Linton, Broughton, Manor and Whitebridge. The Peeblesshire Battalion had its headquarters at the Peebles Drill Hall, where the Peebles Company was also based. As Battalion Commander, Lieutenant-Colonel William Thorburn, DSO, late 1/8th Royal Scots, had returned to the fray. It was quickly realised by Colonel Thorburn that any landings by the enemy on the Berwickshire or Northumbrian coast would attempt to move westwards via the Tweed Valley and Peebles to the Biggar Gap and thence to the west.

In consequence, the town was to be defended to the east. Towards this end a number of ingenious measures were adopted. These included road blocks which were covered by machine-gun posts.

Other posts incorporated the weapons unique to the Home Guard: the Smith gun and the Northover Projector. Between 1940 and their eventual disbandment in 1944, the Home Guard in Peebles and the county trained regularly; in all, the battalion numbered between 800 and 900 men at any given time and altogether almost 2,000 passed through the ranks of the unit.

As the war proceeded, with the British Army largely confined to the United Kingdom, the only overseas campaigns being the Far East disaster and the relative stalemate of the Western Desert, it became obvious that any immediate offensive against a German-held Europe must be from the air. As a consequence of this an ambitious scheme to form an Air Training Corps from boys between the ages of sixteen and eighteen years was launched. The *Peeblesshire News* for 7 March 1941 carried this message and No 330 Squadron, the Peebleshire unit of the Air Training Corps, was founded.

The first commanding officer of the new squadron was Mr Henry Ballantyne, with the rank of flight-lieutenant. The immediate response to the appeal produced fifty; by February 1943 there were 170 in the county. No 1 and 2 Peebles Flights were commanded by Flying Officer Souter with Pilot Officers J. Derrick and J. Rankine. Amongst the first to enlist was Tom Murdoch, No 1, and Alex Walker (later Provost Walker) was No 3 to enlist. Amongst those who became NCOs and who subsequently were to serve in the Royal Air Force or Fleet Air Arm were Flight-Sergeant Hutchison, Sergeant R. Dickson, Sergeant R. Allan, Corporal Alex Walker and Corporal Alex McGill, these being the first promotions on the formation of the unit.

In the course of its existence the Peeblesshire ATC had an extremely efficient pipe-band, formed within the first six months of its creation. Sport also had an important part in the new unit's activities. The football XI played in the ATC Edinburgh and District League, winning it in 1943, captained by Alex Walker, but losing the Cup final against Broxburn; Andrew Naysmith of Innerleithen was capped for the ATC Scotland during his service.[20]

In a more serious vein the corps held weekend training camps at Broughton and annual camps were held at Macmerry and Drem where cadets had flying training in RAF training aircraft, notably Rapides, Tiger Moths and Beauforts. Many aircrew recruits were produced by the ATC. Some were to see active service and indeed were to lose their lives in the course of the war. Similarly, many more served as RAF ground staff.[21]

On 4 September 1939 the Peebles Hydro Hotel was requisitioned and was taken over by the Royal Army Medical Corps as a Military General Hospital. As such, the Hydro Hospital treated Army personnel of those units which were stationed in its immediate area, in the main cases beyond the facilities of the field hospitals.

As a general hospital, it also acted as a training unit for medical staff who would eventually be 'formed' into field hospitals and then posted as complete units where and when required. To accommodate the RAMC orderlies, a hutted camp was created on the ground to the south, where championship tennis courts had been. The main building became a 1,200-bed hospital, with X-ray facilities, a number of wards and two operating theatres. Further, there was a small convalescent unit based on huts at Glentress.

Designed as a hospital to receive and cope with battle casualties on the scale of those suffered in the First World War, the Hydro was only to admit casualties on two occasions. After Dunkirk, in 1940, and from the Normandy Campaign in 1944. This illustrates, if nothing else, the changed nature of warfare in the Second World War.

The number of orderlies, drivers and the like generally numbered about 200 throughout the war. As we have seen, however, it was a changing population, as, on being trained, men were posted away to newly-formed units. The same was true of doctors and nursing sisters. At the end of the war the Hydro was rapidly restored to a hotel. Many of the Army personnel who had married locally returned to make their lives in Peebles.[22]

Like the Hydro, the Peebleshire Red Cross were again mobilised in September 1939. The organisation had continued its good work between the wars but was greatly to expand its efforts between 1939 and 1945. As before, its main effort was directed to the training of both auxiliary nurses and of first-aid personnel. Work parties were also organised and, as in the past, the womenfolk of Peebles and the shire excelled themselves in the production of comforts for the troops, in canteen and other modes of service both to soldiers stationed in the town and to those in hospital. Money also was raised by various means to provide for Red Cross services and more importantly, after the fall of France, to provide Red Cross parcels on a regular basis for local men who had been taken prisoner.

The number of Red Cross workers preclude mention of each individual but not one would forget the service of such organisers as Miss Annie Weir of Peebles who gave outstanding service in both wars.

As in earlier wars, Peebles became host to many and varied individuals and units in the Second World War. In 1939, they received a number of children into their homes, children who had been evacuated from both Glasgow and Edinburgh in the light of the prospect of air-attack on those cities. Although many were to return to their homes when the prospect of air-attack was not realised, a number were to remain in Peebles for the period of the war; some still return to Peebles on occasion, a tribute to the kindness which they experienced in the burgh.

British Army units were early stationed in the area. A Field Regiment RA took over the Tontine in 1939 – 40 as their officers' mess and, for a spell in 1941 – 2, the County Hotel became the Divisional Headquarters of the British 3rd Division, the Division which B. L. Montgomery had commanded at Dunkirk.

By 1941 a Polish armoured division was stationed for training in the Borders. Elements of this formation occupied a hutted camp in Victoria Park; from then on until their departure at the end of 1943 the Polish soldiers were a common sight in Peebles and elsewhere. So also were the 'Matilda' tanks with which they were first equipped. The division moved to the south of England in 1943 for the invasion of Europe. The members of this unit had their revenge for the conquest of Poland when they closed the Falaise Gap to the retreating Germans in 1944. Many of the Poles, bereft of their native land by Russian occupation, returned to Peebles and the Borders where they were rapidly assimilated into the local population.

At the end of 1942, a camp for Italian prisoners-of-war was built on railway ground at the Caledonian Road. By the end of 1942 they became co-belligerents and as such were able to socialise after their daily work as farm labourers was over. This led to a certain amount of friction with local servicemen although there were few serious incidents. The Italians departed for home in 1944/5. As the liberation of Europe progressed, so the human detritus in the shape of 'Displaced Persons' grew. A number of these unfortunates were billeted in Victoria Park Camp in 1944/5.

In marked contrast to the losses suffered in the First World War, the number of Peebleans who were killed or died as a result of Second World War amounted to seventy. Although nonetheless grievous, there was some cause for celebration in Peebles on 8 May 1945.

Footnotes:

1. Ewing, J., *The Royal Scots 1914 – 19* (Edinburgh, 1925) Vol I, pp83 – 5
2. Weaver, Lawrence, *The Story of the Royal Scots* (London, 1915) pp221 – 3
3. Ewing, J., *The Royal Scots 1914 – 19* (Edinburgh, 1925) Vol I, p256
4. Buchan, J. Walter (ed), *A History of Peeblesshire* (Glasgow, 1925) Vol I, pp129 – 130
5. Ibid, p128
6. Ewing, J., *The Royal Scots 1914 – 19* (Edinburgh, 1925) Vol 2, pp773 – 80
7. Ibid, p777
8. Buchan, J. Walter (ed), *A History of Peeblesshire* (Glasgow, 1925) Vol I, pp136 – 9
9. Ibid, pp139 – 41
10. Ibid, p142
11. Ibid, p145
12. Harvie, Christopher, *No Gods and Precious Few Heroes* (London, 1981) p34
13. Watson, William, personal recollections
14. Renwick, James, personal recollections
15. Muir, Augustus, *First of Foot* (Edinburgh, 1961), pp205, 228
16. Ibid, pp268 – 80
17. Keegan, John, *Six Armies in Normandy* (London, 1982) pp166 – 80
18. Martin, H. G., *History of the 15th Scottish Division 1939 – 45* (Edinburgh, 1948) pp104 – 6, 109 – 42, 175 – 80, 199, 226 – 73, 277
19. Brown, Ian, unpublished
20. Walker, Alex, personal recollections
21. Brown, Ian, unpublished
22. McPhater, Dr J., personal recollections

CHAPTER 8

Social Life

THE FIRST HALF of the twentieth century had five distinct periods and each meant a very different way of life for the people of Peebles.

It began with the pre-1914 years which covered the celebrations of two coronations, King Edward VII in August 1902 and George V in June 1911, when the future looked bright and local life was still centred on the activities of the tweed-mills. Then came the First World War, involving every family when the life-and-death struggle lasted longer than anyone at first expected. There followed the 'in-between' years of 1919 to 1938. It was a phase when the life of the town was faced with the uncertainty of work as the tweed-mills gradually moved towards a major recession in world trade and unemployment. Despite the years of the Depression, there were improvements in wages and hours and especially changes in life-style as many families were better housed as new building schemes were completed. Then came the Second World War and Peebles prepared itself to be 'in the front line' like the rest of Britain, ready to defend itself while its sons and daughters were serving in every sector of the wartime life. When the struggle ended in 1945, the last four years of the half-century saw the town and its ex-servicemen and women seeking a return to 'normality'.

However, life could never be the same; it was different after each phase and above all there was from 1914 — and deepened by the years from 1939 — a silent and enduring bond with these never-to-be-forgotten days and with the 293 sons and two daughters of Peebles who had not returned. Chapter 7 gives an account of Peebles during the First and Second World Wars but the story to be told of the life of the town would not be complete without a heart-felt tribute to the widows, the fatherless and the grieving mothers and fathers to whom their loss was irreplaceable.

In the 1920s the Peebles ex-servicemen began to raise funds for the entertainment of widows and children of the men who fell during the First World War. At the final event of an 'At Home' evening in one of the local halls in March 1938, Mrs Tarry extended to everyone the sincere thanks of the widows for all the kindness shown to them. Mrs Tarry's husband, Sergeant Frederick G. Tarry, a tweed warehouseman before the outbreak of war in 1914, served with the Royal Artillery and was killed in 1918. In tribute to him, Dr C. B. Gunn wrote in his *Book of Remembrance*:

> For you, our dead, beyond the sea,
> Who gave your lives to hold us free,
> By us, who keep your memory,
> What can be said?

It can be said, sadly but proudly, that Mrs Tarry and the war-bereaved showed courage and cheerfulness in the years that followed and their bravery of spirit was an inspiration to the town and to the generations that came to know them.

As the century began, the town's population-growth had slowed down from its peak period between 1881 and 1891 when the census showed there were 1,209 additional persons in the town. This represented a growth rate of 34 per cent, comprising 475 males and 734 females. In the fifty years to 1951, the rate of increase was a mere 14 per cent: 747 more people, and about half that increase (314) occurring in the decade which followed the First World War (from 1921 to 1931).

From the start of the twentieth century an endeavour was made to keep pace with the expansion of the population, and there were 157 houses built in the first ten years and just under seventy in the second decade up to 1921. It was in the third decade that the 'march of progressive house building' began through the intervention of the State which enabled the town council to set about improving the standard and quality of the housing stock.

The Government also acted during the years of the Great Depression to encourage a programme of slum clearance and paid the local authorities a subsidy for every person rehoused. It was hoped that the building of these houses would help not only the construction industry but the allied services and trades supplying fitments and furnishings. It certainly proved helpful to Peebles by sparking-off a programme of modern housing with up-to-date facilities, creating more local job opportunities to ease unemployment and helped more money to circulate in the local economy.

A Peebles man in the Government at the time was William Graham. He was born in the town in 1887 and was the Financial Secretary to the Treasury in the minority Labour Government of 1924 and was appointed the President of the Board of Trade in subsequent Labour administration. One of the most respected of the Socialist leaders during the 1920s and 1930s, he was the Member of Parliament for Edinburgh Central.

It was in this progressive period from 1921 to 1951, excepting the war years, that nearly 500 houses were constructed under the provision of these Acts. The new houses provided a greatly improved life-style with homes that had electric lighting, indoor toilets and bathrooms, kitchens with food larders, hot-and-cold-water facilities and gas boilers for washing clothes.

Washing day for many families had previously meant getting the basket of clothes to and from James McCulloch's laundry in Eddleston Green or John Maclaren's in March Street. These were neighbourly meeting places and the gossip of the day was discussed while scrubbing-boards were used. Peebles' homes, however, had been fortunate from the early 1900s to have had gas cookers as well as lighting, and this was due to the enterprise shown by the town council in 1898 in acquiring and developing the Peebles Gas Undertaking. As already mentioned, the council's policy was to supply cookers, grillers and hot plates free of charge or charging only nominal rentals. When the new gasworks were established at Eshiels in 1905, there were about 500 gas cookers and over 800 other appliances in use, including a number of gas fires.

The early years of the twentieth century opened with sufficient work and an adequate level of earnings as the local mills continued to obtain a share of world markets for their quality cloths and tweeds. However, there were occasional short periods when demand slackened off, such as in 1906 – 7.

Apart from the mills providing employment for both men and women in a friendly environment, the earnings improved the standard of life for families and this clearly benefited the whole town and had an impact on its social life. The mills and millworkers held regular dances and other social occasions and all the mills would combine for an annual outing, such as they did in June 1907 when about 700 people went to Portobello in two special trains.

Making your own entertainment and holding community events were an important part of social life before the First World War. These were the days before radio and television and although the gramophone and its collection of records had a pride of place in the home of 1920s, it was outside in the community and in the company of others that entertainment was enjoyed. Social activities covered a wide and interesting programme of events and, at the heart of each year and becoming more popular as it enlarged its pageantry, was the Riding of the Marches and the Crowning of the Beltane Queen. It was the 'centre-piece' of the year's activities — as it is today.

The Peebles March Riding and Sports Committee, for example, arranged an Aquatic Carnival one Saturday afternoon in August 1907. It was held at the Minnie Pool and attracted a very large crowd that gathered on the banks of the River Tweed to see the Wynman Swimming and Humane Society of Edinburgh give an exhibition of the latest style of swimming the 'crawl stroke', and demonstrations of life-saving and water polo. This event raised the hope that something would be done to build indoor swimming baths in Peebles and this happened in 1919 when Sir Henry Ballantyne generously presented the town with its first swimming baths at the Gytes.

The special constables 'Big Trip' was the principal excursion of each year and an event that ranked second in importance to the Beltane Festival. Usually between 500 to 700 went on it each year, visiting Glasgow and the Exhibition in 1901, Ayr in 1902 and 1908, Berwick-upon-Tweed in 1903, Aberdeen in 1904, Rothesay in 1905 and 1910, Dunoon in 1906, St Andrews in 1907 and Helensburgh in 1909 and, in the 1920s and 1930s, the 'Big Trip' was still a favourite day out. Other events in the years before 1914 were visits by the Pierrots, who performed at Ninian's Haugh, and regular concerts, such as the Co-operative Society's 'Concert of the Season'.

The great local medium of entertainment, however, was the cinema which made its appearance in Peebles in January 1907. James A. Scott's 'Cinematography Company and High-Class Concert Party' gave a one-night performance at the Chambers Institute and claimed to show the 'world's best pictures, which included "A Fox Hunt" in twenty-three exciting scenes; "The Stepmother" in fifteen pathetic scenes; and all the latest humorous, dramatic and historical pictures'. Admission was 2s, 1s 6d, 1s and 6d (10p, 7½p, 5p and 2½p).

James Scott, described by the *Peeblesshire Advertiser* as the 'leading cinematographist in Great Britain', became well-established in Peebles, setting up the Burgh Cinema in the Institution Hall and providing the town with a regular programme of silent films which were shown with the accompaniment of piano and violin. Later it became known as the Royal Burgh Cinema and even after the appearance of the Empire and the Playhouse Cinemas it still kept open at the weekends.

Scott built the Empire Cinema in 1914 at the Bridgegate, and it was known as the 'Pavilion' until 1918. Changing to the 'talkies' in the 1920s, the Empire was a popular and homely place of entertainment for over forty years until 1954. The seating at the back of the auditorium, to the right of the projection box, was a favourite courting place for generations of Peebles lads and lasses.

Later, in 1932, the Playhouse Cinema opened in the High Street. It was wall-to-wall carpeted, luxuriously decorated and, although it operated as a rival to Scott's Empire, both were well patronised up to the time of the Second World War. Sadly, the latter was destroyed by fire early in the Second World War but was re-opened in June 1943. As radio and then television became dominant as the main sources of entertainment, there was an inevitable decline in attendances at events outside the home and the local cinemas closed down in the years following the Second World War.

The first years of the century saw the emergence of the car, which gradually became part of the town's way of life by the 1930s. As early as 1907 objections were being made to cars in the town travelling at ten miles per hour. It was claimed that this speeding was a 'danger to the public, created dust and that several roads were very narrow to be used in this way'. In October that year, a motorcar salesman appeared at the Peebles Sheriff Court and was fined five pounds with the alternative of seven days in prison for having driven his motorcar at a speed of between sixteen and seventeen miles per hour. However, earlier that year a delegation from the town council went in Sir Henry Ballantyne's car to look at the possibility of using tarmac on the town's streets. It was reported that for some of them it was a most exciting experience. Treasurer Forester said that they had been somewhat nervous to begin with but he thought they had 'got imbued with the spirit of the motorist'. Sir Henry Ballantyne, who was provost from 1898 to 1907, quickly assured the council that 'We did not go more than twenty miles per hour!'

A new golf course was proposed in 1907 and amongst the reasons put forward was the pause in the town's prosperity as a summer resort and the belief that it was necessary to do something to attract more visitors. The Hotel Hydro was prepared to give £200 towards the estimated cost of £1,000 but in 1908 a new course was constructed at Kirklands for only £761. Kirklands replaced the old nine-hole course constructed in 1892 at Morning Hill, about a mile to the south of the town.

Peebles Rovers just prior to the First World War made a name for themselves as exponents of the five-a-side game with players like Wat Baillie (Peebles Athletic), J. Bain (later of Hamilton Academicals), C. L. Buchan (Queen's Park and Dundee), Jamie Reid (Airdrie) and Arch Cairncross (Third Lanark). Jamie Reid's greatest triumph was at Selkirk when on one occasion he scored over twenty goals during the afternoon. He had played for Airdrieonians in 1912 and was one of Scotland's finest centre-forwards. A native of Peebles, he was the son of Dean of Guild Alexander Reid, and learned his skills with Peebles Adventurers as well as Peebles Rovers before joining Lincoln City.

A notable Peebles 'worthy' and a nippy inside-forward with Peebles Amateurs was Steve Howitt. He was prominently involved in the town's social life for more than half a century, giving generations of Peebleans a lifetime of happy memories that the years cannot dim. Steve Howitt started work in the March Street Mills in 1896 and only retired in 1953. Although that long service is in itself quite outstanding, it was as an entertainer that he will long be remembered. He was our own 'Sir Harry Lauder' and we shared his acclaim with the whole of the Borders where he was very popular.

As a young man, Steve Howitt, along with other local youths, would meet on the grassy banks of the Tweedside — a favourite spot was near to where the Fotheringham Bridge was built — and they held impromptu concerts on Sunday afternoons. They would sing the 'pop songs' of the day, including those of Sir Harry Lauder which Steve particularly made his own with his 'patter' preceding the final chorus.

He had a fine baritone voice and gave many performances but Steve will long be remembered for the 'Store Concerts' which were given for the children of the town. His repertoire was extensive and it was his own songs that were the most popular. He had a wonderful ear for music and having heard a tune he would easily recall it. James Izett, who was the organist and choirmaster at the Old Parish Church, would set down the notes for Steve and help with the arrangements. Favourites were 'Sergeant Dugal', 'Some Wedding', 'Tamson's Wedding Spree', 'Alice' and 'The Message Boy'.

Always appearing with his flaming red wig, he would delight the children by singing one of their favourite 'Steve' songs:

> Come up and see my garret,
> Come up and see it noo.
> Come up and see my garret,
> For it's a' furnished new.
> An auld broken table,
> A chair withoot a leg,
> A cup withoot a handle,
> And an auld iron bed.

It was sung over and over again. Another favourite of the children was:

> Tear in bairns you're at your Aunties',
> And you'll be awfu' glad you came,
> There's a lot of nice things here,
> So make them disappear,
> And what you canny eat you cairry hame.

> The Co-operative Store belongs tae Aunties',
> And she's your dear auld friend,
> So tear in Bairns you're at your Aunties',
> And the mair you eat the mair the dividend.

Steve Howitt's other great interest apart from singing was the Beltane Festival. For many long years he took his place in front of the silver band and led the Cycle Parade dressed in an outrageous costume. Steve Howitt's son, Jim Howitt, tells of the occasion when Steve was 'The Duchess of Kipper Row'. His costume was made of canvas to which kippers had been attached, and as it was a very hot summer's day he became the 'Pied Piper' of all the cats in George Street as he waited there with the silver band to take their place in the parade.[1]

He had turned down offers of professional touring parties,

preferring to be with his ain folk, happy to roam his native hills and to give his special talents freely to all who asked him to perform. It is to be hoped that his collection of songs will find a place in the Peebles Library.

Peebles, in the summer of 1913, enjoyed a lovely spell of hot weather; there was no rain from early July to late August. The Gutterbluid Club, thinking of their kinsfolk overseas, had sent sprigs of heather to Canada and America to be distributed to Peebleans. The Peebles Territorials, about fifty in number and under the command of Lieutenant G. H. Ballantyne, went off to their annual training camp which was at Monzie, near Crieff in Perthshire. A year later, the territorials were preparing to go to France and Peebleans at home and abroad were mustering to share in the long hard-fought struggle of the First World War. In under three months the homes of Peebles families were receiving Belgian refugees who had to flee from their country as the German Army advanced towards France. Dr C. B. Gunn writes most movingly of their arrival at the Caledonian Station on Thursday, 29 October 1914:

> It was a dark and dreary night as the band of exiles crossed the bridge at Peebles . . . They were weary and dejected and their little ones silent in the sleep of exhaustion. The townspeople strove to relieve the tired mothers of their tender burdens. The Provost and Magistrates conveyed the little procession, while on the night wind fluttered the folds of their country's flag. A great crowd pressed upon them, and along the bridge and up the High Street fitful outbursts of cheering stirred the night.[2]

Apparently staying for a much shorter time in the town was the spy named Lodi who was later to be executed at the Tower of London. It later became known that he made an overnight stop in Peebles and then cycled on to Edinburgh, having stayed at the County Hotel as 'Charles A. Inglis from New York, USA'.[3]

Despite the widely-held view that the war would soon be over, it took four long years whilst our young men — and some not so young — faced the dangers of bullet, shell and poison gas and endured the awful conditions of mud and the trenches. At home in Peebles, hearts ached.[4]

In 1917 everyone was asked to eat less bread and meat, to use more potatoes and oatmeal and to avoid waste. The scarcity of certain

141

items led to queues and, to avoid this, a system of rationing was introduced that required registering with a particular shop. By April 1918 there was meat rationing which, at the minimum level, was three-quarters of a pound per person; and tea, butter and margarine were other items that came under controlled distribution. Rationing continued into the post-war years (milk was also added to those items after the Armistice) and only came to an end in October 1919.[5]

During the war the mills were kept busy although during the first week in August 1914 there was a great deal of uncertainty and the mills closed down. Within days they were reopened as orders for khaki and tartan were received and with the menfolk away in the Armed Forces, it fell mainly to the women mill-workers to keep the mills running at capacity.

When the bells of peace rang out Peebles, having learned 'the true meaning and awful significance of war, held herself in proud restraint. There was gladness, but there was also sorrow.' The bells rang out again when the Peace Treaty was signed on 28 June 1919, but on Tuesday, 11 November 1919 there was the two-minute long 'Great Silence',which began with the striking of the eleventh hour on the town clock and the blowing of the mill buzzers signalling work to cease and for pedestrians and drivers of vehicles to come to a standstill, as homage was paid.[6]

The beautiful War Memorial in the Quadrangle of the Chambers Institute was unveiled on 5 October 1922 by Field-Marshal the Earl Haig. On the same day the Morelands War Memorial Hospital was opened by the Rt. Hon. Robert Munro KC. The first was the symbol of the county's remembrance and the other a practical expression of our ongoing indebtedness for the freedom which had been won for future generations.

Since the beginning of the war, there had been an overall increase in real incomes that was sufficient to overtake wartime inflation and in the inter-war years, from 1924 through to 1940, real incomes rose as a whole by about 40 per cent with half coming in the Depression years and half thereafter.[7] Looking particularly at the years of the Great Depression and taking 1930 as the index year of 100, the 1913 weekly wage rates were 52.4 (compared with 82.8 average real earnings, adjusted for retail prices); 1920 — 143.7 (92.2); 1933 — 95.3 (107.6) and in 1938 — 106.3 (107.7).[8] Therefore, despite the long and seemingly endless years of uncertain work and unemployment in the woollen-mills and the effect that these had on local trade during the 1930s, there was a general advancement in social well-being. The inadequate level of unemployment benefit (it was often cut) cushioned the worst effects of long-term unemployment. However, the quality of life was not only a matter of income but also depended on better housing, the local environment and the kind of supporting society that was to be found in Peebles.

In the years immediately after the First World War the Peebles Town Council set about extending its custody of the open countryside and acquired for the 'public enjoyment' extensive areas of land which became the sites for municipal housing schemes as well as parks and playing-fields.

Public enjoyment and the common good were also well served by the enterprise and pioneering spirit of Andrew Harper when he began the bus service which he ran with his two sons, Hugh and Joe. It began its first run to Innerleithen and Walkerburn in April 1923, when Joe Harper drove the twenty-seater bus and young Jackie Elder was the conductor. There was soon to be a regular Harper's bus service to Edinburgh, Biggar and Broughton via Howgate, West Linton and Dolphinton; Edinburgh via Penicuik; Glasgow via Motherwell; Dumfries and Moffat via Carlops and West Linton.[9] William Ramsay supplemented these services with equally enterprising bus-routes to the upper parts of the county.

Harper's, in the days before popular car ownership, opened up the opportunity for many local families to enjoy a new form of leisure: the 'tour', all the more enjoyable in the charabanc coach of the 1920s and early 1930s. Harper's extensive programme included tours to Dryburgh Abbey (6s: 30p), Moffat (7s 6d: 37½p), Abbotsford (5s: 25p); Eddleston, The Meldons and Lyne (2s: 10p); Manor, Black Dwarf's Cottage, and Cademuir (1s 6d: 7½p). His drivers and conductors wore distinctive lapel badges with a red enamel circle and a gold gilt centre-piece of the Peebles coat of arms. John Elder, who became a local bus driver, was on the outdoor staff of Field-Marshal the Earl Haig during the First World War. He had the unique experience of driving the Duke of York (later King George VI) and then drove the Prince of Wales (who became the Duke of Windsor) when they toured the battlefields. In recognition of this service, he was presented with a silver watch from King George V.

James Thomson of Ellerslie also organised trips and conducted a number of summer tours with his horse-drawn wagonettes, replacing these with the luxurious charabancs which provided, as he said, 'more scope'.

Perhaps the first charabanc in Peebles was *The Rover* which was devised by John Richardson, a contractor and bottler at Greenside Place. He was the owner of a large-sized lorry and, being a member of the Peebles Rovers Committee, he came to their rescue in the early 1920s when there was an important Cup-tie to be played at Berwick. The problem arose through the railways being on strike and there being no other way of getting the team to Berwick. John Richardson rigged out his lorry with forms, which were securely roped down, and had a local joiner make a body to enclose them; despite the lack of a top covering, he conveyed the Peebles Rovers to their Cup-tie.

Fred Pearce also used this idea, converting the lorry of his bottling works to take a number of church forms, securely tied back to back, this conveyance being used to take the women's section of the Baptist Church on short outings on Wednesday afternoons.

Horse-drawn vehicles were a part of the local scene up to the 1930s, being used for the delivery of groceries, bread and milk around the town. A regular sight was the Clydesdale horses pulling the tree bogies down from the hills and passing through the town as they made their way to the Dwyer sawmill at the Old Station at March Street. Kit Glendinning was perhaps the last to drive these heavy loads and his horse was kept in a stone-built stable at the Cuddyside which has now been converted into a fine dwelling-house.

Fords across the rivers were a feature of the town and countryside before the advent of bridges but the approaches to the old fords have now mostly been filled in. They were once as important as the King's highway but they fell into disuse as motor vehicles replaced the horse. Cardrona Ford was erased from the list of highways in 1950 but the site of one of the town's fords can still be readily identified at the foot of the Northgate Vennel.

There is still much to be seen in the district of the craftsmanship of the dry-stone dyker. James Marshall, who died in 1937 aged 94, was one of the last of the dry-stone dykers in Peebles, having lived in the town for sixty years. Rising at five in the morning and walking eight miles or so in all weathers, he had first to gather from the moors all the stones he needed for that day's work before he could start building the wall.

James Marshall was only paid 5s (25p) a week and no money was paid to cover the time occupied in walking to Traquair or Stobo or

Leithen Water in the mornings or back to his home at Rosetta Road. He was a poet and observed nature in all her aspects and moods, transferring his thoughts into verse and publishing *A Book of Verse*. James Marshall typified a hardworking and conscientious generation of the early 1900s and was a most worthy and respected Peeblean.

So, too, was Edward Bonong, who died in 1938 in his ninetieth year. He was a native of Peebles and was descended from the French prisoners-of-war that stayed on in Peebles. Edward Bonong started work as a skinner before working in Damdale Mill. Like many Peebleans of the early century, he gave a great deal of time to the many activities that were emerging in the growing town. He was a member of the Peebles Philharmonic Orchestra and also played in the Volunteer Band which took part in Queen Victoria's 'Wet Review' in Queen's Park, Edinburgh. In addition, he was a 'major' in the special constables, having attended about seventy 'Big Trips', and had a long association with the Ancient Order of Foresters and the Board of Management of the Peebles Co-operative Society.

Bailie Thomson was the manager of the Peebles Co-op and was another most able Peeblean who took an interest in a wide range of local affairs, including membership of the town council. It was he and the board of management who developed the 'Co-op', into a huge shopping enterprise that successfully served its large membership with a wide range of goods, services and provided splendid dividends.

Mary Bonong, the daughter of Edward Bonong, was the 'infants mistress' of Halyrude School. It was in her primary department that nearly everyone in the 1920s, and for most of the 1930s, started their education, and she must be fondly remembered by many as their first teacher. Her gentleness and understanding could allay the worst fears of a five-year-old away from home, and to be selected to feed the goldfish was the 'first attainment' in scholastic distinction. It was a matter of great satisfaction to countless former pupils when she was invited to crown the Beltane Queen in 1932.

John Roney, a dairyman at Maybole in the Old Town, painted Edward Bonong's portrait in oils. A fine artist, John Roney had made drawing and painting his hobby since boyhood. His portrait of Provost Anderson was regarded as a masterly work of art. Landscapes were his favourite subject but he will be remembered, too, for his black and white illustrations in Dr C. B. Gunn's *Book of*

Remembrance for Tweeddale: the Burgh and Parish of Peebles (two volumes) which depict *The Last Sacrament of The Royal Scots* and *The Last Church Parade of the 9th Royal Scots.*

Jack and Christopher Roney, his sons, are also well known as local artists. Jack Roney's watercolours of the Peebles countryside, especially of Neidpath Castle, have provided many fine landscape paintings, whilst Christopher Roney's drawings and wood-carvings, particularly his highly-skilled work in restoring ornamental ceilings, is a very special talent. It is a unique contribution to have been made by one local family to the life of Peebles. Another native of the town and an exhibitor at the Royal Scottish Academy, was Andrew Murray, who died in 1937, aged seventy-three. He was a noted etcher and many of his dry-points were exhibited.

The abdication of King Edward VIII in 1936 recalls the story told by Dr Gunn about two sisters, the Misses Bewley, who resided at Rathmore, Springhill Road. They had been commissioned to make a christening robe for the Duke of York's (later King George V) infant son Edward who had been born in 1894. He saw the dress being made, which was of 'the finest mainsook muslin, trimmed with Valenciennes lace; the thread used is as fine as gossamer, and as for the needles, they are like filaments of hair'.[10]

Radio — or rather wireless — was in most homes in the town by the 1930s. In its early days, and before most homes had electric power, there was the regular ritual of having one accumulator connected to the wireless set, one in reserve and the other in the process of being re-charged, possibly by Kid & Veitch at Greenside. The quality of wireless reception was rather indifferent until 1932 when Peebles listeners began to get their transmission signals from a new BBC transmitter at Westerglen, near Falkirk. Accumulators were well charged but alas the new transmitter was not in being for the first broadcast of an evening service from the Old Parish Church in 1931, which was conducted by the Revd Berry Preston. It was relayed throughout Scotland but there was a mixed experience of reception because the local wireless owners tried to find Glasgow on the dial, it being the main Scottish station available to Peebles listeners. However, it was reputed not to perform too well at times 'owing to the close proximity to its wavelength of several Continental stations'. The *Peeblesshire Advertiser* added to its report that possibly the main cause of the trouble was created by listeners with obsolete sets who experienced the difficulty of tuning in, adding that 'tuning controls were still being tuned in a vain search when the service was concluded'. It was a notable local event and quite a number of houses had arranged parties in their homes for the occasion. Nevertheless, just as the 'newsflash' about the assassination of President John F. Kennedy can still be readily remembered, so too can the announcement made on the night of 22 January 1935 which solemnly announced that the 'King's life was drawing slowly to a close'.

Peebles took pride in their own broadcaster, William D. Crichton, who was a well-known actor and took part in many of the Scottish plays that were heard on the wireless. Travelling back on the late-night SMT bus from Edinburgh after being at the broadcasting studios, he could be seen through a cloud of cigarette smoke, well down in his seat and totally engrossed in a script.

William Crichton first appeared in 1921 in the Peebles Philharmonic Society's production of the *Pirates of Penzance*. He instituted the Peebles Players, producing *Campbell of Kilmohr* as their first performance, and also became the stage director of the Peebles Drama Festival. He had the honour of appearing in a Royal Command performance before King George V and Queen Mary in a Brandon Thomas Company production of *Hamlet*.

Peebleans also took pride in the achievements of Margaret Smith, a sixteen-year-old who broke the Scottish Women's 1,000 yards record by one minute and thirteen seconds at Renfrew on 12 December 1934, establishing a new Scottish swimming record of fifteen minutes 25.4 seconds; again, in 1938, she held the Scottish Women's One-Mile record with a time of twenty-nine minutes eleven seconds. A member of the Peebles Amateur Swimming Club, Margaret Smith was in the Scottish team in 1935 competing against England and Wales.

Royal occasions were always loyally marked in Peebles: the restitution of the March Riding in 1897 and the gift of Victoria Park by Sir John Hay of Haystoun, Bart., to celebrate Queen Victoria's Diamond Jubilee; Priorsford Bridge built in 1905 to commemorate the coronation of King Edward VII. These occasions also had special events for the children and the elderly. The Silver Jubilee of King George V and Queen Mary in 1935 was celebrated with a special cinema show in the Playhouse and the Empire Cinemas with 1,270 children attending and each being given a souvenir tin of chocolate.

Also, 200 unemployed and old folks were given luncheon in the Drill Hall, the cost being met by anonymous donors.

Another jubilee that was celebrated in Peebles in 1935 was the fiftieth anniversary of the starting up of the March Street Mills. Sir Henry and Lady Ballantyne gave a dinner in the Drill Hall for 600 employees and present that evening was Adam Dalgleish — the Mill's first employee. There were also four other employees who had started work in 1885 when the mills first opened: Duncan Bennet, Andrew Clyde and Jas Hope who were also at the dinner and Miss Maggie M'Isaac who was unable to attend.

The Coronation ceremony of King George VI and Queen Elizabeth in 1937 was broadcast by radio to the nation but even more spectacular was the Paramount newsreel in the local cinemas the next day. They had been rushed to Edinburgh by aeroplane and brought to Peebles by car. Locally, the Coronation was celebrated with a dinner for the elderly in the Drill Hall which was given by the town council and everyone received a souvenir tin containing tea. The school children in the town were given a copy of the book *George VI, King and Emperor* and a circus performance was also arranged in Victoria Park and a fireworks display at Kerfield.

The King's Coronation Honours List conferred upon Lord Tweedsmuir (John Buchan) the distinction of being appointed a privy councillor, having previously been created a Baron in 1935 when he became governor-general of Canada. A distinguished statesman and author, Lord Tweedsmuir and J. Walter Buchan, his brother, and Miss Anna Buchan, his sister, were members of a family that were held in very special regard by the people of Peebles.

From 1906 to 1948 Walter Buchan was an extremely efficient town clerk of the royal burgh and, in Chapter 13, 'The Law and The Lawyers of Peebles', there is an account of the practice of J. & W. Buchan. It is to his great credit that *A History of Peeblesshire* was produced, having largely written and edited the three volumes. Miss Anna Buchan was also a writer and as 'O'Douglas', her books were widely acclaimed. All three were appointed Wardens of Neidpath — an honour they richly deserved.

Many Peebles folk were given their first opportunity of a flight in an aeroplane one September afternoon in 1932, when Sir Allan Cobham brought 'Britain's greatest air pageant' to Sheriffmuir. A Zeuguied airliner was available for cruises at a cost of 4s (20p). In 1936 Sheriffmuir was again the venue for the 'British Empire Air

Display' which had twelve pilots including T. Campbell Black who had crossed the world in four days in the English – Australian air race held in 1934; flights cost 3s 6d (17½p).

Hiking was much in fashion in the early 1930s, and hints to local hikers contained the following points. Choose your kit carefully. You need one pair of boots or shoes with tackets; one pair of shorts; one general-purpose jacket; no hat; one staff (stout); one haversack, rucksack, or valaise; one blanket, warm; one pencil, complete with cap and rubber; one whistle or mouth-organ; and one round of culinary utensils (Woolworthian). A family trip to Edinburgh in the 1930s generally included a visit to Woolworths, with its wide-range of items conveniently displayed in trays on long counters and nothing costing more than sixpence (2½p).

Another pre-1939 activity was provided by the Neidpath Wheelers cycle club who usually announced in the local papers the route for that weekend, such as: Hawick via Tushielaw, returning via Denholm, Ancrum, St Boswells and Melrose. Alternatively, you could, in the 1930s, play golf on a Sunday and endeavour to be as successful as Alec Kyle who had learned his golf at Peebles and who was chosen as one of Britain's Walker Cup team to play at St Andrews in June 1938. Alec T. Kyle, born in Hawick, came to live in Peebles when he was a year old, his parents residing at Kirkland Street. He won the British Amateur Golf Championship at Hoylake in 1939 bringing great distinction to the town and was accorded a civic reception and chaired through the streets.

In 1922 the Peebles Rugby Club was restarted and W. Allan Taggart elected the first captain. It was only moderately supported in the years before the Second World War, and it is a matter of great satisfaction to followers of rugby to see how well the game flourishes in Peebles today.

Peebles County Cricket was at one time known as 'Thorburnshire', because of an almost complete team of Thorburns. It must be recorded that interest in the 1920s and 1930s in Peebles cricket increased through the support of both the Thorburns and the Ballantynes.

Peebles Rovers, referred to earlier in the chapter, have always had a special place in the affections of local sportsmen. Jock Dodds, who died in 1953 aged seventy-six, was at one time their trainer, after his playing days as a winger were over. He did a great deal to build up the reputation of the Rovers and it was part of their legendary tales that, when they were in the final of the Alliance League Championship they needed both points to win and being a man short, Jock put on his strip to score the winning goal and stake his claim to the 'Flag'. Another distinguished Rovers' player was Robert Carrick, who died in 1963. He was a schoolboy internationalist and played for Scotland against England at Tynecastle in 1925.

In the years before the Second World War there was a nice, steady pattern and quality to life in the town. Peebles, with its wide High Street, had a pleasing atmosphere, especially on a Saturday afternoon busy with shoppers and everyone out seemingly to enjoy themselves. Couples and families on the way to the cinema; dances at the weekends. Veitch's Corner was a favourite standing place for men observing the town's life passing by. The atmosphere and friendliness existing in the town can be gathered from the Christmas message that was read out to the town council in January 1938, having been received from John Caldwell, a well-known street artist. It said: 'This is from John Caldwell, the artist who comes every summer below the Tweed Bridge. I am sorry I could not get there as the Royal Show in Alloa was on the same day. So I wish you's all a merry Christmas and A Happy New Year and best of luck.' John Caldwell's greetings were warmly received.

Christmas was extra special, too, with most shops splendidly decorated. In the windows of J. H. Goodburn, Bakers and Confectioners, and then latterly at Wilson & Sime, a special and popular feature was the display of a magnificent confectionery cake which had been made with great artistry and skill. William Walker, father of Alex Walker who was provost from 1967 to 1970, was the gifted confectioner who took pride and joy in creating those magnificent cakes — the subject was always a great secret until 'the cake' appeared in the window. His artistry produced cakes modelled on Neidpath Castle, Buchan's House, Chambers Institution, the Old Parish Church, the Playhouse Cinema, Snow White and the Seven Dwarfs and the liners Queen Mary and Queen Elizabeth; the most unique was the Wireless Set that played; the most historic was the Coronation of King Edward VIII that had to be changed to depict George VI; his masterpiece was undoubtedly the model of the Peebles Hydropathic. One of the earliest cakes to be put on display was a lighthouse with a revolving light, which caused Dr Gunn to swoop down Goodburn's Close in his usual haste shouting 'Marvellous piece of work, Walker; but whoever saw a robin on top of a lighthouse?' After a quick dip in icing sugar the robin was transformed into a seagull.[11]

On the August Bank Holiday in the summer of 1938, a year before the start of the Second World War, it was reported that the volume of traffic on the Peebles roads was abnormally heavy. There were not just cars, but cycles and tandems out in force. The 'Big Trip' had gone to Campbeltown, in the Mull of Kintyre, and many people were visiting the Empire Exhibition in Glasgow.

Earlier that year Peebles had been shaken by 'severe vibrations' at five minutes to midnight on 21 March 1938, and people in their homes all over the town experienced what proved to be a slight earthquake. It was described as 'starting with a sudden noise, a vibration, a thud, and a tremor that was particular noticeable if you were in an upstairs room.'

Another disturbance in the months before the start of the Second World War was the anti-Jewish statements by the local Member of Parliament, Captain A. Maule Ramsay. He had defeated Joe Westwood at the General Election of 1931 and had been elected as the MP for Peebles and South Midlothian. National and local newspapers were reporting his sweeping allegations that a 'group of international Jews' were behind a movement for world revolution. The local Unionist Association — and the people of Peebles — were by no means pleased with these wild and unpopular views. When war was declared he was detained in Brixton Prison under the provisions of 18B of the Defence Regulations and the constituency was represented for the duration of the war by David Robertson, who was the Member for Streatham.

The tweed-mills had passed through the worst of the Great Depression but they did not get busy until early in 1939 when they received a part of a large Defence Department order for khaki and serge. Nothing can make up for the despair suffered by men and women who were unemployed for long periods but a Personal Service League that was set up in Peebles provided a useful and sympathetic service of support that gave help and encouragement. Machinery and tools were provided in the town hall and, with tuition from Mr Wishart and Councillor Ainslie, there was a wide range of items produced and displayed in the windows of Scott & Rutherford.

Mr James Izett had the responsibility of managing the Labour Exchange during these difficult times. He started his working life with Lowe Donald in 1905 and served with the Royal Naval

Volunteer Reserve in the First World War. He will be remembered for his dedication to music in the town, being organist and choirmaster of the Old Parish Church from 1921 to 1946 and conductor of the Peebles Philharmonic Orchestra.

In the late 1930s the town and townspeople were moving out of the crisis of unemployment into a more fearful climate as the threat of war gathered momentum with each passing day. The *Peeblesshire Advertiser* in October 1938 records the changed mood: 'The defensive measures of Peeblesshire are well under way and her people are ready to do anything human brains and human hands can do to protect their families and their countryside from armed threat.'

To stimulate recruitment for the Territorial Army and other necessary services, The Peeblesshire National Service Committee was set up. It made an early call for the re-establishment of the 8th Battalion The Royal Scots (The Royal Regiment); the 228 Medium Battery of the Royal Artillery was already in Peebles. A recruitment film entitled *The Gap* was shown in the YMCA hall and, after an address by Lieutenant-Colonel William Thorburn, DSO, many young men, including the writer, signed an undertaking to join the 8th Royal Scots if it was re-formed. When Germany attacked Poland on 1 September 1939, the Reserve Forces, including the Territorial Army, were mobilised and once again the Drill Hall was the scene of local men mustering to the Colours. That was also the day Peebles received its evacuated children from Edinburgh and the black-out of all lights from windows and street lamps came into force.

The first air-raid alert in the town happened on the Sunday 3 September, just shortly after the Prime Minister had told the nation that Britain was now at war with Germany. The writer was on sentry duty on top of the tower that was once part of the Drill Hall buildings as the alarm sounded. The Territorial Army volunteers were dressed in the old-style uniform before the days of the 'battle dress' and their webbing equipment was similar to that used in the First World War.

Within three weeks of the war starting, members of the brave Polish community had arrived and later Polish troops were billeted in Victoria Park. They and their families quickly won the friendship of the people of Peebles.

In the town, shopping was done earlier during the day because of the black-out. Pavement edges were helpfully painted white to give guidance during the darkness. The cinemas, initially closed, were reopened after a short period of closure and many heavy lorries belonging to coal merchants were commandeered; garden railings and gates were also removed and collected for the war effort. In due course, signs that could help the enemy, such as directions, were also removed from the approaches to the town.

Ration books were not issued until November 1939 and the rationing of butter and bacon started on 8 January 1940, when it became necessary to register with a shopkeeper for bacon, ham, butter and sugar. Coupons were also issued to control the consumption of clothing which was in short supply due to the limited resources that were allowable for their production. The local newspapers, whilst giving information about the local war effort and advice about air-raid precautions, also featured knitting patterns for balaclava helmets, scarves, gloves and mittens. Veitch's Corner Shop advertised gas-mask carriers in navy blue and dark saxe, 1s 3d (6p); artificial silk, lined and waterproof, in brown and navy, 2s 3d (11p); fancy checks, 2s 6d (12½p).

A soldiers' canteen was opened in the games room and a 'comforts scheme' for the support of local men and women in the Armed Forces were both well supported as everyone wanted to help. An imaginative and very helpful scheme was set up to get local servicemen and women home at awkward times when public transport was not available. This 'Stranded Soldiers Fund' provided a car and valuable hours were able to be spent at home in Peebles rather than waiting at Waverley Station in Edinburgh. William Ramsay's name will always be associated with this valuable service.

The 1st Peeblesshire Battalion of the Home Guard was established in 1940 and, with the air-raid wardens and the Observer Corps who had their post on the golf course, they all shared the responsibility of guarding the town and district from surprise assault by the enemy. The *Peeblesshire Advertiser* commented in 1943: 'Nothing can dim the lustre of those early apprehensive days when the men of the field and factory manned their posts and scanned the evening and morning skies never knowing what they might bring.'

The post-war period of resettlement was made all the more reassuring for the returning ex-servicemen and women because there seemed to be plenty of work opportunities. This was no doubt due to the urgent need to re-establish pre-war markets for goods and services at home and especially overseas.

It gave Peebles special pleasure to greet Their Majesties King George VI and Queen Elizabeth when they visited the royal burgh on

18 July 1947. Some twenty-five years later, when the writer was presented to Queen Elizabeth the Queen Mother, she smiled most warmly and exclaimed 'Peebles for Pleesure, Mr Brown!' A gracious royal tribute to a royal and ancient burgh — and the years down through the centuries have not changed the truth of that proud boast.

The social history of these eventful years must include mention of Dr Clement B. Gunn because he was so much involved in the life of the town. Born in Edinburgh in 1860, he came to Peebles in 1885 to start up a medical practice. His father had been the assistant editor of the *Edinburgh Courant*. He, too, became a distinguished writer and his many books about the history of Peeblesshire and its churches are greatly valued, and especially treasured in many homes are his inspired Books of Remembrance.

Generations of schoolchildren will warmly recall attending Dr Gunn's talk on the history of Neidpath Castle and the Cross Kirk. These were arranged by the school and it was a rare privilege to be taken round these two ancient places and to hear at first hand his detailed knowledge of the history of the royal burgh which he communicated in his unique style with an enthusiasm that made a great impression on young minds.

Many stories can be told about him. His work of carving every letter of the names on the memorial for those who lost their lives during the Boer War, in order that they should not be forgotten. The memorial plaque is still in the building that was once the Drill Hall. He was a dynamic local character and James Brown, the eldest son of the late George Brown, shoemaker, 47 Northgate, recalls one of Dr Gunn's visits to the shop to have his elastic-sided boots examined to remove the cause of a squeaking noise. He would quickly pace up and down the shop, timing the offending noise with the word 'Squeak! Squeak!', and when the boots were repaired the pacing was renewed and accompanied by the words 'Cured! Cured!' Above all else Dr Gunn was an outstanding family doctor and a benefactor to the town's poor and needy; and an outstanding Peeblean dedicated to the well-being of this Auld Burgh Toon. His lasting memorial is the perpetuation each year of his 'Warden of Neidpath' address from the steps of Neidpath Castle by a distinguished Peeblean.

The Beltane Festival which symbolises our rights and freedom is the most fitting memorial for the first fifty years of the twentieth century. The Peeblean men and women who lived in these times and those who died in the defence of Freedom, truly enriched the proud heritage of Peebles.

Footnotes:

1. Howitt, Jim, personal recollections
2. Gunn, C. B., *The Book of the Old Parish Church of Peebles: AD1887 – 1930* pp388 – 9
3. Ibid, pp385 – 6
4. Ibid, p390
5. Stevenson, John, *Social History of Britain: British Society 1914 – 45* (Middlesex, 1984) pp73 – 4
6. Gunn, C. B., *The Book of the Old Parish Church of Peebles: AD1887 – 1930,* p467
7. Smout, T. C., *A Century of the Scottish People: 1830 – 1950* (London, 1986) pp116 – 8
8. Stevenson, John, *Social History of Britain: British Society 1914 – 45* (Middlesex, 1948) p117 ⅜ Source: Aldcroft, D. H., *The Inter-War Economy: Britain 1919 – 39* (1970) pp352, 364½
9. Harper, Huge Geddes, personal reminiscences (1964), supplied by his son Andrew Douglas Harper
10. Gunn, C. B. (ed R. Crockett), *Leaves from the Life of a Country Doctor* (London, 1935) p112
11. Walker, Alex, personal recollections

Part Three

1950 – 1990

CHAPTER 9

Industry, Trade and Commerce

THE SECOND HALF OF the twentieth century began splendidly when the woollen-mills in Peebles were working at full capacity, agriculture was flourishing and the Peebles Hotel Hydro had reaped the benefit from one or two conferences and were reporting a 'satisfying increase' in their turnover for 1951. The only economic blot on the local landscape was the closure, in June 1950, of the Peebles to Symington branch railway line to passenger traffic. It was the first of many changes to the pre-war settled pattern of economic life that Peebles would face in the 1960s.

The local woollen-mills had done rather well as they played their part in the splendid efforts made by the British textile industry to reach their pre-war volume in the overseas markets by 1950. The home market had been controlled up to 1949, as clothes were 'on ration' but when that ended it released a new pressure of demand which benefited the mills. However, a different kind of pressure faced the Peebles mills when, in the middle of 1950, there was a dramatic increase in world wool prices that had been precipitated by the American purchases made at the start of the Korean War (1950 – 53). For the United Kingdom textile manufacturers, there was the additional burden resulting from the devaluation of sterling which had occurred the year before and had put up the cost of importing raw materials. Devaluation should have benefited the export trade but this was offset by the increased competition that was re-emerging in the world markets from the textile industries of Japan, Italy, Czechoslovakia and Germany, which were in the process of recovering from the war. However, the problems for textile manufacturers did not end there because the home market became rapidly depressed when purchase-tax at the rate of 66.6 per cent was levied on clothing. The inevitable consequence of these pressures was the greatly depressed demand at home and abroad.[1]

159

PART III: 1950 – 1990

Purchase-tax and devaluation had been imposed as part of the fiscal policies for dealing with the 'balance of payments' problem. The United Kingdom had realised most of its investments abroad in order to sustain the war effort and in 1950 the earnings from these various overseas enterprises were no longer available to offset the cost of imported food, raw materials and semi-manufacturers that were needed for industry and which were now rising in cost more than twice as quickly as the value of our exports. This became a continuous problem which bedevilled the post-war economic life of the United Kingdom and proved to be a 'brake' on industry and commerce as a range of 'stop-go' fiscal controls had to be applied.[2]

The rapid rise in the price of wool was a serious set-back as wool was about 42 per cent of the value of the finished product and was a high proportion of financing the operation of a mill. In July 1950 Henry Ballantyne gave an example of the fluctuating prices of New Zealand wool: it had been 7s 8d (just over 38p) per pound weight and then rapidly increased by 143 per cent to 18s 8d (just over 93p) per pound, eventually dropping back to 8s 4d (just over 41½p). He made the point at this time 'that it was finance and not orders' that was the main worry.

The number employed in the textile industry in the Borders in 1951 was 11,520, comprising 5,660 men and 5,860 women; by 1961 this had risen to 12,720, with an increase of 180 men compared with 1,020 additional women in the workforce. In 1971 the figure had dropped to 10,670 (a decline of 16 per cent when compared with the 1961 total) and the reduced workforce had virtually the same number of women employed as men (5,370 men, 5,300 women).[3]

The Peebles woollen-mills had a tendency towards an ageing workforce, as the men and women had been either with Thorburns or Ballantynes over many years. The years of the Great Depression had left their mark and, although the mills had picked up in the years running up to the Second World War, the recruitment of younger men and women had become increasingly difficult because the war had changed social values and heightened ambitions for new career and work opportunities. Damdale Mill had taken the initiative in 1945 to establish a hostel at 'The Mount', a large residential house on the south side of the River Tweed, to accommodate about twenty-four women workers who came from Castle Douglas and Kirkcaldy. Workers also travelled from Innerleithen and Walkerburn; in the 1950s they poured into Peebles by the early morning train and in the 1960s they came by special coaches.

There is, with hindsight, a great deal of understanding in the town about the complexity of the problems that had faced the local woollen-mills in the late 1950s. Financing business in post-war Britain and trading in the highly competitive and volatile world markets made life very difficult for many small firms. These were difficulties that not only faced the textile firms but affected a wide range of medium-sized companies at the time, as they, too, resorted to partnerships and consortiums. However, there were two basic problems that confronted the home woollen-mills over the years: the first was the tariff barriers which limited freedom of trading in US markets; and the second, and more damaging in its long-term effects, was the steadily increasing overseas competition which started up immediately after the end of the First World War. In the United Kingdom between the wars there was the inevitable toughening of competition within the Scottish woollen industry and also between the Scottish and English industries. Then after the Second World War they had to trade against keen and intense competition in Europe, especially from Italy and, after the Korean War, Japanese textiles were making strong advances in the American market.[4]

Foreign competition was also affecting the home market and the extent of this overseas penetration can be seen from the value of clothing imports in 1962, which had reached four and half times its 1955 level and most of this increase had occurred in the period 1958 – 60.[5]

Although there had been little advance in machinery between the two wars, Tweedside and Damdale Mills nevertheless kept reasonably up-to-date. However, after the end of the Second World War the situation changed rapidly with the better engineering of machines and the development of a new generation of carding, spinning, weaving and ancillary machinery and this change was led by the Europeans with the United Kingdom lagging well behind. The new automated machinery was much faster, reducing production costs and providing those in Europe — and eventually those in the United Kingdom with the resources to re-equip — with a strong competitive edge.[6]

In retrospect it can be seen that the accumulative effect over the years of toughening competition left the local mills vulnerable in times of cyclic trade recessions, such as those occurring in the early and late 1950s. It was after the marked downturn in trade in 1957 – 9 that the principal family shareholders of D. Ballantyne Bros. & Co.

Ltd sold all of their ordinary shares to Hugh Fraser's investment company, Scottish & Universal Investments Ltd, whilst at the same time acquiring an interest in the new controlling company. The mills at March Street came under new ownership in 1960 but Henry Ballantyne stayed on as chairman and the company continued to trade under its name of D. Ballantyne & Bros. Ltd.

Walter Thorburn & Bros. Ltd merged with George Roberts & Co. Ltd and also with Robert Noble (Woollens) Ltd on 1 July 1962. Each of the firms had low order books, at about 60 per cent of desired capacity, and the idea of grouping together was to enable the closing down of Noble's mill in Hawick and Roberts's production at Berwick so that the Damdale and Tweedside Mills and the two Selkirk mills could operate profitably. It was also the intention to develop a suitable cash-flow to support a newly re-equipped mill from which to develop further yarn-spinning business.[7]

Whilst that plan was being followed it became necessary to face a new problem some thirty months or so after the merger, when RTN had to decide whether or not to rebuild on the Tweedside Mill site after a calamitous fire on 12 February 1965 had totally destroyed it. A reassurance was quickly given by Hunter Thorburn, managing director of the Damdale and Tweedside Mills, that it was the intention to replace the Tweedside Mill with a new and modern woollen yarn-spinning mill in Peebles and, although this would take some time, it had been decided that the Tweedside site would not be used as it was inadequate for the purpose.

However, in August that year (1965) it was announced that the Mill would after all not be rebuilt and that RTN had instead acquired the Black Rock Mills at Linthwaite, near Huddersfield. A new company, RTN Yards Ltd, was formed to handle woollen yarn-spinning from Philiphaugh and Black Rock Mills; the latter being re-equipped with Tweedside insurance monies. Two years later, in December 1967, a further integration of the Border woollen industry took place 'in order to rationalise and modernise production' and this resulted in the formation of Scottish Worsteds and Woollens Limited comprising Wilson & Glenny Ltd, Simpson & Fairbairn Ltd, Henry Ballantyne & Sons Ltd, George Roberts & Co. Ltd, Walter Thorburn & Bros. Ltd and Robert Noble (Woollens) Ltd.

It was at this time that the Damdale Mill closed and was demolished in early 1968. It has to be borne in mind that Damdale was a 'multi-storeyed' mill and was not suitable to be re-equipped with modern machinery, which would need solid foundations and unhampered space and certainly could not be installed on floors supported by cast-iron pillars.[8] Between sixty and seventy had been employed at the Tweedside Mill and forty were offered jobs at Selkirk or Huddersfield. There had been about 200 employees at the Damdale Mill and they were given work either at the March Street Mills or at Henry Ballantyne & Sons at Walkerburn.

These were grim years for Peebles. Its basic industry and economy were most grievously diminished by the loss of Walter Thorburn's woollen-mills — a catastrophe never believed possible.

Since the second-half of the nineteenth century the progress of the burgh owed much to two families — the Thorburns and the Ballantynes. Their entrepreneurial enterprise had largely provided the economic strength to expand and develop the town, and the employment they provided raised the standard of living for its townspeople. Both families gave generously to all the various local endeavours and became personally involved with nearly every aspect of the town's life — its civics, sports and institutions, with Thorburns and Ballantynes listed amongst its provosts, cornets, and Wardens of Neidpath. Fortunately the March Street Mills continued to provide employment and they were reported as faring well under SUI. In 1963 the shareholders of the investment company were told that D. Ballantyne & Bros. & Co. Ltd at Peebles and Innerleithen had a record year 'despite difficult trading amongst textiles generally'. The improved results were said to be due to the successful reorganisation of manufacturing methods, the acquisition of additional plants and the upsurge in knitwear sales.

In 1969 – 70 the March Street Mills again came under new ownership when they were acquired, along with other woollen and knitwear interests, by Dawson (Holdings) Ltd (now Dawson International Plc), D. Ballantyne & Bros. and the other textile firms that comprised Braemar Knitwear within the SUI were acquired by Dawsons at the same time as the firms of Ballantyne Sportswear Co. of Innerleithen and Galashiels, and the Ballantyne Spinning Co. of Innerleithen.[9] However, shortly after this acquisition there occurred a sharp economic recession which placed a considerable strain upon the Dawson Group's resources and to assist liquidity a fairly drastic restructuring exercise took place which closed the Ballantyne Spinning Co. at Innerleithen.[10] Robert Noble Ltd became the new management company at the March Street Mills and their ultimate controlling company of Dawson International Plc had their head office at Charlotte Square, Edinburgh. A programme of investment equipped the single-storeyed mills with up-to-date machinery: in 1974 half of the older looms were replaced by highly-automated Sulzer equipment and the other half by the latest Dornier machinery in 1985/6.[11]

The March Street Mills now employ between 150 to 160 workers compared with the 350 they once employed. They have maintained their high reputation and, through innovative design and production, they are at the forefront of the market with their tweeds, cashmere, pure wool cloth, jacketing and 70/30 weaves of wool/linen and silk mixtures, and currently produce all the tartan requirements for the Ministry of Defence. A major innovative venture is the employment at the mills of their own designer of furnishing fabrics and this has opened up new opportunities which has led to Robert Noble of Peebles supplying airlines at home and overseas with fabrics for aircraft seats.

Lowe, Donald & Co. Ltd whose renown as an international warehouse enhanced the reputation of Peebles between the wars as a supplier of fine tweeds and cloths, also became involved in various changes of structure and ownership in the 1960s. It became one of four cloth merchants in Holland & Lewis (Holdings) Ltd; the other firms were Holland & Sherry, Cagniere and Moffat Bros. In December 1965 all the general administration was centralised at the Peebles warehouse of Lowe, Donald & Co. and this necessitated staff being transferred to Peebles and another fifty local employees being recruited. The export value at that time of those companies, including Lowe Donald, was over £2m. Between 1966 and 1988 the company, which had become Warwick Woollens, was involved in a number of takeovers, mainly by successive property groups. However, in 1988 it returned to the control of Holland & Sherry Ltd as Warwick Woollens. The workforce presently numbers sixty-five, having previously employed 160 in 1965. Its warehouse continues to market high quality cloth with about 80 per cent of its business going overseas.

Looking at local job losses through the closure and restructuring of our woollen industry in Peebles, this has to be seen against the 'deindustrialisation' that Scotland suffered and which was experienced by the United Kingdom as a whole. Both Scotland and the United Kingdom lost approximately one-third of their industrial

164

employment between 1966 and 1981.[12] It also has to be measured against the changes that had occurred in the textile industry in Scotland between 1953 and 1978. At the start of the period textiles employed 106,407 workers but by 1978 the number had fallen by 52,336 to a reduced workforce of 54,071. Job losses in the textile industry in Scotland were therefore 49 per cent over the period 1953 – 78.[13]

In Peebles, Walter Thorburn & Bros. employed about 260 workers and at the March Street Mills of D. Ballantyne & Bros. & Co. Ltd there were about 350 mill workers in the 1950s. In 1989 there are only 160 employed at the March Street Mills, which indicates a loss of employment at the local woollen-mills of about 450 jobs: the disappearance of 74 per cent of local job opportunities. In addition, another ninety or so warehouse jobs were lost at Warwick Woollens, a shuddering blow to the economy of Peebles, primarily through loss of earnings but also the loss of miscellaneous revenues that were generated by having an important company such as Walter Thorburn & Bros. located in the town.

Another change in the early 1960s brought about by the increase in the number of private cars and the convenience and cheapness of the road haulage system, was the closure of the town's last railway line. The British Railways Board had come into being in 1947 and had inherited over 50,000 miles of railway track but, because of rising competition from road transport in the 1950s for both passengers and goods, the railways faced a financial crisis. Dr (later Lord) Beeching pruned the rail network by about one-third and this included a large part of the Scottish and Welsh railway system.

The former LMS line was the first to close down and, twelve years later, the former LNER connection ended; their loss was regarded as a 'vicious stroke' to the future of the town and particularly damaging to the town's commerce and industry. However, the economic consequences of this closure were not as great as was the loss of the social amenity it provided. When the service to Edinburgh and Galashiels ended on 5 February 1962, it was the first time in just over 107 years that Peebles was without a railway.

Local concern that Peebles was no longer a railway town and would be omitted from an 'important map' was real enough in the 1960s but, in fact, the pattern of transportation in Scotland was changing and roadways were assuming greater importance. In 1960 about 52 per cent of freight traffic was carried by road transport,

36 per cent by rail and 12 per cent by the waterways. In 1975 this had changed to 72 per cent being transported by road services (a growth of 38.5 per cent) whilst the volume carried by rail had fallen to 17 per cent (a drop in volume of 53 per cent) and waterways was 11 per cent (down 8 per cent).[14]

Changes, too, were occurring in the pattern of passenger services in Scotland. Car passengers in 1960 amounted to 42 per cent compared with 74 per cent in 1975 (a growth of 76 per cent), while the volume of bus passengers during the same period had fallen from 50 per cent to 19 per cent (a drop in volume of 62 per cent). The rail passengers in 1960 had fallen to 7 per cent in 1975 (a decline in rail usage of about 12.5 per cent).[15]

The post-war decades brought with them still more changes, too, and these were generally unhelpful to the economic environment of Peebles as the shire's 'county town'. Although a new post office was opened in the Eastgate in 1963, it was 'downgraded' as it was believed that in the interests of efficiency and economy the clerical and planning work involved for detailing the services in the Peeblesshire area should be carried out at Galashiels. The Ministry of Social Security office at Peebles was also treated the same way and became a 'branch office' controlled from Galashiels.

Nevertheless, the town's professional services continued to develop. Its well-established law practices were also acting as estate agents and in more recent years they extended their professional services to include both financial and insurance matters. Blackwood & Smith, with an additional office at 15 Eastgate; and J. & W. Buchan opened a special branch office at 2 Cuddy Bridge. These financial services complemented the other local resources that had developed in the town during the years since the end of the Second World War, with more building societies having local offices: Peebles Building Society, 2 Eastgate; Northern Rock, 37 High Street; Halifax, 44 Northgate; and Dunfermline, 7 Eastgate. There were also specialist property agents: Cooper Associates, 11 Northgate; John Sale, 2 – 4 Northgate; and Alan M. Crawford & Co., 5 – 7 Northgate, providing management services.

The British Linen Bank amalgamated with the Bank of Scotland and although its name no longer features in the town, it will be remembered as the first bank to be established in Peebles and the only bank to have had the enterprise to set up a 'sub-branch office', which, in 1936, was located at 68 Rosetta Road and known as the

'Kingsland Sub-Branch'. The two remaining banks are The Bank of Scotland, which is now located at 70 High Street, and the Royal Bank of Scotland, which have their premises at 4 Eastgate. However, another bank that sadly disappeared from the local scene is the Peebles Municipal Bank that was established in 1925. It had a proud record and was one of only seven such banks existing in Scotland in 1967; the fact that it was still in being all those years later was seen as an act of local patriotism.

The *Peeblesshire News*, commenting on the situation in Peebles in 1962, said that it noted with regret that many of the old-established family businesses had faded out or changed hands. They suggested that 'tailors' were then almost a rarity and that there were fewer joiners and masons in the town and many trades had disappeared due to the effect of 'multiple businesses'. This is not so nowadays. The era of the 'small business' has returned and there is now a plentiful supply of small trades firms: joiners and glaziers, painters and decorators, plasterers, building contractors, plumbers, slaters, electrical services and a TV 'doctor'. The lack of local industry has encouraged the development of such trades and services and, indeed, of 'craft skills' generally, including pottery, furniture and jewellery-making and fine art.

There was also regret, in 1962, that the need for the 'local baker' had been reduced by the flood of massed-produced baking coming into the town in the 1950s and that it had gradually brought about the closure of the locally-renowned businesses of J. H. Goodburn & Sons, Wilson & Sime and Robert Johnston. Perhaps future generations will wonder at the verses to be found in the *Peeblesshire News*, written by a Peeblean living in Canada, that longingly recalled the merits of the Goodburn pies! However, a new generation of local bakers have now come into being: The Home Bakery, 55 Northgate; W.T.S. Forsyth & Sons, Eastgate; J. G. Thomson, 21 Old Town; and the Legendary Cake Co., 12 Cuddyside.

Gone are the tailors' businesses of A. W. Stickler, at 11 Northgate, Thos. Skelton, at 17 Old Town, John Elder, at the Veterans' Cottages in Rosetta Road, and A. Inglis at 9 Eastgate. The haberdashery shops and outfitters that once served the families in the town have also disappeared: Jessie Bonsor, 61 High Street; J. M. Hay & Co., 30 Northgate; Miss Hamilton and Miss Somerville, who both had shops in the Eastgate; and Mrs J. Tammi, Northgate. Changed, too, is the once flourishing Peebles Co-operative Society which opted to merge in 1967 with Galashiels and Jedburgh to form the Border Regional Co-operative Society Ltd. The merger now extends as far south as Coldstream but the 'Peebles Co-op' of between the wars, with its many departments and two branch shops in the town, was a major supplier of most of the personal and household necessities. Today it only retails furniture, electrical and fancy goods.

The changed scene includes the disappearance from the town of the Buttercup Dairy, at 50 High Street; Sam Ferguson, at 23 Eastgate (grocers); Henderson & Jardine, at 5 Northgate (grocers); Harris & Johnson, at 59 Northgate (cooked meats); Frank Hogg, at 53 Northgate (grocers); and Scott & Rutherford, 16 High Street (grocers). But a new generation of businesses have come into being: Gateway, the major supermarket in the Northgate; J.& S. Ruffell at 3 Glen Road, Rosetta Road and Dalatho Street (Spar grocers); T. & F. Greenshiels, at 1 Waverley Way (grocer); and Borthwick, in the Northgate (grocers).

A major new business initiative that showed Peebles had not lost its enterpreneurial spirit, is well demonstrated by Graham McGrath. In 1949, when he returned from serving during the war with the Grenadier Guards, he used his modest capital to acquire a car and, having successfully obtained an agency with a tailoring firm in Leeds, he set about obtaining orders. This necessitated many evenings touring round Nissen hut encampments in Scotland where Poles, Ukranians and other nationals had made a temporary home, and measuring between six and fifteen men every night. Although Graham McGrath acquired premises in the Northgate in 1950, for the next two years or so he continued to develop the business by providing a service to the various Displaced Person Camps. He describes how 'suits kept arriving for the men I had measured, so I was out in the evenings and weekends delivering them and I couldn't resist measuring more.' His local business turnover also began to increase as many young men came to take advantage of the 'club' facilities which enabled them to have made-to-measure suits, jackets and trousers.

Newtongrange was the location of Graham McGrath's first shop outside of Peebles, which he bought in 1953 and sold in 1969. He opened up other shops: Penicuik, 1958; Dalkeith, 1961; Morningside, Edinburgh, 1968; St Andrews, 1975; Haddington, 1978; and Bridge of Allan, 1987. The Peebles business was moved from his shop in the Northgate to much larger premises at 27-29 Eastgate in 1965.[16] The quality of his business through the service it gives and the merchandise that it provides, is a reflection of his own high standards as one of the town's leading businessmen. Graham McGrath's success is a credit to his native town and his thriving business today has two sons and one grandson committed to maintaining its reputation. Graham McGrath, with one shop in the Eastgate and six branch shops in other towns, and the Castle Warehouse, with shops in the Old Town and the Northgate, a branch shop in Penicuik and two shops in Galashiels — these highly successful enterprises enhance the business status of Peebles.

Since the early 1950s there has been concern to attract more industry to the burgh. In 1952 the town council set up a committee to consider and report on the possibilities of securing and establishing an industrial estate in or near Peebles. Later, in the 1960s, when the woollen-mills were experiencing a shortage of women workers, there was the added desire to attract new industries with a predominantly male workforce that would bring families into the town and provide additional female labour. Dr J. Dickson Mabon, Minister of State, said in March 1967: 'Peebles is one of the luckiest of the Border Burghs, being positioned very near to Edinburgh's economic expansion which is quite considerable.' That statement was not what we wanted to hear at that time; the idea that the future well-being of Peebles lay — even marginally — as a 'dormitory' town was an anathema.

The Minister of State was being realistic. Of course the ideal solution was to improve the industrial base of Peebles, but that was not very likely given the deindustrialisation problems that faced Scotland as a whole. Nearly every city and town in Scotland was looking for new industries. On the other hand, the town's proximity to Edinburgh was, in a way, a 'natural resource' that could be exploited. Our tourist facilities could 'feed' on the major tourist attractions of the capital and, in a more tangible way, it was a city that could provide career and work opportunities for the town's young people.

The town council continued to pursue the idea of attracting industry and jobs into the town and, towards the end of 1967, they retained a firm of Edinburgh architects to undertake a survey and make proposals for a possible five-year plan of development, covering not only industrial but also housing and recreational facilities. The disused railway goods-yard at March Street (about 8 acres) had already been earmarked as a possible industrial site.

The first firm to move to the March Street Industrial Site was Thos Litster, and they erected premises for their photo-finishing and colour processing business. They are a well-known firm of photographers that first became established in the town in 1923 but, through the growth of colour photography, their business expanded and they are now a major photo-processing company that handles work from all over the country.

When Alex Walker was provost of Peebles during the period 1967 – 70, he established a close liaison with the Scottish Development Department and also held a number of meetings with industrialists in an endeavour to attract new industry to the town. Through these contacts it became known that an American firm, Fidelitone International Ltd of Chicago, was contemplating setting up a factory in Northern Ireland. When it became known that their representative was visiting the area on a fishing trip, he was invited by the Scottish Development Department to meet Provost Walker and Edward Laverock, the town clerk. This first meeting successfully led to a series of discussions with the president and vice-president of Fidelitone, and these resulted in a telegraphed message being sent to the provost on Christmas Eve, 1969, that Fidelitone had decided to locate their new factory in Peebles. Provost Walker sent as his reply: 'Congratulations! There really is a Santa Claus!'

Fidelitone were the manufacturers of needles for the record-playing industry, and these they had developed from the original old-style steel needles to the sapphire and then the diamond styli. In March 1970 they set up a temporary production line in the old post office building in the Northgate whilst the assembly was carried out in St Michael's Wynd, having a very modern tool-room in the gun shed at Walkershaugh. Although it was first suggested that they would need a workforce of about eighty, with an initial recruitment of about fifty, they ultimately employed 276 (this figure included 'outworkers' working at home).[17]

In January 1971 they moved into their purpose-built factory at the March Street Industrial Site and started up with bulging order books but later, when the Japanese magnetic diamond styli came on the market, it caused a gradual decline in the fortunes of Fidelitone. The company was sold to other American interests and the business changed its name to Sonido International Ltd, which diversified into the manufacture of leisure-wear and sweatshirts. This also proved to be a very highly competitive market: in 1989 there was a reduction in the workforce and in 1990 the firm went into liquidation.

The March Street Industrial Site is also the location of Frank Ballantyne Garden Machinery and this provides a repair service and sells garden plants. There are a number of smaller workshop units located on the other side of Dovecot Road in the grounds of March Street Mills, these being occupied by long-established, as well as new, small businesses. The South Parks Industrial Estate also provides a number of units for small businesses. Two are occupied by Barnes of Peebles, who assemble and finish furniture, and Cameo Fine Arts also have two units. They started up a business in 1983 which deals in quality colour-printing which is bought in and from this they produce their finished products.

Despite the success in attracting Fidelitone to set up in Peebles, it has proved difficult to attract any medium-sized industrial companies to locate within or near to the town. Unfortunately, Scotland, as elsewhere, has come to recognise that the American 'branch-plant' type of business mainly relies on importing many of its components and that local directors have had little control over the subsidiary's strategies to develop further local investment.[18] There has been the inevitable realisation over the years that we have of necessity to rely on our own 'natural resources'; whether these be the 'start-up' of small service and tradesmen firms or developing the town's economy by maximising its tourist opportunities.

It was in 1963 that 'tourism' was more openly being mentioned as the 'infant' industry for the town. Commendably, local enterprises over the years since the 1960s have responded to these new opportunities in many different ways to serve and accommodate the tourist; the motorist on tour and day trippers, conference visitors, and families on holiday. In the 1980s it has gradually developed into an important part of the town's economy.

Undoubtedly, the Peebles Hotel Hydro is the 'flagship' of the local tourist industry and conferences have played a notable part in the development of our tourist income. For many years, the mention of 'Peebles' south of the Border, was acknowledged by a quick assurance: 'Yes, I know it! That's the place where the Hydro is — I have been there!' In the early 1970s the holidaymaker was the major market segment and is still today an important part of the Hydro's business, but since then the biggest growth has been in providing

171

accommodation and facilities for conferences. Originally conferences were in the 'off period' between October and March but now they are all the year round except for a few weeks in mid-summer and at Easter and Christmas.

The most recent figures available show that there were 298 conferences in the year to October 1989 and that 305 conferences were anticipated for the following year. The economic importance of these conferences to the Hydro — and to the shops in the town — is the number of nights they stay in the hotel. For example in 1989, 17,500 conference delegates stayed for an average of two nights and, with the accompanying non-conference delegates, that figure was increased to approximately 19,500 – 20,000. That is about 55 per cent of the total Hydro's bed-nights in a year and this ratio of more than half has been fairly constant since 1979.[19]

In the 1960s the Hydro had as many as 163 bedrooms but by 1983 these had been rearranged to provide each bedroom with its own private bathroom. These renovations and the building of an extension with nineteen bedrooms has provided the Hydro with 137 modern bedrooms. Peebles Hotel Hydro, therefore, has kept pace with the changing requirements of guests, providing not only high standards of comfort and service but facilities for leisure and health, thereby maintaining its traditional reputation as one of Scotland's best hotels.

In 1973, apart from the Hydro, hotel accommodation was available at the County, Countryside (Horsburgh), Cross Keys, Dilkusha, Green Tree, Kingsmuir, Park, Riverside, Tontine, and Venlaw Castle. The Langside Hotel on the Edinburgh Road was gutted by fire during the course of that year. In addition to the hotels, there were twenty-one guest houses and bed-and-breakfast establishments in the town. The same number of hotels and guest-houses are currently available and these provide 269 bedrooms — comprising fifty singles, 171 twins or doubles and forty-eight family rooms. Dilkusha, however, has changed its name to Tweedbridge House; and the Park Hotel is now owned by the proprietors of the Peebles Hotel Hydro.[20]

Tweeddale attracted over 120,000 visitors during 1989 and they all spent at least one night. There are about thirty hotels and guest houses in the Tweeddale area and these provide around 800 bedspaces.[21] Peebles itself offers about 550 of the 800 bedspaces available in the district. Tweeddale has also more than fifty bed-and-breakfast facilities as well as self-catering establishments, again a large number of these being in the town of Peebles or its immediate neighbourhood.

Peebles is fortunate in having two outstanding caravan sites: Rosetta Caravan and Camping Park, Rosetta Road, which covers twenty-four acres and has facilities for 200 caravans and thirty tents; and the Crossburn Caravan Park, Edinburgh Road, which has accommodation for seventy caravans and thirty-five tents on a six-acre site. Both these caravan parks featured in the top tourist awards given by the Scottish Tourist Board.

Tourism generates wealth. It is difficult to put an accurate figure on its precise value to Tweeddale, but using the figures based on 1987 and 1988, the Scottish Tourist Board estimates a worth of something like £12m.

Part of the new economy is to earn a large proportion of this spending-power and then to do its best to retain and circulate this wealth throughout the town. A study entitled *Boston 2000* made a survey to establish whether this American city had all the necessary retail outlets within its boundaries to keep the revenue earned from tourism and its local service industries. Peebles has, to a reasonable degree, the resources to fulfil this requirement. It certainly has a wide range of hotel-restaurants (The Hydro, Tontine, Park, County, Green Tree, Kingsmuir and Tweedbridge House) as well as many other restaurants: The Bistro, Northgate; Gino's, the High Street; Joe's Pizza Oven, the High Street; King's Orchard, the Northgate; Nanking (Chinese); Lee Palace (Chinese); The Sheiling Coffee Shop, Elcho Street Brae; Sunflower, the Bridgegate; Tatler, the High Street; and West Port Restaurant. The town also has an attractive array of tourist shops that have evolved over the years, such as knitwear and woollens, in the High Street; jewellery, in the High Street, Northgate, and the Newby Court development; fine art, porcelain, glass, and china, in the High Street and Newby Court; clocks and woodwork, at Cabbage Hall Woodwork, Tweed Green; gifts, at The Couchee Righ, 26 Northgate; and Design Workshops at 9 Newby Court, as well as a number of the larger shops that invariably attract visitors back to them by reason of the quality they offer.

It is now just over forty-five years since the end of the Second World War and Peebles is a town without its railway with only a 'textile' workforce of about one-third it once employed, yet it is far from being a village economy. Much of this economic well-being is due to the foresight and enterprise of the Peebles Hotel Hydro and

173

to the other hotels and visitor services that support tourism. Nevertheless, the town is still dependent on the fortunes of the March Street Mills — managed with flair in what is still a highly-competitive and market-led industry, and with a workforce that can still produce fine cloths and tweeds. We have a comprehensive range of professional services, and they still add to the town's central position within Tweeddale and contribute to the town's economy.

We inevitably need to capitalise on our proximity to Edinburgh and Galashiels and the economic benefits they can provide with their opportunities for young Peebleans to find a worthwhile career and interesting work. In the 1850s nearly 40 per cent of the population were incomers to the town; today we have incomers settling in the town and they, too, can provide an economic contribution by adding to local wealth. True, there can be an off-setting cost when house prices are outwith the reach of local people and other services are stretched but these are problems capable of political solution.

Peebles, therefore, is fortunate in having its 'natural resources' — the magnificence of our valley town with its rivers and hills. People will always want to come to Peebles. It really is a natural tourist centre but it can always be improved by further local endeavour and enterprise in order to maximise what the town and district has to offer. Such endeavours are necessary to safeguard the town's future economy — an assured economy in an age where leisure means business and that business is 'Peebles for Pleesure'.

Footnotes:

1. Rainie, G. F., *The Woollen and Worsted Industry* (Oxford, 1965) p133
2. *Industry and Employment in Scotland* (HMSO, 1951)
3. Turnock, David, *The New Scotland* (1979) p67
4. Thorburn, D. Hunter, personal recollections
5. Rainie, G. F., *The Woollen and Worsted Industry* (Oxford, 1965) p143
6. Thorburn, D. Hunter, personal recollections
7. Ibid
8. Ibid
9. Gulvin, Clifford, *The Scottish Hosiery and Knitwear, 1680 – 1980* (Edinburgh, 1984) p126
10. Ibid, p136
11. Birchall, J. D.
12. Saville, Richard (ed), *The Economic Development of Modern Scotland, 1950 – 80* (1985) p49

13. Ibid, p248
14. Underwood, Robert (ed), *The Future of Scotland* (London, 1977) p136
15. Ibid
16. McGrath, Graham, personal recollections
17. Walker, Alex, personal recollections
18. McKay, Donald (ed) *Scotland 1980* (Edinburgh, 1977) p74
19. Pieter van Dijk
20. Borders Tourist Board Brochure, *Scottish Borders Holiday Guide 1990*
21. Borders Tourist Board

CHAPTER 10

The Burgh

VICTORY IN EUROPE was greeted in Peebles, as elsewhere, with relief and enthusiasm. Although the war in South-East Asia was to go on until August of 1945, it was generally felt that the worst was over. Unlike in the aftermath of the First World War, demobilisation of service personnel had been planned for and, within months of VE Day, Peebleans were returning to civilian life.

Provost Fergusson demitted office when the European War ended to be succeeded by William Cleland. The latter, who had served in the First World War with the 1/8th Royal Scots, was well placed to advise the town council on the problems facing returning service personnel. The first and most pressing of their needs was housing. Many Peebleans, both men and women, had married whilst in the services and were now returning to their native town hoping to set up home and to start a family. In addition, many who had been stationed in Peebles, notably in the General Hospital of the Royal Army Medical Corps which had occupied the Hotel Hydro, had married locally and wished to continue to live in Peebles. Similarly, a number of Polish soldiers who had lost their homes in Poland with the Russian occupation, opted to remain in Scotland; again, many had married Peebles girls and required housing.

Towards this end, the council were empowered to reintroduce the policy of provision of municipal housing which had gone into abeyance in 1939. The first scheme to be built was one of thirty-two houses on part of the Kingsland ground immediately to the north of Kingsland School. The houses were of the type known as 'pre-fabs'. They were three-apartment, well-equipped, flat-roofed, box-like structures whose merit lay in their internal fittings which included fitted kitchens and bathrooms. Indeed the first domestic refrigerator in Peebles belonged to the 'pre-fabs'. The houses, which were mass-produced in aircraft factories, were quickly *in situ* and occupied; another example, if we needed any, of war acting as a catalyst for social change and the application of wartime techniques in production being applied to peacetime needs. The tenants of Kingsland Square were well pleased with their new houses. These were later improved in outward appearance by a permanent cladding of brickwork and with the addition of a pitched, slate roof.

Although in 1946 and up to the 1950s the attention of Government was to exports and the earning of 'hard currency', the problems of housing still had to be faced. Thus, the town council were in an exquisite dilemma. Should they deploy their scant resources purely to housing or should they throw weight behind the local woollen industry. In the end, of course, central government decided and both paths were followed with a degree of success.

Another limited scheme was built on the site of the derelict cattle market in Cross Road. With the market now in the more suitable site in South Parks, the centrally placed Cross Road area seemed ideal. By the end of 1946 twenty-four four-apartment houses were completed at a unit cost of £1,500. Although built by local builders and comprising perhaps the best of local authority houses, the cost illustrates only too well the inflationary consequences of a long war. This scheme became Clark and Montgomery Place.

The final houses which were completed in 1946 were the eighteen built due east of the cemetery on part of Kirklands. Again, like the pre-fabs, these were system-built houses of austere but efficient design. Nonetheless, they cost £1,700 and, although they were extremely popular with their tenants, perhaps because of the high-amenity area which they occupied, they had inherent structural faults which were later to manifest themselves.[1]

It was to be the late 1940s when the next likelihood of extensive building of municipal housing presented itself. Provost Arthur Daniels had succeeded William Cleland. The former, with a banking background, lent his experience to a council still beset by many problems. The council was equally fortunate that on the retiral of J. Walter Buchan as town clerk (1948), he was succeeded by his legal partner, Edward Laverock, thus preserving the all-important continuity of the office.

The plans of the Labour Housing Act of 1949 to boost municipal housing had, by that year, brought local authorities throughout Scotland into conflict with town planners, anxious about the preservation of farming and recreational land. In the case of Peebles, it brought them to a hard decision, the acquisition of building land through compulsory purchase.

Their needs were straightforward. The success of the woollen industry created enhanced labour requirements in the local mills, which had been chronically short of labour since 1945, a shortage which required the bringing in of workers by coach from Midlothian in order to maintain production. To some extent, this shortage stemmed from the years of pre-war Depression, when recruitment was nil, and also to a rapidly ageing workforce. It was felt that the building of more houses would satisfy the bulk of local needs. Further, incoming workers could be provided for, not only for the basic industry but for others as well. Trapped, therefore, between the Scylla of industrial needs and the Charybdis of limited building land, the council were forced to embark on a plan for the acquisition of land by compulsory purchase. The area most suitable was some 139 acres on the south side of the Tweed which comprised the Kingsmeadows policies. Once a royal demesne, it had been in the hands of the Hays of Haystoun until 1920 when the house and policies were purchased by H. N. Mitchell, of the Prize Crop Tobacco family. This compulsory purchase was to cause some acrimony between the parties concerned although, in hindsight, it is difficult to see what other course the council could have pursued. Regrettably, Mr Mitchell, perhaps in reaction to the manner of the sale, left Peebles, subsequently selling Kingsmeadows House and the remaining cottages to the Standard Life Company.

The first phase of the Kingsmeadows scheme involved the building of Kingsmuir Crescent, Glensax Road, Glen Road and on Kingsmeadows Road itself. By 1962, a total of 450 houses were to be built, mostly two- or three-apartment and in traditional style. Later developments of the initial scheme were built in terraced style. As we have seen, the chronic labour shortage which plagued the tweed-mills throughout the 1950s and sixties was tackled in several ways: firstly, as in the case of March Street, by the importation of workers by coach from outside areas; secondly, a programme of recruitment and training directed at school leavers. Finally the council enlisted the aid of the Scottish Special Housing Association. This association, formed in 1920 to provide housing for special needs, now built a number of houses in the Kingsmeadows area, especially for incoming workers. In addition, the council concluded an agreement with the Glasgow Corporation to guarantee housing to selected families. Many of these were found employment in the Tweed mills.[2]

This agreement, which was not confined to the primary industry, brought new citizens to Peebles in a number of different roles. Although a percentage of the new arrivals drifted away over the years, overall the project could be considered a success. The fact of being able to provide housing at this time encouraged new industry such as Fidelitone to come to the town and, equally important, caused existing businesses to expand. Within the provostship of John Duthie (1954 – 7), and the much longer tenure of office by James Lawrie (1957 – 67), a widening of the industrial base was made possible in the town.

Private housing development, which had ceased in 1939, made a slow recovery. With the exception of a few houses on the south flank of Venlaw Hill, the first scheme of any note was the Mount in 1962. The original Mount House belonged to the Thorburn family and had been used as a hostel for young female mill-workers in the post-war period. In the 1960s, however, it was demolished and the land released for private development. Regrettably to many, the fine Douglas firs and sequoias were felled, giving way to modern bungalows. Again, in the same period, the Gallowhill scheme was started. On land purchased from Whitehaugh Farm, this private development was eventually to extend the eastern boundaries of the burgh as far as the Gypsy Glen and the western march of Whitehaugh Farm.

In the post-war period, town planning in Peebles was one of the functions, like the fire service and the police, which were shared by Midlothian. Not unreasonably, this remote control was one which caused a deal of heart-searching by the town council. Aware that many planning decisions were based correctly on the existing regulations and legislation, nonetheless the feeling in view of some of them was of impotence, coupled also with a natural view that, in some instances, the tail was wagging the dog and that, in some decisions, the wishes of Peebleans were being ignored. Much later a Civic Society was to be formed as a pressure group to represent the citizens of the town. Some of the more bizarre planning decisions can be cited, other than the equally annoying apparent irrelevant minutae connected with gable windows and street furniture: the zoning of South Parks as an industrial site, an area of obvious visual amenity and good farming ground; the siting of a new fire station in

179

Caledonian Road, again an area which was to be developed for housing. Many more instances could be quoted.

During the provostship of Alex Melrose (1970 – 3) the town council held firm to their twin objectives: the provision of municipal housing and the attraction of new industry to the burgh. A new industrial site was opened at South Parks with mixed success. The phased development of Kingsmeadows continued with Waverley Way, Ivanhoe and Marmion Drive. To meet the obvious needs of children of primary age on the south bank of the Tweed, a new school was built, close to the remaining stabling and cottages of Kingsmeadows House. This school, to be called Priorsford, along with Kingsland and Halyrude Schools, rationalised the catchment areas for primary schooling in the town. The High School, which had already been doubled in size by the provision of a tower block (another bizarre planning decision) and other extensions, met the immediate needs of secondary education.

By 1961, the population of the burgh had fallen to 5,548; the census figure at 1951 had been at the record level of 6,013. Although there were job opportunities in the town, nevertheless there was an increasing number of townsfolk working outside the burgh as the availability of personal transport and good bus services enabled daily travel to Edinburgh. It was the growth in car ownership — 'commuting' — that increased the recognition of Peebles as being geographically well placed (its original *raison d'être* in prehistoric times) and an ideal centre for journeys to both the Scottish Borders and the north of England and also to Glasgow and the west. In consequence of this, an acceleration of private building took place throughout the 1960s and indeed continues today (1989). The Dukehaugh site had been released with the demolition and clearing of the former Caledonian Railways buildings and the site was built over to the west in the following year. Houses initially were advertised at £2,450 in the early 1970s; an interesting comment on the astronomic rise in house prices.[3]

A further development occurred at Kingsmeadows Gardens and eventually the scheme at the Meadows was to extend to the eastern boundary of the town. Municipal housing also proceeded; with the closure of Damdale Mills, the land became available at Damdale and Damcroft. The town council, as part of the regeneration of the Cuddyside area, completed thirty-four houses at Cuddyside and a further number at Damcroft. In the private sector, a further thirty houses were built in Edderston Road and various gap sites were also exploited. This was the situation which pertained when Robert Kirkpatrick took office as provost of Peebles, the last of a long line. Indeed, not only were the ancient offices of provost and bailies to vanish in 1974 with the Local Government (Scotland) Act 1973 but the Royal and Ancient Burgh itself disappeared as a legal entity.

In 1990 Peebles will celebrate the 850th anniversary of its creation as a royal burgh. Although documentary evidence in the shape of the original Charter was destroyed during one of the English incursions, probably in 1308 when the town was burned, other evidence confirms that Peebles became a royal burgh in the reign of King David I of Scotland (1124 – 53), the likely year being 1140.[4]

The 1973 Local Government (Scotland) Act effectively destroyed the royal burghs and, along with them, privileges which had been cherished for hundreds of years. As the Peebles Town Council disappeared so did the ancient right to create freemen of the burgh and the privileges which that honour conferred. Freemen and burgesses alone had the right, in medieval times, to belong to the burgh; all other inhabitants were unfreemen or indwellers. Thus, they had no right or say in the election of magistrates. Burgesses could be admitted to the burgh and the earliest surviving recorded admission of a burgess to Peebles is dated 2 November 1490 when one 'Will of the Ost' was admitted. On the direction of the council, he paid 'XI shillings at the bailleis wil'.[5]

Until the 1833 Act, only burgesses and guild brothers could become councillors. With the extension of the franchise, the creation of ordinary burgesses became unneccessary. The custom of creating honorary burgesses was introduced in 1840. Among those who received this honour in Peebles for their contribution to the community were William and Robert Chambers, the publishers, in 1841; William Ewart Gladstone, MP (whose forbears came from Hundleshope) in 1880; Andrew Carnegie in 1909; and John Buchan in 1919. Serving soldiers of both wars were collectively honoured, as was The Royal Scots (The Royal Regiment) in 1952. This, then, was one of the ancient rights bestowed on Peebles by its burghal status as a royal burgh, which was removed by a casual 'on the nod' vote of the House of Commons in 1973.

Historically, it is impossible to justify the revival of the custom by the Tweeddale District when they created David Steel, MP (later Sir David Steel) a freeman of the District in 1988. In defence, how- ever, we should accept that, to some extent, the traditional rights of the vanished Royal Burgh of Peebles have been preserved, albeit in a different form.

The reorganisation of local government in 1973 had its genesis in the consequences of the Second World War. As an agent for change, the war had produced an accretion of quasi-governmental boards and committees. These, and the wartime experience of centralised control, brought piecemeal modifications to the 1929 concept of local government. Police and fire services were combined by adjacent authorities and hospital boards followed the same route. Gas undertakings were nationalised, as was electricity. We have already seen that certain functions such as planning, in the case of Peebles, were organised from Lothian. Clearly, since 1929, the creation of units larger than the counties or the burghs had a parallel development in local government. In addition, a number of *'ad hoc'* authorities had been created. It seems familiar to the historian to recollect what had happened in the nineteenth century and it would appear that we had returned to the confusion from which the 1929 Act had been designed to rescue us.

Indeed, the confusion seemed if anything to be compounded. By 1969 there were eleven bodies active in local government, two more than before 1929. The original concept of the all-purpose authority had been completely lost sight of. The principles enshrined in the 1929 Act had been wholly discarded. It was generally felt that local government had become a terrible mess. But it was never made clear whether the mess resulted from the structure set up in 1929, rather than the tinkering with that structure in subsequent years. More importantly, the problem seemed to lie in the provision of local government finance (a problem not yet solved, *vide* 'Poll Tax' legislation) rather than in the administrative set-up. The average burgess of Peebles in 1969, if asked, would probably have expressed satisfaction with his town council.[6]

Nonetheless, a Royal Commission set up in 1969 under the chairmanship of Lord Wheatley produced its report on Local Government in Scotland. Henry Ballantyne, grandson of Sir Henry, served on this commission. Significantly, in the light of later events, local government finance was not included in their remit. The findings and recommendations of the commission were not well received. In addition, there was a not wholly unfounded suspicion that the subsequent Act was pushed through to diffuse the constitutional issues inherent in the upsurge of the SNP. History and tradition were coolly disregarded. The burghs were to vanish, although for hundreds of years a distinction had been drawn between a burgh and a rural area. Further, it was pointed out, though Scots should have learned this particular lesson — certainly it was familiar enough to Burns and Scott — that it is futile to appeal to the Treaty of Union 1707, namely that Scottish institutions expressly safeguarded here were the Law, the Church, the universities, the Register House, and the Royal Burghs.[7]

Not only the burghs but the counties were to vanish. Although the county councils were a nineteenth-century creation, the sheriffdom, from which the county derived, had an antiquity comparable to that of the royal burghs. A small country such as Scotland had been long used to thinking in terms of burghs and sheriffdoms, The Wheatley Report was also much criticised for the laying out of suggested boundaries of the new regions and districts. Indeed, only after a fierce battle was the Borders, including Peeblesshire, granted the right of separate authority, being originally consigned to Lothian.

The final solution dealt a death blow to communities as they had existed from the earlier days. The report demonstrated an obsession with size. Economy of scale was the new god. It was suggested also that regions and districts not firmly based in communities would tend to be bureaucratic and thus unable to resist central government with the necessary backing of public opinion. This latter would seem to constitute one of the major continuing criticisms of the Borders Region by its constituents.

Subsequently, it can be seen, and in particular in areas such as the Borders, that not enough concern had been shown for the pattern of communications in the larger units proposed. Public transport, in the main, had deteriorated mainly with the demise of the railway. Subsidising of bus routes would be an increasing drain on local funds. Improvements to roads, at an ever increasing cost, would add to the heavy burden on local finance. More importantly, no local government amalgamation so far undertaken had resulted in the promised economies of scale. Further, the merging of burghs and districts would, and indeed was to, lead to depopulation of the rural areas.

Despite the criticism and the protests from various groups the White Paper duly became the Reform of Local Government Act in 1973. An undertaking had been specifically given in the White Paper of 1971 that the Government would consider how best to preserve

'Charter rights and privileges, traditional and ceremonial usages'. Again, as we have seen, the obfuscation which strikes the Westminster Government when matters relating to the 1707 Union arise, invariably extends itself to all matters of Scottish tradition which existed prior to that Union and were guaranteed by it. As a sop to public sensibility 'community councils' which might conceivably perform some of the functions previously performed by the burghs were mooted. As a result, the Peebles and District Community Council was duly formed but with no statutory function and no statutory finance. Well meaning as this council is, there remains little that it can do when compared to the old Peebles Town Council.

The Tweeddale District Council formed in 1974 took on the following functions: housing, parks and cemeteries, cleansing and to some degree provision of leisure facilities. Peebles was allocated four members on the new council and towards this end the town was divided into four wards. The new council's jurisdiction extended to former Peeblesshire and members of the council were drawn from this area. The newly created Borders Regional Council assumed all the remaining local authority functions, notably education, roads and drainage, lighting, planning, social work and the rest.

In the fifteen years since the reorganisation of local government, Tweeddale District, based at the former County Buildings, has virtually carried out its functions in much the same manner as the former Peebles Town Council. There was, after all, a certain continuity, since the councillors and many of the officials had served on the town or county councils. Provision of housing in Peebles continued with the provision of forty houses at Connor Ridge, a further extension to Crookston Place and an entirely new development at Drover's Way on land purchased from the Hay estate to the south of Glen Road. This latter was matched by a private development.

The fears expressed by the original critics of the Wheatley Report were justified in respect of housing. With the opening of the burgh housing allocation to rural residents, a steady depopulation of these areas has taken place and the conseqent urbanisation has resulted. Such farm cottages so released have been invariably 'improved' and sold to incomers from furth of the Borders and even of Scotland. Provision of houses in the private sector has also accelerated within the same period, with further building at Craigerne Lane, South Park West, Langside, Kerfield and The Bridges. Again, many of the houses have been purchased by commuters, thus introducing a wholly new factor to the Peebles equation. Once a small mill-town, with its own share of parochialism, the introduction of what has been to many an alien pressure, has brought mixed blessings.

The loss of the functions of the Peeblesshire County Council to the Borders Regional Council has had less happy results. Again, the criticism levelled at the time of Wheatley seems prescient. Certainly the charge that reorganisation would result in more remote bureaucratic control would seem to be borne out. That confusion as to functions would result, could certainly be confirmed. That the removal of the police and fire services to even larger groupings (Lothian and Borders) would result in acrimony and the accusations that the sparsely populated Borders were bearing an unfair financial burden for services: all this has certainly come true.

One other major demographic change has taken place in the years following regionalisation. As a result of the planning 'dictat' from Borders Regional Council, Peebles was designated as an area more suitable for housing than industry, and whose future lay with leisure and tourism rather than industrial expansion. In consequence of this, the advantages of providing sheltered and retiral acommodation became apparent to developers, resulting in the provision of the following complexes: Tweedbridge, St Andrews and Halyrude Courts, a small development at Wemyss Place and a larger one at Rose Park. Two further and similar complexes have recently been completed in Innerleithen Road, Whitestone Court and at Neidpath Road, the Riverside Home. Welcome as these developments are in Peebles with the new residents, most of whom are from elsewhere, the injection of a number of retired persons to a population of under 7,000 has inevitably created an imbalance in that population towards the elderly; an imbalance which has obvious implications in medical care and in the welfare organisations.

But more important for the average person in Peebles has been the loss of burgh identity and the demise of the Royal and Ancient Burgh of Peebles. No longer do the provost and bailies, in their splendid robes, preside over such traditional ceremonies as the shoot for the Peebles Silver Arrow, or even the annual Beltane Festival. Ironically, in a town which has been designated as one with tourist potential, a town which includes a Hotel Hydro with an international reputation as a conference centre, it nonetheless lacks the very civic dignitaries who once welcomed visitors to such conferences and indeed to the town itself. Even the use of the twelfth century 'Three Fishes of Peebles' coat of arms has been called into question, although the matter has been resolved recently (1989) by the initiative of the community council who sought judgement from the Lyon Court on the matter.

As a last word, it might appear paradoxical that the Lord Lyon King of Arms, the arbiter and sole guardian of Scottish tradition, should find it necessary to promulgate the arms of the royal burgh of Peebles. Surely it would have been simpler and more logical to retain the rights and privileges of the burgh in the first instance?

'Contra Nando Incrementum' indeed!

As we have seen, the Tweeddale District Council replaced the Peebles Town Council and took over the Peeblesshire County Buildings for its offices. The new authority was one of the four Border counties that comprised the Border Regional Council located at Newtown St Boswells. Before examining the role of the new authority and its impact on the royal burgh of Peebles we should perhaps examine the demographic changes which took place in the post-war period which is under review.

An analysis of census figures must, of necessity, be speculative. Nonetheless, they provide an interesting comment on the development of Peebles — especially over the period of time which was to prove so crucial to the future of the town. Rarely, if ever, had the rate of social and economic change been as fast and as sweeping as between 1950 and 1974.

In the 1951 census, the population of the burgh rose to its highest number since records started in 1791. There were a number of factors which contributed to this. Firstly, the influx of service personnel who married locally during the Second World War, and of returning servicemen who had married outwith the town and returned to establish a family in the town; the 'baby boom' following the war; and also the increasing trend of rural workers moving into Peebles from the county area following upon the mechanisation of agriculture and the concomitant reduction in the farming labour force. Secondly, the textile industry had re-established much of its peacetime trade. The call was for 'Export or Die' and with an ageing workforce the tweed-mills were forced to recruit labour from outwith the town.

Further, in the 1950s, Peebles was becoming known again as a tourist resort. New hotels were established and those such as the Hotel Hydro and the Tontine were refurbished and extended. The nascent service industries began to expand, bringing to the town labour from outside. The post-war industrial recovery of the United Kingdom, albeit slow, led to a revolution in transport. Motorcars became increasingly commonplace on the roads of Britain. In consequence, towns such as Peebles became more attractive to those prepared to commute to the cities or establish their homes in the town and pursue their careers as representatives and area managers.

Nonetheless, despite the 'baby boom' and other factors, the 1961 census shows a drop in the population of 465, arguably against the trend which we had come to expect as one of continual slow and steady growth. Paradoxically, it was during the 1950s that the biggest municipal housing programme ever attempted in Peebles was embarked on. The reason for the apparent fall in population in the ten years to 1961 seems to be in the considerable emigration of young Peebleans from the town, an outwards movement which was not to be redressed by the arrival of the Glasgow overspill workers and other immigrants until the early 1960s.

Peebleans have a long tradition of emigration, often only as far as Edinburgh and other parts of Scotland, often to the north and midlands of England or other textile areas. As early as the eighteenth century some had followed other Borderers to the newly-born United States of America and Canada. One John Smibert (1688–1751), for example, is buried in the Old Granary Cemetery in Boston, Mass., after a successful career as a portrait painter. A relative of his became the provost of Peebles in 1807. At the end of the nineteenth century, it was the countries of the old Commonwealth which attracted the emigrant, and many young Peebleans in the 1950s had relatives in those countries. It seems, therefore, that a growing number left Peebles to take their chance in the Commonwealth, many to achieve considerable success: Eric Bogle, the folk-singer, might be mentioned here. Ex-Cornets of Peebles, the Raeburns and Clappertons, also spring to mind. In short, the 1950s and early 1960s appeared as a time of stagnation in Peebles for many of the younger generation. They it was who sought wider horizons as a result of the post-war austerity. Many, who had travelled overseas as a result of their National Service, saw the new countries of the Commonwealth as an antidote to the prevailing attitudes of their native town at this time.

Many building workers also found itinerant work. Inevitably, as in previous years, this led to their resettlement in other parts of Scotland or indeed in England. Despite the desperate attempts by the tweed industry to increase their labour force, the loss of the Tweedside Mill by fire in 1965 led eventually to the closure of Walter Thorburn Bros. Ltd with the consequent loss of both jobs and population as textile workers and their families left. This period saw the introduction by the town council of schemes for the housing of incoming workers and the reciprocal scheme run by the SSHA to offer houses to key workers. It must be admitted that these efforts met with limited success.

In 1970, the introduction of a new factory in Peebles contributed to an increase in the town's population. The American-based Fidelitone company (later to be known as Sonido) eventually recruited a workforce of 276, which included outworkers.

By the 1971 census, the burgh's population had recovered to 5,884, and seemed well set to continue this trend. The most important single factor during the 1970s was the great improvements made to the road network outwith the town, more particularly the road from Edinburgh to Peebles. This factor, coupled with the great increase in private-sector building, brought an unprecedented increase in the number of commuters. Indeed, by the late 1970s, Peebles was becoming more of a 'dormitory' town than ever before in its long history. It is important to say at this juncture that the cross-fertilisation of cultures between incomers and Gutterbluids has brought much benefit to the town, if only in a diminution in the somewhat parochial attitudes which it seems were a legacy of the interwar period in Peebles. It also led to an increase in support to many organisations in the town, leading also to a number of new ones.

The 1981 census figures saw the population of the burgh reach 6,705, the highest figure recorded. Again, the two principal factors operating in this instance were directly related to the provision of housing both in the private and public sectors. Again, we see a further increase in the extent to which incomers and residents were prepared to travel daily from Peebles to work elsewhere. The factors of environment, educational facilities and the quality of life in Peebles can be regarded as crucial. The universal trend towards self-employment and the growing service industries caused many to remain in Peebles whereas their forbears had, of necessity, to emigrate. Nonetheless, the number of young graduates remaining in Peebles after qualifying remained low and, once introduced to a wider world, few returned except to visit.

The 1980s also saw the the introduction of specialised housing for the retired and the disabled. As early as 1962 the then Peeblesshire County Council had built Dunwhinny Lodge. This was the first instance of sheltered housing for the elderly in Peebles. It was, of course, designed to cater for the whole county, including the burgh, but not for incoming residents. The new developments, sponsored by the various housing associations, were available to all who qualified under the various regulations laid down. Doubtless this has had an effect on the age profile as revealed in the 1981 census for Peebles. Surprisingly enough, the sixty-five-plus element for Peebles compares favourably with towns in Scotland of a similar size. Nonetheless, the figure exceeds the figure for Scotland by 8 per cent with all the ramifications which this implies in terms of medical care, social welfare and income.

The 1980s also produced evidence of one of the worst fears the critics of the local government reorganisation of 1974 had voiced, that of the urbanisation of the rural population. With the birth of the Tweeddale District and the consequent removal of the strictures on housing applicants from the landward areas, which Peebles burgh had operated, a large number of workers from the district sought and received houses within Peebles. Undoubtedly, this factor contributed to, and continues to affect, the population figures for the town. In the long-term, it may well lead to the collapse of the old balance which happily existed between town and country in former years. With the closure of the rural schools, there has been an increase in holiday houses and a general decline or demise of the rural economy. This trend will accelerate and the whole problem will become exacerbated if the present agricultural policies are carried through and 'set aside' becomes a fact.[8]

In the comparison of the 1971 census with that of 1981, the overall population of native Scots shows a decline of about 100,000. In contrast, the immigrant population, mainly from England and, to a lesser degree, the rest of the United Kingdom, rose considerably. Although it is impossible to extrapolate these figures to include Peebles, there seems little doubt that the alien population of the town has increased. Such changes, of course, have taken place for 200 years. In the main, an influx of other nationalities has been welcomed, bringing, as it does, a different cultural background and fresh ideas to the entire population. Nonetheless, as we have seen elsewhere, there is a danger that current political and social ideology could clash with the long-held beliefs of the natives.[9] This is no new danger in Scotland. It might be remembered, for example, that the wise and good Sir Walter Scott on one occasion said, 'but if you unscotch us, you will find us damned mischievous Englishmen'.

At the time of writing (1989) the main problems facing the Tweeddale District Council remain housing in general but also the question of survival in its present form. In line with the policies of the present government, a considerable proportion of the district's housing stock has been sold to the sitting tenants. In addition, the building of municipal housing has virtually ceased although, as we have seen, housing associations are active. Thus, the proportionate increase in influence of such associations has further eroded the power of the elected authority in the public housing sector.

Further it seems likely that cleansing, parks and leisure functions, such as the swimming baths, the golf course and other sporting facilities, may yet be privatised. Should all such policies be fulfilled it is difficult to see how the district councils can survive in their present form. The future then would suggest a further reorganisation of local government. If such a reorganisation resulted in single-tier authorities based on the present regions, then the cause of local democracy would suffer a severe blow and the worst fears of the critics of the 1973 Act would be more than fulfilled.

Before examining the all-important role of housing associations in Peebles, it would perhaps be productive to comment on the changing aspect of the town in respect of domestic architecture.

In 1922 John Buchan, then a Conservative MP for the Universities, made a speech concerning the future of architecture in Scotland. Sounding oddly like a Scottish Nationalist, the thrust of his argument can be encapsulated in the following quote: 'We are in danger very soon of reaching the point where Scotland will have nothing distinctive to show the world.' We are all regrettably familiar with the depressing aspect of the average council house, at whatever time and whenever they were built. Indeed, only at the recent development of Forest View do we see some local authority houses which do justice to their surroundings. The scheme, however, is marred by the density of the houses on site and the alien facing-brick.

In the same sort of way, the speculative builders have given scant regard to the Scottish vernacular tradition, which dominated the thoughts of the earlier builders within the town. The recent 'gap filling' development at Dovecot is unique in its attempt to blend in

190

with its older neighbours. The developer deserves credit for the sensitivity and quality of the workmanship shown. In contrast, Morning Hill, amongst other private developments could be anywhere in English suburbia and stands out accordingly in the douce surroundings of the original small Border burgh. Given improved building methods and the difficulties inherent in the use of local materials, whinstone and the like, it still seems unfortunate that a suitable compromise has yet escaped the architect of the day. The stark contrast between the old and the new can rarely be more marked anywhere.

There are now (1989) six housing associations represented in Peebles. Of these, perhaps the Eildon Housing Association of Melrose has undertaken most of the work within the town. Formed in 1973 by a small group of staff from Dingleton Hospital, who wanted to provide housing in the community for people ready to leave institutional care, it was for some years run on a voluntary basis. It provided houses for single-parent families, the mentally handicapped, the physically disabled, single people and the elderly.

By 1985, as the only Borders-based housing association, Eildon had a full-time staff and was encouraged to provide a programme of development based on local needs in Peebles. As a non-profit-making organisation, it is controlled by a voluntary committee of management drawn from the local community in the Borders. Also, it receives government grants and is required to be registered by the Housing Corporation. The latter is a governmental body with statutory responsibility for the encouragement of such associations. The Eildon works closely with the Borders Regional Council's Social Work Department and the Borders Health Board to assist those vulnerable groups of people who require some level of care to achieve their full potential to live as near normal a life as possible.

Towards this end in Peebles the Eildon has completed the following developments and has also initiated further on-going schemes. In the Northgate of Peebles seven traditionally-built terrace houses, dating from the 1870s, were rehabilitated in 1982 and have been occupied since then, thus adding much to the amenity of that part of the town. In 1986, fifteen high-quality flats were completed at Crookston Court. This development, close to Crookston Place and Glen Road, is designed for single people. A more ambitious scheme of sheltered housing on Tweedside was completed in 1988. This attractive building, named 'Riverside House', stands on the original site of 'The Personnes Manse', the manse of the post-Reformation parish church minister. Appropriately enough, it overlooks the 'Minnie' or the Minister's Pool, once a part of the glebe. Incidentally, it is best seen from the south bank of the water. Two incised lintels from the original building survive, built into the west-facing boundary wall of the complex. There are thirty-three units in Riverside House, mainly for the elderly.

Future developments planned by Eildon include the rehabilitation of a number of houses on the north side of the Old Town. From Welsh's Dairy, westwards to Young Street, this traditional terrace was built in the 1870s. From 1934, however, it was to some extent under a planning blight since they were scheduled for eventual demolition to permit road widening. In consequence, over the years they tended to become the victims of neglect. The remaining houses in the overall plan lie in a terrace west of Miller's Farm Supplies. Most of them were originally single-storey cottages which were transformed into two storeys in the 1890s; again, to some extent, they were allowed to deteriorate by a planning blight. There is little doubt that such a programme will revitalise the Old Town and enhance the approaches to Peebles from the west; the scheme, due for completion in 1990, will return twenty-nine houses to full use.

The final scheme planned by Eildon relates to the south side of Peebles Water from the Trie Bridge at the foot of the Briggate, upstream to the Cuddyside houses and downstream as far as Cuddy Bridge. Site clearance has already started and the completion of twenty-six houses is scheduled by 1990. Such a development was planned as early as twenty years ago by Peebles Town Council and the whole town will benefit by the restoration of this core site. Indeed, great scope exists for an imaginative and high quality development, one which will be worthy of the town itself.[10]

The Ark Housing Association is also represented in Peebles. This association was formed to channel government and charitable funds to provide a variety of accommodation in Scotland to suit the special needs of disabled people. Further, it was formed by a small group of people in a church in Edinburgh who were moved by Christian concern for the homelessness of mentally-handicapped people. It was thus fitting that the scheme which they backed in Peebles was the attractive complex of single flats which were built at the foot of the Old Town. Known as St Andrew's Court, the scheme is specifically designed for the mentally handicapped. Ironically, the housing is built on the site of the former U.P. Church of St Andrew's. This

Looking towards the Tweed Bridge and the Old Parish Church (c. 1887)

*Aerial view of the Tweedside Mill: in the background is Damdale Mill
(c. 1930)*

*High Street, looking towards the Eastgate (*c. *1900)*

High Street: the ancient Mercat Cross held aloft on the plinth given by Colonel William Thorburn of Craigerne in 1895 (later redesigned to facilitate modern-day traffic) (c. 1900)

Looking westwards up the Old Town: it shows the gates and steps of St Andrew's Church (c. 1895)

The Co-operative Society's main premises at the corner of the Old Town (c. 1900)

*Northgate from Veitch's Corner: William Swanson's hairdressing shop is opposite (*c. *1920)*

North British Railway Station with Venlaw in the background (c. 1905)

*The train from Edinburgh arriving at the North British Railway Station
(c. 1910)*

High School (c. 1900)

High School (c. 1970)

*The Town Council of the Royal Burgh of Peebles prior to the Great War:
Seated beside Provost J. A. Ballantyne (1907 – 13) are J. Walter Buchan
(Town Clerk 1906 – 48), Bailie Dalling (Provost 1913 – 15) and Bailie
Forrester (Provost 1916 – 21)*

splendid church of red sandstone is much missed by its adherents, and its demolition remains a controversial matter within the town. Nonetheless, it cannot be gainsaid that the central site provides an excellent situation for the self-contained flats now occupied by selected people who have learning difficulties and who require special care.

The first complex of housing to be completed for those with special needs was built in the 1970s. Tweedbridge Court was built under the aegis of the Margaret Blackwood Housing Association Ltd and is specifically designed for those who are physically handicapped. Indeed, the association is the brainchild of Margaret Blackwood, who is herself physically handicapped. The building enjoys a unique site on the ground once occupied by the Caledonian Railway station and consists of twenty-four flats and a number of bungalows. It is also well provided with facilities which are common to all the residents.[11]

In addition, there are two further organisations in Peebles that provide private sheltered housing, mainly for the retired. It is only fair to say that such developments have attracted their share of criticism from Peebleans and this stems from a vague sense of resentment that many of the occupants of such housing are incomers to the town. The first such development to be completed was built on the site of the County Hospital in Rosetta Road and is called Rose Court. The site itself is constrained, hemmed in as it is by existing housing and by Rosetta Road itself. Built by the speculative Heritage Housing Ltd, Rose Court consists of eighteen one-bedroom flats, fourteen two-bedroom flats and three two-bedroom houses. Regrettably, when we consider the traditional nature of the housing in Rosetta Road, the new complex is in facing brick, albeit that the brickwork is of a dark sandstone colour.[12]

A similar scheme was completed in 1989 with the building of Whitestone Court in Innerleithen Road, which occupies what was formerly the garden of Whitestone House. The builders, McCarthy & Stone of Glasgow, claim to have pioneered the concept of owner-occupier retirement apartments that are designed and purpose built for retired people. The flats number forty and offer three alternative styles, all based on a one-bedroom core plan and provided with common facilities such as a resident's lounge, laundry and utility rooms. As in the other schemes, there is a house manager. The building itself is perhaps the most attractive to the outside viewer and some thought has been given to the architectural importance of the site and its surrounds.[13]

One other development remains to be discussed, that of the Hanover (Scotland) Housing Association at Halyrude Court. Built on the site of the Parish Church Hall, whose demolition was not without controversy, the scheme comprises a total of nineteen flats made up as follows: eight single-person two-apartment flats; ten two-person two-apartment flats; a separate warden's flat; and communal facilities consisting of a common-room, laundry and guest bedroom. These apartments are for the elderly who are physically capable of leading independent lives, albeit with the background support of a warden.[14]

As we have seen, the concept of housing associations or trusts is not new to Peebles and the speculative 'housing for the retired' can be compared to the housing trusts which flourished in the town before the local authority took on the responsibility for housing in the post-First World War period. However, the wholehearted governmental support of them at the expense of the statutory housing authority is a break with tradition and the local authority's statutory role to provide the housing in the community which, already eroded, is now under threat from external forces. It is, indeed, difficult to see local democracy continuing to thrive when many of its functions have already been taken out of the hands of the duly elected councillors.

There were two organisations which were spawned by the demise of the town council on the introduction of the Local Government (Scotland) Act 1973. The best known was formed under the provisions of the Act: The Royal Burgh of Peebles and District Community Council. The second organisation came into being through the quite natural fear that the unbridled forces of the increasingly remote regional authority could act against the interests of the local community: this latter became the Peebles Civic Society.

The Royal Burgh of Peebles and District Community Council is one of ten community councils set up by the Tweeddale District Council within Tweeddale, and it covers the former town council area and part of the immediately surrounding district that includes most of Eshiels. It has a statutory base but does not have a statutory function; it is not a local authority but nevertheless it is expected to take such action in the community as appears to the members to be desirable and practicable. There are eighteen elected members, one-third of whom retire annually; they represent the whole area and not specific wards. The community council may co-opt up to six more members, including nominees of local organisations.

The aims of the council are: to encourage a sense of community and to maintain local tradition; to ascertain, co-ordinate and express to the regional and district councils the views of the community in relation to matters for which these authorities are responsible; and to act generally in the interests of the community. Monthly, the various sub-committee meetings are held in the council chambers at the Chambers Institute. The community council chairmen since 1977 are: Ex-Provost R. Kirkpatrick; Major R. Ogilvie; Lieutenant-Colonel A. M. Sprot, MC; Mr G. Pennel; Mr W. W. Howitt; Mr I. J. Mewett; and Mr D. Wright.

A major part of the council's function relates to consultation in respect of local planning applications. The Planning Sub-Committee makes frequent visits and provides the full council with recommendations on responses to be made to the Regional Planning Department. The council takes action and applies pressure where it is needed to improve facilities in the neighbourhood. It successfully pressed for the provision in 1983 of a town bus service to the Kingsway/Kingsmeadows area; persuaded the district council to provide a proper play-area at Damcroft in 1987; and along with the other community councils in Tweeddale, gave support to the district council in 1988 to prevent the proposed 'merger' of Ettrick and Lauderdale District with Tweeddale. In 1978 they organised an open meeting regarding the South Parks Flood Alleviation Scheme and, in 1988, held another meeting which gave an opportunity for public expression of opinion against the proposed land-exchange deal which involved South Parks.

In 1988, the council successfully acted to safeguard the traditional coat of arms of the burgh, and these have now been matriculated in favour of the community council. It has also become involved in various projects: taking on the responsibility for the annual Old Folk's Treat, a founder-sponsor of the Peebles Arts Festival, and the 'Peebles in Bloom' garden competition. The council has worked to raise funds for the £1,500 BMX track at Victoria Park (1985); equipment for Hay Lodge Hospital; sports equipment for Peebles High School; and the Gutterbluid Society's Christmas decoration project.

The Peebles Civic Society was formed in 1973 to encourage public interest in the past, present and future of Peebles; to encourage the preservation, development and improvement of amenities in and around Peebles; and to promote public participation in planning decisions. It had its origins as part of the public reaction against

against the Peeblesshire County Council's proposals to widen Cuddy Bridge at the cost of demolishing, in its entirety, Buchan's 'Bank House'. The impact of public opinion in that instance was powerful and effective. The bridge-widening was redrawn in such a way that part of 'Bank House' was retained and tastefully remodelled.

This society, in its primary 'watch-dog' role, continues to be vigilant about planning issues and, after 'regionalisation' in 1974, it established a good working relationship with the Planning and Development Department of the Borders Regional Council and is regularly consulted. During the 1980s the town came under increasing pressure from speculative developers and the society frequently found itself advocating adherence to the 'Local Plan', an important purpose of which was to control and limit the growth of Peebles.

The issues most often confronting the Civic Society during that decade included the expansion of the burgh in respect of population and geographical spread; the need to maintain a balanced population in respect of age groupings and, in particular, to avoid too high a proportion of the 65-plus age group (in 1981 the 65-plus group represented 22.3 per cent of the population); the desirability of providing relatively low-cost housing to meet locally-generated demand; the promotion of good design in respect of housing schemes, in-fill developments and High Street frontages; the development of opportunities provided by the Cuddyside area; the management of traffic; and the protection of trees, regarded by the society as a precious part of the burgh's heritage.

During the last three years of the 1980s there was a renewal of popular interest in planning and development issues. This interest was aroused partly by the general development pressure that was becoming increasingly apparent and partly by issues like the building of sheltered housing complexes; the unpopularity of the district council's exploration of land exchange schemes; the proposal, of unprecedented size and type, to develop a tournament golf course with associated luxury hotel and 'village' of up to 200 houses centred on Cardrona Mains Farm; and by the approaching need to formulate the new 'Local Plan' which was due to come into operation at the beginning of 1992.

There are other external and alien influences at work within the burgh and these are caused by the economic and social changes in the 1980s. We have watched, bemused, the hyped-up house and land prices in the south-east of England: but as we write, houses in

196

Peebles are being built and sold for over £125,000 — prices beyond the dreams of the average Peeblean. Hopefully, there still exists a pragmatism common to most Border Scots which rejects the most irrational excesses of the new culture. Nonetheless, we must bear in mind that the creeping South-East of England syndrome may damage the fabric of our society, both in bricks and mortar and, more importantly, lifestyle. We must remember the historic scale and inherent quality of Peebles as a town. Already the developed villas intrude in the douce townscape.

Footnotes:

1. Bulloch, J. P. B. (ed), *Third Statistical Account of Peeblesshire: The Counties of Peebles and Selkirk* (Glasgow 1964) p165
2. Peebles Town Council Minutes, 1949
3. Census returns of 1961
4. Chambers, W. M., *History of Peeblesshire* (Edinburgh, 1864) p49
5. Ibid, p84
6. Donaldson, Gordon, *Scotland* (London, 1974) pp144 – 6
7. Ibid, p142
8. Census statistics (1984)
9. Ibid (1981)
10. Brochure, Eildon Housing (1989)
11. Brochure, Margaret Blackwood Housing (1980)
12. Information gleaned from Hanover Housing, 1989
13. Brochure, McCarthy & Stone (1988)
14. Information gleaned from Hanover Housing, 1978

CHAPTER 11

Education

THE SENIOR LEAVING Certificate Exam in vogue for over sixty years was in 1950 renamed the Scottish Leaving Certificate and the old system of a pass mark in a group of subjects was no longer compulsory for the award of a certificate; more candidates sat the exam and they were allowed, in their sixth year, to add subjects to passes already obtained. Hence, by 1960 when the High School roll numbered 577 and the prize-giving ceremony was transferred to the Playhouse Cinema because there was no room in the hall, thirty-seven certificates were awarded and seventeen pupils gained additional subjects. It was soon obvious that the two new classrooms opened in 1958 could not contain the increasing intakes resulting from the post-war 'bulge' and by 1959 plans for extra accommodation on a far bigger scale were being voiced abroad. Already, a medical centre had been added which could be used for dental treatment, physiotherapy or first aid, playing fields were extended and visits of architects and buildings sub-committee men to the High School were becoming more frequent. The 1960s were to witness fundamental changes in educational development (some die-hards could only deplore the deluge that ensued!) and so far-reaching were the reforms envisaged that all the schools in the burgh were to be transformed and a completely new one built south of Tweed's stream.

First, a new Scottish Certificate of Education was introduced in 1961 with provisions for Ordinary Grades (IVth year), Higher (Vth year) and Advanced, although the latter, as Sixth Year Studies, were not examined until 1968. More subjects were available, modern studies (i.e. twentieth-century history, geography, economics and politics) at 'O' Grade appeared in 1962 and Higher papers were set for 1968 by which time a new SCE Examination Board had taken over the award of certificates from the Scottish Education

Department. Examinations, at long last, were held more sensibly in May, the number of candidates doubled and many pupils remained at school for four instead of three years in order to sit their 'O' Grades, with further chances to qualify by attending evening classes catering for vocational studies as well as recreational. Several alternative syllabuses were introduced for science, mathematics, classics, modern languages, home economics and technical subjects, all of which meant extra staff and more room.

Rebuilding the High School began in earnest on 20 May 1963: the Rector, who had been ill for three months in 1962, forthwith experienced a relapse and did not return to duty until the end of August. He soldiered on until February 1965 when the death of his wife exacerbated his own ill-health and he retired prematurely in his mid-fifties — a poignant passing of an acknowledged academic who was perhaps unsuited to the hurly-burly of life in the 'swinging sixties'! Happily, he was spared the formidable tasks of tackling the traumas that lay ahead.

One man who took everything in his stride was Charles Blacklaw, MA, who commenced duty as headmaster of Peebles Public School in August 1960. A university prize-winner of the early 1930s, a realist who knew at first-hand what life was all about, he had served as a naval officer for several years during the Second World War and became Broughton Secondary School headmaster in the 1940s before being transferred to West Linton and ultimately Kingsland. A serious student of education, Mr Blacklaw felt compelled to accept a more comprehensive remit than most educationalists and distributed his undoubted talents over a wide field. Thousands would testify to his skills as a headmaster, hundreds remember his deft handling of problems concerning teachers for whom he acted as spokesman on innumerable occasions culminating in his election to the highest professional position — President of the Educational Institute of Scotland. Even that honour could not contain the capacity for involvement of Charles Blacklaw, FEIS, who was also chairman of the Teaching Council which ensured that only qualified teachers could be employed by the Education Authorities throughout Scotland.

Throughout the 1960s Mr Blacklaw busied himself with the endless aspects of education which confront a progressive headmaster in and out of school. He kept up Kingsland's connection with the BBC whose programme pamphlets — pupils' and teachers' notes

— were used for both wireless talks and TV broadcasts (in 1962 a large screen was installed which could also be used occasionally by the children to see such events as the opening of the Forth Road Bridge in 1964). He continued to encourage elocution — i.e. verse speaking — also singing and dancing and sent contingents and soloists to the Borders Musical Festival where Peebles' candidates carried off the prizes with commendable regularity. He arranged annual concerts in the Parish Church Hall. A record player, film-strip projector and screen were acquired early in the 1960s, a tape recorder and duplicating machines a little later — all partly paid for out of the school funds accumulated as a result of pupils' public performances.

Mr Blacklaw was a council member of the Scottish Commonwealth Institute and made full use of their travelling lecturers who gave illustrated talks on countries constituting the Commonwealth to pupils, a few of whom entered the annual essay competition. He was also a member of the Accident Prevention Council, the Consultative Council on educational matters which met in St Andrews House, and the National Joint Council — an Edinburgh-based body which dealt *inter alia* with teachers' salaries — whilst in June 1964 Mr Blacklaw attended as a full member of Peeblesshire Education Committee to which position he had been elected by the primary teachers of the county to represent their interests.

Meanwhile he was not averse to such humdrum tasks as taking a team to Traquair for football, a class to the local mill for an insight into life's prospects for many or an excursion to Edinburgh for some such production as the Vienna Boys' Choir which he did not want everyone to miss. Even journeys across the seas were undertaken by Mr Blacklaw who organised, and occasionally accompanied, educational cruises to the Western Isles, Fair Isle, Norway, Denmark and Poland — but made sure that his school team won the ship's scrap-book and quiz competitions!

At classroom level he kept abreast of the later 1960s by making good use of the Initial Teaching Alphabet and Reading Laboratory courses, visited pilot schools to observe teaching methods adopted in accordance with recent recommendations of the memorandum 'Primary Education in Scotland' but continued 'transfer' examinations in composition, arithmetic, English and verbal reasoning for potential High School pupils. Meanwhile, in September 1964 Mr Blacklaw saw the publication of the *Third Statistical Account* for Peeblesshire and Selkirkshire to which he had been a contributor, said farewell to infant mistress Miss Ker (after forty-five years' service), to Miss Heron in 1966 and Miss Davidson in 1968, welcomed Mr W. D. Smith as Deputy Headmaster, Miss Jean Maule as Senior Woman Assistant, Mr Calderwood as Director of Education and prepared for the introduction of decimalisation at the end of the decade!

During his own presidency of the EIS (1969 – 70) he was to witness a week of teachers' strikes when Kingsland was closed, and to become involved in the revolutionary changes contemplated for local school structures in the early 1970s. The Education Committee had already reviewed future provision for Peebles primary pupils and plans were published for a new Priorsford to take all non-denominational children south of Tweed, for a modernised Kingsland to include infants as well as older 'primaries' and for Halyrude, 'after rehabilitation', to become a new Roman Catholic school in lieu of St Joseph's, where the standard of accommodation was considered unacceptable.

Mr Blacklaw was to become the first headmaster of Priorsford which was not occupied until November 1972 (formally opened by the Secretary of State for Scotland in February 1973) but preparation for the changeover started many months in advance of his switch from north to south of Tweed. Since the new school was to be of the open-plan variety, an appropriate course for teachers had been held in December 1971. The headmaster himself, along with the Director of Education, journeyed to Aberdeenshire to inspect the latest open-plan primary, and teachers were given their chance to express their preference for appointment to Priorsford.

Meantime, Mr W. D. Smith, having obtained a headship at Galashiels, had left Peebles in 1971 to be replaced by Mr Robert Bennet, headmaster of West Linton, on the understanding that the designation 'Deputy' implied automatic headship of the 'new' Kingsland as soon as Mr Blacklaw left for Priorsford. In June 1972 over two hundred parents of potential pupils of the latter attended a meeting where they were given details of 'the revolutionary changes in primary teaching methods and curriculum introduced in the recent past'. Whether they understood or approved is not recorded but at least they would have faith in Mr Charles Blacklaw, that doyen of dominies! Ever aware of history and as if to contrast 'Then and Now', he organised a suitable celebration of the centenary of the Education (Scotland) Act of 1872 by dressing staff and pupils in period costume giving and receiving instruction as per 100 years ago — using apparatus appropriate to the time and demonstrating, with the aid of old photographs, how the whole ethos of education had changed.

Considerable changes, too, took place at the High School where in August 1965, Mr Ian G. Ball slid gently into the rector's chair almost unnoticed. A quiet, self-effacing gentleman (not unlike his predecessor in office, Mr J. F. Soutter, who had been a most efficient interim headmaster since early February), Mr Ball boasted different qualities from those of Mr Rothnie who had been more interested in the past than in the future. The new Rector, formerly Principal Teacher of English at Trinity Academy, Edinburgh, had already written programmes for children's radio, compiled books of plays for school use, was radio critic for *The Scotsman* and served on the Selection Committee for Edinburgh Film Festival. Despite the constant cacophony of constructors throughout the second half of the 1960s Mr Ball remained serene, solving 'leavers' problems by utilising Youth Employment and Careers Officers who liaised with specialised teachers at the High School and by attending appropriate conferences in both the Borders and Midlothian. With an eye to third year pupils' futures and in accordance with principles contained in the Brunton Report, he organised all kinds of projects such as a comprehensive study of the textile industry involving various teachers, visits to mills in Peebles and Innerleithen, lectures by experts and a display of work accomplished.

Another useful study was local government (before reorganisation!) in connection with which many burgh and county officials explained their own roles and even David Steel held a seminar for selected senior students doubtless expatiating on the niceties of proportional representation. Higher geography pupils undertook a land-utilisation survey mapping selected farms, older girls gave a helping hand at a crèche for town toddlers on Friday afternoons, another group from the homecraft department entertained old age pensioners to lunch in the school flat whilst others acted as guides or hostesses at public or parents' meetings.

Mr Ball certainly encouraged integration with the community: Lord Hunt of Everest fame was a distinguished visitor in 1966 and he set in motion the Duke of Edinburgh Awards scheme which was adopted by quite a few pupils who aimed at nothing less than 'gold'. Other groups visited firms like Ferranti's and explored the potential of electrical and electronic engineering, many more limited their activities to inter-school sport, debating and socialising; but all seemed to get the message — education was to be recreational as well as vocational, as catered for by adult evening-classes.

Even before Mr Ball inherited Mr Rothnie's legacy, education had become a political football. By the mid-1960s Government insisted on the implementation of the principle of comprehensive education which meant, in theory at least, a common course and common examinations for all first- and second-year pupils at Secondary level. Then (as now) those who opposed the current legislation, embodied in the famous Circular 600 of the Scottish Education Department, tried either to dilute the implications of the new system or endeavoured to evade it altogether. Although Mr Ball appeared to favour the philosophy behind the new theories — indeed he went so far as to name his first year classes I 'U' 'N' 'E' 'S' 'C' and 'O' instead of the time honoured I 'A' 'B' 'C' etc., so that no pupils (or parents) could claim preferential treatment — nevertheless he realised that some sort of compromise was inevitable and he did not insist that every child learned Latin for two years! On the other hand it must be said that he did not favour the bright pupil at the expense of the slower learner and he was at pains to point out to his staff that he expected parity of treatment for all, that the most backward boy or girl was just as important educationally as the most promising, and that the awkward unco-operative child needed patience rather than punishment.

Not that many of the pupils or staff saw a great deal of the Rector, whose régime of less than seven years encompassed events of momentous importance. He was constantly in conference with architects, clerks of works and builders and undoubtedly helped to mould the shape of things to come: he had a particular interest in the library complex which enhanced at least the base of the new Tower Block. In the end Mr Ball was to attend, as one of the principals, the ceremony on 28 October 1970 to mark the completion of the pro-gramme of modernisation and extension of the High School first envisaged in the heyday of Mr Rothnie who died within a month of its finalisation.

Meanwhile, Mr Ball adopted Radio Vision teaching techniques in 1966, set in motion a whole series of activities for Friday afternoons in 1967, weathered the terrible storm of February 1968 when absent pupils numbered 365 (waylaid by fallen trees), inaugurated a biology course thus adding another dimension to the ever-expanding science department, installed audio-typing equipment and a new cine-projector and witnessed the closing of the secondary departments of Broughton, West Linton and Innerleithen schools whose senior scholars and several staff were incorporated within the confines of the new High School in 1969. Yet again the Rector had to rise above both a bus strike in March 1970 when some 300 were unable to get to Peebles and a teachers' strike when twenty-six staff absented themselves for a week later that year.

In 1971 Mr Ball arranged for a very wide variety of visiting speakers for potential 'leavers', obtained the services of Captain Keeling, Army Director of Music Scottish Division, to instruct band instrumentalists, and began to reorganise existing staff in accordance with the new policy of promoted posts when he resigned and left the High School in March 1972 just as quietly as he had arrived in the summer of 1965. His departure almost coincided with that of Mr Calderwood who had directed proceedings from County Buildings for five years and left for the south to face further educational challenges.

Peebles could hardly hope to hold such an omniscient administrator who had already planned the new Priorsford 'Open Plan' Primary School to suit the needs of pupils in the expanding area south of the Tweed and had been consulted in connection with the reconstruction of Kingsland along similar lines. Priorsford, started in November 1971, was occupied one year later and Mr Blacklaw, as if fore-ordained to hold the highest primary post locally, assumed the headship of the ultra modern school supposedly for the remaining years of his working life. Alas, years proved to be only months and, tragically, Mr Blacklaw passed away, still in his prime, in June 1973. His hallmark had been one of selfless dedication to the exacting tasks of teaching and organising within the classroom and without: the last of the pre-war brigade!

But there was still much to be done by builders and other tradesmen as they together transformed Kingsland from a two-storeyed, galleried complex, so well known to thousands of Peebleans for over seventy years, into a modern 'Open Plan' design reflecting 'current trends in primary education' and providing 'facilities comparable with those of a new school at a substantially lower capital cost' according to the Scottish Education Department's

Building Study published by the HMSO. Until June 1974 Kingsland pupils and staff were accommodated in Halyrude, Church and Drill Halls, but were amply rewarded for their endurance when most of them were housed in the revolutionised Kingsland in August of that year. During that long summer holiday, Halyrude itself was redecorated, after the installation of a new heating system and the addition of carpets for the comfort of Roman Catholic children and staff who had been waiting patiently in the wings for rehabilitation — and parity with the other two primaries. At last they were included in the annual Beltane honours!

In fact, local history was made in 1974 when Claire Dubar was chosen Beltane Queen as a result of a new method of selection which has obtained since that year: all six pages and two members of the court from St Joseph's accompanied her. Two other queens and two first courtiers have been products of the new Roman Catholic school housed in Halyrude from whence, on Beltane Saturday morning, sets out that unique procession of primary pupils who walk quietly to the High Street to take their allotted stances on the steps of the Parish Church. Exactly one hundred years before Claire Dubar assumed historical importance, St Joseph's opened its doors to accommodate Catholic children who were obliged by the 1872 Act of Parliament to attend school. Independently run at first for over forty years, it was included in the local education system only after 1918 and even then it was still influenced for some time by St Catherine's Convent in Edinburgh — an institution which secured suitable staff, usually married ladies who satisfied the required religious standards.

The first lay headmaster was Mr Pat O'Neill (1946 – 64) who did not limit his activities to Catholics but busied himself in the affairs of his adopted burgh, became a member of the old town council and was already a senior bailie when, in 1962, he was honoured by being chosen as Warden of Neidpath. During his time, St Joseph's gradually entered the post-war era. Electricity was installed in 1952 so that film shows were now possible, a film strip projector was obtained, wireless provided BBC programmes and a new automatic boiler ensured uniform heating. In 1953, with a roll of over seventy, a new classroom was added and a separate staffroom made possible for what became a three-teacher school. It must be borne in mind that Catholic children from outside Peebles attended St Joseph's — or occasionally failed to do so! Truancy in the landward areas created awkward administrative problems. In 1959 a tape recorder was added to the school's apparatus and the new Radio Relay was adopted. The roll had risen to eighty and an extra hut had been erected in the precincts before Mr Pat Connolly took over in 1964 and thus continued the line of lay headmasters. A keen footballer and deft dribbler in his younger days, Mr Connolly encouraged the boys' sporting activities and usually accompanied his team when playing away.

Soon after he assumed the headship, St Joseph's older pupils joined the audio-visual series of French lessons provided by the BBC whilst another specialist teacher improved musical standards to the extent that the school choir gave an excellent performance at the Beltane concert and won the Challenge Shield at the Borders Musical Festival. The school roll reached eighty-six in 1970 and Mr Connolly was all set to move to the promised new premises — in the offing for so long. The actual transfer took place during the brief headship of his successor, Mr Bonnici, (1973 – 74), and Halyrude, from time immemorial an infants' department, became the final and most appropriate abode of all Catholic children of pre-secondary school age.

A Parent-Teacher Association was started in 1973 and Halyrude took its rightful place alongside the two other Peebles Primary schools. Mr Brian Nimmo, a young enthusiast, took over in 1974 and for a couple of years Halyrude boasted four class teachers as well as visiting specialists including Pipe-Major Pryde and his chanter lessons. In 1975 the school held its own sports, assisted by the parents who took an active part in the innumerable educational visits and outings organised by the headmaster and his helpers. Even Edinburgh Tattoo was on the list! Meanwhile, instrumental instruction (cello and violin) was added to the normal musical repertoire so that, when Mr Nimmo handed over the reins to Mrs Inglis in April 1979, the old St Joseph's had well and truly become the new Halyrude — an integral part of the primary school system in Peebles — and District. So it has remained for the last decade in the very capable hands of May Inglis and her 'composite class' teachers.

Mr Graeme J. Murray, Deputy Head, who took over temporarily at Priorsford on the sudden death of Mr Blacklaw, was officially appointed headteacher in September 1973 and has held the position with aplomb for some sixteen years. A personable young man, he was ideally suited for the immense changes that were about to be seen in primary school educational methods. One of these changes had already occurred: a Parent-Teacher Association had been formed in November 1972 and Mr Murray kept in close contact with this new phenomenon, occasionally consulting its seven General Purposes Committee members as to policy, putting on diverse displays for their delectation and organising social events where parents mixed with teachers and/or pupils in order to help perpetuate that liaison which would appear to have been created in the first instance to eradicate some of the errors perpetrated by existing educators!

Priorsford 'Open Plan' School became a showpiece almost in world terms! Apart from visits by local and Scottish school heads, advisers and teachers, training college lecturers and research students, directors of education and administrative officials — including a posse of HM Inspectors — we read of educationalists from as far afield as London, Cyprus, Canada, the Caribbean Islands, America, India, Australia, New Zealand, Hong Kong and even the Gilbert and Solomon Islands! The Queen herself and the Duke of Edinburgh met and spoke to Priorsford pupils during the royal visit of 1988. Why such a universal interest? We were not the first open plan primary school (others, e.g. in Aberdeenshire, had pilot schemes) but, with Peebles being such a perfect place to visit and Priorsford having been designed, newly built and open for inspection to the public from the early 1970s, it gave it a certain mystique which magnetised many who were just curious and a minority who were genuinely interested in this new educational project. Gone were the classrooms of yesteryear — with doors firmly shut and teachers talking to pupils passively 'sitting up straight'! Here were 'bases' and 'areas' without doors and pupils in small groups talking if they wished to teachers or to each other but working away on assignments already set.

But not for one instant did Mr Murray and his single-minded staff rest on their laurels, however widely acclaimed. He himself, as elected representative of large primary schools in Peeblesshire, attended national conferences for open-plan schools at Callender Park and Jordanhill Colleges of Education as well as art and craft working parties in Galashiels. Several of his staff updated themselves on modern methods by attending 'Reading Workshop' and other in-service courses at St Boswells Teachers' Centre, becoming familiar with computers and adopting the latest techniques favoured by the Scottish Primary Maths Group. Miss Fleming, infant mistress, gave a talk to parents on the Initial Teaching Alphabet and the Downing Reading Scheme, whilst Borders Regional Council held a language policy course, started audiometric testing, added a teacher of environmental studies to Priorsford and, with the aid of a music adviser, introduced pupils to the electronic keyboard and involved many of them in both an opera and a drama workshop. The emphasis seemed always to be on extending the experience of the new generation, long before they reached adulthood. Aside from local history, industry, forestry and farming projects, there were day trips to Edinburgh (ballet, Ingliston, art galleries etc.), Glasgow (transport museum) or up Tweed to Talla and Fruid, with a week in London thrown in for good measure in the month of April. In school, films were shown by the police on Safety First, by SSPCA on 'Never Go with Strangers' and, more vocationally, by bodies such as the Forestry Commission. In 1976 Border Television came to Peebles to make a film which included Priorsford children in full song: later an even larger unit from STV arrived to film pupils and teachers at work and Mr Murray had to take three of his pupils to the Glasgow studios for their solo performances.

Self-reliance must have been one of the results of open-plan teaching for we read of youngsters entertaining the old folks at Dunwhinny, operating their own school savings bank and conducting their own morning assembly! They were encouraged to take an interest in all kinds of organisations and activities: indeed, one of their many projects was 'People's Jobs' which was a fairly wide remit and must have familiarised them with an adult world denied to earlier generations of schoolchildren. Mr Murray and his staff continued to collaborate with parents to provide a brand of education which has been universally acclaimed. The good citizens of Peebles can bask in the reflected glory!

The last meeting of Peeblesshire County Council Education Committee took place at the end of April 1975. Its members could claim to have seen the completion of all the constructive changes conceived in the 1960s. Only one month earlier the ageing Mr Lawrie, ex-Provost and Emeritus Headmaster, must have had mixed feelings as he addressed the assembled adults and children at the official re-opening of Kingsland, metamorphosed as it was from within the building he had known intitially. The secluded classrooms downstairs had been thrown open to contain infants and the huge hall, built over at the former gallery level, housed the older pupils who were now provided with almost futuristic furniture and facilities. Here could be found a quiet/noisy room, a library/study, a kitchen area and 'drama well', besides interconnected classroom bases, an administrative suite and a visiting-service room. Mr Lawrie may have avoided the mound, stepping stones and playing steps when he entered his old school, possibly noticed the flower beds, the climbing wall and football pitch in the distance, but would most certainly have appreciated the carpets for all to tread. What a transformation for Mr Bennet and his staff who had been waiting with anxious optimism since 1968 to be rehoused.

Mr Bennet, an experienced headmaster before his Kingsland appointment, was already *au fait* with open-plan methods and he was at last able to implement all the latest teaching techniques. Some parents comprehended the changes introduced, joined the Parent-Teacher Association and even acted as auxiliaries. Mr Bennet and his chosen staff knew quite well what they were doing and soon the children were organised into houses for work and play, into groups (ideally of eight) for most lessons and reading was taken at each child's own pace. Except for maths and languages, the old subject divisions were abandoned: topics and themes took over. Environmental studies supplanted history, geography and general knowledge as pupils studied various aspects of their neighbourhood, their river, their forests or whatever, finding out as much as they could for themselves. Word processors were available and were used but handwriting (joined-up script) was still taught, as was spelling.

Mr Bennet's senior staff are agreed that everything then felt freer, looked lighter and brighter, the new furniture more comfortable and, as for those carpets, what a change from the stone stairs of yesteryear! No wonder that the children were guided more easily into self-expression — even school sports' days became much more fun as novelty events alternated with the more serious business of running races, for competition was still encouraged and a house system, which operated on the sports field as in the classroom, was a motivating force which, to an extent, replaced corporal punishment. Discipline was simply deprivation of privilege and only a minority stepped out of line: the occasional extreme case would involve parents' participation in the exercise of sanctions. Mr Bennet is quoted as saying that 'Education is a fascinating mixture of problems and opportunities'; he met these challenges head on and, before he retired in 1988, he had, with the help of a dedicated staff, transformed Kingsland and its clientele from a regimented to a congenial, more communicative school where children feel at ease.

Mrs Marlene Galashan, the first female headteacher of Kingsland, succeeded Mr Bennet in August 1988. Originally from

PART III: 1950 – 1990

Aberdeenshire (home of the open plan school) where her adviser was Mrs Mary Tawse, who hailed from Kirkurd and Newlands, Mrs Galashan has continued contact with the Parent-Teacher Association and engages local mothers as auxiliaries. Inevitably, she has added a 'woman's touch' to the inside of the building — flowers, posters, photographs of school trips add a new dimension to the décor whilst her talent for organisation and her reputation for knowing every child in the school augur well for the future. It's not easy to envisage the return of the slate and the strap!

The initials RSM connote respect to ex-Army and national servicemen and so it was when Robert S. Morton became Rector of the High School on 29 May 1972. Customarily, Mr John F. Soutter had held the reins since the surprise departure of Mr Ball to Biggar High School early in April but Mr Morton needed no deputy to ease him into his role as Rector of an expanding complex comprising Victorian, neo-Georgian and modern Elizabethan architecture which would have bemused the normal newcomer. Mr Morton had served an acceptable apprenticeship before coming to Peebles. Successfully teaching English in the west of Scotland for over twenty years — a tough assignment by any standards — he seemed ideally suited for his new post, having experienced the usual brickbats and bouquets of an organiser of his own subject and its presentation to the public. He was a past-master of the art of communication and no one was ever in any doubt as to his educational policy: there were frequent assemblies for pupils, staff meetings for teachers, other occasions when he could meet and talk to parents for whom a special bulletin was prepared periodically, plus a monthly Newsnotes feature in the local paper, whilst he himself was soon in frequent demand by organisations as a public speaker. Mr Morton inherited the new promotion structure whereby certain teachers had been appointed Assistant Rectors, Principal Teachers of Guidance etc. and, with these aides, he held weekly consultations: his heads of department he met monthly, groups of form teachers from time to time, whilst a system of staff circulars was established in the interests of communication. Unlike his predecessor, the new Rector was no Scarlet Pimpernel!

He had to address himself almost immediately to the problems connected with ROSLA (the Raising of the School Leaving Age to sixteen), an obvious offshoot of which was an increased pupil roll. New courses were devised for 'Young School Leavers' (YSL) involving extra staff, auxiliaries such as health visitors, Youth and

Community Service officers, Department of Employment officials and careers advisers who were able to grant individual interviews to teenagers. The former Civil Defence premises below the new hall were transformed into a guidance centre cum office for lower and middle schools, 'social accommodation' was provided for the upper school whilst all pupils benefited from a spacious games hall which was added to give everybody much more elbow room. In the course of time, more classrooms were erected on what had long ceased to be the girls' hockey pitch, including an isolated group of four in an effort to contain the ever expanding history and modern studies department.

Meanwhile the Rector, as if he did not have enough to do, had to cope with teachers' and bus strikes, which severely limited pupils' attendance for several weeks, and solve the mysteries of the break-ins which occurred only too frequently for his peace of mind: the latter he tackled successfully with admirable *tour de force*! The time-honoured adage that 'the only constant is change' proved a little wearisome for the older members of staff but Mr Morton's most characteristic quality was his versatility; he never rested on his laurels but adapted to the numerous educational changes which evolved in the late 1970s and early 1980s. Possessing a comprehensive command of English and Scottish language and literature, he was able to pay a memorably moving tribute to his predecessor, Mr Ball, who died early in 1973, yet more light-hearted but sincere farewells to the several staff who left or retired during his decade or so in office; nevertheless he did not mince his words when addressing miserable miscreants who managed to bring two fire-engines to school on a hoax call! A little of this literary ability must have rubbed off on the editors of the school magazine which was judged third equal in 1974 by *The Scotsman* and was an outright winner of that paper's trophy in 1975.

In the mid-1970s the reorganisation of local government resulted in the transfer of the headquarters of educational administration from the County Buildings to Newtown St Boswells. Fortunately, Mr McClean from Peeblesshire became the Director of Education, Borders Region, and he was joined by High School's Assistant Rector, Mr Paterson, who was appointed Assistant Director of Education specialising in secondary work. Further staff enlargements — chiefly of an administrative nature — followed in the wake of the move to Newtown St Boswells; the multiplication of manpower appeared to be an inevitable concomitant of eductional change and many deplored the demise of the old cosy connection with the

County Buildings which had existed for forty years — yet seemed eternal!

One practice which dated from 1972 (Mr Morton's first year in office) was that of liaising with primary schools: this was elaborated in succeeding years until all primary-VII children and most of their parents had been initiated into the hitherto hidden mysteries of the High School — staff, curricula, recreational facilities, the lot — long before first-year pupils set foot in the place officially. Presumably the practice was designed to ease the transfer of youngsters from primary to secondary education and the psychological traumas associated with such a move but, nonetheless, it was typical of the Rector whose watchwords were 'anticipation' and then — 'organisation'. Long before they had completed their 'comprehensive' common course, second-year pupils were being badgered to choose certain subjects for their third year and very soon they were subjected to the advice and blandishments of a multiplicity of minions from farms, factories, shops, hotels, the services, the professions plus local and central government.

Reviewing these later years it would seem that educational policy was structured solely to smooth the path for children of all ages and thereby facilitate each big step into life. Certainly their knowledge and experience were widened by links with other schools in Scotland, England and Europe, whilst their chances of further education or future employment were catered for by a whole army of helpers, amateur and professional. Self-expression was encouraged and took various forms in and out of school: Gilbert and Sullivan operas, opportunities to learn musical instruments (instruction provided), Duke of Edinburgh Award schemes, innumerable activities plus school parties, dances and discos. Pupils became less inhibited, corporal punishment was phased out and learning was more and more a matter of assignments, worksheets and the increasing use of teaching aids. At the same time, a new examination — i.e. Standard Grade — was mooted so that no child should leave school without some sort of certificate; the idea was not universally welcomed by the teaching fraternity and took several years to become adopted. But the traditional and alternative 'O' Grades and Highers continued in the meantime, making life a little confusing for Rector and staff alike.

Fortunately Mr Morton was, above all else, a consummate organiser and he coped with all exigencies — even when the school roll topped the thousand mark and still further extensions were necessitated. Meanwhile, Messrs Munn and Dunning demanded consideration and ultimate implementation. Mr Munn's report dealt with the structure of the curriculum whilst that of Dr Dunning concentrated on assessment of pupils' abilities. It took several sessions for the powers that be to mull over Munn and Dunning's ideas but eventually, in 1982, the Scottish Education Department issued a 'Framework for Decision' based on the findings of these two erudite gentlemen and Peebles High School, ever to the fore, piloted a science scheme of work which would lead to the award of a certificate of sorts for every single candidate. Other subjects followed suit until all academic skills could be adjudged worthy of a certificate of mixed merit and no pupil need leave school without paper qualifications!

More meaningful was the publication, in 1983, by the Scottish Education Department of an 'Action Plan for the 16s – 18s in Scotland'. This framework made available for students in further education colleges, as well as the later level of secondary schools, new educational opportunities based on short courses of work (or modules) leading to the award of yet another national certificate (known as SCOTVEC). Pupils of Peebles High School were presented for this latest accolade in 1985, by which time extensions had been made to the science laboratories which now numbered nine and severe structural damage of the 'new' Tower Block meant extensive (expensive) repairs.

Even the redoubtable Mr Morton gave up at this juncture. For fourteen years he had been held in high regard by pupils, parents and staff who had learned to respect him for his pragmatism, his resilience to change and the resolution he revealed when resolving the consequent problems of reorganisation that came his way. He left the field free for a younger man who was to face up to unprecedented challenges from the government but Dr Kerr, a Borderer to boot — albeit with no particular claim to having taught locally — was alert to the new philosophy of education with which most of us are nowadays familiar. For this is the age of the computer and even the time-honoured commercial department has abandoned its typewriters for word processors and become a veritable hive of business studies. In the meantime, and since Dr Kerr took over, the former remedial course classroom has been transformed into a computer centre and its pupils 'with special educational needs' have been integrated into the life of the secondary school: structural additions have made this possible.

Grandparents who gravitate Springhill-way nowadays find

themselves bemused by the plethora of computer and technology rooms more reminiscent of a TV space-age programme than a school. But that's not all, for increased funding and staffing have led to the adoption of a system known as Technical and Vocational Education Initiative, which apparently equips students better to enter employment by providing them with more practical application of skills and knowledge than heretofore, engendering more initiative, motivation and enterprise and giving them direct contact with the world of work — equal opportunities for male and female. It's a wonderful world! No more the three 'Rs' but TVEI.

And yet with all its futuristic flamboyance, education may be edging towards its earlier evolutionary ethos. Back to School Boards (remember them?) with parents deciding what's to be done, how much it will cost and who's who! Teacher assessment and even 'opting out' of the local authority would mean only that 'Bonnington Academy' reverted to its earlier penny-pinching status of semi-independence. The High School Magazine was last issued in 1980; in its place have appeared countless columns in the local newspaper from the pen of Mr Morton or Dr Kerr. But, if you really want to be updated on all the High School miscellanea, get hold of a recent prospectus, a comprehensive compendium which tells all — very similar to the annual prospectus with all its minutiae provided by Dr Pringle over eighty years ago. As for 'testing', the very word summons the spectre of the old Qualifying Exam which divided pupils into A, B and C — yet it is to return, according to the latest dictum of the Secretary of State for Education (in London!). National testing of every primary-IV and -VII pupil in Scotland has now been imposed, plus a common curriculum from ages five to fourteen, presumably followed by yet another test at the end of the second-year secondary.

So as the story of education unfolds and we are once again in a 'Nineties' situation, it would appear that history repeats itself and that politicians and parents have taken from the professionals the torch of learning. The revolution has indeed completed its circle: *Plus ça change, plus c'est la même chose.*

Sources:

EIS, *The Scottish Educational Journal* (November 1988)
Halyrude Infant School [St Joseph's since 1973] Log Books, 1950 – 89

Kingsland School Log Books, 1950 – 73 (thereafter discontinued)
Peebles High School Log Books, 1950 – 75 (thereafter discontinued)
Peebles High School Magazines, 1950 – 80 (thereafter discontinued)
Priorsford School Log Book, 1973 – 89
Scotland, James, *The History of Scottish Education*
Peeblesshire News — especially *Peebles High School Supplement* (July 1972)
The Scotsman educational articles and *The Weekend Scotsman* — e.g. December 1975 – May 1989
Scottish Education Department 'Standard Grade', 1984
Scottish Education Department's 'Building Study' ('Open Plan') for Kingsland School

CHAPTER 12

Social Life

Ye may gaun east,
Or you may gaun west,
If on the hunt for treasure;
But Peebles beats the very best,
If ye be oot for pleasure.

THESE LINES WERE proudly quoted by Robert W. Jack of Edderston Farm — an enthusiastic supporter of the March Riding and a popular Cornet in 1924 — when he was interviewed on Richard Dimbleby's *Down Your Way* on the BBC's Light Programme one Sunday afternoon in late January 1951. It was a widely acclaimed radio programme and on this occasion it featured Peebles and the verse referred to had appeared at the top of the West Linton Agricultural Society's Show poster in the early 1900s. 'Clayboddie', in days long past, was famed for his rhyming on the Yarrow Show posters, and the late Fred Dyson, who had been Secretary of the West Linton Show, thought he would go one better so he approached Robert Watson and these lines were written for that purpose.'[1]

The radio programme was about the life of the town and the surrounding area, and included interviews with Miss Agnes Brunton, a darner in the March Street Mills; William Hunna, a yarn store foreman at Damdale and Bailie J. P. Duthie, of Lowe, Donald & Co. while J. Walter Buchan, the former Town Clerk, told listeners about the town's traditions and its history, and Miss E. B. Turner, physiotherapist, and W. B. Brown, Secretary and Resident Manager, spoke about the Peebles Hotel Hydro which was in the process of re-establishing itself as one of the leading hotels in the country with the ending of the Food Control Regulations and petrol restrictions. Mr J. Wilson, a champion sheepdog trialist, was also introduced to the radio audience. In the days before television made sheepdog trials popular viewing, both J. Wilson of Whitehope, Innerleithen, and D. Murray of Glenbield, Peebles, were making their way into the leading ranks of the sheepdog-trial world during the 1930s. After the war David Murray was still an active competitor and won the *Daily Express* international two-day sheepdog trials in June 1963, winning the supreme championship trophy when at the age of 73 he was the oldest competitor!

However, the idyllic 'pre-war picture' broadcast in 1951 about Peebles and its settled life of work and social activities was about to end. Sadly, a series of radical changes lay ahead and one after the other they created an air of uncertainty as each event seemed to threaten the quality of life for the town and its townspeople: the closure of the town's two railways; changes in the ownership of the woollen-mills with larger outside firms becoming involved; the disastrous fire at the Tweedside Mill which preceded the closure of the Damdale Mill; and then the insidious policy of 'regionalisation' which effectively down-graded the town as an administrative centre, culminating in the 'reorganisation of local government' which finally removed the autonomy of the Royal and Ancient Burgh, with its town council being replaced by the Tweeddale District Council.

The years immediately after the war gave no indication of these pending changes; indeed, the town and Peebles folk were in good heart. The town was said to be 'more strongly on its feet', because the captains of our main industry had 'kept the wheels going', as the *Peeblesshire News* reported at the time. There was plenty of work for all and the general well-being of the town seemed to be more secure than it was in the days of the 1930s. There was clearly a local determination to get things back to the way they once were and to throw off the wartime restrictions. No private or municipal houses had been built during the war and as discussed earlier, the supply of housing was the most pressing local social need. The town council quickly reacted to the situation and had acquired, in 1946, thirty-two prefabricated houses to be erected at Kingsland Square. These two-bedroom houses were delivered on to the site in sections and came equipped with a range of well-designed fitments that were generally not available at that time and these were greatly admired and envied.

Fourteen traditional houses were also built at Buchan Gardens, four at Eliot's Park, twenty-four at the site of the old Auction Mart and a start made on one of the largest housing schemes ever tackled in the burgh as twelve houses were erected at Kingsmeadows. By 1950 there were eighty-four houses built or in the course of erection and it was a good start to the post-war period, reflecting well on the early initiatives taken by the town council and its officers.

The Peebles Hotel Hydro also responded quickly to the opportunity of getting back to business and it was reopened during August 1946, only four months after being de-requisitioned. It took a little longer to restore the Chambers Town Hall as a venue for public functions. Immediately after the war this had been a store for building materials which were in short supply as it was prudent policy to obtain these supplies whenever they became available so that there would be no delay in the building programme. The building needed extensive restoration, having inevitably suffered damage during this time and when used as a canteen for the troops before that. The virtually new tip-up seating, belonging to the Royal Burgh Cinema, had been removed in 1942-43 and sold towards the cost of reopening the Empire Cinema which had been destroyed by fire. The post-war restoration work completely transformed the hall from its pre-war cinema days replacing the old elevated flooring and reconverting the balcony to its original use as a stage. The cost for the work was largely met by a donation from the Town's Entertainments Committee with money raised from local dances.

The editor of the *Peeblesshire News* — the redoubtable guardian of local tradition, Will Kerr — in a strongly-worded leader, admonished Peebleans against the growing tendency for the 'Chambers Town Hall' being referred to as the 'Burgh Town Hall'. Taking this admonition to heart, it was appropriately reopened on 8 September 1950 to mark the 150th anniversary of the birth of William Chambers.

In 1953, despite the attractions of radio and the early days of television, Peebles folk turned out to celebrate the occasion of the Coronation. There was an Eve of Coronation Dance in the Drill Hall, a united service in the Parish Church on Coronation Day, a children's treat in the afternoon in Whitestone Park which was followed by an Old Folk's Tea, open-air dancing, bonfire on Morning Hill, fireworks at Kerfield Park and another dance on Coronation Night. It was hoped that the accession of our young Queen Elizabeth would herald the start of a bright and enterprising future for the country — and the ascent of Mount Everest was seen as a glorious start to this new era!

The 'Elizabethan Age' did not, however, herald great new endeavours or bring about an economic transformation but it did boost the age of television. The ceremony of the Queen's Coronation was televised and those without a receiving set crowded into the Chambers Town Hall where a television was provided by T. Watson Bracewell. Viewers witnessed the unique ceremony in Westminster Abbey and were caught up in the happy atmosphere of the huge crowds cheering the royal procession.

Over the years in the decades that followed, it seemed that the people of Peebles, whilst remaining in their homes, could be at any of the great events wherever and whenever they were taking place. Inevitably, television, with its compulsive attraction, dominated the leisure time of the family and this consequently had an effect on the social life of the town as it led to a gradual decline in organising and supporting local events during the 1960s and seventies. A well-supported programme of events had always played a part in the general well-being of the town and Peebles, in the decades after the Second World War, owes a great debt of gratitude to the dedicated leadership of the March Riding and Beltane Festival Committee for keeping alive a strong sense of community by maintaining and not curtailing the traditional programme associated with the Beltane festivities.

Whilst some reassurance may be gained from the idea that in the late 1980s the impact of television is diminishing and that there is now a renewed awareness of the enjoyment and unique pleasure of participating in community activities, nevertheless the history of the social life of the burgh shows that the festivities in June each year are a necessary and well-established pivot around which the quality of life in Peebles revolves. The March Riding and Beltane events provide momentum, setting a standard of organisation as a pattern for the community to follow, and their importance has never been more crucial as Peebles moves into the last decade of the present century and sets course for the years of the twenty-first.

Returning to the first years of peace, it was a time when everyone was having to accept much of the austerity and shortages of the war. The *Peeblesshire News* wrote in 1952: 'The nation had endured much during the War and whilst these hardships were gladly accepted as necessary, we lived in hope that when peace came matters would improve.' In time, the restrictions slowly melted away

219

and the deprivation of earlier years was miraculously forgotten, as rationing ended and sweets, eggs and clothing could be readily purchased and the 'utility' range of furnishings gave way to a wider choice of furniture for the home.

It was recognised during these early post-war years that many young people held the expectation of a brighter future than a life centred on the tweed-mills and were seeking employment and career opportunities outside the town. Some left Peebles to make a life overseas and it was at this time that a 'little corner' of Peebles became established in Perth, Western Australia, where their 'Peebles Society' has maintained strong links with the Auld Burgh Toon.

Changes wrought by the passing of time were sadly brought home to those who had grown up in the town during the 1920s and thirties as they mourned the loss of 'Auld Worthies true and guid'. These men and women had contributed a great deal to the life of the town and their passing signified the end of the pre-1939 era. They included many notable 'leaders of local affairs'. Provost John Fergusson, a fishmonger in the Northgate, will be remembered as a very fine provost of Peebles (1933 – 45) who died in 1949. George Anderson, who died in 1951, was provost from 1926 to 1933 and was the founder of the Castle Warehouse. William Cleland, a freelance reporter, died in 1952; he had a long association with local government and education in the burgh and was provost from 1945 to 1949. Robert Johnston was a well-known baker and an equally respected bailie. A story that always brought a warm smile concerned the poacher who appeared in the Magistrates Court and was fined five shillings. The offender quickly retorted to Bailie Johnston: 'Ah! weel, Bailie, you can stop delivering my rolls for a fortnight!'

A true 'worthy' was the former Pipe-Major John Sterricks who died in 1953, aged seventy-three, having held that rank in the 6th Volunteer Battalion The Royal Scots and with the 1/8th Royal Scots during the First World War. Peebles will always be grateful to him for starting the local Federation of Ex-Servicemen's Pipe Band which was more commonly known as 'Jock Sterrick's Pipe Band'. A recording of the sounds of Peebles during the 1930s would surely bring back to mind the sound of the bagpipes drifting down from Venlaw Hill on a summer evening as Jock Sterricks played his pipes — often it was the stirring tune of a march but sometimes it was a lament that in fond retrospect seemed as if Peebles was weeping for its sons of the First World War that 'lay not beside the silvery Tweed but near some foreign stream'.

Daniel (Danny) Shiels was also a founder-member of the Ex-Servicemen's Pipe Band and he died in 1950 aged eighty-six. He had served with the 1st Battalion the King's Own Scottish Borderers and had been awarded the Medal and Bar for the Chin-Lushai Campaign in 1889/90 when he saw service under the command of Lord Roberts. Alf Dodds was another well-known musician who died that same year, an accomplished violinist and the musical director of the Peebles Philharmonic Society Orchestra. He was also an expert angler and his advice was readily available in the 'angler's emporium' that was part of the jeweller's business that he and his brother George carried on in the Eastgate and which had been started by their father, William Dodds.

William J. Whitie, who died in 1954, was a member of a long-established and respected business family. He was an accomplished pianist and secretary of the Peebles Choral Union, another of that distinguished group who did so much to encourage musical interests in the town. Three other outstanding men also enriched local life. Steve Howitt was a well-loved entertainer who gave fifty years of happiness to the townsfolk, died in 1957. James A. Scott will also be associated with the bringing of the cinema to Peebles at the time when he was regarded as the country's 'leading cinematographist'; he died in 1962. And William (Will) Kerr died in 1963 which was a great blow to Peebles; an account of his distinguished work as the editor of the *Peeblesshire News* is recorded in Chapter 19.

Peebles also mourned the loss of two highly respected 'leaders': James Walter Buchan died in 1954 and Lieut.-Colonel William Thorburn, DSO, TD, in 1959. The three volumes of *A History of Peeblesshire,* published in 1925 and 1927, are an outstanding memorial to Walter Buchan's love and service to the royal burgh and to Tweeddale. 'Colonel Willie' Thorburn, with a long and successful career in the management of Lowe, Donald & Co, had a unique place in the affections of the men of the town, having commanded the 1/8th Royal Scots during the First World War. He took a leading role in local defence activities during the Second World War and was appointed Lord-Lieutenant of Peeblesshire in 1945.

Miss Mary Bonong and Miss C. Williamson, both of whom had the honour of 'crowning the Beltane Queen', were greatly respected and their passing in 1958 was marked with great sadness. Miss Bonong was cherished for her kindly way with the infants at Halyrude School — a kindness that is still remembered by men and women who are now in their sixties and seventies — whilst for thirty-one years, Miss Williamson had been an outstanding burgh chamberlain held in the highest regard by town councillors and ratepayers alike for her tremendous efficiency and management of the town's treasury.

Another part of the changing scene of the town's life was the closing of the Empire Cinema in January 1954 due to the lack of patronage and in the same year the *Peeblesshire Advertiser* ended its long life of service having lost much of its commercial strength during the war. By 1969 the Playhouse Cinema was changing and there were bingo sessions on Tuesday and Thursday evenings. When these changes occurred they were all accepted as being inevitable casualties of the times, but there was quite a different reaction when the decisions were announced by British Rail that they were closing down the local railways.

The Peebles to Symington branch railway closed in June 1950 but freight was carried for a time until the goods depot was closed down nine years later. In February 1962 the railway line between Eskbank, Peebles and Galashiels was also closed, despite an attempt to run diesel trains to reduce the cost of the service. On the occasion of each announcement there was great concern about the 'viciousness of the stroke' as this was not what the people of Peebles expected of nationalisation! A fear was felt about the burgh's ability to maintain its quality of life — a quality that was identified with the facilities the railways had brought to Peebles in 1855 — and there was a belief that the future would be bleak for the town having to rely solely on the motor car and road-transport services.

The days of the train in Peebles are now gone but certainly not forgotten are the great 'train events' like the mill trips. Amongst the last of these was when the employees of the March Street Mills went to Butlins at the Heads of Ayr in 1951 and again in 1953 when they went to Gourock and Rothesay Bay. There are memories, too, of the family outings on the 'Big Trips' organised each year by the Special Constables; the years of the Sunday School picnics, more often than not entrained for Stobo; and the crowded evening excursion-trains with their cheaper fares. The generations of the 1930s will be able to recall the activity at the LNER station heralding the arrival and departure of trains, particularly the busy train which arrived in

Peebles during the early evening; the atmosphere of the station platform with its well-stocked newspaper kiosk and the array of chocolate and letter-punching machines; the parcel trolleys being noisily trundled along the platform into position ready for the goods van and near to them the post office trolley with the mail bags to be exchanged for the incoming mail for Peebles and district; whilst outside the station, in its usual stance, was the Hydro bus, resplendent in its livery of gold and brown.

Despite the loss of the railways in 1962 there was a momentum about the late 1950s and early 1960s as people in the town became better paid and there was a reduction in the hours of the working week. Local shops during these 'boom' years sold many new luxurious gas and electrical gadgets for the kitchen and there emerged a revolutionary change in what became to be regarded as 'necessities' for a household. In Britain washing-machines were installed in 10 per cent of households in the early 1950s but this had increased to 64 per cent by 1971. Over the same period, the installation of refrigerators had risen from about 8 per cent to 69 per cent whilst television sets rose from 11 per cent to 91 per cent by 1971. The expansion of car ownership really began in the 1950s with 2.3 million cars and vans rapidly increasing during the 1960s to just over 9 million, and to 11.8 million by 1970.[2]

Despite the material improvement in the standard of living, these were uncertain times. Although the local newspaper was reporting in 1962 that the town's 'staple industry carries on despite the departure of the railways', there was in 1960 the surprise announcement that the March Street Mills were no longer to remain under the control of the Ballantyne family. This change was unexpected and the cause of considerable regret throughout Peebles, although there was some consolation that the new owners would be Scottish — Hugh Fraser's Scottish & Universal Investments Limited. However, the workforce were reassured about the effects the change might have when it became known that Henry B. Ballantyne would remain as the chairman. Nevertheless it was only a matter of time before there was another change in the ownership and, resulting from this and from the installation of highly mechanised machinery, the number employed at these mills is now 160 compared with the 350 or so that once passed through the March Street entrance and the Dovecot gates.

Having come to terms with the idea of 'outside' owners at the

PART III: 1950 – 1990

March Street Mills, Peebles faced up to another major set-back to its established pattern of industrial life when the Tweedside Mill was completely gutted by fire during the early evening of Monday, 6 February 1965. The fast and furious blaze lit up the whole town and the mill was virtually rased to the ground within a matter of two hours — but there was a great sense of relief that no lives were lost and that the neighbouring Parish Church had escaped damage. This destruction put about seventy spinners out of work, but they were given kind consideration and received full pay until alternative arrangements were made to find them work in the company's other mills. The town was delighted when the Thorburn management quickly reassured everyone that another yarn-spinning mill would be built on a new site in Peebles.

However, the Damdale and Tweedside Mills were already in a consortium with other Border woollen-mills and the decision was no longer one to be made solely by the former local owners but by Roberts, Thorburn & Noble. Six months after the fire, RTN acquired a mill at Linthwaite, near Huddersfield, and announced that they had decided against building a new woollen-mill in Peebles. The consortium of George Roberts & Co. Ltd, Walter Thorburn Bros. & Co. Ltd, and Robert Noble & Co. Ltd, said: 'Sheer economics left us no alternative.'

This was deeply disappointing news for Peebles and sadly it heralded the end of work at the Damdale Mills. They closed down during the last months of 1967, when alternative employment was offered at the March Street and Innerleithen Mills of Henry Ballantyne & Sons. It was a grievous loss to the town and to the way of life that it had known and valued since 1869 when Damdale was built. Many generations of Damdale workers could tell of the happy comradeship that had existed in all the departments, and the undoubted pride they had taken in the quality of the cloth they produced for Walter Thorburn and for the succeeding generations of his family.

Despite the loss of its railway and two of its woollen-mills, Peebles did not allow itself to look 'run down'. Instead, the town showed a spirit of enterprise in response to these unfortunate events by developing the former sites of the woollen-mills and the railway stations and brought about attractive changes for the benefit of its inhabitants. In 1963 there was a belief that tourism was an 'infant local industry' and this also highlighted the importance of making

224

these changes, as they were entirely supportive of the idea that visitors could make an important contribution to the local economy if the town retained its attractiveness as a beautiful and historic place.

An imaginative change took place at the former LNER site as the station and its railway track gave way to a greatly improved road system that could cope with the flow of traffic that had increased so much since the end of the Second World War. In making this change it opened up a splendid new vista to show the lower aspect of Venlaw Hill, which became the location for a number of additional private houses. Similarly, the Caledonian station, with its yard and railway tracks, provided ground for many new houses and some of these had facilities for the disabled. The changes made possible an enhanced approach from Ninian's Haugh and Tweed Bridge to the south side of the river and to the pathway up the south bank leading to the Fotheringham Bridge and Hay Lodge Park. The removal of the railway track and the provision of a car and coach-park, with its entrance from Kingsmeadows Road, opened up the accessibility of Ninian's Haugh with Tweed Green, these improvements enhancing the setting for the River Tweed as it flowed through the town.

Equal enterprise was shown in adapting the Tweedside Mill site which was acquired and developed, along with the old gas works area, to provide a new swimming pool. The beautiful landscaped entrance-area, leading to the pathway along the north bank of the River Tweed, provides a lovely walk from the town to Hay Lodge Park. It is an imaginative use of the site and has proved an asset to the town's life that benefits Peebleans and visitors alike.

Damdale Mill was also demolished and a new vista opened up from the Cuddy Bridge which showed splendid new houses and provided a pathway along the Cuddy where the old dam used to be. It also opened up the approach to historic Biggiesknowe.

> Look o'er to St Andrews and what see we there
> But a Gutterbluid lad in a Professor's Chair,
> And Chambers we have only to mention his name
> Baith Biggiesknowe Callants well known to fame.[3]

Some twenty-five years after the end of the Second World War, the town stretched out from Rosetta to Gallowhill, developed in a way that showed flair and vision. It was an attractive place to visit and equally it was still a wonderful place to live . . . even if you had to travel to work in Edinburgh, Galashiels or elsewhere.

PART III: 1950 – 1990

There had been a decline in the number of people living in Peebles during the ten years to 1961 — the first time there had been a drop in the population since 1851. The census of 1961 showed a reduction to 5,548, a decline at the rate of 7.8 per cent when compared with 6,013 in 1951; in 1971 the figure was 5,884 (an increase of 6 per cent); by 1981 it had increased by 14 per cent to a new high of 6,705.

In the years before Peebles suffered the reduction in its woollen industry, the mills for a time in the 1960s had great difficulty in recruiting adequate levels of female labour and in 1963 an 'overspill agreement' was made with the Corporation of Glasgow in an endeavour to attract families to live in Peebles and help reduce the shortage of women workers. In addition to the Glasgow families taking up residence at Kingsmeadows, where a number of houses had been specially built for their occupation, there was an increasing tendency for 'incomers' to the burgh buying up newly-built private houses. Peebles was now being regarded as an attractive dormitory town and this development was seen as a threat to close-knit social life. Although as time passed there was a tacit acceptance of the overspill agreement, the 'dormitory' aspect of the town's development has always been resisted, with the townsfolk keeping a watchful eye on each new development proposal.

Letters to the editor in December 1989 commenting on planning applications connected with three major private housing developments, indicated that local opinion was clearly opposed to these schemes with their 'up-market' houses that would encourage more dormitory families to live in the town. The real concern was that these developments would exert even more pressure on local property prices, pushing them out of the reach of local people and causing young Peebleans to leave Peebles to find affordable housing elsewhere.

The *Peeblesshire News,* in highlighting the housing problem during 1989, reported there were 227 families or individuals on the waiting-list for a vacant tenancy occurring at any of the 801 council houses in Peebles. During the 1980s, young local married couples wanting to live in the town had to wait something like two-and-a-half years before they could get a house to rent and during that long wait they had little prospect of purchasing a suitable property at a price they could afford. That is why the current development at the

226

Cuddy-Bridgegate corner site (Provost Walker Court) is widely welcomed, as it will provide twenty-six flats for single persons and couples.

The town gradually adapted to its role as a tourist centre as a number of the larger houses — Minden, Dilkusha, Lee Lodge, Kingsmuir — became hotels and other property owners provided differing forms of residential accommodation. Peebles had always attracted visitors, even before the advent of the railways, but now in an age when there was much more leisure time and also a growing proportion of retired people with the means to enjoy holiday breaks, the town's closeness to both Edinburgh and Glasgow made it a popular place to visit and to shop. It was also well-placed as a centre for touring the Border country and its close proximity to Scotland's capital city was an added facility for visitors from overseas and other parts of the United Kingdom.

Peebles folk were also becoming tourists as the 'affluent society' provided the means for more extensive travelling and holidays. Car ownership had become more general and touring was a popular pursuit — sometimes with a caravan in tow — whilst television advertising boosted the attractiveness of 'holiday packages' to foreign resorts.

The long 58½-hour working week in the woollen-mills at the start of the twentieth century, from 6 a.m. to 6 p.m. with the two forty-five-minute breaks during weekdays and from 6 a.m. to 12 noon on Saturdays, gave way to a forty-five-hour week in the 1960s (7.45 a.m. to 5 p.m. with one break of forty-five minutes).[4] Today it is thirty-nine hours (7.30 a.m. to 4.30 p.m. with a break of forty-five minutes each Monday to Thursday; 7.30 a.m. to 1.30 p.m. on Friday). Weekly wages for men in 1906 were 27s 7d (£1.38) and women earned 18s 6d (92½p) whilst today men and women are paid at the same rate of £110 to £120 per week in 1989, excluding shift allowance.[5]

'The car' absorbed part of the leisure time and became a new hobby as it extended the range of visiting for the family and enabled participation in a wide range of social events; this often involved 'ferrying' members of the family to their various interests. Car maintenance and cleaning also became an essential part of the new hobby, being tackled with various degrees of enthusiasm.

As the post-war decades progressed there was more time for relaxing and participating in sport. More people played golf; bowling, too, gained in popularity and during 1989 the Peebles Bowling Club celebrated its 160th anniversary in strong heart. Sadly, the Peebles Quoiting Club closed down in 1950 due to a lack of interest, despite having been provided with a new ground at the Gytes Park. There is still a strong curling interest in the town though now mostly on indoor rinks. Perhaps the most notable change is the greatly increased participation in rugby and the number of local XVs that the town can now field. A fuller account of the activities of the local associations and sporting clubs over the years will be found in Chapters 17 and 18.

The quality of Peebles life in the 'leisure society' of the 1980s is well reflected in the activities of the Arts Festival which brings together various Border crafts from violin-making to wood-carving, spinning and knitting to calligraphy. The Hobbies Exhibition shows the interest being taken in embroidery, lace-making, stained-glass, photography, book-binding, painting, wood-turning and fly-tying, not to mention activities of the Tweed Theatre, the Floral Art Club, the Camera Club and other societies.

In the 1930s and forties the level of local crime, perhaps more aptly referred to as 'misdemeanour', could be judged from the annual figures produced for Peeblesshire giving the number of persons locked-up overnight in police cells; and over the years these ranged from between fifty-four to eighty-two persons each year — about one person per week. In the 1920s many householders did not feel the need to lock their front doors but it became prudent to do so as time went by and today many houses have installed burglar alarms. Local newspaper reports during recent decades show a regular pattern of occurrences involving the occasional house burglary and the more frequent petty disturbance as well as the almost inevitable range of traffic offences and car break-ins. The incident level is neither a matter for satisfaction nor for too great a concern when compared with other towns.

A matter of concern over the years for households in Peebles, as elsewhere in the country, has been the acceleration in the cost-of-living. However, it was not just prices that drastically changed but also shopping habits, with self-service shops taking over from the traditional grocers. J. L. Renwick & Sons in the Old Town, founded in 1899, was one of the first to adapt to self-service when it became the Centra Licensed Grocers. The Centra organisation consisted of a large number of grocers who owned their own shops but acted together to purchase their requirements in bulk and thereby with low self-service overheads the shoppers were able to buy at keener prices.

'Fine Fare' (later changed to 'Gateway') became established in the town when it was opened by Miss Andrea Currie on 2 April 1984, providing shoppers with a major self-service supermarket. It was built on the site of 'Glencorse House' in the Northgate, which was the location of the first bank in Peebles and then became the residence and surgery of Dr G. Harper Wilson and later of Dr Robin Wilson. This supermarket provides a wide range of merchandise and is well patronised. It is good to note, however, that many of the town's shops still provide a counter service and this custom still gives pleasure to local shoppers as well as being an attractive way to look after the needs of the visitors.

Most homes have become equipped with refrigerators and many have freezers as well, enabling Peebles households to pursue their own form of 'bulk buying'. Shopkeepers nowadays are not expected to provide a delivery service, so the family car has become a necessity for carrying the heavier loads. A major shopping expedition tends to reduce the need for daily visits to the grocers and the butchers, but fortunately there is still a steady pattern of shoppers on most days making their way along the High Street and the Northgate and taking the opportunity of exchanging news and greetings just as Peebleans have always done. This is a particularly important aspect of local social life, and nothing can ever replace it.

The railways have gone and the employment value to the town of the woollen trade is now only about a third of its former capacity; just as these changes have affected the quality of the life of the town so has damage been wrought by the insidious policies of 'centralisation' and 'reorganisation'. These policies made claims about increased efficiency through the creation of larger units of administration that would be more economic to run and control. It is to be hoped that these policies will be reassessed and evaluated on their performance and that there will be a back-trekking to a structure that removes the remoteness of centralised control and a return to good economic performance based on local control and accountability.

It began when the new post office in the Eastgate was 'downgraded' in 1967 and the work of planning the county's detailed services was transferred to Galashiels, the new headquarters. The reasons given for this action were improved economy and efficiency. Also at that time Peebles lost its Ministry of Social Security Office which was replaced by a 'Job Shop' and the new centralised Social

Security Office was established in Galashiels. The police force also reduced its establishment and the importance of the local police station, which was once the county headquarters and the office of Superintendent Ninian Notman, Superintendent Sonny Dickson and Inspector James Attridge.

Even the co-operative movement in 1967 decided on a policy of 'mergers', with the societies of Peebles, Galashiels and Jedburgh becoming the Borders Regional Co-operative Society Ltd. Undoubtedly there were commercial reasons for this happening, but regrettably the Co-op in Peebles today is a mere shadow of its former greatness.

A Royal Commission appointed to inquire into the structure and future of local government led to the Local Government (Scotland) Act, 1973, which replaced county and town councils in Scotland with a structure comprising nine large regions, fifty-one districts and a general-purpose authority for the Orkneys, Shetlands and the Western Isles. Peebles, with Selkirk, Roxburgh and Berwick, formed the Borders Regional Council but of more concern to the future life of Peebles was that it lost its town council in the reorganisation of 1975 and got, in its place, the Tweeddale District Council and a local Community Council.

The autonomy of the people of Peebles to decide their own affairs was removed. In future, what had been done by the former town council with great flair and local understanding, would be subject to the decisions and policy of elected representatives that were not solely accountable to the people of Peebles, even to determining whether or not a street in Peebles should be named to commemorate the late Dr C. B. Gunn. As Will Kerr, in exasperation, would often exclaim in his Tittle-Tattle column: 'Ye Gods and little fishes!'

A major example of the loss of local autonomy to safeguard Peebles' interests was clearly demonstrated when approval was given by the Borders Regional Planning Committee to a planning application for the development of private housing on land which was part of Dunwhinny Lodge Old Folks Home — a local facility dear to the heart of Peebles folk. Despite the justifiably strong views held in the town about the decision and the protests that were forcefully conveyed to the Planning Authority, the substantial weight of local opinion was unable to influence the outcome of this purely local matter.

Other contentious issues which have concerned the people of

Peebles during recent years began with the demolishing of St Andrew's Church at the foot of the Old Town. This was a local decision and one taken by the Church Council but it was a decision that disappointed, as it was the hope of many in the town that this beautiful red sandstone building could have been adapted for other uses that would have benefited the social life of the town.

The second issue which raised local hackles and was strongly debated in 1973 was the proposal to demolish Buchan's House to facilitate the widening of the Cuddy Bridge and make more road space for traffic. A petition was presented by 600 residents against any alteration to the 'House with the Red Door' and they had the support of the Council of the Society of Antiquaries who were at that time expressing concern about major road changes in other burghs and cities in Scotland. However, the bridge could not be widened on the Sheriff Court side because the Parish Church and the Sheriff Court buildings were 'listed' due to their historic interest, but fortunately public opinion prevailed to the extent that the plans were changed so that only a small part of Buchan's House was affected.

The greatly increased volume of cars and lorries that had developed over the years became a major problem and sparked off a debate about the desirability of an 'east-west bypass' to relieve the heavy traffic congestion on the High Street — a hazard to motorists and pedestrians alike! Four hundred attended the meeting, held in the Chambers Town Hall early in 1973, to discuss the matter with the representatives of the Peeblesshire County Council and the Peeblesshire Roads Committee. However, a survey showed that of 554 vehicles counted in the High Street, only 91 were 'by-passable' and that the remaining 463 vehicles per hour in the High Street were due to locally generated traffic. However, it was decided to ease the overall traffic flow by introducing a one-way system at Young Street and Rosetta Road. Fourteen years before this change occurred, Rosetta Road, which is the longest street in the burgh, was by some mischance the last to have electric lighting installed and that took place in 1959.

There were 2,404 (62.1 per cent) households in Tweeddale in 1981 with a car and 845 (35 per cent) of these had at least two.[6] This high proportion of car ownership created a need for more private garages to be built, particularly in high density areas like municipal housing schemes. Most private and council houses were built at a time when a car was a 'pipe dream' for many householders but this modern-day requirement was incorporated in the Violetbank Scheme of 1970 when fifteen garages were provided.

Another result of the increased traffic on the life of the town was the need to provide an improved island for pedestrians and motorists, particularly the drivers of smaller saloon cars, at the busy junction of the High Street and the Eastgate. The plinth for the Mercat Cross was redesigned by Schomberg Scott who retained the beautiful stone setting for the plinth whilst the work was carried out by James Clyde & Sons in 1965.

Another change that went largely unnoticed in 1960, partly through misuse and a reflection of changing times, was the removal of the beautifully-polished granite drinking-well with its brass cup on a chain that was located on the wall of a shop at the top of Bridgegate at 'Cunzie Neuk'. Other old 'Dalek-shaped' drinking-wells have also been removed and now appear as 'decorative' features, one in the small garden in the Northgate and another is to be seen at the Tweed Green.

Whatever else has changed in the social life of Peebles from the pre-1939 years, there has not been any shortage of local leaders. Miss Anne C. Weir, who retired in 1966 after fifty-five years' service with the local Red Cross as a VAD and Detachment Commandant, is a fine example of leadership given to a local cause; and Miss Jessie Ferguson, MBE, who gave forty-four years of service and inspiration to the young people of the town through her life-long interest in the Scout and Cub movement is another notable example. John S. Veitch, who died in 1972, also gave outstanding service to Peebles. He served with 8th Royal Scots during the First World War and was a reserve policeman during Second World War; was a member of Beltane Committee; chairman of Peebles Social Club; served on Peebles Rovers Committee and was a keen footballer, athlete and sportsman; was a founder member of Peebles Entertainments Committee that arranged the 'Hydro Treat' for the elderly people; was Dean of Guild; and Cornet in 1930.

Since the 1960s the town has benefited from Alex Walker's leadership in local government affairs. He has held every elective office as a town councillor and was provost of Peebles from 1967 to 1970. As one of the town's four elected representatives to the Tweeddale District Council he has helped to bridge the transition from the days of the Peebles Town Council to the new District Council and in this capacity he has rendered great service to his native town. Honorary sheriff and honoured in 1971 when he was installed as a Warden of Neidpath, Alex Walker is still involved in virtually every aspect of the town's life.

Douglas Edgar, who died in 1989, was another tireless organiser and worker who was involved in a wide range of local activities, and he earned the unique distinction of being the first Cornet (1950) to be appointed a Warden of Neidpath (1987). John Veitch and Douglas Edgar followed in the splendid tradition of service and leadership that has been the hallmark of ex-Cornets. Renwick Sanderson, too, is another Cornet (1955) who has served Peebles with distinction and his record as a local sportsman is second to none; he played for Peebles Rovers from 1950 and Hibernians (1951 – 53) and has the unique record of having scored 550 goals.

Peebles took pride, too, in the fine example and inspiration given by James Veitch, who turned to writing in 1949 when the door of his tweed warehouse was closed to him and who, by 1952, had written four novels. His acclaim as a novelist maintained the town's literary heritage and brought credit again to the local name of 'Veitch'.

The town's local institutions have been sustained throughout the years by the enthusiasm and service given by men and women like Mrs Kempsell, who served for sixteen years with the local branch of the Scottish Old Age Pension Association; like Neil Brown, Donald Johnston and T. Yule, who each received in 1969 the long service medal of the Scottish Amateur Band Association for their fifty years' service with the Peebles Silver Band; and like countless others who have been the mainstay of local clubs and activities. The quality of voluntary service shines through the town's tradition of kindness and generosity for local causes and charities and it is to the Peebles lasses that tribute must be paid for their unstinted enthusiasm in support of the numerous annual events with their coffee mornings and other fund-raising activities.

Another Peeblean who was greatly admired was William W. Howitt. Warden of Neidpath in 1976, he was an outstanding Chairman of the Peebles March Riding and Beltane Queen Festival from 1982 to 1984. He had the charisma of his father, Steve Howitt, and was in the same 'Peeblean mould' as Will Kerr — each of them loved and thoroughly entered into the spirit of the Beltane and they were loth to let the enjoyment and sing-song end. Willie Howitt's late evening 'gathering' in a local hostelry at the conclusion of the Beltane Week would have pleased the 'worthies' of auld land syne with its

PART III: 1950 – 1990

spirited renderings of the Beltane Song and 'Come ower the hills tae Peebles'.

Institutions like the Peebles Guildry Corporation and the Peebles Callants, with their succession of distinguished Deans of Guild and Chief Callants, continue to flourish in the 1980s. They still meet to enjoy a 'wee drappie o't' and like to have their evening of song and sentiment. Perhaps the local minstrels — and there are many, as in former years! — will add to their repertoire of local ballads which currently includes the tale of the 'Dalathie and North Street Gangs', by including songs about that day in April 1989, when HRH The Duchess of York 'dropped in' for tea with twenty-two-month-old Rhianna Scott and her parents at 50A Rosetta Road; or tell about the occasion when Cornet Andrew Williamson and the Beltane Queen of Peebles (Sarah McGrath), resplendent in her regalia, were presented to HM The Queen and HRH The Duke of Edinburgh on the occasion of the royal visit to Peebles on 1 July 1988; or about the visit by HRH The Princess Royal to Cuddyside in September 1990 to open 'Provost Walker Court'.

The *Peeblesshire News* in 1969 paid tribute to the life of a very popular mill-worker, James (Sykes) Miller, who had joined the Royal Scots early in the First World War when he was under the age of eighteen. He was recognised as a fine cricketer and notable footballer, having played with Hearts and as a trialist for Scotland, but, above all, Sykes Miller was described as a man who 'loved to joke, laugh and no trouble ever daunted him'.

These fine qualities of courage, humour and undaunted spirit sum up the characteristics of generations of Peeblean men and women who, in their day, have been the 'architects and soul of the town'.

Footnotes:

1. *Peeblesshire News,* January – February 1951
2. Marwick, Arthur, *British Society since 1945* (The Pelican Social History of Britain, Middlesex, 1984) p121
3. Poet Tait, Peebles Gutterbluid Club Minutes, dated 2 February 1905
4. Bulloch, J. P. B. (ed), *Third Statistical Account of Scotland: The Counties of Peebles and Selkirk* (Glasgow, 1964)
5. Birchall, D. J.
6. Borders Regions in Figures, 1988 – 9

Part Four

CHAPTER 13

The Law and The Lawyers of Peebles

PEEBLES, as a royal burgh and the county town of a large, though sparsely populated, area had perforce, and understandably, its fair complement of lawyers from 'a long time back'.

Their designations varied — Writers to the Signet, Writers, Law Agents, Solicitors — or known to many as simply their 'man of business', these lawyers practising in Peebles were all solicitors — that was, and still is, their qualification and justification of their right to practise the law. From 1672 there exist direct traceable records of Peeblesshire lawyers, through apprenticeships initially, generation to generation, giving unbroken connections down to the lawyers who practise in the town today — over 300 years later.

Certainly in Peebles, and probably in most similar towns throughout Scotland, they (or some at least) invariably served three almost separate functions. First, they practised the law for all who needed advice; they made wills; they carried through all executry business to wind up and distribute a person's estate on his death; they bought and sold property and dealt with the all-important transfer of title to all such property; they represented anyone who so required it in court, whether defending a criminal charge or pursuing a civil action for 'A' against 'B'; and, in general, were available to all to give help whether a person could afford to pay or not (the latter under the age-old Scottish Poors Law, where representation at least, and much else was done for nothing).

Second, several throughout the years became clerks to the county or burgh councils (or their predecessors such as the Commissioners of Supply — or The Roads and Highways or The Education authorities), running the whole administration for these bodies.

Third, with the advent of banks in the town in the 1820 – 40 period — initially The British Linen Company, The City of Glasgow Bank and the Union Bank, one (or more jointly) were appointed agents (i.e. managers) of these banks.

All these three functions they carried out simultaneously from their individual offices, which thus came to be established in one of the several bank buildings — the 'Bank Chambers' or offices above or behind the bank itself and with, in some cases, also in the same building a bank house.

For well over one hundred years there were basically three separate such banks at any one time and so partnerships of lawyers developed, each based on the chambers of the respective bank of which one or more partners in that firm acted, in addition to his law practice, as the 'bank agent.'

John Welsh of Mossfennan was the first agent of The British Linen Company (later Bank) when it arrived in Peebles in the early 1820s — situated in what became Glencorse House in the Northgate. He was followed in his practice and in the bank by a William Stuart and William Blackwood I who came to Peebles in 1839, and this was the foundation of the firm of Stuart & Blackwood, later Blackwood & Smith.

John Bathgate, to 1864, and his nephew James Bathgate, to 1881, were concerned with the Union Bank in the building at the N.W. corner of the High Street with Cuddy Bridge, and practised latterly as Bathgate & Stevenson. In 1881 John Buchan, grandfather of the 1st Lord Tweedsmuir, became agent for The Commercial Bank, successor to The Union Bank, and moved then into what later became known simply as 'Bank House'. He, who until then had previously practised from premises further east along the High Street, was founder of the firm of J. & W. Buchan.

Robert Thorburn of Springwood in 1867, or very shortly after, succeeded his father who had been agent for the City of Glasgow Bank, although not a solicitor and later, from 1857, agent for its successor the Bank of Scotland. Robert Thorburn was the founder of the firm of Thorburn & Lyon.

Each of these three firms survives to this day and with an occasional exception, all the Peebles lawyers in the last one hundred years were in partnerships constituting one or other of these firms. In the case of Buchan's and Thorburn & Lyon, there were periods of a 'sole partner' (however much that may appear as a contradiction in terms).

To give a short account of the thirty or so lawyers who practised

238

their profession in Peebles in the last one hundred and fifty years it is thus simplest to treat them by firms.

Blackwood & Smith is the oldest of the three, and throughout has been the largest firm. It dates, as stated, from the first of three generations of Blackwood, William Blackwood I who came to Peebles in 1839. Direct roots or connections through John Welsh (qv) 1786–1843 go back, as mentioned, to 1672. Agents from John Welsh's time for the British Linen Company, William Stuart and William Blackwood (1843) were the first of the firm's long line of partners to be agents for that bank right on to 1965.

Initially called Stuart & Blackwood (which included latterly William Blackwood II), after William Stuart and William Blackwood I's deaths in 1881 and 1884 respectively, the firm became, following the assumption of John Ramsay Smith in 1884, Blackwood & Smith. First in the bank chambers in the Northgate, it moved with the bank to its still-present site at 39 High Street about 1887. William II died in 1892 while John Ramsay Smith continued in practice until 1947, a period of sixty-three years. A second partner, Robert A. Milne, served almost as long — 1893 to 1944 — and with the assumption of William Blackwood III and Alexander Fyfe, it became, from just post-First World War, and remained, a four-partner firm, with only short exceptions, for the next sixty years.

In 1947 Robert Weir Goodburn, and in 1949 James Gordon Fyfe, both returning from the Second World War, were assumed as partners and made up the continuing four-partner firm. William Blackwood III (full name actually William Thorburn Blackwood) died in 1957. Alexander Fyfe retired in 1965. Aged 82 at retirement, he was thought to be one of the last old-time lawyer-cum-bank agents in Scotland. He died aged 94 in 1978. R. W. Goodburn, latterly Clerk of the Peace and an Honorary Sheriff-Substitute, retired in 1979 and died in 1980.

J. G. Fyfe was a Deputy Lieutenant of the county and held numerous other local appointments during his years of practice. He retired in 1983, leaving the business in the hands of the next generation, the present partners (now six in number) William M. Goodburn (1969), David G. Fyfe (1971), Donald C. Strathairn (1976), Morris Anderson (1981), Patricia Watson and Alan H. Blair (both 1983). Patricia Watson has the distinction of being the first woman solicitor to have practised in Peebles.

Three generations of Blackwood, three of Fyfe and two of

Goodburn (who were linked back by marriage to R. A. Milne) give a fair continuity.

Blackwoods I and II, J. Ramsay Smith and then Blackwood III were all clerks to the county council — 'County Clerks' — until that office became a full-time appointment in 1936. All general administration and finance of the county council was done until then in or through the Blackwood & Smith office for not much short of one hundred years.

John Buchan, grandfather of the 1st Lord Tweedsmuir and of J. Walter Buchan, was born in Kincardine in 1811. He is first recorded as being a 'Procurator before the Court of Law' in Peebles in 1851. He lived and presumably practised from a house/office half way along the north side of the High Street. His second son, William (born 1851) ultimately joined his father in the 1870/80 decade to found the firm of J. & W. Buchan.

It was in 1881 that the Buchan father and son took over the previous firm of Bathgate & Stevenson of which the two Bathgates — uncle (John) and nephew (James) had been agents for the Union Bank at 90 High Street. John Bathgate, Town Clerk 1853 – 63, went to New Zealand where he became Judge Bathgate. James, Town Clerk 1863 – 1880, ceased practice when The Union Bank gave way to the Commercial Bank and when the Buchan firm took over the practice and became agents for the Commercial Bank. It was then that the first Buchan connection with the later Bank House (and its famous red door) first started.

John Buchan died in 1883 and following the death of William in 1906, his nephew, James Walter Buchan (son of William's elder brother, the Revd John Buchan and brother of Lord Tweedsmuir), took over the business in that year which he continued until his death in 1954. Walter Buchan was Town Clerk and Procurator Fiscal for most of these years until succeeded by Edward Laverock, whom he took into partnership in 1945 and who succeeded him as both Town Clerk and Procurator Fiscal. Buchans, until the reorganisation of local government in 1975 thus 'ran' the administration of the royal burgh just as Blackwood & Smith, until 1936, 'ran' the county.

In the early 1940s J. & W. Buchan acquired the practice of William Gordon, a sole practitioner, on his death and in the 1950s the practice of Dunbar Nicholson, Solicitor, Innerleithen, on his retirement, and the firm still practises there to this day.

Edward Laverock and another partner, John Gibb (1949) who, incidental to his law practice was for a long time concerned with, and latterly for several years, Chairman of the Borders Health Board, practised still as J. & W. Buchan after the death of Walter Buchan and until their respective retirements in the mid-1980s, but with the firm still continuing in the younger hands of Walter Murray Charters and Robin Hill. Edward Laverock and John Gibb were also appointed Honorary Sheriff-Substitutes.

The Buchan partners ran, as joint managers, The Peeblesshire Savings and Investment Building Society, the one local building society, founded in 1859, until it merged in the end of 1979 with the Dunfermline Building Society. In 1982, the Commercial (by then The Royal) Bank left 90 High Street for a completely new building, at 2/4 Eastgate, which was built on the site of the long-known and largest bakery and tea-room of Peebles, Wilson & Syme, facing down the Northgate — with, as in past days, 'Chambers' above the bank now Buchan's new home.

J. Walter Buchan, despite being for years a 'sole partner' of the firm, still found time to edit and, to a considerable extent, write the three-volume *A History of Peeblesshire*, both burgh and county, from earliest times up to 1925.

Walter Thorburn, some of whose descendants down through several generation were identified much with the wool and cloth mill owning family of Peebles, is described as Banker and Merchant. His merchant business, primarily in woollens and textiles, is said to have operated from a building on the south side of the High Street, roughly opposite the present Bank of Scotland, or a little further east. As presumably one of the sound and reliable citizens of Peebles, he was appointed agent for The City of Glasgow Bank in 1840. In 1857 this bank gave way to the Bank of Scotland whose agent Walter then became until his death in 1867.

His eldest son, Robert Thorburn of Springwood, which he built as a residence, qualified as a solicitor and succeeded as bank agent in 1867 or very shortly afterwards. He was born in 1841 and died in 1911.

He entered into partnership as Thorburn & Lyon, Solicitors, with William Lyon, said to have come from Moray. William Lyon succeeded his partner as bank agent. He was also, apart from his solicitor's practice, Secretary to the County Education Committee, or the equivalent co-ordinating committee of the still-parish-run schools, which meant that Thorburn & Lyon, in effect, ran the administration of the education of the county from then on. William Lyon, although retired for some years, died in 1936.

His son, John Lyon born about 1880, succeeded in partnership with his father to the secretaryship of the Education Committee which thus continued with that firm until the set up of the County Buildings and independent administration in 1936. John did not become bank agent which had by then been made a full-time appointment.

John Lyon, carrying on the business as 'sole partner' after his father's death, took into partnership in 1946, Donald Brian Shaw who had served in World War II in the Royal Navy (Fleet Air Arm) and he, D. B. Shaw, continued in practice until his retiral in 1985. John Lyon was remembered by many for his Gilbert & Sullivan enthusiasm and his playing of Jack Point and other roles in the operas put on in the 1930s by the local Philharmonic Society.

John Lyon having died in 1953, Brian Shaw took into partnership Michael Claude Ogilvie-Thomson. Of slight eccentricity and of apparently reasonable means which could have precluded him working at all, he was nevertheless a good and pedantic lawyer (of the old school — in conveyancing) but sadly died before the age of 50 in 1967.

Continuing with some help in the intervening years, Brian Shaw took into partnership in 1970, Alastair Keith Christie and for a short time in the 1980s, Ronald Cobham. In 1985 when he retired, he left the business in the hands of Keith Christie who continues to this day as 'sole partner'. Brian Shaw took on the duties of Town Clerk of Innerleithen in 1956, until the demise of local government in 1975 and the firm in more recent years opened a branch in Galashiels which continues today in addition to the main office in Peebles. This main office has been throughout in the Bank of Scotland Chambers (now 72 High Street) — a new building superseding the older bank on the same site in the 1930s.

William Gordon was in the 1920 – 40 period a lone practitioner, unlike the partnerships with their bank connections. His office was above 'Wemyss the barber's shop' in the High Street some few doors west of Veitch's Corner Shop at the junction of High Street/ Northgate. The business was taken over by J. & W. Buchan on his death. He was described to the writer by someone who once worked for him — 'He was an awful nice old man — far too decent to be a lawyer' — what better epitaph!

And so from, say, 1840 to 1990 — 150 years — the law was, and still is, being practised in Peebles by, over the period, some thirty individual lawyers. What tales could they tell, but that was what they were never allowed to do!

Peebles Sheriff Court, now and for many years at the south-west end of Cuddy Bridge next to the Parish Church steps, has functioned for the whole period with which we are concerned, and still does. It is now the 'Sheriff Court of the Lothians & Borders at Peebles'. Sitting basically only one day per week for both civil and criminal cases (though five days for all administration and executory purposes), its presiding sheriff has invariably been Edinburgh-based (and resident) who sits as sheriff also in the Edinburgh Court.

Until the mid-1970s, the Peebles sheriff was not involved in Edinburgh but also covered the court in Selkirk and in view of this, one Sheriff James Aikman Smith, chose, as happened in earlier days, to live in Peebles for his time of about ten years here from 1949/50 onwards. Not only did he run his court well and strictly, but took part and rode in the March Ridings of both Peebles and Selkirk.

Of the several sheriffs succeeding him, should be noted Sheriff Isabel L. Sinclair who held the office for a number of years in the 1970s and was the first woman sheriff in Peebles.

The Sheriff Court still continues as part of the Lothians & Borders Sheriffdom, to this day, its sittings much as above.

243

CHAPTER 14

Medical Practice in Peebles

1900 – 1920

AT THE BEGINNING of this period, medical practice was in what might be called a more or less static state. Few drug treatments were really effective and the family doctor was limited in what he could do for his patients. In those days the doctor did much more home visiting than is the custom now and he was dependent on his horse and trap for country calls and on his bicycle for visits nearer his surgery. The first motor vehicle I remember my father possessing was a 2.75-horsepower Douglas motorcycle. This he acquired in 1913 and it served him well for seven years. He must have had many a difficult journey — the Peebles folk gave it the name of the 'Glencorse Express' after Glencorse House in the Northgate where we lived.

The outstanding event of this twenty-year period was the First World War. During most of it Dr Gunn and my father were the only doctors in Peebles, the other two doctors, Dr Bremner and Dr Marshall, being on military service. This involved the doctors in extra duties. Venlaw House, the residence at that time of Lady Erskine, whose late husband had been an admiral in the Royal Navy, was used as a hospital for military personnel and it was supervised by Dr Gunn. Two houses on Tweed Green which had, prior to the war, previously been used as a nursing home, were taken over by the Red Cross and used as a hospital for soldiers requiring medical care. These patients were under the care of my father. None of these patients were, of course, acute war casualties but it did mean an extra workload on two already very busy doctors.

Just at the end of the war Peebles was struck, like everywhere else, by the pandemic of influenza. This must have been a terrible experience for the whole community, for there were something like forty deaths in the space of two months, and, in some cases, death came very suddenly. The doctors were helped by Mrs Mitchell, the wife of one of the United Free ministers who was medically qualified (a rare being in those days) and by Dr A. E. Gow, who was then on the staff of the Hydro which had been taken over as a hospital for Naval officers. He later became physician to St Bartholomews Hospital in London, so no doubt the Peebles folk were in good hands. Another helper was Dr T. D. Luke who, before the Hydro was taken over by the Royal Navy, had been physician to the Hydro. He was seconded to the RNVR for the duration.

1920 – 1945

After the war, life settled down to a more normal routine. The two houses on Tweed Green, mentioned above, were acquired and converted into a cottage hospital with a small operating theatre and maternity unit. It was opened in October 1922 and became known as The War Memorial Hospital. This must have added interest to the work of the local doctors. Visiting consultants came from Edinburgh and carried out quite major surgery there — assisted by the local doctors who also acted as anaesthetists. The maternity department, too, must have eased their workload considerably and saved them many a journey and perhaps a long wait in a country cottage.

During the 1930s there were two notable advances in medicine, namely the advent of the sulphonamide group of drugs, which greatly improved the outlook in many cases of pneumonia, and the immunisation of children to diphtheria. Prior to these advances, deaths from pneumonia were common, not infrequently in young fit men, and diphtheria caused deaths among children.

Towards the end of the 1930s the war clouds were again gathering and, in September 1939, war against Germany was declared following the invasion of Poland. Britain expected early and massive air-raids on its cities, and large numbers of children were evacuated into country areas. Kingsmeadows House was requisitioned and taken over to be used as a hospital for expectant mothers from Glasgow, to which they would come before delivery and be looked after during and after delivery. The hospital was under the care of Dr A. Temple, one of the local practitioners. The massive air-raids did not come about, at any rate in Scotland, apart from the Clydebank and Greenock raids in the spring of 1941, and the Glasgow mothers for whom it was primarily intended soon became less in number and the hospital was not used to full capacity. The local practitioners were permitted to use the hospital for their own patients; this arrangement continued till the hospital later closed down.

The Hydropathic again played its part in the war effort. It was taken over by the military and the 22nd Scottish General Hospital was set up there until it was mobilised and sent overseas. Afterwards it continued in its work until the end of the war.

Peebles was fortunate in escaping the ravages of war. The only occasion on which bombs fell anywhere near was on the night of the raid on Clydebank when a few incendiary bombs fell over the Hamilton Hill area to the north-west of the town.

In May 1945, the war with Germany came to an end and in August, Japan finally surrendered following the fateful dropping of atomic bombs on Hiroshima and Nagasaki. Then followed the General Election and the formation of a Labour Government with Mr Attlee as Prime Minister.

1946 – 1990

Great changes were soon to come about in the medical set-up. On 6 July 1948, the National Health Service was introduced. With its inception the voluntary hospitals came under Government control and family doctors, too, came to be paid out of the taxpayers' money. In so far as Peebles was concerned, this meant that the War Memorial Hospital ceased to be administered by the former Peebles Nursing Association, but by a body known as the Borders Hospital Board of Management — this was centred at Peel Hospital — a 'temporary' hutted hospital near Galashiels originally intended to serve the large numbers of expected war casualties which happily did not materialise.

A medical superintendent was appointed, the first holder of this office being Major-General Stanley Arnott, DSO, who was to prove a wise and caring leader during the early years of the NHS. He had responsibility not only for Peel Hospital but also for all the small hospitals throughout the Borders area. Each hospital, or group of local hospitals, had its own House Committee which met at monthly intervals. The Borders Hospital Board of Management consisted of medical and lay members approved by the Secretary of State.

During the first forty-five years or so of the twentieth century, there had been in Peebles the County Infectious Diseases Hospital. During this period infectious diseases were an important cause of illness particularly amongst children. Outbreaks of scarlet fever occurred at fairly regular intervals and quite a few patients were seriously ill as this infection could cause damage to the kidneys. Diphtheria, too, as has been mentioned above, was not uncommon and could be lethal. So it will be seen that this little hospital of twenty beds could at times be quite busy and certainly fulfilled a useful purpose in the community.

But the history of disease never stands still — diphtheria was practically wiped out by mass immunisation of children. The streptococcus, the causal organism of scarlet fever, started to lose its virulence and the need for an infectious diseases hospital became much less. So in 1946 the hospital was put to a different use — namely the care of the long-term sick. In practice this meant that it really became a geriatric hospital, although there were at times a small number of patients who would not qualify for geriatric status. The hospital was at first administered by the county council under the Medical Officer of Health but in 1948, it was, like the War Memorial Hospital, taken over by the Borders Hospital Board of Management.

A major advance in medicine which took place shortly after the end of the Second World War was the discovery of how the antibiotic streptomycin was effective in the treatment of tuberculous meningitis. This disease had previously been fatal in 100 per cent of cases but, under treatment with this new antibiotic, patients were found to be recovering. Arising out of this, other substances were developed and so arose the effective chemotherapy of what had hitherto been a very difficult disease to treat with any real or certain effect. In the first half of the twentieth century every family doctor must have had several known cases of tuberculosis in his practice — and in addition a number of undiagnosed cases. Since the advent of chemotherapy, the incidence of tuberculosis fell drastically and patients formerly requiring long periods in hospital may now frequently be treated as outpatients. Hence, as with fever hospitals noted above, many TB hospitals have closed and been put to a different use.

GENERAL PRACTICE UNDER THE NHS

While doctors working in the NHS were permitted still to continue private practice, in Peebles this never developed to a large extent as the great majority of patients elected to be attended under the NHS. The doctors were paid by capitation fees and, in addition, received a mileage allowance for all patients residing at over three miles from the doctor's residence. For maternity services, the doctor received a special fee and to obtain this he had to send to the executive council (the body responsible for medical payment) a written record of the number of ante-natal examinations carried out — whether the confinement was managed in the cottage hospital or in the patient's home. All this relieved the doctor of much book-keeping and also did away with any financial embarrassment which might occasionally arise and possibly undermine the doctor-patient relationship.

TRAINEE ASSISTANTSHIPS

These were introduced in the early 1950s. For doctors to engage a trainee assistant, the practice had to be approved by the executive council. The doctor's surgery was inspected and it was to his advantage for approval to have a reasonable number of maternity patients. The doctor was responsible for the payment of his trainee but this was refunded to him by the executive council. The scheme had many advantages — it encouraged the trainer to maintain a high standard in his practice and to try to give the young doctor a good example of what general practice could and should be.

It also worked the other way. These young doctors were fresh from their pre-registration hospital appointments, were up-to-date and the trainer could certainly learn from them. It was rewarding, too, from the trainer's point of view when he could see how, at the end of their year, the trainee's confidence had grown and how they were better fitted to deal with the various problems arising in the course of their work.

APPOINTMENT SYSTEMS

In the late 1960s general practitioners were beginning increasingly to see patients by appointment and this entailed employing one or more receptionists in a practice. By this means a doctor would know in advance the work facing him on any particular day, and also which of his patients to expect. The receptionist would have the patient's case-notes laid out ready for each consultation. On the whole the new arrangements worked well, though some of the older patients preferred the old way of just 'turning up to be seen'. Sometimes a patient might have to wait a day for their appointment but if their case was deemed to be urgent they were always fitted in.

THE NEW HEALTH CENTRE AND HOSPITAL

For many years it had been realised that the War Memorial Hospital had many shortcomings. It had not been designed as a hospital, being simply a conversion of two semi-detached houses. There were two separate staircases and the many awkward corners round which to manipulate a stretcher was a real problem. Occasional serious flooding occurred when the River Tweed came down in spate. So the provision of a new purpose-built hospital had always been a dream. The Borders Hospital Board of Management had long since acquired the property known as Hay Lodge at the top of the Old Town. The house they had used as a physiotherapy department and the kitchen-garden was used for growing produce to supply the hospital. Here was an opportunity — they had a site suitable for building and it was decided to build there. It was quite a number of years before the plans materialised, not, in fact, until 1983 when it was officially opened by HRH Princess Alexandra. Within the building, consulting rooms were also incorporated for the local practitioners and visiting consultants who continued to hold outpatients clinics, physiotherapy services, chiropody and dental services.

No major surgery is undertaken in the new hospital, all such cases being dealt with, up until April 1988, at the Peel Hospital and after that date the new Borders General Hospital near Melrose. Nor is there any longer a maternity department and for delivery, patients are transferred either to the Simpson Memorial Maternity Pavilion in Edinburgh or to the Borders General Hospital. Ante-natal care is shared by the general practitioners along with obstetric consultants.

So it can be seen that over the years in which the author was in practice, great changes have come about. These, I feel, are for the most part advantageous, though there are some fields in general practice which have, to a large extent, passed out of the hands of the family doctor and this, to some of the senior ones, may give cause for some regret.

CHAPTER 15

The Church in Peebles

PREFACE

I OFFER THIS modest and fragmentary study of one hundred years
in the life of the churches in Peebles with hesitancy born of different
considerations. It is modest, since format demands it. It is
fragmentary, for it has been easier to gain information relating to
some churches than to others.

Here I acknowledge the assistance of all who have contributed
information, not least the help of Mr Allan Macdonald and Mrs
Margaret Alexander of St Andrew's Leckie Parish Church, and of
Mr Alasdair I. Macdonald of St Peter's Episcopal Church. Nor can
one write of the Old Parish Church of Peebles without voicing
profound gratitude to a former elder, Dr Clement Bryce Gunn.

Finally, it has been difficult to write objectively. I am of the period
— too close to a theme and people I hold in affection. So simply
I write of our buildings and of what men and women have sought
and still seek to do in a holy ministry which I hope fulfils its
essential purpose by spilling over into the common life of community
and nation.

THE WITNESS OF THE BUILDINGS

The Old Parish Church of Peebles

The Old Parish Church offers a varied continuity of Church history
through the centuries. Founded by St Kentigern (518 – 603) or by one
of his disciples, that tapestry can be traced vaguely at first, then by
the tangible evidence of St Andrew's Church (1195), the Cross Kirk
(1261), St Andrew's Church on Castlehill (1784), to the present
building replacing its predecessor to guard the High Street from

1887. From this notable and dominating building (generally held to be the fifth building of the Parish Church) stems the contemporary chapter of a long and sustained story.

Built in the thirteenth century Gothic style of the Scottish type to the design of William Young of London, the building carries many material links from the 1784 church, and is distinguished by its crow-stepped gables and crown tower. Spacious within, it seats 1,300 people comfortably, and is composed of a vestibule, nave, north and south aisles, and a raised chancel. There are large galleries to the north and south and rear. It is astonishing to realise that such a large and fine building was raised and initially furnished for £9,500.

The church has much to admire both without and within its walls and tells much of the history alike of Church and burgh. Those many features are too numerous to mention in the compass of this brief account. To list a few of those attractions, however, illustrates both the rich provision of its builders, and, when dated, demonstrates the sustained care and continuing generosity of succeeding generations of worshippers who have offered an uninterrupted evolution of devotion and enhancement through the past century.

Much stained-glass provides silent Scripture Lessons. Most admired is the work of Cottier of London. The great 'East' window was installed in 1887; that in the south and north galleries followed in 1893; while the twenty-two lancet windows of the aisles, and the rose window above the chancel arch, date from 1899.

Prior to the building of the present church, a harmonium had been used while the congregation worshipped in the Chambers Town Hall, and when opened, the gift was made of the present organ, built by Auguste Gern, by members of the Thorburn family. Its extensive pipework filled both sides of the chancel till 1937. Then it was removed to a newly-constructed chamber when the instrument was rebuilt by Henry Willis by the kindness of Mrs Winifred T. Mitchell. In 1972, the organ was rebuilt again and extended by Rushworth and Dreaper. 1988 saw further extension when a new choir section was housed in the south gallery and when the console was taken from the chancel and a new one placed in the south aisle.

The lectern was gifted in 1897, and the Austrian-oak pulpit replaced the original one in 1913. The Colours of the Peeblesshire Militia raised in 1808 came to the church in 1921, while war memorials were erected in 1921 and 1954. Thirteen bells were gifted in 1946 and the regular ringing of them is a much commented

251

upon feature of the town. They were founded by John Taylor and Co. of Loughborough and hung 'dead' in the tower of the church.

The chancel was reconstructed, first in 1937, to accommodate the Choir. At this time the Communion Table, chairs and prayer desk were gifted. Tapestries were given in 1965, and a Cross was hung behind the Holy Table in 1968. Also in 1965, the splendid entrance screen, which contains as comprehensive Christian symbolism as can be seen in Scotland, was gifted by the Misses Madge and Eleanor Ramsay-Smith. The ladies were responsible also for the enlargement of the vestibule, the broadening of the aisles, the reflooring of the crossing and the redesigning of the chancel steps.

The north aisle was developed as a side chapel by the raising of a memorial screen in 1972. This illustrates the history of The Old Parish Church. The area was furnished in the following year. Also in 1973, a book and table of remembrance were gifted; while twenty-two scriptural paintings — the gift of the artist — were hung in 1977.

Once again in 1987, when extensive additions were made to the fabric to celebrate the centenary of the building, the chancel was reconstructed by the removal of the choirstalls and their replacement by elders' stalls set around the walls. This was made possible, as was the extension of the Holy Table and adjustment to the marble flooring, by a gift from Mrs Agnes S. W. Cairns. In the same year, kneelers at the ends of the Holy Table were gifted by another member of the congregation. New choirstalls were built in the former crossing in 1988 by the generosity of Miss Ella Bain, while in 1989 a sound reinforcement system was installed in the church.

A song school was attached to the church in 1895, while extensive church halls were built adjacent to the Cross Kirk in Cross Road in 1899. The latter served well the busy organisational life of the congregation through the century, until they were replaced by the Church Centre in 1982. The newer building stands behind the church, sharing with it the site of the twelfth-century Castle of Peebles, and, more recently, that of the town bowling green. The former halls cost £2,543. The later building cost £87,000. The first seated 900 people. The present accommodation seats 350.

Saint Andrew's Leckie Parish Church

Matthew Arnold suggested that Presbyterianism 'is born to separation as the sparks fly upwards'. It might be offered in mitigation of this doubtful, if doubtless deserved, distinction that many divisions of earlier centuries from the Reformation never sprang from debate of the fundamentals of the Faith. Some — Presbyterian agnostics among them! — might even claim those differences are but proof of zeal for religion! Whether or no, the story of the churches in Peebles well illustrates both that feud and fusion.

Of all the congregations of the town, it is that which is now St Andrew's Leckie Parish Church which best and happily encompasses this complicated history of reunion. Happily, too, for this chronicler, by 1900 the complexities of origins and mergers had been simplified and the century opened with only three Presbyterian churches in addition to the Parish Church. These were St Andrew's Church (now the Eastgate Hall), the Leckie Memorial Church (above Tweed Green), and the West Church (formerly in the Old Town). In that very year, the United Presbyterian Church and the Free Church had united to form the United Free Church. In 1918, St Andrew's Church and the West Church were to merge, taking the name of the former, and worshipping in the building of the latter. With the great union of the Church of Scotland and the United Free Church in 1929, St Andrew's Church and the Leckie Memorial Church both became charges of the Church of Scotland, and the Presbytery allocated to each a parish area within the burgh. Finally, and after extended discussions, St Andrew's Parish Church and the Leckie Memorial Parish Church united under the name of St Andrew's Leckie Parish Church in 1976, and from 1977 employed the Leckie Memorial Church as their place of worship.

The original St Andrew's Church in the Eastgate, a product of the Disruption of 1843, was retained for many years after union with the West Church, until it was let to the Peeblesshire County Council in 1950 for use by youth organisations and sold to the same council in 1966 for £1,300.

The West United Presbyterian Church, which had succeeded the Relief Church of 1827, was built in 1847, and which became St Andrew's United Free Church in 1918, was a familiar and loved landmark standing at the east end of the Old Town at the corner of Elcho Street Brae. Built of red sandstone, entrance was gained by a flight of steps from the main road to doors on either side of the south gable. Vestibule doors led to aisles on the ground floor and by stairs to side galleries and a back gallery. The ground floor sloped downwards to a dais and central pulpit, flanked by choirstalls, behind which was an organ console with pipes above. The church sat some 600 people and was distinguished by its fine Kauri pine woodwork — the gift of a former member. Attached to the west was a hall seating about one hundred, a session room and kitchen.

When, in 1977, it was decided to use The Leckie Memorial Church buildings for the then united congregation, an offer to use the building for community purposes was declined, and later the church was sold to the Ark Housing Association for £4,000 for demolition. The site now houses a sheltered complex. The fine pine pews and balustrade were sold to a firm specialising in exporting church fittings to America.

The Leckie Memorial Church was built in 1877 as a remembrance of the Revd Thomas Leckie, the first pastor of an Associate Burgher Church. It stands between the Eastgate and Tweed Green, is graced by a tall spire, and originally its centre and side pews and gallery pews sat about 400 people. A dais at the north end of the building held an organ console with choirstalls to the east side, while a large wooden screen stood in front of an apse and supported the pipework of the organ. The building has an attached hall accommodating around eighty people.

It was this building that became the home of the united St Andrew's Leckie Parish Church in 1977. The restrictive trust deed by which the properties are held by the congregation demands that properly it is referred to still as the Leckie Memorial Church. At this time of renewed readjustment of charges in the area, and because it was realised that hall accommodation was inadequate to house organisations attached to the united congregation, the main church building underwent major refurbishment to provide a flexible layout for varied use both as a church and as a hall. The entire ground floor was carpeted, while stacking chairs replaced the pews. This considerably reduced the seating capacity of the building. An Allen Computer Organ replaced the pipe organ. The removal of the pipework of the latter, and of the screen that had supported it, allowed the apse to be opened and incorporated again within the whole church. A large Cross, made from the Kauri pine of a pew of the former St Andrew's Church, was hung in the apse above a fine tapestry. The pulpit and font from St Andrew's Church were brought within the rearranged sanctuary, while the vestibule was renovated. Hall accommodation was more than doubled by the acquisition and conversion in 1980 of an adjacent and disused bakehouse. Now known as the Old Bakehouse, this transformed building now provides a second hall, committee room, and other facilities. This was done at a cost of some £12,000, by the availability of much voluntary labour.

Saint Peter's Episcopal Church

The Episcopal community in Peebles began in homes and halls in the town early in the nineteenth century and later met in the upper floor of the Town House where now the silver band gathers. It is interesting to note that this 'neat, elegant and appropriate Chapel' included 'a fine organ'.

The foundation stone of the present church in the Eastgate was laid on 30 March 1836, and the building was consecrated by the Episcopal Bishop of Edinburgh, Glasgow and Fife on 19 April 1837. Stairs and a gallery at the entrance to the building were removed, and an attractive new chancel, with offices behind, was completed in 1884. Otherwise the church remained largely as we enjoy it today.

The handsome chancel is built of finely-hewn ashlar with an open timber roof. The floor is paved with mosaic tiles, and there is a matching reredos. Choirstalls are fashioned in oak, and there is a piscina on the south side. The altar is of oak and was gifted to the church in 1926 by the widow of a local physician, Mrs Marshall. Fine stained-glass fills a triple lancet window in the east end of the chancel. The subjects of the glass are Christ calling His apostles, our Lord's charge to St Peter, and St Philip baptising the Ethiopian. This glass is to the memory of Charles Mackenzie, the first Bishop of Central Africa. He was born at nearby Portmore. A window on the south side of the chancel is the gift of Mrs Edward Potter, while two windows in the south and north walls of the nave were gifted by Mrs Marshall in memory of her parents and sister. The first glass depicts the Holy Family. The second, a St Christopher window, shows the globe with both Scotland and New Zealand carried by the Christ Child. (Mrs Catherine Begg drowned in New Zealand.)

The vestry was enlarged in 1932, and the organ is enclosed within an oak-pane screen and separated from the chancel by two arches of stone supported on a pillar of polished Peterhead granite. The organ of St Peter's is noteworthy. One of the smallest three-manual instruments ever built, it was installed in 1909 at a cost of £640 by the famous builders, Harrison and Harrison. It has been much admired for its compact nature and tonal quality. This was the organ that replaced the 'fine organ fitted up in the Town Ballroom' which had been built by Brinley and Foster.

St Joseph's Roman Catholic Church

The present building of St Joseph's Church in Rosetta Road was blessed by Bishop Gillis, and High Mass celebrated by the Vicar General, Dr Macpherson, on 29 December 1858.

Earlier, on 30 July 1850, and for the first time since the Reformation, some 200 members heard mass in their own chapel. Previously, they had used the private chapel of Traquair House. The Peebles chapel had been provided by the Earl of Traquair in the doubtful rented accommodation of an old loft partly over a carpenter's shop. Then the congregation struggled. In five years, only once did the yearly offerings realise £15 — the rent of the priest's house. The Catholic Directory described it as 'being unquestionably among the poorest in the Eastern District'.

With the coming of the railway, an appeal for funds for a new church was made in 1855. Contiguous to it was the priest's house. A school followed in 1865, at first administered by the priest himself, there being no means to pay a teacher. This St Joseph's School moved to Halyrude Primary School in 1974.

Today, murals in the entrance porch of the church depict the visit of King James IV to the Cross Kirk in 1507, and the reception by St Columba on Iona around 580 of a cross — The Great Jewel — from the hands of seven monks sent by Pope Gregory.

Within, the church enjoys a couthy atmosphere. A central aisle passes through open-backed pews and between plastered walls below a timbered roof. There is a small, open, wrought-iron pulpit to the north of the sanctuary steps. A major change, reflecting the theological and liturgical thinking of the day, was made in 1971. Then the altar was dismantled, moved off the east wall, and resited as a free-standing pedestal. The original Greek Cipollino marble was retained. Romanstone marble tiling completed the flooring and provided a base for the new podium of green marble and Westmorland slate.

The north-east end of the nave opens into a small chapel, while a stair at the west end leads to a back gallery containing a small, electronic organ. Beneath this gallery is the font and a most attractive baptismal window showing the baptism of our Lord. Other stained-glass is in some lights of the east window in the chancel, while, within the nave, windows remember St Margaret and St John Ogilvie, St Michael and the dead of two world wars. The Holy Family and a Descending Dove enhance the small window of the side chapel.

The church includes statues of our Lord, the Virgin Mary and the Holy Child, and St Joseph, together with the fourteen Stations of the Cross. The only plaque — adjacent to the inner entrance door — was given with a chalice by the Polish community in Peebles in 1944 and carries the poignant inscription, both in English and Polish:'Give us back, O Lord, our country in freedom.' The Polish community remains to hold a warm place in the affection of the burgh.

The Baptist Church

The birth of the Baptist Church in Peebles was on 19 September 1889, when a few people holding Baptist principles gathered in the Masonic Hall.

The leading spirit in a movement which was to face much discouragement and opposition was Mr A. M. Crooks, an insurance agent, who 'combined business acumen with godly enthusiasm'. In the early years of the cause, he served, not only as secretary and treasurer, but undertook many ministerial and pastoral duties. From 1890 the congregation met in the Good Templars Hall. A Church Building Fund was established in 1891, and a site was obtained in Greenside from Mr William Ramsay in 1893. The subsequent opening of a simple and unadorned church, at an estimated cost of £387 6s, is notable testimony to the 'courage and faith' of no more than twenty 'humbly situated people'.

Admission was sought to the Baptist Union of Scotland in 1894 and the first minister was inducted in the following year with a stipend of £75. The longest ministry known to the congregation — that of the Revd James Dewar, which extended to twenty-one years from 1899 — took the small, poor church through its difficult period of growth and through the war years to see it established firmly as a congregation within the burgh. That it remains so today is tribute alike to the courage and determination of its pioneers and to the dogged faith and perseverance of its membership through the years. That congregation again faces the daunting prospect of building a new church and premises as a result of the Greenside property being declared unsafe. The probable site of the new church would seem to be in the Victoria Park on the south bank of the Tweed. At present members worship in Priorsford Primary School since the church at Greenside was vacated in 1988.

Others

At the outset of the century a branch of the Railway Mission was established by Mr John Sked. First meetings were held in the waiting rooms at the Caledonian Station, now Dukehaugh. In 1902 a hall — 'The Tin Kirk' — the gift of Miss Hay of Hay Lodge, was built at the junction of March Street and Edinburgh Road. Purposely, services were not conducted at the hours of Church worship. People from all denominations and of none supported the venture. At different periods there were active meetings for ladies and children. When the town's railways closed in 1960, the name was changed to the Peebles Gospel Mission and services continued until 1982. The hall was dismantled in 1989.

At present, the Peebles Evangelical Church is active, having built recently a new church building in Tweedbrae and, still more recently, having added adjoining halls by the conversion of the former public baths. Services are conducted each Sunday with many invited speakers from other similar groups and gathered congregations, and enthusiastic evangelistic work is directed towards young people.

SOME TRENDS OF WITNESS

I have written much of stone and mortar. Temples proclaim the faith of folk. The evolution of buildings relates the development of that confidence. The material symbols reveal the inward conviction and growth, the liturgical style and stress.

By some examples only, let me now seek to disclose a little more of the activity and mood within those walls I have described, and throughout our swiftly changing period which has seen both the bold march of materialism, and a rash of ecclesiastical enterprise and fashion to match its swift pace.

Our span, which encompassed such diverse change as the repeal of patronage in 1874 (Matthew Gardner in 1893 was the first minister elected to the Old Parish Church after its abolition), and the 'revolution' of the Second Vatican Council in 1962 (which so dramatically was to colour change in almost every branch of the Church) was to witness a new birth and growth of organisational life within the churches. Church halls were to house fresh fashions of enterprise. On a site given by Sir John Hay one such was opened by the Parish Church in 1899 at a final cost of £2,543. The work of ladies was focussed by the establishment of the Woman's Guild. Branches were formed locally. One within the Parish Church, founded in 1894, was affiliated to the national movement in 1904. It is but one illustration of this development. Ladies Work Parties and Flower Missions were only symptomatic of a desire to care practically.

Sunday Schools and Bible Classes reflected an anxiety to lead the young, and represented an attraction that would be the envy of today's response. In 1905, 440 children were on the roll of the Sunday School of the Parish Church, while 265 attended its Bible Class. A Young Men's Guild numbered 128, while the Band of Hope, formed in 1879, drew more than 400 and later was to thrive in all three congregations of the United Free Church. A Girls Guildry opened in 1928. Youth Fellowships prospered in the years after the Second World War. The Boys Brigade was most popular in the same period, while groups of Boy Scouts were often affiliated to particular congregations, or enjoyed the facilities of their properties.

The Woman's Guild was later to share its earlier, more comprehensive roll, by the proliferation of more specialised groups, such as Flower Committees and Guilds, and Young Wives and Mothers Groups. The latter became Young Womens' Groups. At the Old Parish Church, a Guild of Friendship was formed in 1955. This was to have a practical and pastoral roll with the housebound and others in particular need.

Such a wealth of diverse activity has continued in varying forms, and to varying degrees, in every branch of the Church to this day.

A continuing and notable care for education was to be pioneered by the Church. This was extended later by local authorities and by the State itself. Most commendable concern for the poor and socially disadvantaged was well exemplified by the scheme for the Long Close of Peebles (an area to the north of the Eastgate). This was undertaken by the Old Parish Church in the early 1900s and, as in the case of the educational involvement of the Church, was to induce great national schemes of social reform.

In all of this sensitive exercise of organisational activity, however, we might do well to consider, in every age, the caveat of a notable historian: 'Organisations may do much to foster Christian life; but it is possible for them to be mere parasites of the Church.'

So what was happening in the sanctuaries?

Nationally, there had been a gradual broadening of theological outlook through the nineteenth century. A relaxation of formulas at ordination in the United Presbyterian Church in 1879, in the Free Church in 1892 and in the Church of Scotland in 1905, was followed by change in attitudes to The Lord's Day. The ordering of public worship in the Reformed tradition had been redirected by the sway of notable individuals and by the formation of such influential societies as the Church Service Society (1865) and the Scottish Church Society (1890). The Euchologian (1867), containing orders for different sacraments and ordinances, was to have far and long-reaching effects throughout parishes. This was to reach a peak by the publication of *The Books of Common Order* of 1928 and 1940. Currently, new forms and orders abound in the Episcopal and Roman Churches.

This trend to order in public worship and to Catholic forms of worship continues to this day in the Church of Scotland, though some might say perhaps less effectively and not without challenge. It has also been developed dramatically in the Church of England and in the Roman Church in more recent years. Though again it must be said, and perhaps of every branch of the Church, that there are those today who would say we are losing dignity and direction in public worship, allowing it to be replaced by a tawdry and careless absence of order and less wholesome evangelism. Something of all this can be traced and is clearly reflected in the Churches of Peebles in the past century and today. Truly it can be said of our burgh that it presents a diversity of worship.

Perhaps nowhere is such heterogeneity of choice more apparent than in the sphere of church music. Musically, Peebles was notorious at one time. Pennecuik, the historian, declared that 'it was hardly possible to find one in six of its inhabitants who could tell one tune from another — who could differentiate, for instance, between "God save the King" and "Scots wha Hae"! Yet such a state of affairs was to contrast with the later fame of the town's vocalists and the all-male choir of the Old Parish Church, which was not only then the sole such choir in the Church of Scotland, but described by one as 'the most highly acclaimed in the United Kingdom'. This was the achievement of Mr J. J. Finlay, the choirmaster of the Old Parish Church for twenty years at the outset of the century. Clad in black jackets and trencher caps, the choir reached sixty in number, and replaced an earlier mixed choir. This was the unique forerunner of the present robed choir of that congregation introduced in 1975. It was at the same time that the *Third Edition of the Church Hymnary,* published in 1973, replaced the *Revised Church Hymnary* of 1928, as it had done in the St Andrew's Leckie congregation.

A musical tradition remains strong despite contemporary difficulties — such as an unwillingness to cede a regular commitment on the part of many of all ages, and in the face of competition for the loyalty of the young, a rivalry not least keenly felt on Sunday mornings. Despite such obstacles, the congregation of the Old Parish Church is affiliated to the Royal School of Church Music, with boys being trained under its schemes, and with a few gaining its highest award in Scotland — the Saint Andrew Award.

Earlier, it had been the Episcopal Church that led the introduction of the pipe organ in local churches, 'with a fine organ fitted up' in the Town Hall as early as 1828. Then a precentor held sway in the Parish Church, until, not without objection, a harmonium was introduced while the congregation worshipped in the Chambers Hall during the building of the present church from 1885. Pipe organs were installed in St Andrew's Church, the Leckie Memorial Church, and in St Joseph's Roman Catholic Church. After the union of those two congregations of the Church of Scotland, an Allen Computer Organ replaced the pipe organ in the Leckie Memorial Church. There too, to a degree, as in the Roman Catholic and Baptist churches, an increased use is made of the guitar in leading congregational praise.

It is interesting to read of special mention being made of Christmas in 1892 and of two carols being sung in the Parish Church, of the church being decorated for Easter in 1898, and of the Lord's Prayer being repeated in 1900. In 1903, a Watchnight service was conducted at the close of the year; a Good Friday service was introduced to the Parish Church in 1954; and a full celebration of Holy Week from 1971. The practice in the Reformed tradition (the exception being the Episcopal Church) was to celebrate the Sacrament of The Lord's Supper but infrequently throughout the twentieth century. Now in both congregations of the Church of Scotland, the celebration is at least monthly.

The other great event and trend of our period has been, and remains, the move towards union. The Union of the United Presbyterian and Free Churches opened the century. The Union of the Church of Scotland and the United Free Church dominated it in 1929. Professor G. D. Henderson wrote of the latter union, saying: 'it was not so much an end as a beginning; and all the strength and consecration of all the elements combined in the new body will be

261

required in order to face the problems and tasks of the changed world in which we live'.

The prophetic words are more true today. Yet Peebles has a basis upon which to face such challenge. It enjoys the twin foundations of a notable community spirit and a kindly neighbourliness. Both the reality and the greater hope of consolidating unity were given gracious expression by the words of Dr Thomas Martin, Minister of the Parish Church, who was to be Moderator of the General Assembly of the Church of Scotland in 1920, who said this on the occasion of the semi-jubilee of the present building:

> I would not forget Churches in this town other than our Parish Church, Churches respected by us and with a record of good works behind them. Within the last century these Churches, for motives honourable and for reasons that seemed just to them, parted from us, but I believe only for a time . . . I am sure that as we celebrate our semi-jubilee we rejoice in the movement that is now working towards a greater reunion. I am confident that under the constraining influence of a fervent desire to be one, means will be found for a corporate union that will conserve to all the Churches what is best in their respective parts, and strengthen them for common warfare against the enemies of Christ.

That warfare rages more fiercely today. Through the past century, countless expressions of that oneness, on local and national occasions, have countered petty congregationalism, and been modest steps to that end. A chain of co-operation can be traced through trivial and inconsequential rivalries among the Presbyterian churches of the town. Happily, this joint action was to broaden to include all the branches of the Church, and this long before a fashionable stress was laid upon ecumenism. This concurrence extends in our days by regular joint devotional exercises and services, by combined discussion, and, not least, by practical united ventures such as Christian Aid. It is exercised and focussed by the friendly meetings and pursued discussions of the Peebles Churches Joint Committee, on which all the principal churches of the burgh are represented.

Presently too, there continues, what some would see as a less happy consequence of the warfare of materially-orientated days. This is the process of the readjustment of parishes and churches, and is the result — in part — of dwindling resources of manpower and finance.

Our period has witnessed the union of St Andrew's and the West Church in 1918. St Andrew's Church and the Leckie Memorial

Church became charges of the Church of Scotland in 1929. In 1976, the two congregations united as St Andrew's Leckie Parish Church. In the same year, St Peter's Episcopal Church revived a practice of the nineteenth century and appointed a part-time rector. In 1977, Eddleston Parish Church sought linkage with the Old Parish Church of Peebles, while in 1984, Lyne and Manor Parish Church was thus linked, and an Associate Minister appointed, to serve in all three charges. In 1987, St Joseph's Roman Catholic Church united with St James' Roman Catholic Church in Innerleithen to become the Roman Catholic Parish of Tweeddale.

If there be regret, let it be set in the right context. It was in 1901 that one citizen mused ruefully in St Joseph's Church: 'How changed! One modest chapel represented St Andrew's, St Mary's, the Cross Church and St Leonard's, all flourishing at one time within the Parish of Peebles in pre-Reformation days. All the representatives of the old faith easily found room within its walls.' Surely better to know the Real Presence still wherever He appears?

> What blessed peace the Real Presence gives
> To those who have that gift Divine, true faith,
> To apprehend our Saviour really lives
> Within the shrine, and that the Heavenly breath
> Breathes on and animates the living death
> Of deadened hearts . . .

I hope the examples I have given of activity within the walls of the churches serve to indicate a varied wealth of enterprise and sustained effort, the benefits and rewards of which have not been confined to the bounds of any building. Rather that that energy has served both congregations and community, for indeed the Church exists for those outside her. Hopefully too, that work of many has been the influence of the One Holy Catholic and Apostolic Church imparted through various channels, and her healing touch that has been enjoyed by folk of every branch and of none.

POSTSCRIPT

Should one — or dare one whose ministry is incomplete! — draw any conclusion?

Perhaps not since the days of the great Border abbeys can our region lay claim to ecclesiastical distinction. Native pride in its churches tends to be exercised from without rather than demonstrated from within. Caution rather than commitment is the manner of most. 'You will never see me in your church, but I do welcome you most warmly to Peebles, and I do hope sincerely you will be very happy among us!' It was the first, honest and kindly welcome I received in the High Street of Peebles, and perhaps most aptly it illustrates an ambivalent attitude.

Distinction of leadership and faithfulness of pastoral care has not been absent. During the ministry of the Revd Alexander M. Maclean at the Parish Church, the popular adage 'Peebles for pleasure' was challenged by the claim 'Peebles for preaching'. Yet I suspect the counter slogan was evolved as much by the conviction of a reflective community as by the experience of a contemporary people! An acceptance of the Church; a satisfaction that she is present; the expectation that ever it shall be so, outrun vocal or demonstrated enthusiasm for her cause, or consistent support of her worship. Or so would appear to be the passive assumption and practice of most.

Yet, as in so many other communities, and through the entire history of the Christian Church, there exists a devoted minority — composed alike of natives and newcomers, and from every denomination — who valiantly and graciously defend the Faith, meet her needs with unparaded liberality, and quite splendidly sustain her worship, work and witness. They — often 'the quiet of the land' — are the strength of the Church and the salt of the earth in every generation. Peebles has her share of such good people, as well as an abundance of caring neighbours. As in every place and age, they far outshine the careless.

THE SUCCESSION OF CLERGY SINCE 1900

The Old Parish Church of Peebles

Ministers
1893 Matthew Gardner
1907 Alexander Miller Maclean
1911 Thomas Martin
1926 Berry Preston
1952 James Hamilton
1970 David Cockburn
        MacFarlane

Associate Ministers
1984 Andrew Paxton Lees
1988 Nancy M. Norman

Leckie Memorial Church

1868 Robert Burgess
1908 Oliver Russell
1916 Kenneth Edward
1928 Alexander Brown
1937 James Kerr
1947 George Bayne Wilson
1953 William A. L. Hutchison
1957 William Guthrie Tran
1964 James Eaglesham Dott
1966 Alexander Mackenzie
        Sutherland
1973 James Mackintosh
        Alexander (Locum.)
1975 Calthorpe Emslie
        (Locum.)

St Andrew's Church (Eastgate)

1880 Robert Ballantyne
1913 David Cecil Mitchell

The West Church

1876 David Young Currie

St Andrew's Church (Old Town)

1918 David Cecil Mitchell
1921 John Alexander Baird
1938 William Galbraith Taylor
1955 James Henderson Taylor
        Boyd
1961 Alexander John Geddes
1967 Albert Craig

PART IV

St Andrew's Leckie Parish Church

1976 Albert Craig
1977 Duncan MacGillivray
1983 James Henderson Wallace

St Peter's Episcopal Church

1881 J. Llewellyn Evans
1905 Edmund T. R. Johnston
1908 Reginald B. LeB Janvier
1913 John H. Watt
1917 Stuart D. Morris
1919 E. Hugh Samwell
1930 J. Arnold Towers
1951 Frank E. W. Weeks
1963 A. Kenneth Mathews
1969 Wilfrid B. Currie
1976 Robert Haslam
1981 A. Wilson McCay

St Joseph's Roman Catholic Church

1883 J. McCartney
1912 James S. Lyle
1919 J. Turner
1926 J. A. McIntyre
1929 C. E. Rooney
1941 J. Harold
1953 T. P. McGregor
1954 J. McKee
1963 Peter Donati
1977 Alex. Bremner
1985 James Myers
1988 David McCann

The Baptist Church

1899 James Dewar
1921 A. Campbell Dovey
      (Student Pastor)
1921 R. G. Black
      (Student Pastor)
1923 A. Campbell Dovey
1926 G. Hardie
1930 F. Price
1937 R. Burnside
1938 Douglas Robb
1945 James Taylor
1947 James McLean
1951 John McMillan
      (Layman)
1956 Andrew MacRae
1958 Alexander Duncan
1959 William Tregunna
      (Layman)
1963 George Cruickshank
1965 James McLeod and
      Alexander Hardie
      (Student Pastors)
1966 Fergus G. Little
1968 Jack Spiers
      (Lay Pastor)
1976 David Mullen
      (Lay Pastor)
1980 Keith Crozer
1989 Peter Firth

CHAPTER 16

The Beltane Festival

TO PEEBLES FOLK Beltane means instant recall: middle-aged men remember when they were 'little mice peeping out', women have more detailed memories of being 'Belgian ladies', 'Rainbow girls' or maybe 'Maids of Honour'. Older generations (we live a long time in Peebles!) can hark back to the twenties (1927 to be exact) when the heavens opened and it rained 'like steel rods' causing the abandonment of the children's procession and the curtailment of the subsequent sports. To 'incomers' — and their name is legion — the Beltane is a mystery and at first they are bemused by its nuances and take time to absorb its traditions.

Let's not be too modest about our celebration of the summer solstice for we boast a festival second to none — some would say unique in the annals of Border history. But in describing it we must distinguish between Peebleans who, like old soldiers you can always tell — but you can't tell them much! — and newcomers, bless them, who are mystified by the 'goings on' of Beltane week in the little old Burgh of Peebles. Festooned with flags, bedecked with bunting and huge hardboard coloured cut-outs, the town resounds to the music of silver and pipe bands with cheering children in their wake, crowds of grown-ups too make their way purposefully to points north and west of the High Street or just stand and shout 'Hooray!' when vast processions pass. Something must be happening.

This chapter then is written both for the locals who will forgive the writer for stating the obvious — 'what's aye been', and for those who have made Peebles their commuter town, visitors' centre or retirement residence. The latter, understandably, may well be perplexed in the third week of June to find on the Saturday morning, the High Street closed to traffic, the populace cheering vociferously, most shops shut and loud music wafting from the steps of the

PART IV

Tontine! Take heart, you are witnessing Peebles Beltane Festival and sooner rather than later the 'Queen' accompanied by her Chief Maid and Pages will most assuredly proceed round the burgh resplendent in her Victorian landau to be acclaimed by all. Generations of visitors have queried the name Beltane and we make no apologies à propos its pagan origins — long before written records the bonfires of Baal figure in folklore in connection with the advent of summer. But few nowadays have the inclination to delve into the prehistoric origins of national or local holidays be they Beltane, Christmas, New Year or even Easter! Suffice it to say that for centuries the merry month of May meant the beginning of summer (witness the May Queen celebrations in England) but that, in the course of time, Midsummer became the preferred holiday to be recognised as Beltane. This synchronised nicely with the end of the school session by which time the name of the Dux girl in the burgh school could be divulged and from 1899 she could be hailed as the Beltane Queen.

Although the first one was crowned at the Mercat Cross (only a few yards from its present position), from 1900 the church steps became the ideal setting for the coronation which for some years took place on the Friday nearest Midsummer Day at noon. The subsequent procession included *inter alia* 'Fire Brigade and Engine', whether as a precaution, a gimmick or genuine display of Burgh apparatus is not clear! The sports were held in Kingsmeadows Park where they had been wont to take place in olden times. Many procedural changes have occurred over the years, most of which have enhanced the annual festivities or enlarged their scope. In 1906 the Scots Greys took part and staged a mini tattoo at the sports: not to be outdone, the Navy arrived in the following year in the form of a band and ratings from the north of England who put on a gun drill display to delight the crowd. This probably influenced the committee's decision to celebrate Beltane on the Saturday as from 1910 so that more visitors could witness our unique spectacle. Although Victoria Park was the venue in 1911 for a special children's fête (commemorating the Coronation of George V) the sports have reverted to Hay Lodge Park as nowadays: Peebles is fortunate to have so many recreation grounds — even Whitestone Park was to play its part in the Beltane celebrations in due course.

But we must not anticipate events too soon. Before we become involved in the twentieth century, think back to Queen Victoria's Diamond Jubilee in 1897 for then it was that the town council made its momentous decision to resuscitate the age-old 'Riding of the Marches'. Not that the burgh boundaries were in danger of being encroached upon but simply as a re-enactment of a ceremony which had lapsed for centuries. The 'Citizens' Committee' (as it was labelled long before it became 'Peebles March Riding and Beltane Queen Festival Committee') appealed to all local horsemen to 'hook their spurs and mount their saddles' and 'make a grand display'. Judging by old photographs this 1897 March Riding was indeed 'Something worthy of the occasion!'

The leader of the mounted Cavalcade was known as the Cornet — not necessarily a young man but one deemed to be a worthy son of Peebles representing local manhood and on occasion acting as ambassador for the old royal burgh. The annual choice of Cornet was undertaken by the Citizens' Committee whose members, after 1909, submitted their selection to the town council for official approval before any public declaration was made — a system which obtained until the mid-1970s.

Apart from a children's fête in Victoria Park on George V's Coronation Day in 1911 replacing the customary Hay Lodge Sports, the first innovation was in 1913 when a time honoured horse race for the Beltane Bell was revived. The original Course had been from Nether Horsburgh to the East Gate, which the exigencies of modern traffic obviously preclude, so the race was transferred first to Hay Lodge and later to the golf course. The handsome trophy linked with this exciting event was donated by exiled Peebleans in USA; it is a silver replica of the historic 'Liberty Bell' of Philadelphia which was rung in 1776 to proclaim American independence. Another 'change' was necessitated by the incidence of the First World War which intervened in terms of the appointment of annual Cornets but 'Queens' were still chosen yearly — successive Dux girls of Kingsland School.

1919 did not see the complete restoration of pre-war pageantry: on Wednesday the Cornet led his supporters from Tweed Green via Craigerne Lane to Edderston Farm where he entertained them to curds and cream. He took no part in Concert or Fancy Dress Parade but simply received his flag on Saturday morning at the church steps after the Crowning. The 1920s however witnessed several embellishments and elaborations which became firmly established traditions. The first of these was the adoption of the Beltane Festival song which embodies the veritable essence of 'Peblis to the Play': its

269

music and words have been played, sung, whistled and hummed ad infinitum for seventy years. We all owe a debt to Messrs James Hope Brown and Fred Purvis for their inspired joint effort. Unforgettable.

The second contribution came from South African Peebleans who in 1922 presented a coronation chair for 'Her Majesty's' use! Upholstered with leopard skin, it was skilfully carved by the well-remembered woodwork master A. C. Mackay who flourished between the wars. Another innovation took place in 1923 when for the first time the Cornet was installed at the Mercat Cross where his Colours were 'bussed' by the provost's wife who also crowned the 'Queen' that year. (For readers who are not well versed in these terms — 'bussing the Colours' means pinning on to the new Cornet's standard the coloured ribbon bearing his name). The exquisite silver casket used every year since 1925 came from Canada; made of maple and beautifully embossed it contains a scroll listing the names of former Queens. The next gift was from New Zealand where exiles 'stirred by memories dear' were inspired by the late James Caldwell to ensure that the 1926 Queen appeared resplendent in her new robes adorned with a gold medallion.

More gifts and changes in procedure followed in quick succession before the end of the 1920s. In 1927 for the first time the Cornet was installed at the Parish Church steps so that the ever increasing number of visitors could view the ceremony. In the same year a new crown, cushion and sceptre were gifted by Mr (later Provost) and Mrs Daniels to supplement the robes of the previous year. The sceptre must be unique in that its head was deftly designed by Mr Mackay to match the Parish Church steeple! Within a year further appurtenances appeared in the form of a VIP Indian carpet for the Queen and her entourage to tread from top of steps to waiting carriages — a gift this time from Darjeeling. In 1929 Wednesday evening became the alternative highlight of the week to Saturday in that the Cornet, after his installation, was 'welcomed' at Neidpath Castle (just follow the crowd to get there!) by a new personality — the 'Warden' who thereafter made a speech to the assembled crowd from the steps of the Castle. This innovation which has continued annually except for the war years was the brainwave of Dr Gunn who was its protagonist not only in 1929 but for the next three years. The ceremony has proved particularly popular whenever the Warden has been a Peeblean or a returned exile — so long as the rain does not descend like the proverbial steel rods!

Still further changes or rather extensions of events during the Beltane week took place in the 1930s. Dr Gunn was involved in the first of these in 1930, viz., the Cross Kirk service on the Sunday at 6 p.m. Similar to the symbolic Warden of Neidpath another new title was invented, that of Warden of the Cross Kirk, sometime Parish Church of Peebles, nowadays a respectable ruin whose precincts are well preserved and where, on a usually sunny evening in the third week of June, a service is held to inaugurate Beltane. Christianity had thus triumphed over paganism! And since the death of Dr Gunn in 1933 (who presided over the first four services) ministers of all Christian religious denominations have taken turns at being Wardens of the Cross Kirk.

1931 saw the first Tuesday evening Children's Sports in Hay Lodge Park — quite a noisy night but a necessary supplement to Saturday's Sports which cater more for adults. The weather unfortunately has proved to be the catalyst on more than one occasion when the Children's Sports have been postponed. In 1934 the wonderful words and nostalgic tune of 'Come ower the hills to Peebles' were first heard at various Beltane functions and we are indeed indebted to Messrs Binnie and Inglis for such a superb compilation which has been sung sincerely and with verve at many a Callants' Supper in Peebles and at Beltane celebrations overseas.

From the mid-1930s to the outbreak of war Peebles March Riding and Beltane Queen Festival Committee received more gifts from patrons far and near. In 1935 the Fotheringhams of South Africa (later famous for their footbridge over the Tweed) presented a new hand-embroidered flag for future Cornets' use whilst in 1936 a fine Challenge Shield to be competed for annually arrived from India — the gift of Maharajah Kumar who had been a guest earlier. It is awarded to the shop deemed to be decorated in the most original and pleasing manner. From much nearer home in 1937 came a new saddle cloth and head plume for the Cornet's mount — a token of appreciation from Mrs Mitchell of Kingsmeadows. Another local lady made history that year by being appointed Warden of Neidpath: Miss Anna Buchan was followed thirty years later by her relative Lady Tweedsmuir, perhaps a third lady will get a turn in 1997! Mr James Forrester, OBE, JP, who was Warden of Neidpath in 1939 donated a sash for the occasion; its use was postponed for six years because of the war but thereafter it was worn with pride by successive 'sashed' Wardens in the post-war years.

271

PART IV

Two years before the outbreak of World War Two the senior pupils of Kingsland School were transferred to the High School: this meant that Beltane Queens from 1938 would be eleven or twelve years of age instead of thirteen or fourteen as they had been for the past forty years. But with war came inconvenience and abbreviation: the young Queen of 1940 found herself crowned in the school playground! The second wartime ceremony was held in Hay Lodge Park, but a semblance of the usual setting was used for the remaining years of the War, viz., the steps and balcony of Whitestone Park Pavilion. Meanwhile the 1939 Cornet was deemed to have remained in office until 1945 (although in fact he had a distinguished wartime career!) but the first years of peace saw a return to pre-war pageantry plus the chance to choose ex-servicemen to lead their troop of horses.

In 1948 a useful, indeed decorative table was added to the Beltane accoutrements courtesy of Mr Tom Murray, a local worthy. Known as the Coronation Table it bears the burgh coat of arms carved in colour and is the temporary resting place for the Canadian casket during the crowning ceremony. 1949 was celebrated as the Jubilee Year of Beltane: Will Kerr, editor of the *Peeblesshire News* produced an appropriate book to mark the occasion and there was an assemblage of former 'Queens' numbering thirty-eight who posed for a photograph which is still treasured by many Peebleans. Since those heady days of local girls annually hogging the limelight there has been a tendency in post-war years for incomers to 'steal the show' and quite frequently children of 'stoorifits' have been chosen Queen, First Courtier or Chief Maid to the discomfiture of the locals; but these occurrences are inevitable concomitants of the constant shift of population during the decades following 1950.

In 1951 Miss Bonong, known to three generations of Peebleans as an able administrator and dedicated teacher, donated the Beltane Queen's Standard, carried first by Master Ron Runciman — Warden of Neidpath in 1989 and veteran town (District) councillor. In 1953 interest switched to the Wednesday evening when for the first time the ladies competed for a handsome trophy given to the winner of their exclusive horse race by the Royal Burgh of Peebles Callants Club — that exclusive body of men which is 'renowned for its generous gifts and support . . . to the Beltane . . . and proudly heads the list of patrons in the programme each year' — as its secretary Ken Howitt wrote at the time of its Jubilee in 1985. The exciting ladies' gallop on the golf course has since continued to draw droves of spectators most of whom have just witnessed the fording of the Tweed by the Cornet and his mounted followers of both sexes. A couple of years later the Merchants of the town awarded a shield to the winner of the best decorated house: difficult decisions have had to be made by those expert professionals, chief judges Jim Mackison and son Graham, because there is always intense rivalry and standards are extraordinarily high. (Take a dander round the town on Beltane Saturday afternoon and see for yourself.)

Several Border festivals are confined to two days' celebrations and such an experiment was tried in Peebles in 1966 and 1967 when a condensed version of Beltane took place. But tradition dies hard and the purists persuaded the powers-that-be to revert to the established system in 1968. As Provost Alex Walker wrote in his 1968 programme message: 'With so many people working out of town, the whole week would enable more folk to participate in evening events.' One of those events was a portrayal of the centenary of Peebles Fire Brigade and a number of engines dating from the mid-nineteenth century took part in the Beltane procession as had happened on a smaller scale in the parade at the beginning of the century. The previous year saw the first horse race for junior riders who since 1967 have competed for a special trophy given by Bailie Stewart Smith, chairman of the March Riding Committee during the war and for long afterwards. He was the worthy reputed to have made the remark that he had seen 'hundreds of Beltanes!'

So the Beltane continued into the 1970s when more momentous events took place in terms of local government. From the beginning festivities had occurred only with the blessing of the town council under whose auspices they had flourished. But what was to happen when the burgh's 'twelve good men and true' were abolished and the more nebulous, less numerous District personnel took over? The hypothetical question became a reality in 1975 when District Councillor Sandy Melrose (ex-Provost) prefaced his message to Peebleans in the 1975 programme with an apt quotation from Lord Tennyson, 'The old order changeth, yielding place to new.' He went on to say, 'Minor alterations may be effected in our traditional ceremonies, but rest assured — an enthusiastic March Riding Committee will retain . . . the well established traditions of bygone years.' Thus it was that the reorganisation of local government made little difference to Beltane. On Beltane's seventy-fifth Anniversary thirty-seven Queens were guests at the lunch held at the Hydro,

273

(only thirty-four appear in the photograph). From 1975 we lacked the colour and robe splendour of provost and bailies — even halberdiers for a time, but the chairman of the committee whose predecessors had held office for well nigh eighty years continued to deputise for defunct dignitaries despite all Lord Wheatley could do — and the show went on!

Never doubting that all would be well the indefatigable secretary of the Beltane Committee Dennis Tammi gave in 1974 a sash to be worn by future Queens. This was the year, incidentally, in which the first Roman Catholic girl was chosen to be crowned. This innovation was due to the reorganisation of primary education in Peebles whereby three schools, Kingsland, Priorsford and Halyrude, now became possible sources of Beltane principals and other ranks. Since 1974 the Queen has been chosen from a short leet consisting of six girls from each of the three schools; the headteachers take into consideration other criteria as well as academic merit when making their choice; they tend to look for a good 'all rounder' acceptable to her peers.

Another change concerned the Cornet and his Supporters. Previously the custom had been that his two predecessors acted as Right and Left-hand Men but since 1974 the Cornet and his Supporters have been chosen altogether, the previous year's Cornet acting as Fourth Man and adviser. Both Supporters may be re-elected either for a second term as Supporter or as Cornet. It was also in 1974 that the manager of the Tontine Hotel, Mr Ian Buick, who was himself a member of the Beltane Committee and who rode the Marches with the best of them, presented a trophy to be competed for annually on the Wednesday night. A third gift dating from 1974 was a Stirrup Cup for the Cornet who can quench his thirst from its contents after the dancing of the reel and then pass it on to his fellow performers — not forgetting the drum-major of the Pipe Band. The Stirrup Cup came from those staunch Peebleans who constitute the Western Australia Beltane Society.

In 1976 another 'prize' was donated in the name of the late Mr George Irvine who had himself won the Beltane Bell Race in 1948: his memorial Trophy is confined to young lady riders. In 1976 with the departure of Dennis Tammi for South Africa, ex-Cornets Allan Beveridge and David Turnbull agreed to act as joint secretaries and one of their tasks was to endorse the decision to substitute a children's disco for the old-fashioned dancing to the Silver Band outside the Queen's house on the Monday evening. The event was confined to primary-school children and first took place in the Drill Hall in 1977. Nowadays they are led by the Pipe Band along the High Street on their way home via the Queen's house and are able to wave to their Daddies who leave the Callants' Supper Table temporarily to stand on the steps of the Tontine and wave back!

1978 witnessed further changes in procedure or revivals of old customs. Realising that provosts and bailies were personalities of the past, the committee re-introduced two halberdiers to add a little more colour to the head of the procession. Tuesday evening children's sports assumed a new look with team events such as a middle distance relay race round Hay Lodge Park for a special prize — donated once again by our good and faithful friends in Western Australia. As an extra embellishment a brand new burgh flag was dedicated by the Warden of the Cross Kirk and formally unfurled by the chairman of the ex-Cornets association who handed it over to the Cornet of 1978 for safekeeping. The concert on Thursday, for many years staged in the Old Parish Church Hall was, in 1978, transferred to the Burgh Hall where it was no longer possible to get a seat on one of the window sills! As for Friday's Fancy Dress Parade, the prize money was doubled and our two Joint Secretaries — policeman both when more gainfully employed — could congratulate themselves on having completed their two year stint in office to the huge satisfaction of all.

They have remained at the helm ever since and during that decade or so enthusiasm for Beltane has grown apace with more young people taking an active part and quite a few ladies on the General Committee. Without being guilty of tautology one could boast that Beltane has improved as a spectacle throughout the 1980s as will be shown. The late David Wright who was Cornet in 1954 donated a trophy in 1981 to be competed for by Cornets, ex-Cornets and Supporters who show their mettle on the race-course annually. Witness also the new landaux used for conveying Queen, Maids and Pages on Beltane Day. For some years the Callants Club had borne the cost of hiring these but the annual charge increased astronomically over the years until it was felt that enough was enough and the decision was made to purchase two new Victorian carriages outright. Whilst they were being built Peebleans and innumerable friends raised the necessary funds — a mere £11,000(!) and the beautiful maroon, black and grey vehicles were at last acquired in time for June 1987. They epitomise the spirit of Beltane and show the world how highly we value our Festival: obviously only the best is good enough. The same thoughts must have influenced other organisations because objects of splendour continue to arrive from near and far. The inestimable and indispensable Silver Band on the occasion of its 150th anniversary presented to the March Riding Committee two silver-plated horns for Heralds of the Beltane Court. Likewise the ex-Cornets' Association in 1984 presented a new saddle cloth for the Cornet's horse to which was added in 1989 a replica of the original (1937) jowel-plume which was tracked down after months of research by an anonymous member of the Beltane Committee. Attached to the harness at the chin and known also as a dress beard it consists of a silver cone and a length of red horse-hair — a unique adornment for the smartest steed in the Borders at Beltanetide! From the ex-Cornets' Association also, a new cushion for 'Her Majesty's Coronation' replaced the original one mentioned earlier, whilst the Queen's sceptre was given a face-lift, i.e., it was regilded. So no expense has been spared in recent years in pursuit of perfection, even the Queen herself was clad in new robes (1988) courtesy of the Callants who felt that after sixty years it was time for the old dress to go into mothballs. The embroidered gold medallion was transferred to the new robes which surely must now make Peebles Beltane Queen the 'Jewel in the Crown'.

Just as the valuable New Zealand gold badge with its dual coats of arms preserves the long link with the Peebleans resident in that country, so do the several gifts and annual telegrams from the Western Australia Beltane Society link us with its members who have chosen to live in that particular antipodean paradise. In recent years it has gifted to the March Riding Committee a lectern, a new sash for the Warden of Neidpath and a handsome contribution to the landau appeal. Even more recently Alex Robertson, himself a winner of the Beltane Bell in 1954, presented a silver tray to the 1988 winner as a commemorative token of Australia's Bi-centenary. Not to be outdone, Margaret Thomson (Mrs McKenzie) of California donated a model horse trophy for annual presentation to the Cornet's Lass to remind her of the equestrian nature of her temporary calling! Other gifts have included a scroll holder in memory of the late Bob Shearer, a chain of office for the chairman of the March Riding Committee from Mrs Isobel Howitt in memory of her husband, a former chairman — the inimitable W. W. — and a Crowning Lady's Brooch from Lieutenant-Colonel Sprot who was Warden of Neidpath in 1981. Periodically the Callants Club provided new costumes for the Maids and miscellaneous male Members of the Court. It is indeed difficult to imagine any further improvement in the 1990s and yet, even more lavish embellishments will doubtless be added to the ceremonies which already must surely be acknowledged as 'Abune then A'.

Dear Reader, if you have managed thus far to assimilate this historical eulogy you will realise that what had been a twenty-four hour holiday — according to the original Proclamation of Beltane Fair — has developed in the course of a lifetime into a week-long festival. (Mr William Shortreed, who was First Courtier in 1909 and a First World War veteran to boot, can recall his primary school days more than eighty years ago.) The fact that Beltane has not changed fundamentally is evident from a fascinating booklet that has but recently come to light; it was written by the Revd T. D. Miller who was Minister of Kirkurd and printed by Allan Smyth of Peebles. It refers to the celebration of 1906 and already the writer was able to say: 'The festival has become a popular one and thousands of people from country and town throng to the ancient burgh to witness the sight and take part in the general merry-making.' The booklet contains a photograph of the Queen and Maids of Honour, all of whom were known to an earlier generation. After comparing Peebles Fair with that at Lanark the writer continues: 'The Queen is the cynosure of every eye — she is elected to the proud position . . . on account of her vivacity of spirit and intelligence of mind, and because she has gained the highest place of honour for the year in the Public School.' So it would appear that selection criteria have changed little in over eighty years! 'The crowd of youthful processionists tricked out in all their finery of muslin, millinery, "ribbons, bibbins and lace" and bearing "knots of flowers and buds and garlands gay" gives for the day all the beauty, brightness and loveliness of May Fair to a town that used to be described as being "quiet as the grave".'

The Reverend gentleman refers to the sports by briefly mentioning that 'the day does not close without the customary contests on the Green which date from long before the Christian era', and he concludes that the Beltane Queen Festival is not only a fête which brings delight to thousands of old and young but 'is a link with a venerable past and ministers to a deep-seated desire manifested both in social and religious life'. Human nature does not change and there is little doubt that in another eighty years the oldest inhabitants will reflect on 1990 and rejoice that their forebears had the prescience not only to preserve traditions but to improve on them for posterity's enjoyment.

Whilst the week's timetable caters in the main for children cheering, singing, dancing, racing, dressing up and parading in fancy or character costume, there is a great deal on offer for adults. Before breakfast on Sunday morning the town is transformed and elaborate decorations, which appear as if by magic wand, engender an atmosphere of carnival. Early in the evening the unmistakably brisk tones of the Silver Band summon citizens to watch the procession as it marches to the old Cross Kirk for the inaugural service. Quite a colourful occasion and one which gives official blessing to Beltane: it has been averred that modern members of uniformed youth organisations attended by their Colour parties replace the pilgrims who, for centuries, visited the shrine to view the relics contained in the ancient church founded in 1261. Wednesday evening could be quite a long one if you witness first the installation of the current Cornet on the Parish Church steps and then make your way to Neidpath Castle where he is welcomed by the new Warden who will thereafter make a thought-provoking speech to the assembled throng. Next you can meander down to Hay Lodge Park and see the Cornet and his cavalcade fording the River Tweed, with all the bravura imaginable, after the riders have completed their perambulation of the burgh boundaries. If you still have energy to continue enjoying the evening's entertainment, follow the crowd to the golf course and watch the half dozen horse-races which are always exciting, and then make your way back to the High Street for the dancing of the reel — if you cannot get near enough to spectate, just listen to the loudspeakers and the Pipe Band! Thursday should see you in the Burgh Hall for the grand concert — a mixed bag of professional and local artistes plus the stately little ceremony of the Queen's Standard halfway through the proceedings — not bad for 60p! Soon after tea on Friday (no time for dinner that evening) go down to Tweed Green for the Fancy Dress Parade, a kaleidoscopic montage of the excellent and the outrageous such as you never before have witnessed — some on cycles, some singly, some in mounted sections or on lorries but most on shank's mare! The procession which follows the judging is an extraordinary sight and if you miss it first time round it will be back 'ere long before dispersing on Tweed Green. For the energetic and young at heart there is a Dance in the

Burgh Hall — but don't be too late home and risk oversleeping because Saturday's programme gets off to an early start. Before your alarm goes off the judges are out and about assessing the standards of decorated houses, whilst you are still at your toilette hundreds of children are traipsing up to Halyrude School where they will be 'made up' for their innumerable parts in the Beltane Show. Whilst you are having your breakfast the Cornet's mounted followers have commenced their ride-out over Cademuir whence they will return during the forenoon to join the main procession. Make your way first to the east end of the High Street and soon after nine o'clock you will witness the never-ending line of youngsters walking demurely towards the west end to take up their pre-arranged stations on the steps of the Parish Church — a motley crew indeed! Not so quietly the official party and guests emerge from Chambers Institution headed by the Silver Band to attend the Proclamation of Beltane Fair. The Pipe Band (which has led the children's crocodile thus far) now joins forces with the Silver Band to make a grand sound as they lead the official party to their reserved seats facing the children. The Crowning Ceremony must be seen rather than read about and most first-time spectators become instant and complete converts.

Afterwards there is the bustle of Beltane; the bands and their 'unofficial' rivals outside the Tontine or further along the street, the enormous floats loaded with their happy human freight, the unfamiliar sound of horses' hooves and the accompanying shouts of 'Hooray!' The sports in the afternoon at Hay Lodge Park continue the atmosphere of Beltane Fair which long ago included archery, horse racing and football; today you will see the latter plus foot racing, hockey and Highland dancing. But don't miss the Saturday evening climax to the week: by 7 p.m. both sides of the High Street are lined with people and very soon is heard approaching military music — Beating Retreat has begun. It continues for nearly an hour and, with the haunting sounds of the 'Sunset' air still ringing in one's head, metaphorically the curtain comes down on yet another Beltane Festival. As we stated earlier there's plenty on offer for adults and you still haven't made a tour of the town to see those exotically decorated houses — hurry!

Beginning long before broadcasting added a new dimension to Beltane, it has since been filmed and even televised for the folk who are unable to make the pilgrimage to Peebles. Many of these 'loyal sons of a fearless race' are thousands of miles away and, like the

PART IV

Western Australian Beltane Society (where the ladies are as keen as the men), re-enact their own version of the highlights of the Festival. That it has a history we hope has been demonstrated; that it has a future is certain for it is verily a microcosm of Peebles itself — and in another ninety years, generations as yet unborn will be 'little mice peeping out!'

CHAPTER 17

Local Associations and Social Interests

THE GUILDRY CORPORATION OF PEEBLES

The Guildry Corporation still exists in Peebles but only for social and philanthropic purposes. As early as the sixteenth century, however, it had specific powers conferred on it and in its own sphere was second only to the town council in importance within the burgh.

An Act of the Scottish Parliament in 1593 approved of the power of the Dean of Guild and his Council 'quhilk is to the great furtherance of justice . . . in all actions and maters concerning merchands . . .' By the Royal Burgh of Peebles Charter of 1621 the burgh was empowered to have a Dean of Guild and Council; it was not until 1647 that the burgh records show such an appointment. In 1649 the Dean's duties were more clearly defined, his principal duties being certainly in connection with the weights and measures used by the traders in the town. It is from about this time that the 'Peebles Pint' dates. The 'Pint' was a measure for the sale of cereals and now rests in the Museum of Antiquities in Edinburgh.

The earliest minute book of the Guildry Corporation no longer exists; but the rules and regulations have been copied into the second minute book which begins in 1705. Here we learn that the Dean of Guild must be a councillor and a merchant of the burgh; he was to be chosen annually. His original council consisted of four merchants and two from the trade guilds. Further, the Dean was given a key to the Town Charter Chest.

A Guild Brother's oath was as follows: 'I doe here protest before God that I shall be a faithful Gild Brether. I shall not collour ony unfreeman's goods under pretence of my owne. I shall not pack or peill with any unfreeman . . . and so oft as I break ony part of this my oath I shall be lyeable and pay into the Gildrie of Peebles the soume of forty punds Scots money.'

281

In February 1698 the guildry was given permission to have seats in the Parish Church (then the Cross Kirk) the 'south syd of the town loft' being enclosed for that purpose. This custom continued and the present Parish Church still has seating provision in the north loft for the Guildry Corporation.

The corporation, composed of six members was later increased to fourteen and by 1834 eighteen. At the turn of the present century the membership was again increased to twenty-five and it is now confined to a membership of fifty. With the demise of the Peebles Town Council, the loss of the offices of provost and bailies, the Guildry Council and Corporation of Peebles is now selected from the Guildry members; the office is taken seriously and the Guildry Council meet regularly to discuss the affairs of the burgh and to recommend action where necessary.

The Brethren of the Corporation meet annually for a general meeting and hold a dinner yearly for the 'Guildry Supper'.

THE TWEEDDALE SHOOTING CLUB

Although strictly speaking the Tweeddale Shooting Club is a Peeblesshire club, its roots are firmly in Peebles and its various dinners and meetings are still held in the Tontine Hotel. The club was established in Peebles in 1790 and remains one of the oldest continuing clubs of its kind in the United Kingdom.

In 1790 the French Revolution was a year old. In Peebles Dr Dalgleish was the minister of the Parish Church. The town clerk was William Little; the provost, James Reid. The Cross Kirk had been abandoned and the new Parish Church occupied Castlehill; Tweed Bridge, dating from the fourteenth century, was still as narrow as its humpbacked neighbour over the Peebles Water or 'Cuddy'.

The origin of the Club dates from a shooting party at Cardrona House, 'to enjoy the "sport" on Glendean banks on the Quair'. Here proposal was made to establish a club amongst those owning or taking part regularly in shoots in Peeblesshire and so the club was born. Amongst the founders were Lord Elibank, Sir James Naesmyth of Posso, Walter Williamson of Cardrona, James Wolfe Murray of Cringletie. From its inception the club consisted of not more than thirty members and adopted a uniform to be worn by all members. It was agreed that it must be: 'A coat of green colour with a dark green velvet cape, and a silver button with the letter "T" engraved on it.' In 1792 the button was altered in design, having 'a pointer dog and letters "TSC" engraved thereon, the button to be of silver'. In 1806 the uniform colour became dark green. In the main this latter is still the club uniform.

The club originally met in Miss Ritchie's Inn, now the Cross Keys. On completion of the Tontine, the club changed its 'home' to the new establishment, where it has remained ever since.

In 1790 the club established its wine cellar and purchased six dozen of port and claret glasses and four decanters all engraved with the letter 'T', with also a handsome book for the minutes of the club. The cellar, later established in 1808 in the Tontine, was well stocked with port and claret, 'Madeira' and champagne. All was under the supervision of Mr Lenoir the then manager of the Tontine. This cellar is still maintained today.

In 1822 Mr Paterson of Birthwood presented 'A very handsome ram's horn snuff mull mounted with silver.' The mull is still in the possession of the club and is used on all formal occasions. The club still flourishes, and although the number of their dinners, which still feature the appropriate game-bird as main course, i.e. grouse, partridge, pheasant, are now reduced to two in each year they are still well attended. More importantly perhaps they provide in the setting of the table furnishings and the uniforms of the diners, a glimpse into part of a tradition that has now been maintained for 200 years.

PEEBLES GUTTERBLUID CLUB

It has been said that the nineteenth century was the century of the 'Gentlemen's Club' and certainly this could be true of Peebles. In addition to the Gutterbluid Club founded in 1823 the following were active during the period: the Incomers Club, the Peeblesshire Society, the Edinburgh Peeblean Club and so on. Of these only the Gutterbluid Club has survived, having being resurrected by the late George Thomson in the 1960s.

Gutterbluid is unique to Peebles and it is a word used to describe one who was born in Peebles, often from a family whose forbears were in Peebles for several generations. The formation of such a club, one of whose original members resolved in 1823 to allow only those born in Peebles to become members, may have reflected a certain feeling of insecurity in the members that was engendered by the number of incomers as a result of the changes that were increasingly taking place during the nineteenth century.

The club met annually in February and each meeting was preceded by a committee meeting when arrangements were made. The early meetings were held in the home of William Robertson, Old Town, then part of the 'West Indies' of which Mr Robertson was the publican, 'he being the only publican born in Peebles'. William Robertson was the great-grandfather of the late Mrs Leila Ogilvie of Crossland Crescent. The club over the years met in various other venues: Gideon Wallace, Old Town; Mr Hotson, Old Town; the Masonic Lodge; the Commercial Hotel (now the County Hotel); the Cross Keys; the Crown Inn; and the Tontine.

Originally, and for many years, the fare was simple. In 1840 threepenny-pies, provided by James Dickson. In 1842 the more substantial gigots of boiled mutton and 'minced collops' with turnip and potatoes. In 1845 the price of the supper stood at 'one shilling each, and drink at pleasure'. By 1870 the supper included 'a Scotch haggis, also a capital salmon, both of which are now considered to be indispensable at the annual festival' — this for 1s 9d (just under 9p) per head. In 1873 roast beef is mentioned as the main course, the price of tickets being 2s (10p).

Traditionally the club provided its own entertainment. In the 'West Indies' in 1830 'the Club spent the evening with much mirth and harmony enlivened by songs, toasts, sentiments and memories'. In Alexander Tait, the club had its own poet laureate. Tait was succeeded by James Grosart, the author of *Tales of the Briggate.*

At the supper of 1881, in giving the toast of the evening 'Prosperity to the Gutterbluid Club', the chairman, Mr William Buchan, town clerk (uncle of John Buchan and a later Town Clerk J. Walter Buchan) concluded by referring to the value of its minutes, no similar register being kept in the burgh. The toast was drunk with tremendous enthusiasm. This last sentiment would be endorsed by anyone who has had the opportunity to examine them in full. They provide, not only a fascinating record of life in the royal burgh of Peebles in the nineteenth century, but include valuable information regarding the social and economic conditions of the period. The minutes extant date from 1823 – 1914 when they come to an abrupt halt with the outbreak of war.

THE GUTTERBLUID SOCIETY

The revived Gutterbluid Club owes much to the inspiration of the late George Thomson. It is a very different club from that started in

1823. The main activities of the re-formed club relate to voluntary work by the members in support of their native town. For a number of years they have laboured to improve and enhance the floats and street decorations for the Beltane Festival; their recent efforts culminating in the purchase of a landau for the Queen's Court.

Similarly, they are responsible for the ever-improving Christmas lights and seasonal decorations which enhance the appearance of the High Street at festival time. They also conduct a cleaning campaign of the Peebles Water on an annual basis.

THE PEEBLES SPECIAL CONSTABLES

It is not known precisely when the Special Constables were formed to support the regular police in Peebles and Peeblesshire. The nearest date we can arrive at is sometime in the 1860s. What remains of interest in the early days of their existence lies in the role they played in the life of the town outwith their official duties. In the days when annual holidays were confined to perhaps two separate day holidays in the course of the year, the Peebles Special Constables appear to have taken it upon themselves to organise a summer outing to take place in July on the Trades' Holiday.

As early as 16 July 1870, the 'annual pleasure trip of the Special Constables' is reported in the local press, on this occasion by rail to Stirling. By six o'clock on the appointed day 'the Constables headed by the Volunteers' Band and accompanied by the Provost and magistrates led a merry troop of excursionists to the railway station'. It is uncertain how such trips were funded but there is no question that the organising of them fell to the constables.

Such trips continued on an annual basis until the outbreak of the First World War when the practice ceased. In 1881 as many as 500 citizens of the burgh took advantage of the trip to again visit Stirling and in 1882 a similar number travelled to the Clyde Coast on the annual trip.

Needless to say the Special Constables still exist in Peebles, and they still act in support of their regular colleagues. But it might be said that in the more innocent days of the nineteenth century they played a more worthy part in Peebles society as the organisers of the 'Big Trip'.

PART IV

ROYAL BURGH OF PEEBLES CALLANTS' CLUB

Chambers' Scots Dictionary defines a 'callant' as a stripling, a young lad, or youth. Such a description could hardly be applied to the Peebleans who founded the Royal Burgh of Peebles Callants' Club in 1935. The founder members were Will Kerr, Ross Dodds, John McCormack and Jock Preston — veterans of the First World War. The early Callants were all mature men, but nonetheless, they were Gutterbluids and in their time had been 'striplings' or 'youths' in Peebles.

It is said that the draft constitution of the club was written on the back of Will Kerr's cigarette packet in the old Peeblesshire Social Club. Indeed the Social Club became the unofficial headquarters of the Callants. The more formal constitution states that the club exists to preserve and stimulate interest in the history and traditions of Peebles; to encourage and foster local sentiment; to foster local song and literature and in general to safeguard their heritage as Peebleans.

Membership remains high and is restricted to those born in the town or who have a fifteen year residence within the town. Once a year the Callants Supper is held in the Tontine Hotel on the Monday of the Beltane Festival week. Other than an annual general meeting, the Callants only meet to carry out community ventures in furtherance of their stated aims. Such ventures over the years have been the restoration of Tweedside walks, notably at the 'Sliders' and on the south bank of Tweed through the South Parks Wood; the planting of masses of daffodils at St Ninian's Haugh, Tweed Green and in Hay Lodge Park; also hardwood trees in Hay Lodge Park.

Further, they have given tangible support to the Beltane Festival in the form of costumes and dinner for the principals. They have also provided financial backing to local authors whose work has been concerned with Peebles. Considerable money for such purposes has also been raised through coffee-mornings, raffles and slide shows on local history, all the money raised later being applied to 'good works'.

The club also formed a close association with the members of a Welsh club from Ystrad based on the common interest in rugby football. Contact is made with the Welsh on the bi-annual trips to Murrayfield for them and the Callants to Cardiff Arms. The late Mr William Howitt in particular will be remembered amongst other Callants in respect of the success of the Welsh visits.

286

The club continues to thrive with sons following fathers as members, carrying on the traditions of their native town and supporting the many worthy enterprises which the club embraces.

THE TWEEDDALE SOCIETY

Strictly speaking, the Tweeddale Society is an organisation which embraces the whole of Tweeddale. Since its revival in 1967 the Society has attracted a membership which is drawn almost exclusively from Peebles. The society was founded in the 1880s and like so many organisations in Peebles became a victim of the First World War. In its earlier existence the names of Dr C. B. Gunn and later J. Walter Buchan are prominent in the early records.

The revival came in 1967 under the aegis of the University of Edinburgh who supported one of their faculty members, Basil Skinner, in the enterprise. The society, from the beginning, was fortunate to have the guidance of the late J. H. Hendrie who lent his considerable knowledge of the pre-history of Peeblesshire to the reborn society. One of the early office-bearers, C. Morrison, and the financial guidance of Angus Drummond and James Buchanan will be associated with the successful development of the society.

The aims of the society include the continuing study of the history of the area, including the archaeology and geology of Peeblesshire. Further, the natural history and literature of Scotland also claim the interest of the members, with particular reference to the Borders. The society also encourages research in the field of local history and the place-names of the area. The late Mr Liddell will be remembered for his interest in place and field names, and Mr Morrison for his research on 'cess' and other forms of medieval taxation. Miss Sheila Scott has also contributed to the corpus of local history whilst an office-bearer with the society.

The Tweeddale Society have always attracted an extremely high standard of speakers to their monthly meeting, many of them from academic institutions within Scotland. Summer outings and some local field-study outings are also arranged.

PEEBLES BURGH SILVER BAND

The genesis of the Royal Burgh of Peebles Silver Band would seem to be in the 'bands of music' which the militia regiments, including the

Peeblesshire Militia, maintained during the Napoleonic Wars. Antique instruments, including the military 'Serpentine' in the possession of the Peebles Museum, would seem to confirm this.

The first mention of a town band appears in the town council minutes for 1834, when it was agreed that subscriptions should be solicited and a town band formed. This approach was eminently successful and on 24 August 1835, the newly-formed band led a political procession of around 2,000 through the town.

From then on, and indeed to this day, the band assumed a semi-official status within the town, a status which has been supported over the years by public funds. Amongst the public functions which the band attended were the laying of the foundation stone for St Peter's Episcopal Church in 1836, the County Hall in 1843 (now the Sheriff Court), the Peebles East Station in 1853 and the subsequent arrival of the first passenger train which inaugurated the railway line in 1855.

By 1870, although the town council minutes noted the presence of a newly-formed flute band in the town, the burgh band was at full strength with many of its members also belonging to the Peeblesshire Rifle Volunteers. In consequence, the town council was approached by the Volunteers in 1871 to hand over the instruments to the Corps. This they did on the understanding that the band would continue to play for public functions within the town.

Between 1871 and 1888 the band functioned as the Volunteer Corps Band, attending both military occasions and also the public duties demanded of them. With the Army reforms of 1888 the Peeblesshire Volunteers were unable to maintain the band and its instruments. As the result of a public meeting held in 1889, and with the agreement of the military, the instruments were returned to the town. By the end of the year it was as the Peebles Brass Band that the band performed in the town.

The first of many contests were entered in 1891 under the Scottish Amateur Brass Band Association Rules. New instruments were obtained in 1895 and in 1897 the band played an important part in the festivities connected with the Diamond Jubilee of Queen Victoria. The following year marked the first occasion when the Beltane Festival in its present form was celebrated. The band with the exception of the war years has taken a prominent part in the festival ever since. In 1902, with the receipt of silver instruments the new title became Peebles Silver Band.

Between 1900 and 1914 the band attended national and Borders contests with mixed success. In 1900, the tradition of playing Christmas carols round the town was started, a tradition which has survived. The return of the Peebles men who had served with the Royal Scots in the South African War was also marked by a band performance in 1901. Invariably, the band was to play round the town, to waken the townsfolk at 5 a.m. for the day trips arranged by the Special Constables and other local organisations, a custom which has died.

In 1914 with the outbreak of war the band enlisted almost to a man: their instruments were then handed over to the Army who used them to form a regimental band of the Royal Scots. With the war over in 1919 the band re-formed and played, as one of their first post-war engagements, in the Beltane Festival of that year. New instruments were again purchased in 1923, the cost being £412 which was borne by subscriptions and an annual grant from the town council.

In the Second World War the band again disbanded to rise again in 1946. By 1949 the band became the Peebles Burgh Silver Band and as such was a charge on the domestic rates. The instruments were refurbished at this time and revalued at £2,000. The long years of hard work and contesting bore fruit between 1957 and 1961 when the band represented both Peebles and Scotland in the Silver Band Finals in London. An astonishing achievement for local musicians from a small burgh.

The band has always been well supported by the townspeople and by the former Peebles Town Council. The Tweeddale District Council also extends financial support in line with that given to the other bands in the District, but Peebleans were particularly pleased when the Royal Burgh of Peebles Common Good Fund recently provided a donation of £10,000 as well as an interest-free loan of £20,000 to enable the Silver Band to replace its instruments. This was generous help but fully justified as the band makes a valuable contribution to local events and through its role of offering musical tuition to the youth of the burgh.

PEEBLES EX-SERVICEMEN'S PIPE BAND

The Peebles Pipe Band was formed in 1919 from returned ex-Servicemen. There had, however, been an earlier pipe band since photographic evidence shows the Peebles Company of the

8th Royal Scots leaving the town in 1914 following mobilisation, led by a pipe band. Presumably this was formed from local 'Territorials' belonging to the Royal Scots.

The re-formed band came under the aegis of the Peebles ex-Servicemen's Club which had been formed in 1919 before the advent of the British Legion to which it was later affiliated. The band was based on the club premises in the School Brae. It first paraded as a unit in 1919 and for a time played in civilian clothes. By 1920, however, the band was fully equipped, their dress based on the Black Watch (Royal Highland Regiment) comprised Royal Stuart kilts and plaids, green doublets, Glengarry bonnets with a cap-badge bearing the 'three fish of Peebles'.

In 1920 the pipe-major was Jock Sterricks and the pipers Jas. Stirling, George Hall, Alex Sterricks and David (Danny) Shiels. The drum corps were Frank Bain, William Todd, Edward Todd and James Stavert. A member of the band who achieved fame furth of Peebles was John Garroway who became the principal of the Glasgow School of Piping.

Between the wars the first drum-major to be appointed was William 'Drummy' Irving and to him fell the honour of carrying the mace which had been presented by Mr Mitchell of Kingsmeadows House. Later drum-majors were W. McGrath, R. McGrath, J. Mitchell, R. Raeburn, A. Smith, J. Nicol and the present incumbent Sandy Brown. Over the same period the pipe-majors were Jock Sterricks, Ross A. Dodds, George Hall, John Connor, J. Wilson, Andrew Hall, Robert Veitch, Graham Aitchison, the present being Bruce Campbell. George Hall was to continue to play in the band during the Second World War and in the post-war period to become the longest serving piper.

During the Second World War many of the younger members served in the Armed Services. For example, they again formed the nucleus of the Pipes and Drums of the 8th Battalion The Royal Scots. The pipe band continued to serve the people of Peebles throughout the Second World War, many of the older players returning to keep the band in existence. Re-formed in 1945 and reinforced by the returning Servicemen they were able by 1946 to parade in Princes Street Gardens with a fully-equipped band comprising sixteen pipers and nine drummers.

In the twenty years since the celebration of the Golden Jubilee of the Pipe Band, it has steadily improved its playing performance and has been successful in a number of band competitions. More importantly, perhaps, the band continues to attract to its ranks a flow of the youth of the town willing and anxious to learn the art of piping or the skills of drumming.

THE BOYS BRIGADE IN PEEBLES

The First Peebles Company was formed in 1887, only four years after Sir William Smith founded the Boys Brigade 'for the advancement of Christ's Kingdom amongst boys'. Attached initially to St Andrew's Church (in the Eastgate), the company — the oldest in the Borders — was from the outset interdenominational.

Unable to continue during the last year or so of the Second World War, it was re-formed when its officers returned from the Services. Over the years W. Fairbairn, S. Fergusson, J. Phail, A. Hamilton, D. McKenzie have been associated with the First Company; D. Davidson, D. O'Hare, G. Johnstone, Revd James Hamilton and Mr Geddes were connected with the Second Company attached to the Parish Church. In time these two Companies amalgamated and today (1990) the members of the First Peebles Company proudly rally round their Queen's Colour which was presented in 1950.

THE BOY SCOUTS IN PEEBLES

On 26 March 1910, Boy Scouts from all the Border towns paraded at Wilton Park, Hawick, for inspection by their Founder, Sir Robert S. Baden-Powell. Amongst the 300 on parade were four patrols of the Peebles Boy Scouts under the command of their scoutmaster, R. H. Thorburn.

In September of the same year the Peebles Troop had their first annual inspection in Peebles, thus marking their first full year of existence as a youth organisation. They were to go from strength to strength in the eighty years which followed. The first Boy Scout headquarters of the Peebles Scouts was in a small hall on Tweed Green (now replaced by a dwelling-house to the west of the Tontine Hotel car park). Although taken over by the military in the First World War these headquarters served the Scouts well and were in use until the new headquarters, made necessary by the continued growth of the movement, opened at Kingsmeadows in the 1920s.

During the First World War along with the Girl Guides and other local organisations, the Boy Scouts were to lend their services to the war effort in many ways; not least they gave direct assistance to the military as messengers. Many former members were to be the first to volunteer for service with the Armed Services. In the post-First World War period the Peebles Boy Scouts were to languish somewhat as were many other local organisations due largely to the aftermath of the war and the depressed times which followed. The appointment of Captain Alex Anderson, MC, as scoutmaster was to revitalise the Peebles Scouts. Alex ('County') Anderson as he became known, was to devote much of his leisure to the Boy Scouts, a dedication which was to last for his lifetime. His organisational ability as county surveyor and his experience in the Army was to serve the Scout movement well. 'He ran the local Scouts with military precision,' one former member still recalls.

The Peebles Scouts were also fortunate during this time in having a new headquarters built for them, thanks to the generosity of Mr H. Mitchell of Kingsmeadows. This Scout hut in what is now the Moss Park was to serve them well until the move was made to their present headquarters at Dean Park.

The intervention of the Second World War saw the Peebles Scouts involved in 'national service', many of them gaining the appropriate badge for this service to the community, and again many were to see service in the Armed forces. Before leaving the post-war period, we should note that a group of Rover Scouts had been formed and they met in premises off School Brae, and they became a permanent feature in the Peebles Group. Nor should we forget the Wolf Cubs whose name in Peebles is generally linked with Miss Jessie Ferguson who had a near lifetime association which started in 1930 through to 1970, and received the MBE for her work with the junior movement.

The Peebles Scouts were prominent in the field of international scouting. In 1955, Robert Boyd and Elliot Jardine represented Peebles at a World Jamboree in Niagara, Canada. At the Fiftieth Anniversary Jamboree at Sutton Coldfield the Rover Scout leader David Ritchie was a member of the Scottish team responsible for the running of the camp. In 1963 at the Eleventh World Jamboree Allan Forbes journeyed to Marathon in Greece to represent Peebles. At the Fifteenth World Jamboree, again in Canada, Ferrier Pryde and Allan Ramsay were present; at the Sixteenth Jamboree in Sydney, Australia, Mark Begbie was the sole representative from Peebles.

The First Tweeddale Peebles Scout Group is in good heart and in the late 1980s it continues to grow and to provide a focus for the activities and aspirations of the youth of the town.

PEEBLES GIRL GUIDES

In February 1990 the First Peebles Girl Guide Company will celebrate their eightieth anniversary. The Boy Scout movement had been formed in 1908 under the aegis of Baden-Powell, but the new movement actively discouraged the participation of girls. In reaction to this attitude, and perhaps as a reflection of the burgeoning 'suffragette' movement, young girls and women throughout the United Kingdom sought to emulate their brothers in having an outdoor organisation which would cater for the new sense of freedom.

In Peebles the girls were fortunate in having Lady Erskine as a patron and mentor. Lady Erskine of Venlaw was a personal friend of Lady Baden-Powell and her daughter, Veronica, knew of the Girl Guide movement which had started in England. As a result the first Girl Guide company to be registered in Scotland was the First Peebles founded by Lady Erskine. The first meeting took place on 26 February 1910, and there were three patrols, under the three Miss Thorburns. By the close of 1910 a number of these guides had been presented with merit certificates at the opening of the new Girl Guides' hut at Crossburn.

From such early beginnings the new organisation was to blossom and flourish over the years and in the late 1980s there are three Guide companies and three Brownie packs active in Peebles. Both Golden and Diamond Jubilees of the Peebles Guides have been marked by the planting of flowering cherry trees as an avenue at Neidpath Castle, thus enhancing the already spectacular surroundings of the castle.

Youth movements have a habit of retaining their adherents for life. Mrs E. Laverock, to mention but one, was District Commissioner at the time of the Peebles Guides' Golden Jubilee. In the course of a Guide career which eventually spanned sixty years, Mrs Laverock held every rank from fledgling Brownie to county president.

The corporate minutes of the Peeblesshire Girl Guides in the near thirty years following the fiftieth anniversary of the inception of the movement in Peebles present a catalogue of activities which span the whole gamut of the aims and objects of guiding, including fashion shows in 1969, 1974 and 1976 — enterprises of obvious appeal to the teenage girl which also encourage pride in personal appearance, enhance individual self-confidence, and, of course, the shows were for charity.

Contribution to their own community was also encouraged and is in evidence. In 1973 further tree planting took place in Hay Lodge Park. The annual Daffodil Day which takes place in April is also supported; the daffodils, donated generally by Dawyck House, are bunched and sold by the Girl Guides in aid of various charities. Other community service events include 'Thinking Day'; 'Year of the Child' (1979); Adventure Day at Ingliston (1979); involvement in Blue Peter Christmas Appeal (1979); Carol 'Sing-a-ling' in aid of 'Shelter'. In addition the Summer camp at Penicuik in 1973 and International camps in Belgium and Norway in 1979 were held. The Girl Guide Movement in Peebles still flourishes and this can be seen by the array of merit badges earned by the Brownies, Guides and Rangers.

PEEBLES HORTICULTURAL SOCIETY

As early as September 1850 enthusiasts in Peebles had formed a Horticultural Society and in that month were able to mount a 'Horticultural Exhibition of flowers, fruit and vegetables, composed of gardeners, amateurs and cottagers in the County'. This show took place in the Burgh Hall and was reported in the local newspaper as a splendid occasion that was 'attended by all the beauty and fashion of the neighbourhood', adding that during the afternoon 'about sixty gentlemen dined in the Tontine'.

In the following year (1851) the Horticultural Exhibition was held in the Tontine Hotel and again it was well attended with nearly 800 visitors. In 1852, the date of the Horticultural Show was put back to July and on this occasion 'a large and elegant marquee' was erected on Tweed Green; again the Show was supported by about 800 people.

From such early beginnings the Peebles Horticultural Society has gone from strength to strength. They continue to sponsor an annual Show and before the event their silverware, cups and trophies provide an impressive display in the window of a local building society. Much of the success of the present society over the years is due to the dedication of the late James Derrick and his sister Miss Lizzie Derrick. Amongst the most prolific of prizewinners over the years must be William Greenshields for both vegetables and flowers; for superb flowers, J. D. Runciman; and the late Jack Duthie will also be remembered.

PEEBLES FLORAL ART CLUB

In the drab post-war years colour began to return to women's lives through the use of flowers as a medium for creative art. By 1952 Glasgow and Edinburgh both had a Floral Art Club. The third club in Scotland was inaugurated in Peebles by a group of ladies led by Mrs Minette Hamilton, a minister's wife, aided and abetted by Mrs Joan Mackison, herself a florist, and other enthusiastic flower arrangers. The first meeting of Peebles Floral Art Club was held on 8 November 1954. Its objectives were: '(a) To encourage interest in the Art of Flower Arrangement and the educational, cultural and charitable aspects of it; (b) To support the decorative section in all Horticultural and Produce Shows; (c) To give pleasure to the sick and the elderly through regular arranging of flowers in hospitals and to assist worthy causes by organising exhibitions.' Over the years these objectives have been faithfully carried out. Peebles ladies have been given monthly demonstrations of floral art by experts. Practical classes have been well attended. Flowers have been arranged weekly in churches and distributed to the sick and elderly. Worthy causes have been assisted by exhibitions such as 'Face the Music with Flowers' 1971, 'Flower Fare into Europe' 1973, 'The Tweeddale Way with Flowers' 1982 — all in the Burgh Hall.

Spectacular Church Festivals stand out in the memory. In the Old Parish Church, 'Flowers for the Christian Year' hit the headlines in 1968. This was a communal effort by flower arrangers from all over the county. In 1978 a similar undertaking, 'Music, Art and Flowers', celebrated the Queen's Silver Jubilee year. There have been others.

In St Andrew's Leckie Church 'Christening Robes and Flowers' 1983 followed by 'Wedding Dresses and Flowers' 1986, were fund-raisers for church and charity. In 1988 'Floral Song', a unique effort by the Floral Art Club and the Rullion Green singers, attracted over 200 people to the church to listen to singing of unsurpassed quality and to feast their eyes upon the floral tableaux staged down opposite sides of the nave. It was an emotive experience for all present. Floral artists and musicians had achieved the pitch of perfection. Voices and flowers blended in colour, rhythm and harmony. The singers were inspired by the beauty of their surroundings. Likewise the flower arrangers were touched by the sensitive musical rendering of the songs they had expressed in their particular medium. Each art had been a light to the other.

At the invitation of Mr and Mrs Maxwell Stuart of Traquair House, flowers were arranged on two consecutive Spring Holiday weekends in 1983 and 1984. 'Flowers in a Country House' attracted many visitors from over the Border and elsewhere. These two displays were presented also as part of Peebles Arts Festival in September 1984. Entitled 'Wine and Roses, Plants and Posies' — a slide show with a lively commentary — this event turned out to be a social occasion. Floral pedestals decorated the Parish Church Centre, wine and savouries were served, produce stalls did brisk business.

Since 1955 the club has provided the flowers for making what have come to be known as the 'Beltane Bouquets' for Queen and Maids. This pleasant activity is carried on, invisible from the populace outside watching the Friday night fancy dress parade, 'on the nicht afore the morn'. A chaplet to be worn by the uncrowned Queen, the bouquet which she carries and which is later given to the Crowning Lady, the six posies to be carried by the Maids of Honour, are delivered to their homes. In the past two years silk flowers have been requested, so that mementoes may be handed down to posterity. So the 'Beltane Bouquets' need not be made now at the last minute and the parade can be watched by the ladies of the Floral Art Club!

TWEED THEATRE

There has been a tradition of theatrical performance in Peebles since the French Napoleonic Prisoners introduced the burgesses of the royal burgh to Racine and Molière in 1811. In Victorian times a local company existed. In the manner of the times they offered both 'Peebles Amateur Darkies', musical soirées and dramatic plays. Before the First World War, the Peebles Players had been founded, amongst the principals being J. Walter Buchan and Dr Clement B. Gunn and later William Crichton. The company thrived until the late 1950s when the attraction of television caused the demise of the company.

It was fitting, therefore, that a new theatrical company should be founded on 29 March 1980, to be known as Tweed Theatre. Amongst the founder members were Paul Taylor, Marion Ewart, Lilani Ashmole, Peter Anderson, Joan Harvey, Chris Carney, Andrew Macnaughton, Sandra Marshall and Wilson McCay.

The first venture in 1980 comprised three one-act plays: *Careful Rapture*, *After Midnight Before Dawn* and *Irresistible Albert*. By 1981 *Blithe Spirit* had been attempted. By 1982 the company were taking part in the Peebles Art Festival with great success. In 1983 pantomime was introduced when *Dick Whittington* was presented;

pantomime is now an annual event. A further step forward came in 1987 when Tweed Theatre offered *Between Mouthfuls* in the Borders Scottish Community Drama Association Festival for one-act plays.

It was in April 1988 that Tweed Theatre made dramatic history at the Tontine Hotel. It seems appropriate that the Tontine, whose assembly rooms (now the dining room) owe something to the French Prisoners who introduced theatre to Peebles, should be the venue for an evening of Supper Theatre. This imaginative concept consisted of the Borders première of *Wha Daur* by Howard Purdie coupled with a dinner whose menu reflected the nature of the production, suitably framed in the Border tongue. This new idea seems set fair to become an annual event.

PEEBLES AND DISTRICT ART CLUB

On 16 March 1965, thirty-two people interested in art met in the Park Hotel. It was explained that the idea of having an art club in Peebles was in order to form a body of people interested in art which would meet regularly during the winter months for lectures, discussions, etc, and also encourage and assist the project of regular exhibitions in the Picture Gallery.

The inaugural meeting was held on 9 April 1965, and fifty people attended. The objects have been achieved by holding a programme of winter lectures and by organising an annual Members' Exhibition as well as exhibitions sponsored by the Scottish Arts Council and Open Exhibitions. In 1989 a junior section was started and their exhibition is held in May each year. In 1989 the membership of the Peebles and District Art Club had reached over ninety.

THE PEEBLES ARTS FESTIVAL

The imaginative step of first organising an Arts Festival was taken in 1981. Timed to coincide with the close of the International Edinburgh Festival, it is held annually during the first week in September. It is now well established as a local event and given unstinted support by Tweed Theatre, Burgh Silver Band, Ex-Servicemen's Pipe Band, Peebles Folk Club, and the 'Buskers' (drawn from the ranks of the Silver Band). The local children's groups are featured in a children's concert, and the Peebles Singers also have their own concert.

CHAPTER 18

Sporting Activities

THE PEEBLES BOWLING CLUB

Bowling like curling has a long history in Peebles. As early as the sixteenth century there is mention of the bowling green on Castlehill. Indeed, John Buchan uses the Peebles bowling green in *John Burnet of Barns* as the venue for Plenderleith's warning of the onset of the great Tweed Flood of the seventeenth century, Plenderleith having run from Tweedsmuir to carry the warning to the burgesses of Peebles.

In 1874, the bowling green was moved from Castlehill to the present site at Walkershaugh. The present clubhouse was opened in 1914 and it has recently been extended. Many sets of bowls have been left to the club by past members and amongst them are pairs marked 'John Grieve 1786', 'John Marshall, Surgeon, 1786' and 'Francis Russell, Esq, 1786'. Many more of similar antiquity bear only initials.

The game itself is perhaps even more popular than it was in earlier times, the club being well supported locally, and providing a welcome both to visiting clubs and holiday visitors.

THE PEEBLES CURLING CLUB

Curling has long been a sport in Peebles and Peeblesshire. The present club dates from 1821 and as early as 1823 Sir John Hay, Bart, of Haystoun, had presented a silver medal to the club to be competed for annually, and to be worn by the successful competitor.

In 1830 the same Sir John Hay further presented a massive silver buckle embellished with suitable insignia and a leather belt. The 'Belt of Victory' was contended for annually by the married men versus the bachelors on the town curling pond. The pond was created on

St Ninian's Haugh. Lined with blue clay to render it impermeable, it could be readily flooded and subsequently drained from the nearby River Tweed. The Kingsmeadows car park now occupies the site of the curling pond.

There were other venues within the town. A curling rink once occupied the site of the 'old' tennis courts and to the north in Victoria Park stands a single Canadian maple, one of two planted in 1897 to mark the occasion of a bonspiel between Peebles curlers and Canadian Peebleans. The cleared area of the rink can also be seen. The Moss Hole was also much used for curling although obviously only in really severe weather.

The Peebles Curling Club still competes now much more regularly than in its earlier years, the provision of indoor rinks making this possible. It has added also to the number of medals and awards competed for.

THE PEEBLES RUGBY FOOTBALL CLUB

It was in 1823 that William Webb Ellis, then a pupil at Rugby School, picked up and ran with a football in the course of a school game. Thus, effectively, the game of Rugby Football was born. Just before his death Sir Walter Scott, who was familiar with the new game, was asked his views on it by some of his Selkirk friends. Sir Walter opined that it was more suited to the martial spirit of the Borderers than any other ball game. As in the case of the retention of the Scottish banknote and the consequence of the loss of a Scottish Parliament, the good Sir Walter was correct in his opinion.

By 1841 the new game had been codified and was being played at schools and universities. In the Borders a number of *ad hoc* games were being played. It was 1875, however, before the first Border club was formed in Galashiels. Many others were to follow. By 1880 a club had been formed in Peebles and in the following year it was accepted into the Scottish Rugby Union. At first the matches were played at Kingsland Park where Kingsland School now stands. Regrettably the club ceased to function just before the First World War, doubtless a consequence of the outbreak of war.

In the spring of 1922, largely due to the efforts of James Carruthers of Crossland Crescent, the club was re-formed. In this he was assisted by similar spirits from the Border towns, notably Walkerburn, and these efforts resulted in the club being permitted to rejoin the SRU.

PART IV

In support of the revised club a representative game was arranged between Gala RFC (Border Champions) and a Walkerburn Select reinforced by a number of Scottish Internationalists, amongst them W. C. Bryce (Selkirk), A. Wemyss (Edinburgh Wanderers), D. S. Davies (Hawick) and W. G. Dobson (Heriot's). This match was played at the new venue of Whitestone Park and was watched by over 2,000 spectators; the score was Walkerburn, twenty-eight; Galashiels, five. The surplus gate-money of £58 was donated to Peebles RFC.

The Peebles side returned to their traditional colours, the ancient scarlet and silver of the Royal Burgh of Peebles. Their first game was at Kingsmeadows Park (now Glen Road) in October 1922. It was played against Watsonians. In a later game on 28 October 1922, G. M. Irvine was the first to score a try for the new Peebles RFC against Edinburgh Borderers. In 1934, the club moved to Hay Lodge Park where they have played ever since and where the original changing accommodation has been augmented by a new pavilion in 1967.

By the 1938/9 season the club was able to complete the season with only one defeat at the hands of Melrose by three points. A 'Second XV' had already been formed by 1923. In the post-1939/45 period both XVs were able to be raised again and by the 1960s a 'Third XV' and by the 1980s a 'Fourth' was turning out regularly. Also during the 1970s, in 1974, a 'Colts XV' was formed, providing a useful recruiting agency for the senior XVs. In the 1980s, sixteen as well as fourteen-year-old teams, both midi and mini levels, were all turning out (usually on a Sunday) for their respective games. The moving spirit of Don Ward remains prominent in this enterprise.

When the National League was introduced in 1974, Peebles joined the fifth Division East in 1974/5. In the 1984/5 season Peebles were moved up in Division 5 and promoted thereafter to Division 4. As in the rest of the Borders, Peebles sponsor and run a seven-a-side tournament. They now (1988) run a 'sevens' for under sixteen-year-olds and for the primary schools.

No Peebles player has yet won an international cap but many players have moved to more senior Border Clubs and have received recognition playing for the South of Scotland. The club has played against teams from all the home counties plus the USA, Canada, Sweden and Holland. A 'Welsh Tour' takes place every two years to coincide with the International Match. In 1987 there was a successful tour of the Isle of Man and in 1989 a tour of Holland took place.

The club opened a social club in the Northgate in 1971 and later moved to more suitable premises in the Eastgate in 1985. Much of the success of Peebles RFC in recent years reflects the dedication of the committee and the office-bearers, together with the flow of keen playing members.

In 1972 the Peebles RFC successfully marked their fiftieth anniversary of the club's resuscitation, with commemorative games against their old opponents Watsonians and another match with a 'Peebles-Walkerburn Select XV' playing Gala.

THE PEEBLES GOLF CLUB

On 8 October 1892, the *Peeblesshire Advertiser* intimated that a public meeting was to be held to discuss the institution of a golf club within the burgh. On 11 October the meeting was held under the chairmanship of William Thorburn of Craigerne; twenty-five 'gentlemen of the town' attended. They were to hear the events leading to this inaugural meeting of the Peebles Golf Club.

For some four years a number of individuals within Peebles had worked towards the founding of a golf club. In 1893 they were able to lease a suitable site at Morning Hill, which is about one mile to the south of the present golf course and lies on the other side of the Tweed. In due time a nine-hole course was laid out under the supervision of William Park, a professional golfer and perhaps the first golf architect. The new club had Lord Wemyss as its president; Sir Henry Ballantyne of Minden as the first captain; W. Lyon, secretary; and A. Yellowlees, treasurer. The annual subscription was to be 10s (50p), with artisans and boys admitted for 5s (25p). By 1893 a clubhouse had been built for £102, and a professional/greenkeeper, John Duncan, appointed. Mr Henry Ballantyne had presented three monthly medals to the club, and the 'gentleman's medal' is still in the possession of the club.

With the formal opening of the club on 8 April 1893, a silver-mounted club was presented to W. Thorburn, and this valuable club by R. B. Goudie of Edinburgh is in the possession of the present members. 'The Captain's Putter' is played for annually in the first competition of the season. The layout of the 1892 course can still be discerned since the tees survive on Morning Hill. It looks very short to the modern golfer but then the ball in use was the 'gutty' and the clubs were all wooden shafted. At the successful conclusion of the first year, membership of the club stood at 248.

By 1908 it was thought that the existing nine-hole course was inadequate. In consequence, ground at Kirklands was leased from the Wemyss Estate and a completely new eighteen-hole course was laid out and opened on 1 July 1908, with a fine new clubhouse located at the top of the present Kirkland Street; the total cost being £761. By 1910 the Peebles Golf Club was able to have James Braid, the Open Golf Champion, to play three rounds on the Kirkland course.

During the First World War part of the course was given over to the Army. In the course of the war, as was to be expected, membership fell and by 1918 plans had been made to dissolve the club and dispose of such assets as it still retained. Fortunately for Peebles it was found that the Earl of Wemyss was prepared to sell the lands of Kirkland and Jedderfield and the town council had first choice to purchase. In accordance Kirkland was purchased in 1918 for £3,500, the farm of Jedderfield in the same year for £2,250.

In the event the club agreed that a municipal golf course should be formed with the Peebles Town Council taking over control of the club with the following responsibilities: firstly, the appointment of a clubmaster, who would run the clubhouse including the catering and licensed facilities; this under the control of the Town Chamberlain's Department; secondly, the appointment of a greenkeeper and the maintenance of the course by the staff under the control of the parks superintendent. Naturally, the playing members would retain their autonomy and office-bearers. Over the years the system has worked to the advantage of both the local authority and the club. Again the club was fortunate in having such dedicated staff as Jimmy French as greenkeeper and his father before him in the same post. Indeed, the late Jimmy French spent all his working life in the service of the golf club.

In 1933, ground to the north of the clubhouse was given up to enable the town council to build municipal housing (the present Connor Street). As a result the existing course was redesigned and extended. This work was carried out to the design of H. E. Colt, with a total length of 6,205 yards. At the end of the day the course could claim to be one of the finest inland courses in Scotland.

In its history the Peebles club has produced many fine golfers; perhaps none better than A. T. Kyle. Born in Hawick, Alec was brought up and educated in Peebles. All his early golf was played on the Peebles course. In 1930 he won the BGA Spring competition, the BGA foursome, the Peebles Open, the Peebles Club Championship and the BGA Championship. By 1938 'A.T.' had progressed to and helped win the Walker Cup at St Andrews — the first of his twenty-one appearances in the Home Internationals. In 1939 he returned to Peebles as the British Amateur Champion of that year. Only the outbreak of war prevented 'A.T.' achieving additional honours in golf.

The Peebles Club also produced such gifted players as T. T. Sanderson in the post-war years; Kenny Wells in the 1960s and 1970s, others of the younger generation being Paul Gallagher and Alan Turnbull. The club has acquired a number of trophies which are annually competed for. Included is a magnificent rose bowl, the Weil Trophy, which having been won outright left the club but was restored in later years. Other trophies include the Anderson Trophy, Thorburn Cup, McGregor Cup and the Factory Cup.

Threatened with the loss of the present course in the 1950s in favour of municipal housing, good sense prevailed and this superb course survives; long may it continue to be so.

FIELD HOCKEY IN PEEBLES

The game of hockey flourished in Peebles before the First World War, when the local club produced an internationalist in Alex Smith. Between the wars, however, Peebles was strongly represented in the game but by ladies' sides only; the ladies competing against other Border sides. Much of the interest shown was due to the influence of W. E. Bryce of Selkirk who was to become an international player of note. In the ladies hockey XI who played at the Gytes both Mrs E. Laverock and Mrs Mary Nicholson played for a time in the 1930s.

The peak of interest in the game in Peebles was reached in the 1930s when three international games were played in Whitestone Park: in 1933, Scotland were the host to England; in 1936, Scotland played Ireland; in 1937, Scotland played Wales. The greatest occasion was undoubtedly the first one in 1933 when W. E. Bryce represented the Borders for Scotland.

The adult game has only recently been revived in Peebles and again this is due to the ladies. The present ladies' club is a member of the East of Scotland League and having started in the sixth Division the club has successfully reached the third Division; they also won the Scottish Women's Hockey trophy in 1989.

PART IV

PEEBLES AMATEUR SWIMMING CLUB

Swimming as a sport has always been popular in Peebles. As early as the turn of the present century, and when Tweed was at its original height, swimming galas were held in the Minister's Pool or 'The Dookets'. In addition to races, young men wearing a chest harness played 'salmon' to rod anglers who endeavoured to 'land' them!

It was only with the gift to the town of swimming baths by Sir Henry Ballantyne in 1919 that swimming and indeed competitive swimming could take place all the year round. Further, diving events which had hitherto been held in Tweed at 'The Dookets' were also transferred to the indoor venue. The first baths were built at the foot of Tweed Brae and it was here that the Peebles Amateur Swimming Club was instituted on 13 July 1922. The secretary and treasurer was J. Jardine and amongst the first office-bearers were Mrs Borthwick, and Messrs Runciman, Scott and Flint (YMCA). It is important to note that at this stage outdoor galas and other events continued to be held in the Tweed at 'The Minnie'.

The first bathmaster appointed was Joe Lamb and it is a testimony to his ability that he was to remain in the post until after the Second World War when he was succeeded by Joe Brock. Over the years both of these early bathmasters were highly influential in the encouragement of the youth of Peebles in competitive swimming. In 1934, for example, Margaret Smith held the Scottish 1,000 Yards record at fifteen minutes and twenty-five seconds. The same girl held the Scottish One Mile record in 1938 with a time of twenty-nine minutes and eleven seconds, and indeed Margaret Smith represented Scotland in the One Mile in 1935.

In the post-Second World War period and before the opening of the present baths at Castlehill, under the guidance of Joe Brock, Lynne Ellis and Jamie Murray will be remembered for their achievements in competitive swimming. Only with the opening of the new pool in 1984, a pool which meets international standards, could the swimmers of Peebles reach their full potential. In consequence, the membership of the swimming club has increased, and in general the sport of swimming has become even more popular.

PEEBLES TENNIS CLUB

Although a tennis club flourished in the 1930s, from which time the Club Championship trophies date, the present club was only reconstituted in 1956. Two of the original five blaes courts were converted to all-weather surfaces in 1970, when a practice wall was also constructed.

It is interesting to note that thirty years ago the club committee was concerned whether Sunday play should be permitted, the question of appropriate 'clothing' requirements, and looking into complaints from the public about the behaviour of younger members!

Many well-known Peebles family names feature in the extant records in honorary or playing capacities but the club's most notable member was the late Scottish Internationalist, Mrs Helen Proudfoot. Her club connection and her special interest in junior coaching were commemorated in 1975 by her family's donation of a trophy for annual junior competition. The Peebles Helen Proudfoot Memorial Competition for Under-Sixteen Mixed Couples is held every May and has now been established as one of the main events in the Borders for younger players.

The club itself has always encouraged its younger members and as a matter of policy readily supports, and occasionally initiates, Borders and even National Youth Schemes. In recent years, Peebles and Innerleithen have been particularly to the fore in introducing and developing 'short tennis'.

The courts and pavilion are leased from the Tweeddale District Council and the club average thirty-five to forty senior members and over forty junior members. Senior Men's, Ladies' and Mixed teams along with Junior Boys' and Girls' teams represent Peebles in all the Border Competition Leagues.

TWEEDDALE ROVERS

The name Tweeddale Rovers is synonymous with Jimmy Grant. Before retiral Jimmy Grant was a successful shopkeeper in the Eastgate, but for forty-one years following the Second World War he devoted much of his spare time to the Rovers. Amongst the founder members of the club were the late Joe Brock, 'Buster' Brown as well as Jimmy Grant.

Originally the club was a member of the Peeblesshire Amateur Football League, an organisation which regrettably is now defunct. In the early days the club operated on a shoestring. Joe Brock, who was at that time the bathmaster, washed and laundered the team strips himself in his spare time; such was the unselfish spirit of the original members.

PART IV

The first name of the club was the Tweeddale AFC but the late Will Kerr, editor of the *Peeblesshire News* added 'Rovers' to the title and so it became. From its inception the club was a family affair. Of the players there were three Frenchs, three Kilners, two Frasers, two Grants, two Tullochs, and two Rathies — all well-known Peebles families.

From such beginnings the club blossomed to become the outstanding amateur club in the Borders. Their record speaks for itself: they have won more cups and league finals than any other football team at their level. They have won the South of Scotland Cup a record seven times. On a number of occasions they have held the Cleland Cup (named after Provost Cleland), the County Rose Bowl, and the Benigno Cup (gifted by the Benigno family). Most impressive of all is the Dudley Cup, which rivals the Scottish Cup in size; sadly the Dudley Cup now has been relegated to the custody of a bank vault.

With the demise of the Peeblesshire League the club successfully applied for membership of the Lothian Amateur League, winning in succession the Hamilton, the Logan and the Mackinnon trophies. In addition, they reached the top of tne league and added the American Cup, the Brunton Cup and the Paul Shield to their spoils. Perhaps the Rovers' best run was in the competition for the Scottish Amateur Cup when they reached the quarter-finals only to be defeated by the eventual runners-up.

In the history of the Tweeddale Rovers there have been many players of note. James French who played eventually for Raith Rovers. Douglas McDonald who was approached by senior clubs but preferred to remain loyal to his club. The brothers Tulloch, who emigrated to Australia, joined Gregor Grant (another former Tweeddale Rovers player) at his adopted club Chelsea. Both George Nichol and David Drummond had international trials at Lesser Hampden. Alistair Grant received international honours playing for the Scottish Banks against England, a game they won. The youngest player was 'Cookie' Cockburn who at the age of fifteen scored twice against Pencaitland.

The club added to its reputation in the Borders by winning the Braw Lads five-a-side tournament on one occasion against a number of senior sides. In its forty years the club has been fortunate, not only in its players, but in its dedicated committee members and officials,

306

notable club secretaries such as H. E. B. Davidson and by having careful and frugal treasurers.

After these impressive achievements and the expansion of the club to be able to field three teams, the apogee under the chairmanship of Jimmy Grant came in 1962 when through the efforts of the committee, the players, their many friends and supporters, they were able to build their own pavilion in Kerfield Park. Funded by local subscription, built by local tradesmen and Tweeddale players, entirely in their own time and without any pay, it is an excellent example of community effort. The pavilion is testimony to the club and particularly to Raymond Scott, the club captain. The excellence of the club's facilities was recognised when the French World Cup squad used the pavilion and grounds of the Tweeddale Rovers Football Club for their preparation in June 1985.

CHAPTER 19

Local Newspapers and Media

IT WAS DUE to the foresight and the enterprise of Alexander Elder that the first printing-press was brought to Peebles in 1814. He was a stationer and bookseller, with a shop on the south side of the High Street. Two years before that he gave Peebles its first circulating library, which contained over 2,000 books. It was there that William and Robert Chambers developed their love of books and most likely caught the smell of printer's ink that was to capture their lives and to add a lustre to Scottish publishing and to the literary heritage of the English-speaking world.

Alexander Elder printed and published a small pamphlet entitled *The Concise History of the Origin and Progress of the Art of Printing*. This first publication produced in Peebles was described as a 'quaint production, the printer having considerable difficulty with his capitals and the spacing of words'. Nothing, however, can detract from his worthy effort in bringing the art of printing to the town. It may well have inspired the idea of a locally-produced newspaper.

Two names are closely associated with the starting of the first local newspaper. Andrew Murray, a printer and publisher of newspapers with a business in Edinburgh, was the first 'publisher', but, the newspaper had a 'local agent' and he was Alexander Scott. It proved to be a timely initiative that was most likely due to the foresight of Alexander Scott, because the newspaper came into being shortly after he had acquired Elder's business. Certainly J. Walter Buchan gives him the credit for starting the newspaper but it is clear from the first copies that Alexander Scott was not the publisher but the 'local agent'. The fact that the *Peeblesshire Monthly Advertiser and Tweedside Journal* quickly became established in the town was undoubtedly due to Scott with his local connections and his knowledge of Peebles and its affairs.

Alexander Scott, known as 'Booky' Scott because he was a bookseller, was reputed always to have worn a white shirt, had shaggy locks and was remembered by many old Peebleans for his practice on Hansel Monday (the first Monday after New Year's Day) of scattering ballad sheets from an upstairs window of his house in the High Street to the children waiting below. Although 'Booky' Scott sold literature, he did not stock new books or new periodicals. In that respect he was unlike his predecessor, Sandy Elder, who had in 1812 such periodicals on sale as the *Edinburgh Review,* the *Quarterly Review,* and the *Scots Magazine.*

Only two or three newspapers came into town each week in the early years of the nineteenth century. They were expensive and it was local custom for various persons to share the cost and they were passed from hand to hand until they were in tatters. Various tax duties were payable on every copy: stamp duty at 4d (1½p) which was reduced to 1d in 1836 and abolished in 1855. There was also a tax payable on advertisements of 1s rising to 2s and then 3s 6d (17½p) and, in addition, an excise duty on newsprint of 3d (1p) per pound weight of paper. However, a public reading-room was opened in 1846 for the 'gratuitous admission of all'. It was established in the old Town Hall, which was next to the Town House in the High Street and the same stair led to both. It had been opened at the suggestion of William and Robert Chambers and it was they who undertook to keep it supplied with newspapers.

When the various taxes on newspapers came to an end in 1855, it led to a flood of new national, regional and local newspapers starting up. Clearly it was good news for newspapers like the *Peeblesshire Monthly Advertiser* but it was even more welcomed by the national newpapers and there followed the start of the 'penny press'. When *The Times* had successfully developed the technique of rotary printing it became possible for national newspapers to develop very large circulations.

The local press primarily existed to serve its own immediate community but in order to gain a viable circulation it extended into a wider area to make itself an attractive medium for advertisers. However, circulation was generally only a few thousand copies and there was a need to develop general printing services to ensure a reasonable level of profitability for the business.

The first issue of the *Peeblesshire Monthly Advertiser and Tweedside Journal* appeared on 4 February 1845, when 1,100 copies were printed and distributed free, and thereafter it was published and sold on the first Tuesday of each month. The *Monthly Advertiser* began by raising support on its front page for the 'Improvements of Peebles' fund which had just been launched. Costing about £1,100, the improvements were the lowering and repaving of the street and entrances to the town, the laying down of convenient foot pavements on both sides of the street, the removal of some projecting buildings, the introduction of a more abundant water-supply, the renewing and repairing of drains, and the levelling and beautifying of Tweed Green. It would have been a major local news story at any time but, for the launching of the town's first newspaper, it was an ideal start. There were other items of news and general interest, consisting of small paragraphs like 'The town council had given two guineas [£2 10p] to the testimonial fund for Rowland Hill, the originator of the penny postage.'

Newspapers in Britain around the 1840s did not use much in the way of illustrations because they slowed down the production. There were, however, a number of weekly magazines that specially provided illustrations and one that started up in 1842 was the *London Illustrated News*. The *Monthly Advertiser* printed its first illustration on 5 October 1846, being an artist's drawing of Neidpath Castle and was reproduced from a wooden block (a woodcut). Later, there appeared a line-engraving of Jenny Lind, which the editor said was being published because of the 'consequence of the wide-spread interest excited by this musical genius'.

The first newspaper picture appeared in the issue of 22 June 1907 and this was printed from a metal plate which had a surface of dots of varying size and their gradation reproduced the image from a range of tones from black to light grey. It showed Jessica Taylor, the Beltane Queen in 1907, Jeannie M'Kay (Chief Maid) and Betty Ker, Gracie Muir, Sadie McNeill, Minnie Clark, and Robina McCormack (Maids of Honour).

Apart from news items and much-valued comment, there were in the early years of the monthly paper a great deal of 'homely' bits and pieces like 'The Nine Points of Speech':

1 Three little words we often see
   Are article — a, an, and, the.
2 A noun's the name of any thing —
   As school, or garden, book, or swing.

3   Adjectives tell the kind of noun —
    As a great, small, pretty, good, or brown.
4   Instead of nouns the pronoun stands —
    John's head, his face, my arm, your hand.
5   Verbs tell of something being done —
    To speak, read, write, sing, jump, or run.
6   How things are done the adverbs tell —
    As slowly, quickly, ill, or well.
7   Conjunctions join the words together —
    As men and children, wind and weather.
8   A preposition stands before
    A noun — as by or through a door.
9   The interjection shows surprise —
    As Oh! how pretty! ah! how wise!

After the newspaper had been in existence for about eight years and had a monthly circulation of around 2,000, the initiative was taken by William Chambers, in conjunction with 'Booky' Scott, to set up a newspaper printing-press in Peebles. This move coincided with the transfer of the stationers and printing business to Robert Stirling in 1853, Scott having sold the business prior to his departure to America. Having become the 'local agent', Robert Stirling quickly reversed the roles and became the publisher and arranged for the *Peeblesshire Monthly Advertiser* to be printed in Peebles and appointed Andrew Murray as the newspaper's 'agent' in Edinburgh.

The newly-acquired printing-press was described by Robert Stirling as an 'engine for good' that was 'capable of throwing off a newspaper sheet'. It was an American-designed Columbia printing-press, manufactured and supplied by Mr T. Long, Paul's Works, Edinburgh, at a cost of thirty pounds. It was made of iron and stood some 7 feet in height, having a type-table that wound below the printing platen to produce a print impression of the type when power was applied by hand using a large wooden lever. New types were also used and a scroll title-piece for the newspaper was designed by Alexander Kirkwood, St Andrew Street, Edinburgh. In modern terms, the newspaper was completed 'redressed' and began a new phase of its existence. It still remained a monthly publication but was published on the first day of the month, except when it fell on a Sunday.

At the time when these changes were made, the newspaper was

looking forward to the recovery of the town's prosperity. It said: '[Peebles was] at one time a place of much greater importance than it is at present', and had 'enjoyed considerable celebrity and profit as a market-place'. It was the hope of the publisher that the coming of the railway would prove to be the 'means of drawing local and general attention to the benefits of a regular market in Peebles'.

On 20 July 1858, the first issue of a new opposition monthly newspaper appeared with the title *Peebles County Newspaper and General Advertiser*. The title-piece contained the line:'The more a man knows the more he is open to conviction.' The publisher was John Paterson who was the other stationer in the town, as well as being an ironmonger, and the newspaper was printed by William Clark, who now owned the Columbia printing-press and was in business to print both newspapers. Edited by Mr Russell of the Grammar School, the *Peebles County Newspaper* was not successful and, in January 1860, after a short life, it merged with Robert Stirling's monthly paper, which then became a weekly publication, the *Peeblesshire Advertiser and County Newspaper*.

In 1871, William Clark, the printer took over as the sole proprietor of the weekly newspaper and, when he died in January 1875, it was acquired by James Watson who was a bookseller. Watson leased the publishing and printing to a professional journalist, James Young, but this proved to be a short-term arrangement which ended on 24 January 1880, when Mr Watson took on Allan Smyth as a partner.

Two years prior to this in 1878, Allan Smyth had started up a rival weekly newspaper with the title *Peeblesshire Herald,* and this he published and printed at the former offices of William Clark in the High Street, adjoining the Chambers Institution. The *Herald* did not survive very long and it stopped publication. Only about thirty issues of the *Herald* remain today and these are in the possession of Mr T. Litster who acquired them in the 1950s when he took over the premises of the former Neidpath Press at 26 Eastgate.

The firm of Watson & Smyth set up a new printing plant on the first floor of the engineering premises of T. W. Wallace in the Bridgegate. Up-to-date machinery was installed and the size of the newspaper sheet was enlarged. When the partnership was dissolved on 24 June 1889, Allan Smyth became the sole proprietor and the fifth owner of the *Peeblesshire Advertiser* in its relatively short life-span of forty-four years. His policy was clear:'We hope always to be on the side of progress; and will advocate as best we can those measures which have for their object the redress of grievances, social and otherwise, and the inauguration of reforms wherever necessary.' He was the publisher of the *Peeblesshire Advertiser* for well over forty years, and he lived and ran the newspaper in true accord with these high ideals, serving Peebles in this unique way.

The *Advertiser* acquired its own premises at 26 Eastgate before the First World War and again new and up-to-date machinery was installed. It established a high quality general printing department and many fine publications about Peeblesshire carry the imprint, 'The Neidpath Press'. Without doubt, the finest of the books that were printed there were two volumes of *The Book of Remembrance for Tweeddale* written by Dr Gunn for the burgh and parish of Peebles (1920 and 1921).

The *Peeblesshire News* under its earlier title of *The Peebles Commercial News,* first made its appearance in Queen Victoria's Jubilee Year of 1887 when it was started by James Alexander Kerr. Coming to Peebles in 1881 he became the foreman printer at the *Advertiser* Office when he was about twenty-seven years of age. Then, in 1887, he started up on his own account and with a small hand-operated printing-press located in premises at the Eastgate, he produced a four-page quarto size 'gratis' weekly publication containing a lot of advertisements and a few brief news paragraphs. Soon afterwards he moved his business to 55 Northgate. This quarto publication developed into the *Peeblesshire News* and once J. A. Kerr had acquired a suitable press capable of printing a newspaper sheet and had established his School Brae printing works, he made known that 'reform' was the aim of the newspaper and his editorial policy was to: 'Fear no man's frown, court no man's smile.' A contemporary wrote: '[As a publisher and editor he] assuredly and strenuously fought for what he believed was right, and friend and foe alike felt his rapier-like thrust, if in vain judgement they diverged from the straight path of duty.'

In January 1907, J. A. Kerr appeared before the Court of Session, to answer for his editorial efforts on behalf of an angler who was seriously injured when he was alleged to have been trespassing. The judge complimented Mr Kerr on his honesty of purpose and personal disinterestedness but the verdict went against him and he was fined £275 with costs. In Peebles it was deemed an occasion to raise a fund to present Mr Kerr with a public testimonial.

PART IV

The *Peeblesshire News* established a format that had a number of features like 'Sanctum Notes', which commented on the issues of the week and 'Current Topics', which covered national news items of particular local interest; local news was arranged under the heading of 'District Doings'. Avid readers who enjoyed Will Kerr's 'Tittle-Tattle Column' in the 1930s through to the 1950s, will be interested to know that his father produced a similar feature that was written in a humorous and pointed style. It took the form of a 'Letter to the Editor' from 'Maister M'Pen':

We'll gang to Edinburgh an' hae a doonricht day's enjoyment. At Embro' the first man I cappit up against was ma' auld frien' Treasurer M'Crae, the new member o' Parlymint for the East Division. He was rael gled tae see us, an' aifter introducin' him tae Betty an' Wullie we a' adjourn't tae the Royal Hotel in Princes Street.

We hadnae been lang there when wha shou'd turn up bit General Wauchope, happy an' smilin' after his defeat in South Edinburgh. He shook hauns wi' Maister M'Crae, an' askit tae be introduced tae Betty an' me. 'Man, General', says the MP, 'dae ye no' ken Maister M'Pen. He's yin o' the maist distinguished men in Peebles'.

When I cau'd get in a word, I says, says I, 'Man, General, ye made a grand fecht an' aw wis sorry ye didna' get in, but I suppose in Embro' they dinna want heroes for members o' Parlymint, it'll be men wi' brains they want'. 'You are more plain than pleasant, Maister M'Pen', says the General.

After knockin' aboot the maist part o' the day fechtin an' cattin' oot wi' each ither as bitterly as the thrae wives at Rosetta, wha are aye screitchin' aboot pittin' a bucket on 'my side o' the walk, ye hussy', we daundered aimlessly on.

Man thirs graun' shop windys in Embro' but Melrose o' the High Street o' Peebles dinged them a' for Tweeds. An' Bob Veitch's new hat shop wad stand formist wi' ony o' them. Shairly a' the men folk in Embro' are tilers or printers — puir seik lookin' fallows — (nae offence tae the 'PN' staff) — but talkin' o' tilers, aw ne'er saw sic ill-fittin claes. My certy, Mr Henry Ker, the tiler in oor toon wae blush tae pit oot sic work.

We saw a wheen grocer's shop — cheap in Embro? Dinna tell me that! Russell at 33 High Street ding's them a'.

The typesetting of the pages of these early newspapers was a task carried out by hand and using movable type, which was assembled letter by letter into words. The newspaper pages consisted of columns of hand-set type that could easily be knocked over (when this happened the pile of jumbled letters were referred to as 'pie'd'). Therefore, it needed care and skill to assemble these large areas of type into newspaper pages within metal frames for placing on the printing-press. This task went on week-by-week in the printing offices of the *Peeblesshire Advertiser* and the *Peeblesshire News*. When the type pages had been used to print the newspaper, the individual letters had to be 'distributed' back in to the type-cases ready to be used again; uppercase for capitals and a lowercase for the remaining letters, punctuation marks and figures.

This laborious type-setting work ceased to be employed for news pages when composing machines became available. In major newspaper offices that happened towards the end of the nineteenth century but, for many of the smaller weekly newspapers, this did not occur much before the 1920s. Composing machines originated in America and they were relatively expensive, but when machines were manufactured in Britain it made available many of the older models which found an extended life in local newspaper offices.

The printing-presses in Peebles were designed to print direct from the type-formes and the folding and cutting was done on a separate machine. It required the printer to hand-feed the newsprint sheet into the machines and this was a laborious process when compared to the automated rotary presses that were eventually designed for the high-speed printing, cutting, folding and counting of large circulation newspapers. In Peebles, newspaper-printing machines were generally utilised for other work and in the Neidpath Press they were used for printing books, the Valuation Roll, Voters' Roll, Abstract of Accounts, and such work as the Beltane Festival Programme. A good general printing department could enhance the profitability of the publishing business.

When James Alexander Kerr died in 1908, his eldest son, Charles S. Kerr, took over the running of the business but, when he decided to emigrate in 1920, the firm of J. A. Kerr & Co. was taken over by A. Walker & Son Ltd, Galashiels, the publisher of the *Border Telegraph*. William Christie Kerr, the second son of the founder, was then appointed editor. William Kerr (better known as 'Will' Kerr) carried forward all his late father's high ideals and within ten years he had made the *Peeblesshire News* a strong paper that was gaining the ascendancy over the *Peeblesshire Advertiser*. Peebles was a fortunate town to have such an outstanding editor.

The new ownership meant that the newspaper was now printed in Galashiels and the printing works at School Brae were kept solely for general printing. The *Advertiser* then rightly made the claim in its title-piece that it was 'the only newspaper printed in Peebles', and this was part of the friendly rivalry that existed between the two newspapers and their staff. Frank Bain was the chief reporter of the *Advertiser* at that time and he and Will Kerr were close colleagues.

The transfer of ownership led to a more secure financial future for the *News* as it now shared its overhead costs by improved utilisation of costly capital machinery and had better production facilities. In 1951 Walkers installed a Cossar flat-bed rotary printing-press at the Galashiels works and it was the only one of its kind in the south-east of Scotland at that time. It had some of the facilities of the rotary press because it used reels rather than sheets of newsprint and printed faster with improved quality.

The *Advertiser* changed ownership in November 1931 when it was acquired jointly by John Parmley and W. G. Mitchell. Mr Parmley had been the general manager of the *Darlington and Stockton Times* and Mr Mitchell had been the president of the National Union of Journalists in 1930. In an editorial statement, the new owners said: 'Comment is justly subject to a self-imposed restraint, for while it is well to be frank, it is even better to be fair.'

When the new proprietors took over, Mr Allan Smyth stayed on as manager and tributes were fittingly paid to him and to his newspaper's past service to Peeblesshire. Mr M. G. Thorburn (later Sir Michael), Lord-Lieutenant of the County, commented that it was 'a healthy, well-conducted paper'. Provost George Anderson said 'it had a long and honoured history behind it', J. Walter Buchan, Town Clerk, adding that 'from the beginning the *Advertiser* had a beneficial effect, supporting schemes of progress'.

The *News* in the mid-1930s overtook its rival as the dominant local newspaper in terms of circulation and readership. It had a better service of news coverage and it was a much more interesting paper to read. Will Kerr took a tremendous interest in all aspects of local life and his undoubted love of the town gave him a special insight about Peebles and Peebleans. This reflected, week by week, in the newspaper. Seated at an old, well-used typewriter and working in a haze of cigarette smoke, his editorial office had an atmosphere of dynamic clutter. Despite the piles of typed pages scattered about his desk and elsewhere in the room and generally lying on the floor, he could reach out and unerringly find the piece of 'copy' I had to receive from him. His son, Ronald Kerr — also a writer and author of verse — summed it up when he quoted the reactions of a titled lady who arrived in Will Kerr's office and exclaimed 'What a glorious mess!' I have since visited many cluttered newsrooms all over the world but Will's office was 'abune them a', because he was completely, superbly and very happily in control of 'his' newspaper — 'Wee Kerr's Paper'!

His Tittle-Tattle column was popular with the readers; it was unique, and a piece of good writing that was 'truly' Peebles. It was widely read and often quoted in the town, appearing regularly as the last column on the front page. It is difficult to single out one item but the Amalgamated Poachers' Union frequently featured in the column and a fine impish piece by Will Kerr about the APU appeared in the issue dated 3 February 1950:

Now just imagine the Amalgamated Poachers' union is disunited — there's a split in their ranks, and all over nothing at all. The row started over Burns Suppers. Evidently some member thought it would be a good thing to have a hail-fellow-well-met sort of affair. An APU nicht wi' Burns.

The President didn't think it was up to them to honour the Scottish bard because he never wrote a poem about salmon. A very prominent member thought there must be some sort of reference and informed the President that he would look it up. He arrived back some time after out of breath. He kent fine Burns has written an appropriate song and he produced 'Roaming in the Gloaming'. Was the President mad?

The APU entered into the discussion and when the member stated: 'Aw didna ken oney better, ye see Aw canna read', why the air got thicker and thicker. A few thought the President had overstepped himself in pointing out the fellow's ignorance, but when the President retorted: 'The idea's rideculous, its nothin' mair or less than a plot to introduce women into the Union, the members looked at each other. It was when the Secretary hummed over 'Roaming in the gloaming wi' a lassie by your side', that the great split asserted itself.

Half the company thought it a great idea and that the fellow wasnae sae very ignorant after a'. The wee APU member in the corner took up another attitude; said he: 'Sae like women, coming between us and a Burns Supper.'

PART IV

> The APU's not concerned about who wrote the song, they're wondering which of the two sections will introduce a women's section. It looks as though it will be the President's group as he is using hair oil.

In August 1935, J. K. Robertson became the proprietor of the *Peeblesshire Advertiser*. He was a newspaperman and a native of Dundee. Then the business was sold to Mr Simpson, a retired grocer from the north of Scotland, who became an enthusiastic newspaperman. Then it was acquired by two journalists who had worked on the *Scottish Daily Express* in Glasgow, and they later bought the *Dalkeith Advertiser* and thereafter the *Peeblesshire Advertiser* was printed in Dalkeith at the works and offices of the Scottish County Press.

The Second World War, with its newsprint restrictions and fall-off in advertising revenue, counted badly against the *Peeblesshire Advertiser*. It became a mere shadow of its former self and it ceased publication in 1954. All who had for a time served the newspaper during its long years of life, were proud of its early beginnings and great traditions. For those who had worked alongside Allan Smyth, including the writer, it was indeed a great privilege to have known him and to be linked in this way with those early days of the newspaper's life in the 1880s.

Will Kerr paid this tribute to the *Advertiser* when it closed down:

In the newspaper world there is always a rivalry which must be maintained at its uttermost pitch, but notwithstanding there has generally been between ourselves and our contemporary, a friendliness and collaboration, as there must be with small town newspapers. The *Peeblesshire Advertiser* has played its part in the progress of the County and Burgh; it was noted for its integrity and soundness of opinion. It served well its readers and advertisers. It has had good Editors, who served every section of the community. Age did not show; rather it ripened and was well printed and an excellently produced newspaper.

The whole town was pleased and delighted when Will Kerr was appointed Warden of Neidpath in 1959. It was an honour he richly deserved and the people of Peebles took the opportunity to demonstrate the great warmth and affection they had for him and to show their appreciation for all he had done for the town and for its institutions. He was proud of the distinction of being Warden of Neidpath, which he held in the same special regard as the distinction and honour of having served alongside his own generation of

Peebleans in the 8th Battalion The Royal Scots during the First World War.

Undoubtedly, there were the two newspapermen of outstanding ability that greatly contributed to the well-being of Peebles in the twentieth century: Allan Smyth, who died in 1936 at the age of eighty-one, and William Kerr who died on 12 September 1963, aged seventy-five. Both were kindly men and worthy Peebleans; both had given over forty years dedicated service to the recording and commenting on the life and development of the royal burgh.

In February 1963, at the time Alex Walker retired from business, the firm of A. Walker & Son Ltd, was acquired by the proprietors of the Hamilton Advertiser Ltd. The ownership of the newspaper group based at Galashiels again changed hands in 1969 when it was acquired by Scottish & Universal Newspapers Limited, who were the proprietors of the *Glasgow Herald.*

Robert M. Shearer succeeded William Kerr as editor in 1963. He was a native of Peebles and had previously worked with Lowe, Donald & Co., but had always been interested in journalism and was a freelance contributor. He had a great knowledge of the town's affairs, having served on the town council, was a bailie and will be long remembered as a first-class secretary of the Peebles March Riding and Beltane Queen Festival Committee, having held the appointment for fourteen years.

Richard Pringle became the editor after the death of Robert Shearer in 1973, succeeded by Atholl Innes in 1978 and then, in 1982, Sheena Stavert became the next occupant of the 'editorial chair'. In October 1987 the *Peeblesshire News* was acquired by Kenneth Whitson, a past-president of the Scottish Newspaper Proprietors Association and chairman and managing director of the *East Lothian Courier* which is based in Haddington. He set up Border Weeklies Ltd as an independent and private company to manage and publish the *Peeblesshire News* and the *Border Telegraph* and they are both printed at Galashiels.

The *Peeblesshire News* continued during the 1980s to reflect local opinion and showed the newspaper's spirited roots when it withstood the onslaught of bureaucratic pressure from the Borders Regional Council when they reacted to the newspaper's campaign against the regional council's decision to allow private development in the grounds of Dunwhinny Lodge Old Folk's Home. The granting of planning permission for the building of housing in front of

319

Dunwhinny House was a decision that was strongly opposed by the people of Peebles, and it was argued that if local opinion had been properly taken into account, the statutory permission would not have been given. Although permission was granted, the full scheme, which included blocks of flats, was modified in view of the vigorous opposition.

Another important issue which the newspaper successfully campaigned against was the projected idea that the Tweeddale District should be amalgamated with the Ettrick and Lauderdale District. Again local opinion was strongly opposed to such a proposal and the newspaper did an excellent job in focusing attention on the issue and ensuring that public opinion was kept well-informed and that their views were clearly made known through the columns of the newspaper. It showed that the editor's coverage and comment on these issues were fully in accord with the founder's declared intent: 'Fear no one's frown, court no one's smile.' J. A. Kerr would have been well pleased with his newspaper!

Apart from the local newspaper, the other 'local medium' for news about Peebles is BBC Radio Tweed. It is a Scottish Community Radio Station which started up in April 1983 and is located at Selkirk. A commercial radio station is currently being established at Galashiels and will be 'on the air' early in 1990. Border Television also provides news coverage of major local events but as the catchment area for the station's news coverage is so extensive there is little scope for more than a brief reference.

A ' brief reference' would not have been good enough for 'Booky' Scott, Robert Stirling, Allan Smyth or J. A. Kerr. If that was the measure of the coverage that the town's affairs would receive — and if no newspaper existed to properly cover the news — they would be clamouring to start a newspaper, or a radio station, or a Peebles community television station . . : and demonstrate again their dedication to local affairs and love of their town that each had shown in their time during the 145 years of the 'Local Press of Peebles'.

CHAPTER 20

The Peebles Railways

AMONGST THE TOWNS which featured in the earliest rail-based schemes to serve the south of Scotland, Peebles was one of the most prominent.

In 1810 the celebrated engineer Thomas Telford (1757 – 1834) proposed a horse-drawn tramway to link Glasgow and Berwick by way of Peebles. Next, in 1821, another prominent Scotsman, Robert Stevenson (1772 – 1850), put forward a similar proposal.

Amongst the many schemes promoted in the 1830s and 1840s, six involved rail links between Newcastle and Edinburgh and Glasgow serving Peebles, whilst another, grandly entitled 'The National Railway of Scotland', proposed a line from Lancaster and Carlisle, up Liddesdale and through the Borders to Peebles, dividing there to continue to Edinburgh and Glasgow. This scheme actually originated in Peebles and copies of correspondence about it dated February 1841 from William Turnbull writing from the 'Stamp Office' Peebles (the Revenue Office) to John Rooke of Wigton in Cumberland are held in the Scottish Record Office in Edinburgh. Turnbull's letters exemplify the practice of the time when facts were falsified to serve the ends of the promoters, mileages, traffic potential and prospective revenue being distorted in order to present a favourable proposition.

In order to discriminate between these schemes, a royal commission was appointed. Its report, published in 1841, declared that only one Anglo-Scottish route was necessary, finding in favour of the newly-formed Caledonian Railway Company's proposed line from Carlisle to Glasgow via Beattock with a branch from Carstairs to Edinburgh. Despite this the North British Railway Company opened its line from Edinburgh to Berwick in 1846.

The Caledonian Railway's line was opened in 1848, and in 1849 the North British Company's Edinburgh and Hawick line was opened.

Despite a branch from this line to Peebles having been put forward, it was struck out of the Bill. Even before the opening of its main line the Caledonian Railway had in 1845 proposed a line from Ayr to Berwick via Douglas, Peebles and Kelso. This proposal was dropped, but it marked the beginning of the fierce competition which eventually developed between the North British and Caledonian Railway companies and so characterised the pattern of Scottish railway history. Later, an Act of 1847 authorised the Caledonian Railway to construct a railway from Symington to Broughton but powers were allowed to lapse.

It is necessary to bear in mind, therefore, in gaining an appreciation of railway developments around Peebles that the North British regarded the counties of Peebles, Selkirk, Roxburgh and Berwick as its own inviolable territory. Peebles thus became one of the notable frontiers betwen the two largest and most powerful railway companies in Scotland.

In 1845 an independent group was formed to promote a double line of railway between Edinburgh and Peebles by way of Penicuik. Capital was assessed at £250,000 and the preamble to the Bill went through Parliament in 1846. However, this coincided with a general proliferation of schemes, many of them hare-brained, the period becoming generally known as the 'Railway Mania'. Inevitably the bubble burst and many proposals including the Peebles one were abandoned.

THE LIGHT DAWNS

There the matter rested until 1851 when some Peebles residents, frustrated by the unsatisfactory horse-drawn transport serving the town, and, noting the rise in prosperity which the coming of the railway had brought elsewhere, got together to reconsider a rail link with Edinburgh.

These well-intentioned men were William Chambers of Glenormiston; Walter Thorburn, the banker; and John Bathgate, writer in Peebles. The railway was to be a local line founded on the most economical principles of construction and operation. The services of Mr (later Sir) Thomas Bouch were secured to conduct a survey of the suggested route which was from Eskbank on the Edinburgh and Hawick line by way of Bonnyrigg, Hawthornden and Leadburn, just south of which the summit at 930 feet above sea-level would be reached, and thereafter down Eddleston Water to Peebles, a distance of 18.75 miles. Bouch, noted for his ability to produce inexpensive railways, reported favourably on the route and assessed its cost at £49,065 including bridges and stations. Parliamentary and ancillary costs were estimated not to exceed £10,000.

A committee of local gentlemen was formed to carry through the proposals, comprising Sir Graham Montgomery, Bart., of Stanhope, MP for Peeblesshire; Lord Elibank; William Chambers; Anthony Nichol of Kerfield; William Anderson of Hallyards; A. Buchan of Haystoun; and Walter Thorburn. The secretary was John Bathgate.

A Parliamentary Bill was duly presented and the Peebles Railway Company received the Royal Assent on 8 July 1853 (17 Vic. Cap. lxxvii), the authorised capital of the company being £70,000 in £10 shares with an additional borrowing capability of £23,000 on mortgage or bond after one-half of the share capital had been paid up.

It was stipulated that the railway must be constructed within five years of the Act being granted. The first directors were Sir Graham Montgomery, Bart.; Sir Adam Hay, Bart., of Venlaw; William Chambers; Anthony Nichol; R. B. Wardlaw Ramsay of Whitehill (Rosewell); Charles Cowan of Penicuik; William Anderson; Walter Thorburn; and John Ballantyne.

That the Peebles Railway had got off to a good start there was no doubt; no less an authority than *Herepath's Railway Journal,* making good use of pun, praised the company for its lack of pretension — 'It bids fair to deserve the name of the "People's Railway",' — and congratulated it for having obtained its Act of Parliament at a cost claimed to be the lowest yet accomplished by a railway company. Negotiations with landowners over its construction had been conducted with diligence, goodwill and economy, thanks largely to the zeal and ability of the secretary, John Bathgate, and the Board had also demonstrated considerable ability in its dealings with the officials of the North British Railway over the junction with the latter's Hawick line at Eskbank.

CUTTING THE FIRST TURF

On 9 August 1853, a mere month after incorporation of the company, the public ceremony of 'Cutting the First Turf' took place in Dovecot Park, Peebles, amid great rejoicing. The following is a synopsis of a report published in the *Peeblesshire Advertiser:*

Early that morning the rural population for miles around were astir and in they poured in hay carts and every sort of vehicle until the usually quiet streets of the burgh were awakened to an extraordinary state of vivacity. The shopkeepers had been rubbing up their shop fronts and dressing their windows to the best advantage the whole week before. The mills at Innerleithen were stopped and the villagers marched en masse to Peebles; not a child was left behind who could walk the distance. The strains of the Innerleithen band added to the excitement, which was still further enlightened by the ringing music of the Penicuik Band as they marched up the street, fifteen strong, playing 'In the Garb of Old Gaul'. It was bewildering how such a multitude could be gathered together in Peebles. Carriages upon carriages added to the throng.

At precisely 12 o'clock the procession started from Tweed Green in a long column three deep, preceded by the Innerleithen Band, flags, banners and floral decorations. The Yearly Benefit Society, Hammermen and Weavers, and Penicuik Band preceded Peebles Lodge Kilwinning, accompanied by delegations from the Lodge Canongate and Leith, the Journeymen, Edinburgh; the Operatives, Biggar; from Stow, the Celtic and others, the brethren all decorated with sashes of the livery of their respective Lodges. Then followed the Magistrates and Town Council of the Burgh, preceded as in the days of yore by three officers carrying halberds. The clergy followed, then came Sheriffs Napier and Burnett, preceded by a large banner bearing an elegant device — the arms of Edinburgh and Peebles united, with the motto: 'Tandem Triumphans'; and three navvies following, bearing a mahogany barrow of tasteful design and a new Sheffield spade to be used for the occasion.

The procession was by way of Old Town, the Ludgate and the Cross Kirk to the Dovecot Park. A large platform held the dignitaries. There were Directors, shareholders, elegant ladies, the crowds massed all around in holiday attire; everywhere gay with bunting, flags and designs, eight or ten flagstaffs displaying the arms of England, France, Belgium and other countries, and a huge Union Jack.

Mr Bathgate, Secretary, opened the proceedings reading a preamble of the Act. The Revd Mr Monilaws conducted the service and invoked the Divine blessing on the undertaking. Sir G. Graham Montgomery, Bart., MP, Chairman of the company, introduced Lady Montgomery, who, taking the spade, lifted the first sod and with great dexterity and spirit filled the wheelbarrow amidst the acclamations of the crowd. Sir Graham then, with great humour took off his coat and wheeled the loaded barrow a regular navvie's run and emptied it. On bringing it back, he filled it again himself and again discharged his load with a will, amidst long and repeated applause.

Short addresses, cake and wine in the marquee belonging to the Horticultural Society, a distribution of biscuits and Galashiels beer to the people congregated outside, and a dinner in the Tontine Hotel concluded the occasion.

CONSTRUCTION

Work began immediately at the Eskbank end. By March 1854, 250 men were employed but progress was slow. The secretary wrote to the contractors Bray & Dyson urging them to press forward 'so that they might be finished within a twelvemonth of getting possession of the first lands in terms of agreement'. The Peebles Railway minute book records for 18 April 1854 that the directors took much pleasure in renouncing remuneration for their services. Mr Bathgate was awarded £150 per annum for his (considerable) services.

Having calculated that the shareholders would be worse off by 2 per cent per annum if the North British company was contracted to work the line, and having unsuccessfully ventured into an arrangement for operation by one of the contractors of the day who undertook comprehensive operation of railways, the Peebles Board resolutely decided to work the line itself.

Locomotives and rolling stock were ordered, staff were recruited and the supply of all manner of equipment, plant, tools, uniforms, lamps, clocks, etc, were investigated with a thoroughness that was the hallmark of the Peebles Railway Board. Mr Knox, station master on the NBR at Portobello, was appointed to the combined posts of station master at Peebles and general manager of the railway at a salary of £110 per annum; and John Blackwood of the Caledonian Railway was appointed locomotive superintendent at the same salary.

In March 1855 Bray & Dyson, having overrun their agreed completion date of December 1854, announced that the line would be open for May, and in April their locomotive 'Soho' became the first to enter Peebles, not surprisingly being the object of interest of much of the populace. The *Peeblesshire Advertiser* was able to report that on 29 May the first actual train comprising two first-class carriages, two third class carriages and a number of wagons had been hauled through from Eskbank by one of the contractor's locomotives.

The newspaper described the first-class carriages as containing two centre compartments elegantly fitted for first-class passengers and two for second class, each capable of carrying thirty-six passengers. The third-class carriages could each accommodate sixty passengers. The carriages were of varnished mahogany, the centre panel of each being emblazoned with the arms of Peebles. For their wagons the railway company had adopted a white arrow with a red scroll, the newspaper commenting: 'The "silver arrow" is most appropriate for anything connected with our ancient burgh.'

The Board of Trade wrote announcing that Captain Tyler, RE, would inspect the line on 28 June, and the Board arranged for its newly delivered locomotive 'Tweed' to draw first-class carriages to Eskbank to meet the government inspector, and for lunch to be ready at the Tontine Hotel between twelve noon and one o'clock. Captain Tyler was reported as being highly pleased with the works. However, the railway company received a letter from the Board dated 2 July which only agreed to the opening of the line provided that a 'One Engine in Steam' arrangement was introduced. For a line 18.75 miles long this was clearly unpractical and the Peebles Railway objected. The Board of Trade consented to the route being divided at Pomathorn, a 'pilotman' being appointed for each section to ensure safe working.

THE LINE OPENS

On Wednesday 4 July 1855, without any ceremony whatever the Peebles Railway opened for passengers and goods traffic, the first train leaving the March Street terminus at 7.30 a.m. in the hands of Driver George Wilson and Guard John Goodwillie.

The *Peeblesshire Advertiser* commented in its August edition:

> It is quite possible that many among us may have considered this a tame way of inaugurating an event so pregnant with great results to the district, but we believe that the Directors were so disgusted with the tardiness displayed by the contractors in the execution of the works that they resolved—and we think rightly—to continue business at once and in earnest. We have entered upon a new epoch in the history of Peeblesshire.

Three trains were run each way daily between Peebles and Edinburgh at single fares of 4s (20p) first class, 3s (15p) second class and 2s (10p) third class. The town benefited immediately from the reduction in cost of transporting coal, minerals, building materials and agricultural produce, and a weekly grain market was started. The movement of livestock increased, the cost of transport by rail being 5s (25p) per truckload of cattle, and 7s (35p) per truckload of sheep.

The railway prospered and its directors were soon advertising 'building tickets' 'to induce parties to erect dwelling-houses in the vicinity of Peebles', granting a 'free ticket' for a term of years to the principal occupant of each house of a certain value. Two villas at Springhill were also advertised for sale or let with a 'free ticket' over the Peebles Railway for seven years.

In 1857 the Peebles Railway Company was granted a further Act of Parliament (20 & 21 Vic. Cap. 14 of 26 June) to raise additional capital of £27,000 in 5 per cent preference shares and £9,000 on loan, also to convert mortgage debts into debenture stock not exceeding 4 per cent.

WAR AND PEACE BESIDE THE TWEED

It was not surprising, the expectations of the promoters having been so demonstrably realised, that a scheme was soon being floated for an extension of the railway to Galashiels. The editor of the *Peeblesshire Advertiser* wrote: 'The wakened life in our little valley is about to receive a fresh impulse from an extension of our means of railway communication. Those who only know Peebles as it appeared before 1855 will scarcely recognise the town, bursting from its confines and extending its array of gay and comfortable villas on every side.' However, he complained that this was chasing out the poorer classes and that there was insufficient housing for workers. 'Houses must be found for our sinews—the workers.'

By Act of 21 May 1858, a small independent railway company was incorporated — the Symington, Biggar and Broughton railway — an event which probably appeared to the Peebles Railway Board to be innocuous enough. However, this ostensibly local enterprise had the backing of the Caledonian Railway in furtherance of its design on the territory of the Borders which, as remarked earlier, had been exclusively staked out by the North British company.

With the benefit of hindsight it hardly comes as a surprise that only eighteen months later, in November 1859, the SB & B company applied to Parliament for a Bill to extend its as yet uncompleted Broughton line by 11.25 miles to Peebles. Also, that same November, Richard Hodgson, chairman of the North British Railway, who had been assiduously courting the Peebles Railway, promoted two Parliamentary Bills, the first for a Galashiels, Innerleithen and Peebles Railway and the second for an Innerleithen & Peebles Railway.

Reading between the lines of Hodgson's course of action, one comes to the conclusion that if the first Bill for the full line failed, the second one for the much smaller part had some chance of succeeding on its own, and that whilst the extension of the Peebles Railway to Innerleithen would hardly on its own be considered a commercially viable proposition, it would fulfil the North British Railway's prime objective, namely the preclusion of a further extension of the Broughton line beyond Peebles. As it turned out only the application for the Bill for the line right through to Galashiels went forward.

To Hodgson's dismay it was thrown out by a casting vote in the House of Commons after being twice unsuccessfully opposed in the Lords, the case having been lost in the Commons on grounds of likely residential damage. This was the hand of the Caledonian's supporters at work, the Symington, Biggar and Broughton directors having made a public pledge that if the Bill was defeated they would extend their line to Galashiels. This company had actually lodged petitions as far away as Wishaw, Carluke and Douglas as well as on the Peebles Railway's doorstep in Peebles and Eddleston.

To the rapture of those in the Caledonian camp the Peebles Extension of the Symington, Biggar and Broughton Railway received the Royal Assent on 3 July 1860 (21 & 22 Vic. Cap. XV), just four months before the line was opened to traffic between Symington and Broughton on 5 November. The North British chairman hastily set about putting together a new Bill the following year for the incorporation of the Galashiels and Peebles Railway with powers to construct a line from a junction with the NB's Hawick line just north of Galashiels to a junction with the Peebles Railway's line just north of its terminal station.

This time round, however, the two railway giants, realising somewhat belatedly that continuing competition was both expensive and essentially unproductive, had come to an agreement that the North British would include in its proposals the construction of a

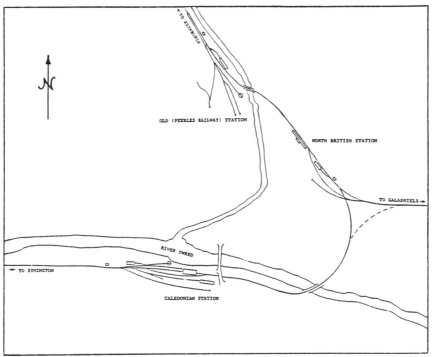

Sketch-map depicting the basic layout of railways in Peebles. (Due to the small scale some sidings have been omitted.)

connecting line between its new line and the future Caledonian terminal at the west end of Tweed Bridge.

This connecting line would be provided with junctions to enable direct running both to the North British station and to the line southward to Galashiels, as shown on the accompanying diagram. In exchange for its agreement not to oppose the Bill, the Caledonian was empowered to establish its own mineral depots at Galashiels and Innerleithen if so desired, and the North British was required to convey mineral traffic from the Caledonian to these depots at set rates. Rating conditions on other traffics were also included.

The Peebles and Caledonian Railway companies were each given running powers for their locomotives over the connecting line and junctions to be constructed by the North British. Finally the agreement required that, in exchange for the concessions made, the North British would not oppose the purchase of the Symington, Biggar and Broughton Railway by the Caledonian.

As late as March 1861 the *Peeblesshire Advertiser* averred that the

Caledonian was about to renege on the agreement. However, on 28 June the Bill became the North British (Galashiels and Peebles) Railway Act 1861 (24 & 25 Vic. Sess. 1861), and with that the Caledonian finally gave up the quest for a line into the Border country beyond Peebles.

MANAGEMENT CHANGES

Early in 1860 it became known that the North British was proposing to present a Bill to Parliament for the amalgamation of the Peebles and Jedburgh railway companies with the NB. A guaranteed dividend of 3.5 per cent was offered which would be raised to 4 per cent in perpetuity after three years. Convinced that this was as much as the Peebles Railway could be relied upon to yield, the directors recommended acceptance.

Following the Peebles Railway's statutory half-yearly meeting on 21 April a special meeting considered the Bill before Parliament. The chairman, Sir Graham Montgomery, considered that the North British should and would pay 4½ per cent. George Arbuthnott, for the dissenting shareholders, upheld the retention of the Peebles Railway as an independent company, and in this he was supported by the company's engineer, Thomas Bouch. Provost Stirling on behalf of the town council also opposed the amalgamation, although he personally supported it. Mr Chambers spoke as the only dissenting director. A vote was taken and as the three-quarters majority was not obtained the Bill was lost, but the result was the resignation of the chairman, Sir Graham Montgomery and three other directors.

William Chambers of Glenormiston presided over an extraordinary general meeting of the railway company in Peebles in January 1861. The North British were by now proposing a 5 per cent guaranteed dividend and certain improvements to the train service in exchange for the lease of the railway which would be operated and maintained by the NB. Moreover the proposal involved the retention of the corporation of the Peebles Railway and its directors. A temporary working agreement would apply for eighteen months with effect from 1 February pending a permanent lease being granted by Parliament. The resolutions were unanimously adopted, and Mr Chambers was applauded for all his efforts on behalf of the shareholders.

It is perhaps worth recording that the Peebles Railway Board had become fairly knowledgeable in the working and management of railways, and Mr Chambers, the publisher, particularly so. In 1866 he was the author of a book entitled *About Railways* in which he dealt with legislation and management, construction, operation and finance, not just from a local viewpoint, but covering also foreign and colonial railway undertakings.

Following the temporary leasing arrangement, formal authorisation was received on 11 July in the form of the North British Peebles Railway (Lease) Act 1861 (24 and 25 Vic. Cap. CXIV). Only three weeks later, on 1 August, Royal Assent was given to the amalgamation of the Symington, Biggar and Broughton Railway with the Caledonian.

THE PICTURE IS COMPLETED

During the lead-up to the application to extend the Broughton line to Peebles, the editor of the *Peeblesshire Advertiser* had queried the sense of running an indirect line along the sparsely-populated Tweed valley to connect with Symington, a place which, he opined, no one would want to go to anyway. He had preferred the option of a direct route up Lyne Water and by Garvald and Dolphinton 'as taken by the old Hawick carriers', thereafter linking into the Caledonian's main line at Carstairs, already an important junction. Travelling, as he put it, 'on the string of the bow' this would not only provide a faster route to Glasgow but would also provide a beneficial link between Peebles and the Dolphinton area. He had forecast that the direct route would ultimately be taken, claiming that 'it appears injurious to make that part of the line from Lyne Toll to Broughton, a distance of eight miles, seeing it will eventually be of little or no use'. The editor's strictures went unheeded by the Caledonian.

However, in June 1862, going some way towards vindicating the editor's opinion, the independent Leadburn, Linton and Dolphinton Railway Company received its Act of incorporation. Construction work on the Peeblesshire lines continued and in 1864, a notable year, the following lines opened: the Caledonian's extension from Broughton to Peebles on 1 February; the Leadburn, Linton and Dolphinton Railway on 4 July; and the Peebles to Innerleithen section of the proposed line to Galashiels on 1 October.

Perhaps as an indication of prevailing influences, the *Peeblesshire Advertiser* made no reference whatever to the opening of the Caledonian line. The company's timetable appeared tersely on the pages of the paper headed 'Broughton – Symington on 30 January and Peebles – Symington on 6 February'. On 20 February fully one and a half of the paper's broadsheets were devoted to a report on the arrival in New Zealand of John Bathgate, former secretary of the Peebles Railway!

On 1 October that year the Peebles to Innerleithen section of the Tweedside railway was opened following examination by Captain Tyler. Goods traffic had already been passing for some weeks. Four trains each way were run on week-days between Innerleithen and Edinburgh and two each way on the Sabbath. Contrary to earlier prognostications the running of Sunday trains gave no rise to any outrages or drunkenness.

It was 1866 before the final link was forged when the line from Innerleithen to Galashiels opened on 18 June. The North British immediately commenced the running of through trains from Edinburgh to Galashiels via Peebles.

A new station had been constructed on the through-line just off the Northgate near Dean Park, the Peebles Railway's March Street terminus being closed for passengers but retained for goods traffic, being referred to thereafter as 'Peebles Old'.

The opening of the Caledonian line had caused a decline in the Peebles Railway's goods traffic receipts on account of the loss to the 'Caley' of the Peebles – Glasgow traffic but passenger carryings had actually improved.

THE PEEBLES TRIANGLE

The terms of the North British (Galashiels and Peebles) Railway Act 1861 had dictated, as mentioned earlier, the construction of a link line between the Caledonian and North British systems. This ran on the south bank of the Tweed through Ninian's Haugh, crossing the river on a bridge at Priorsford and dividing thereafter into lines giving direct access to both the North British station and to the line southward to Galashiels to form a triangle adjacent to Venlaw Bank.

Until it was uplifted in 1961 the connecting line ran from the Caledonian terminus over the Tweed at Priorsford and round the west to north curve to join the Galashiels line at Peebles Caledonian Junction signalbox not far from the North British station.

There has for a long time been speculation as to whether the west to south curve was in fact ever laid with track. A contemporary lithograph by H. Paterson, Edinburgh, dedicated to Sir G. Graham Montgomery, Bart., MP, depicts the full triangular layout, and until the early 1970s, at least, one could trace the track bed of this curve under the bridge carrying the Innerleithen Road. However, no reference could be found locally or in early railway publications to indicate whether the curve had ever been used by trains.

Recent examination of the Board of Trade Inspecting Officers' reports, which are lodged at the Public Records Office at Kew, reveals the following situation: when Captain Tyler, RE, inspected the line between Peebles and Innerleithen on 22 September 1864 he made no reference to the junctions demanded by the Act. However, on 24 May 1866, Captain Rich, RE, examined the Innerleithen – Galashiels section and also the link line in Peebles between the North British and the Caledonian, both of which had been notified as being ready on 16 April 1866.

The captain did not like the west-north curve as it crossed the sidings in the NB goods yard on the level. He commented that the west-south curve 'was laid down — part of it still remains, but the points have been taken out. I recommend that it be replaced and the present junction [i.e., the west-north curve] be taken out.' The NB chairman, Hodgson, wrote to the Board of Trade stating that it was not the intention to open the connecting line for passenger traffic in the meantime, but he stressed that passenger trains could not conveniently be worked in the west-south curve 'as they would require to be backed into Peebles station instead of running direct into it as proposed by the branch executed'. Captain Rich responded that the sidings crossed by the west-north curve should be moved. They remained in place with the link line crossing them on the level until the latter was removed in 1961!

The conclusion to be drawn is that the NB neither intended that the link line by the Tweed should ever be used by passenger trains nor that the opportunity should ever be presented for through trains to be run to the south from the Caledonian line. In short, the NB built the line to observe the requirements of the Act and, without having the slightest intention of fulfilling its purpose, they promptly put it out of commission. The Caledonian cannot have pushed the matter either, but for over a hundred years the earthworks remained as a reminder of the follies wrought in the age of railway competition.

DEMISE OF THE PEEBLES RAILWAY

In 1876 the Peebles Railway, still an independent undertaking though leased to the North British, finally succumbed to takeover, the proud little company along with several other small railway companies in the South of Scotland being amalgamated with the North British under the North British Railway (Additional Powers) Act of 13 July 1876, (39 & 40 Vic. Sess. 1876), the actual amalgamations taking effect on 1 August 1876. Mortgages of the Peebles Company became mortgages of the North British, Peebles preference shares and ordinary shares becoming respectively 5 per cent and 8 per cent lien stock of the North British.

INTO THE TWENTIETH CENTURY

In 1905, the Jubilee Year of the coming of the railway to Peebles, the North British let a contract for a new station on the site of its 1864 predecessor. The new structure, complete with 240-feet-long covered verandah, offered commodious offices and accommodation and provided on its upper floors a house for the station master, or agent as the NBR then termed the post.

In the Edwardian era the railways of Britain reached what is often regarded as their zenith. Life was leisurely until the First World War intervened to make heavy demands of the system. This war brought with it the development of road transport, and although the railways in the after-war years continued much as before, changes were in the wind.

THE GROUPING

In 1923 Britain's many railway companies were grouped into the 'Big Four'. The North British was absorbed into the London and North Eastern Railway, and the Caledonian became a part of the London Midland and Scottish Railway. Despite the change in ownership the separate railways continued to glower at each other across the Tweed.

The 1920s and thirties marked the increasing ascendancy of the motorbus, and the *Peeblesshire News* carried regular illustrated advertisements for Harper's coaches and for the SMT Company. The railway companies, either indifferent to or failing to apprehend the growing competition, took no action to improve their services, not even appearing to advertise what they had to offer.

Between 1937 and 1938 the former Caledonian engine shed was closed.

The Second World War came along, and the splendid viaduct over the Tweed at Neidpath was strengthened to carry anticipated heavier loadings. Both the LNER and LMS lines witnessed much wartime traffic. The tunnel at South Park was used to shelter the Royal Train when the King and Queen came to Scotland to view the damage caused by the German air-raids on Clydeside.

POST-WAR: NATIONALISATION AND DECLINE

On 1 January 1948 Britain's war-torn railway system was nationalised and given the title 'British Railways'. Peebles at last, after over eighty years, ceased to be a centre of inter-railway company rivalry. Sadly, a number of rural lines had reached a very low ebb, and in 1950 the passenger-train service between Peebles and Symington was withdrawn. The official closure date was 5 June but the final train was the 8 p.m. from Peebles on Saturday 3 June. This closure was the subject of impassioned correspondence in the press, culminating in an appeal in the House of Commons in October 1950 by Mr David Pryde, MP for Midlothian and Peebles. The Minister of Transport's response was that it had been decided that transport facilities in the area could best be provided by road transport. It was a litany that would be oft repeated over the ensuing twenty years.

On 25 September 1950, for reasons which remain quite obscure, the remaining (ex-North British) station was officially renamed 'Peebles East'. Two years later, in September 1952, equally obscurely, the former Caledonian station, by now of course only in use for goods traffic, received the new title of 'Peebles West'.

On 7 June 1954, the former Caledonian line was closed completely between Broughton and Peebles though Peebles West Goods Station remained in use, served by the link from the former North British line. The signalbox was closed as a blockpost but was retained as a lever frame to work the remaining points and signals. Despite the fact that the former Caledonian Railway Peebles engine shed had closed in the late 1930s, the turntable still remained in operational condition.

The *Peeblesshire News* carried an intimation of the closure of the Broughton – Peebles line a week after it had actually taken effect!

The centenary of the opening of the Peebles Railway occurred in

1955, and by way of marking the event British Railways closed the former North British engine shed adjacent to the old terminus. Locomotive workings were transferred to Galashiels and Hardengreen Junction (Eskbank). Messrs John Menzies, newsagents, also celebrated the centenary by closing the station bookstall.

NEW HOPE

The year 1958 heralded an attempt by British Railways to revive the flagging fortunes of some of Scotland's rural lines by introducing lightweight diesel railcars.

On 17 February in that year these units began officially on an experimental basis, to operate a new and greatly improved train service between Edinburgh and Galashiels via Peebles. They ran as twin-car units capable of seating a total of 128 passengers. They were cheaper to operate than their steam-hauled counterparts, dispensing with the need for a fireman and causing less wear and tear on the track, presenting at the same time a bright, clean alternative to steam trains, and a grand opportunity for the appreciation of the delightful scenery along the Peebles line.

Shortly after the diesels arrived Peebles East station, having carried its extended title for only eight years, was shorn of its suffix.

GOODBYE TO THE 'CALEY'

On 1 August 1959, after a decade of decay, Peebles West Goods Depot was closed together with the link line through Ninian's Haugh and over the Tweed. Goods traffic had been very light in its latter years, the yard dealing mainly with livestock traffic and the occasional storage of redundant carriages. Since the closure of the former North British engine shed the link line had been used by locomotives on the daily goods train from Galashiels which were turned on the still extant ex-Caledonian 50-foot turntable — a bitter irony in the light of the fierce rivalry of earlier years.

Also in August of that year Mr James Logan, station master at Cockburnspath, was appointed station master at Peebles in succession to Mr E. Middleton who was transferred to Stonehaven.

THE LAST GOODBYE

In November 1961 the *Peeblesshire News* reported that the lines in the former Caledonian Station had been uplifted and that the 'loopline between there and the former NB station was currently being removed'. The paper also reported that Provost Lawrie had at the Convention of Royal Burghs put forward a plea that the threatened closure of the line from Hawthornden to Galashiels be opposed, asking that it be fought relentlessly as a matter of national importance. Earlier, in September, Peebles Town Council and Peeblesshire County Council had planned an all-out offensive against British Railways' closure proposals which had been published during the previous month.

A BR spokesman was quoted as saying: 'We haven't decided on closure; we have just asked for opinions to the proposal.' Hardly a credible remark when he followed it up with: 'The traffic on the line is just not sufficient to justify its existence.' The truth of the matter was that the diesel railcars had failed to gain sufficient public support on the Peebles Branch. Despite the opposition, county councillors backing moves to retain the service by twelve votes to two, the die was already cast, and with that familiarity of procedure which haunted the 1960s, the winding up process began.

The fateful day eventually dawned, Saturday, 3 February 1962. The normal service operated culminating in the 11 p.m. 'Saturdays only' from Edinburgh which was met at Peebles by a piper and nearly 200 onlookers, the diesel setting off detonators which had been placed on the line. Earlier that afternoon, a special, last-day steam train, organised by the Stephenson Locomotive Society and carrying 150 enthusiasts, had arrived at Peebles hauled by a forty-four-year-old ex-North British locomotive (0-6-0 No. 64587 of Dundee Tay Bridge Depot).

The crowd of 300 which gathered at the station on that dreich February afternoon to meet the train and to witness Wendy Wood of the Scottish Patriots planting a symbolic Saltire on the windswept platform was in complete contrast to the jubilant throng whose rejoicing had celebrated the 'Cutting of the First Turf' not so far away nearly 109 years before. Indifferent to the feelings of its denizens, 'No. 64587' tugged out of Peebles into the grey evening, sending its shower of steam and smoke into the Tweed Valley for the last time.

The official date of closure was 'on and from Monday, 5 February 1962', the line closing to all traffic between Hawthornden Junction

337

(Rosewell) and Kilnknowe Junction (Galashiels), and Peeblesshire becoming the first county in Scotland without passenger trains. Such is the march of progress. The sole railway remaining in the county was the goods line from Symington to Broughton which was retained until April 1966 to handle railborne meat traffic for London.

The two signalboxes in the town, Peebles Engine Shed box and Peebles Junction box, were closed on 3 and 4 February respectively and soon disappeared at the hands of the contractors who almost immediately set about demolishing the railway.

Messrs Robert McGillivray & Son, Northgate, who had been operating a carrier service between Peebles, the Border towns and Glasgow, extended their collection and delivery services to Edinburgh.

Mr Logan, whose daughter had been Beltane Queen in 1961, moved on from Peebles to be station master at Broughty Ferry in Angus.

ENGINEERING WORKS

Both the Caledonian and North British (1905) stations were fine structures, the former being in the Victorian-Tudor style with a train shed spanning one of its two platforms, the latter having a wide platform facing on to the single through line between Peebles Engine Shed signalbox and Peebles Caledonian Junction signalbox. There was a loop at the former to enable up and down trains to cross. A signalbox adjacent to the engine shed controlled the Caledonian's terminus and adjacent sidings.

Being the hub of a small railway network, there were a number of interesting engineering works in the vicinity of the town. The most notable of these was, and happily still is, the eight-arched sandstone viaduct which carried the Caledonian line across the Tweed near Neidpath. Some 414 feet in length, this is a superior example of bridgework which incorporates skew arches on ashlar springing courses together with decorated piers and parapet rails. Trains bound for Peebles crossed this viaduct and instantly plunged into a 674-yard-long tunnel under South Parks Wood before emerging near the signalbox on the approach to the Caledonian terminus. Like the viaduct, the tunnel remains intact.

The link line between the Caledonian and North British stations crossed the Tweed at Priorsford on a bridge 257 feet long formed of four spans of wrought-iron bowstring girders. Traces of its abutments can still be detected, and the embankment which carried the line remains for part of the way separating Kingsmeadows Road from Ninian's Haugh and the river. The NB Railway's extension line to Galashiels crossed Eddleston Water on a wrought-iron girder bridge, eighty-six feet six inches in length. South of Peebles the line to Galashiels ran through a short tunnel under the Innerleithen Road before emerging at Peebles Gasworks which was served by a private siding.

There were goods depots at the Caledonian and the North British stations both of which were equipped with the usual goods shed, loading bank and crane and facilities for livestock and coal, as was also 'Peebles Old', the former March Street passenger terminus from where private sidings branched off to serve Ballantyne's March Street Mills and Dyer & Company's sawmills, both private sidings being extant in the 1950s.

TRAIN SERVICES

The Peebles Railway initially ran three trains each way between Peebles and Edinburgh. By 1856 the service had increased to four, two each way being 'mixed trains'. The timetable explained: 'Mixed trains are goods trains (having first- and second-class carriages attached) taking on and leaving off goods at all stations and sidings if required.'

In April 1860 the following passenger trains were run:

Peebles depart	7.45 a.m.	11.10 a.m.	4.45 p.m.
Edinburgh arrive	9.15 a.m.	12.42 p.m.	6.17 p.m.
Edinburgh depart	9.00 a.m.	12.30 p.m.	4.25 p.m.
Peebles arrive	10.35 a.m.	2.15 p.m.	6.00 p.m.

A horse-drawn coach provided Innerleithen with a connection with the 7.45 a.m. departure and the 6 p.m. arrival. When in October 1864 the line was extended to Innerleithen, a service similar to that above was operated between Innerleithen and Edinburgh.

By 1876, the year in which the Peebles Railway was amalgamated with the North British, there was a basic service between Edinburgh and Galashiels via Peebles of four trains each way on weekdays, one of which in each direction ran only between Edinburgh and

Innerleithen. In April 1910 five trains ran each way on weekdays whilst on Sundays there was one train each way between Edinburgh and Innerleithen and one each way between Edinburgh and Peebles.

In July 1938 there were five trains each way except on Saturdays when additional services operated, including a departure from Edinburgh as late as 11.03 p.m. which reached Peebles at 11.59 p.m. and Galashiels at 12.32 a.m. This train became known, amongst railway staff at least, as 'The Globe', reputedly because it ran out to Galashiels via Peebles and returned to Edinburgh via Stow — thereby circumnavigating the globe! Regular Sunday trains on the line had by now been discontinued and were never restored. By September 1951, the service was a mere three trains daily from Edinburgh-Galashiels augmented to five on Saturdays, and four trains from Galashiels to Edinburgh on weekdays and five on Saturdays.

Introduction of diesel railcars in 1958 heralded a new era of rail travel for Peebles, the service being eight trains from Edinburgh to Galashiels on weekdays, and nine on Saturdays, including restoration of the old 11 p.m. Saturday night train from Edinburgh, and seven trains from Galashiels to Edinburgh on weekdays and Saturdays. The 1958 basic service continued essentially unchanged until the line closed.

In its heyday the North British ran the 'Peeblesshire Express' which left Galashiels at 8.01 a.m., stopped at all stations to Peebles except Thornilee, departing from Peebles at 8.44 a.m. and reaching Edinburgh after a limited number of stops at 9.37 a.m. On its return trip from Edinburgh at 5.31 p.m. it ran with limited stops to reach Peebles at 6.24 p.m., stopping thence at all stations except Thornilee to arrive at Galashiels at 7.05 p.m. On Saturdays the return journey left Edinburgh at 1.33 p.m. reaching Peebles at 2.28 p.m. having stopped only at Leadburn.

When the line from Symington – Broughton was extended to Peebles in February 1864 there were three trains each way daily between Peebles and Symington, but by October that year the service had increased to four trains each way, the journey time being around 45 minutes. Trains left Peebles at 7.45 a.m., 10 a.m., 3.50 p.m. and 4.45 p.m. Trains to Peebles left Symington at 9 a.m., 11.20 a.m., 5.40 p.m. and 6.20 p.m.

In 1881 trains left Peebles at 6.25 a.m., 7.50 a.m., 10.45 a.m., 2.30 p.m., and 4.04 p.m. These ran through to Carstairs, taking in most cases just over an hour for the journey. Trains returned from

Carstairs to Peebles at 8.21 a.m., 11.34 a.m., 3.25 p.m. and 5.21 p.m. By 1910 there were four weekday trains from Peebles with an additional one at 8.20 p.m. on Saturdays. The same number ran in the reverse direction, the last arrival at Peebles being at 6.25 p.m. during the week and at 8 p.m. on Saturdays. There were no Sunday trains.

In July 1938 there were still four weekday trains each way. On Saturdays there were five trains to Peebles and four trains from Peebles. On Sundays there was one train in each direction between Peebles and Edinburgh Princes Street station where it arrived at 12.25 p.m. and from which the return trip departed at 8.04 p.m.

Before the First World War the Caledonian Railway Co. ran the 'Tinto Express' from Peebles and Moffat with through carriages from both places to Edinburgh and Glasgow. The 'Tinto' left Peebles at 7.45 a.m., Edinburgh and Glasgow both being reached at 9.30 a.m. Departures on the return journey were from Edinburgh Princes Street at 4.45 p.m. and Glasgow Central at 5 p.m. After detachment from the Moffat portion at Symington, the Peebles carriages ran forward to reach the town at 6.46 p.m. Over the years certain trains conveyed the odd through coach from Peebles to Glasgow or Edinburgh, though in the case of the latter it was certainly the long way round compared with the direct North British route.

By 1948 Peebles still had a 7.40 a.m. departure which enabled travellers to reach both Edinburgh and Glasgow at 9.30 a.m. Except on Saturdays there were departures at 9.55 a.m. to Carstairs, 1.50 p.m. to Symington and 4.19 p.m. and 7.05 p.m. to Lanark. On Saturdays a train left Peebles at 8 p.m. for Carstairs. In the reverse direction there was a basic service of four trains daily from Symington. Sunday services were not restored after the Second World War.

Over the years both railway lines serving the town catered for a goodly demand in what would now be termed leisure-market traffic, and trainloads of trippers descended on the town. There were Sunday School trips to the town as well as a variety of special trains conveying clubs, guilds, works outings, etc. In the 1950s the town was host to BR's innovative 'Television Train' which arrived at Peebles East double-headed by a couple of B1 4-6-0 locomotives.

Peebleans too enjoyed their own excursions from both of the town's stations to many and varied destinations in those less hectic times when a day trip to Largs, Ayr or Berwick-upon-Tweed was one of the big treats of the year.

PART IV

LOCOMOTIVES

The Peebles Railway Company's first locomotives were two 2-4-0 tank engines built by Neilson & Co. of Glasgow for the opening in 1855. These were named 'St Ronans' and 'Tweed'. They were followed by two 0-4-2 tender engines built by Hawthorns & Co. of Leith in 1856 – 7. These were the Peebles Railway's goods engines named 'Neidpath Castle' and 'Roslin Castle'. These locomotives worked trains betwen Peebles and Eskbank where North British engines took over.

They were all incorporated into the North British locomotive fleet when the leasing arrangement of 1861 took place, the Peebles Railway being the first independent company to contribute to the North British. After the Peebles line was extended through to Galashiels in 1866, North British locomotives worked passenger services throughout. NBR 0-6-0 No. 82 (later LNER Class J33) became the regular goods engine based at Peebles (NB) engine shed.

After the First World War NBR Class C 0-6-0 (later LNER Class J36) 'Mons' became a regular Peebles goods engine. It had acquired its name after being shipped out to France for war service. 'Mons' spent much of its life on Peebles goods trains until the engine shed beside the Cuddy closed in October 1955, having survived the fire which gutted the building on 27 September 1934, the locomotive being stripped of its paint as a consequence.

A variety of locomotives worked the North British line over the years including NB 0-4-2s and 2-40s also classes (LNER classification) B1; C15 and 16; D11, 25, 26, 27, 29, 30, 31, 32, 33, 34 and 35; J31, 32, 33, 34, 35, 36 and 37; K3 and V1. Lightweight ex-LMS 'mixed traffic' class 2-6-0 locomotives were regular performers during the 1950s. In the 1930s and forties the LNER experimented with steam railcars on the Peebles – Galashiels section, but these were never considered to be much of a success. The ex-NBR 4-4-0s (Classes D29, 30 and 34) bore names from Scott's novels and of Scottish glens.

Named locomotives seen regularly on the Peebles Branch were 'Hal o' the Wynd', 'Claverhouse', 'Dominie Sampson', 'Dugald Dalgetty', 'Quentin Durward', 'Laird o' Monkbarns', 'Glen Falloch', 'Glen Arklet', 'Glen Gour', 'Glen Aladale', and 'Glen Fintaig', these often evocative names adding a piquancy to the experience of a train journey on the line.

The author entertains fond memories of several journeys behind a 'Scott' or a 'Glen', chugging up Eddleston Water to the summit of the line at Leadburn, and then galloping downhill between stations to join the Hawick line beneath the towering signalbox at Hardengreen Junction.

At the outset the line from Symington to Peebles was worked by the Caledonian Company's vintage 2-4-0 and 0-4-2 locomotives. Later the various classes of 0-6-0 and 4-4-0 tender locomotives of Drummond, Lambie and M'Intosh design worked the services, and the engine shed adjacent to the Caledonian station is reported to have housed one 4-4-0 and two 0-6-0 engines outbased from Carstairs.

In the 1930s the large 2-6-0 locomotives built by Peter Drummond for the Glasgow & South Western Railway worked the Peebles goods (Control No 123) and Broughton meat trains. Latterly Pickersgill's 4-4-0 'Caley Bogies' and LMS 4-4-0 'Compounds' worked passenger trains, with Fowler and Stanier 2-6-4 and ex-Caledonian 0-4-4 tank engines also putting in appearances.

In LMS days at least one excursion arrived in Peebles behind a 'Jubilee' 4-6-0, and Hughes 'Moguls' were regularly on the Peebles goods train which was also worked occasionally by a Fowler 0-6-0 'Standard' goods locomotive.

During the last war ex-Caledonian '60' Class 4-6-0s worked military freight specials for Stobs Camp as far as Peebles.

The Caledonian engine shed was closed and demolished sometime between the summers of 1937 and 1938.

IN RETROSPECT

Perhaps Peebles suffered as a result of the piecemeal development of its railway system. The Peebles Railway, conceived and run on the most economical principles by Peeblesshire people for Peeblesshire people, was an admirable enterprise of that age, and proved to be a major contributory factor in the growth and prosperity of the town.

But suppose that one of the 1830s proposals for a railway from Newcastle to Edinburgh and Glasgow by way of Peebles had materialised or that the vision of William Turnbull of Peebles with his 'National Railway' had found favour with the Royal Commission. Almost certainly this would have become the major Anglo-Scottish route, supplanting the Caledonian's West Coast line via Beattock and pre-empting the North British line from Edinburgh to Carlisle via Hawick.

Peebles would have become the principal junction linking both Edinburgh and Glasgow with the Border towns and with either, or

PART IV

maybe even both, Newcastle and Carlisle and the South. It is interesting to reflect upon whether a double-line railway with electrically hauled Anglo-Scottish express trains sweeping along the Tweed Valley would today have presented a happier prospect to Peebleans than the overgrown earthworks of those rustic branch lines which eventually joined hands so reluctantly at Ninian's Haugh. Many might have resented the scale of development that would almost inevitably have resulted. Many may now regret that the opportunity was missed.

Sources:

Robertson, C. J. A., *The Origins of the Scottish Railway System 1722–1844* (John Donald, Edinburgh)
Thomas, John, *A Regional History of the Railways of Great Britain,* Vol 6
   Forgotten Railways: Scotland
   The North British Railway (two vols) (David & Charles)
Allen, C. J., *Titled Trains of Great Britain* (second edition) (Ian Allan, London)
Railway Correspondence and Travel Society, *Locomotives of the LNER* (ten parts: 1963 – 89)
Stephenson Locomotive Society, *The Locomotives of the North British Railway*
Clinker, C. R., *Clinker's Register of Closed Passenger Stations and Goods Depots in England, Scotland and Wales 1830 – 1977* (an Avon Anglia Publication)
Bradshaw's Railway Manual, Shareholders' Guide and Directory (various years)
Deposited plans, books of reference, gazette notices of the various railways referred to in the text
Acts of Incorporation, amalgamation, etc, as referred to in the text
The Minute Books of the Peebles Railway Company and railway correspondence held in the Scottish Records Office, West Register House, Edinburgh
Chambers, W. and R., *Peebles and Its Neighbourhood with a Run on Peebles Railway* (second edition) (1863)
Scott, Sheila, *John Bathgate: A Sketch of His Life and Times in Edinburgh, Peebles and Dunedin.* (Sheila Scott, Peebles, 1977)
Pascal, Mrs Joan, article on Peebles railways in the *Peeblesshire News,* October 1980
Peeblesshire Advertiser and *Peeblesshire News* 1853 – 1962
Official publications of the North British Railway, the Caledonian Railway, the LNE Railway, the LMS Railway and British Railways

CHAPTER 21

Local Government in Peebles and Peeblesshire
1920 – 1989

NO HISTORY OF the Royal Burgh would be complete, whatever the period under review, without some reference to what is known as local government, its structure and its effects on the life of its citizens.

Historically the burghs of Scotland were one or other of the following: royal burghs created by royal charter, parliamentary burghs (which were essentially electoral constituencies) or police burghs both of the latter being creations of statute.

Peebles is known to be a royal burgh by a charter of King David I in the twelfth century and this is reaffirmed by charters granted by later Sovereigns. It was thus a place favoured by Kings and royalty in general, hence such local names like Kingsmuir, Kingsmeadows and Dukehaugh.

The authority for the existence of the town council, thus was by royal charter and records of the town council can be traced with accuracy as far back as the fifteenth century. It is also clear that there was a close liaison and communication from that century between the town council and the tradesmen and business community of the burgh. The various trades guilds were an influential force in the promotion of council policy and their regulatory influence on daily life was immeasurable. It should however be emphasised that functions of the town council were strictly limited to local issues and powers where necessary were delegated to them by central government.

In these earlier centuries, from the fifteenth to the nineteenth, there evolved the existence of two distinct offices that of provost and town clerk. It is clear from earlier protocol books and court books that the Lords Hay of Yester, having traditionally the sheriffship of the area, exercised along with it the provostship of the burgh. The first recorded reference to any other as provost was in 1609 when one John Dikisoun is named. Chronological records of provosts began in 1620 with James Williamson, and are recorded with accuracy until 1975 when Robert Kirkpatrick demitted office on the reorganisation of local government.

The word 'provost' has been of considerable significance to local government in Scotland. Derived from the Latin *praepositus*, it means in simple terms 'the leader'. Thus until 1975, the provost of a burgh was its civic head to whom deference and respect were paid and who by usage became chairman of the town council. By contrast, the chief officer of the town council, the town clerk, was less in the limelight, but yet influential. He was the adviser to the council with no vote but expected to proffer wise counsel on many matters. He was also the keeper of the minutes, documents and insignia of the council. Records of clerks to Peebles Town Council began with John Donald in 1459 and end with the writer in 1975. The penultimate Town Clerk was James Walter Buchan who was the younger brother of the first Lord Tweedsmuir and who edited an erudite *History of Peeblesshire,* which covered earlier centuries up to 1922.

For the purposes of this summary we can now pass over a few centuries and consider briefly the implications of one or two relevant statutes. These are as follows:

> The Town Councils (Scotland) Act 1900;
> The Local Government (Scotland) Act 1929;
> The Local Government (Scotland) Act 1947; and
> The Local Government (Scotland) Act 1973.

The first of these Acts virtually placed royal burghs, parliamentary burghs and police burghs on a par with each other for local government purposes. The Act of 1929 brought into being a structure for the division of local functions between town councils and county councils. The Act of 1947 was little more than a revamp of the earlier Act re-defining the relationship between town councils and county councils, revising electoral procedures and times and the representation of town councils on their appropriate county councils.

Under the 1947 Act, municipal elections were switched to May instead of November. Peebles Town Council comprised twelve members, one-third of whom retired each year in rotation and the council was required to hold a statutory meeting immediately after each Election, when vacancies in the offices of provost, bailie, Dean of Guild, treasurer and police judge were filled as necessary under the statutory conditions set forth in the Act.

The powers and duties delegated to the town council were multifarious. Housing, health matters, libraries, water, sewage and drainage, maintenance of unclassified roads, building control, licensing, recreation (tennis and golf) while the major functions such as education, planning, trunk and classified roads were controlled by the county council. There existed a close liaison (if not always agreement) between the county council and town council. Peeblesshire County Council comprised twenty-six members and that number included eight appointed by Peebles Town Council from its membership and three from Innerleithen Town Council.

In retrospect then, what can local government claim to have achieved in Peebles and Peeblesshire in the half century spanning the years from 1920 to 1975? The earlier of these years, namely the period up to 1939 were influenced by the aftermath of the First World War. Municipal housing was perhaps the number one priority and a first essay into the provision of housing with government subsidy brought into existence the 1919 scheme at Eliot's Park which was followed by similar developments at Dalatho, North Street, North Place, George Place and George Terrace areas. The rapid expansion in housing made necessary a new sewage-treatment plant and this was erected adjacent to the gasworks, which were at that time a municipal undertaking which lasted until nationalisation of the industry under the Gas Act 1948. On the recreation front, the municipal golf course was reconstructed, a licensed municipal golf club formed and the tennis courts upgraded.

The first municipal swimming baths were built at the foot of Tweed Brae through the largesse of the late Sir Henry Ballantyne.

The advancing prosperity of the burgh was shattered however by the recession of 1929 – 31 as the textile industry, on which the basic prosperity of the town depended, was badly hit. It was the only industry of any moment and the principal employer of labour and its recovery was slow. Various schemes were promoted with government grant to provide employment such as the formation of Venlaw Quarry Road. As the years passed, the Second World War loomed nearer and in the war years, it was very much a question of the 'status quo', the suspension of municipal elections, essential services maintained but all other resources directed to the war effort.

The post-war era began with the election of a new town council in November 1945 and continued until the reorganisation of local government became effective on 15 May 1975. As in 1918, the first priority was housing to provide for returning ex-Service men and women, many of whom had married during the war years and rightfully expected both housing and employment on their return from active service. An emergency statute of 1944 led to the provision of thirty temporary houses at Kingsland Square later to be converted into permanent dwellings, which to this day continue to be in much demand. There followed housing developments at Montgomery Place, Buchan Gardens and of course Kingsmeadows, by far the largest of the post-war schemes.

Simultaneously there was a clearly detectable shift in the type of population. Whereas previously, newcomers to the town were in the main those taking up employment locally or new professionals joining established practices, the advent of the modern reliable motor-car in the post-war era attracted a new clientele — the commuters whose work took them all over but allowed them to spend weekends and leisure time in a rural area. The population figure of the 1931 Census of some 5,853 persons has slowly pushed towards 7,000 or above and the housing need was substantially met by an ever-increasing provision of housing in the private sector (although this sector was also fairly active in the pre-war era) and such post-war developments were provided in the main by local firms, such as James Clyde & Sons, Peebles; Johnston & Smith, Peebles; Murray & Burrell, Galashiels; and James McLellan, Peebles.

At the same time, the Town Council had to keep pace with the provision of complementary amenities and modernisations. Improvement grants were provided to bring many old houses up to date. In the pre-war era Peebles Gasworks were run by the Town Council and this was a successful revenue-generating undertaking. The Town Council was its own best customer as all street lighting and lighting in all municipal housing schemes was by gas! When the Gas Act 1948, assumed responsibility for gas distribution on a national basis, the Town Council proceeded to convert street lighting and municipal house lighting to electricity as soon as possible.

The town's water supply, abstracted from the confluence of the Kirkhope and Manor Burns at Langhaugh high in the Manor Valley, had limited storage facilities at Bonnycraig, and the council proceeded to up-grade the whole scheme, duplicating the pipeline from Langhaugh, doubling the storage capacity at Bonnycraig and installing for the first time, full filtration of the public water-supply.

Meanwhile on the social side, civic amenities such as the library service (where previously a statutory limit of expenditure of three pence [just fractionally more than 1p] of each £1 rated had applied) was improved as was the Chambers Town Hall, a tourist information centre provided and the local museum completely overhauled with the assistance of a Carnegie Grant.

A much used facility was provided shortly after the Second World War by the erection of a footbridge in Hay Lodge Park linking the north and south banks of the River Tweed, known as the Fotheringham Bridge. It was the gift of a Peebles man John S. Fotheringham, who established a prosperous business in South Africa and was at one stage of his career Mayor of Johannesburg.

Despite such progress, depopulation of rural areas such as the Borders was a matter of concern and in an attempt to ease labour shortages particularly in the textile industry, an overspill agreement was entered into with the Corporation of Glasgow which brought in about fifty new employees of whom a fair proportion remain in the town to this day having made Peebles their permanent home. Also in an attempt to provide diversification of employment, councils were given statutory powers to assist incoming industries by rating concessions and the provision of loans for the erection of industrial premises on sites designated for the purpose. Under these provisions, the town council developed industrial sites at March Street and at South Parks and at the former, this led to the establishment of the business originally known as Fidelitone Inc. of Chicago and then as Sonido. In its heyday, this firm provided a substantial number of local jobs, but the business declined and went into liquidation in 1990.

Meanwhile the activities of the county council were both relevant and complementary to those of the burgh. There were advances both in the provision of housing and housing improvement in the landward area. Up-grading of classified roads continued apace to cope with the ever-increasing volume of traffic. An active Social Work Department was established to look after the care and health of the elderly and the provision of old peoples' homes at Dunwhinny, Peebles and St Ronan's, Innerleithen, well illustrate the county's success in this field.

PART IV

Likewise tourism was not forgotten and the county council provided such facilities as Rosetta Caravan Park with all modern amenities, and this today continues as a successful venture in private hands. Meanwhile, some major services became too costly and extensive to be undertaken by a single authority with modest rateable value and these were made available on the basis of joint funding with neighbouring counties. Such services were Town Planning, Police, Fire and Valuation these being major functions, all of which were absolutely essential to rational development in the post-war era.

The most expensive service provided by the county council was education. The county had to meet the challenge laid down by the provisions of the Education (Scotland) Act 1944 which for the first time opened up the opportunity of higher and university education to all, irrespective of means. Not only were schools modernised and upgraded throughout the county to meet the demands of the increase in pupil population, but the Burgh and County High School in Peebles was vastly extended, a new primary school was provided at Priorsford, Peebles, Kingsland Primary School in Peebles reconstructed and a new junior secondary school opened at the Pirn, Innerleithen.

Throughout the half century under review, and indeed both before and after that period, the services provided by local government were funded on the one hand by the rating of heritable property and on the other by government or exchequer subsidy. Such grants calculated on the basis of abstruse formulae, were an effective weapon which central government could wield to control local spending. The basis of rating (now abolished in Scotland so far as domestic property is concerned and replaced by the Community Charge) always reflected a degree of absurdity. By statute, county councils were required to establish Assessors' Departments whose *raison d'être* and sole function was to provide a roll of rateable values calculated on a basis which was entirely fictional, and that for the solitary purpose of fund raising.

The system *vis-à-vis* county council and town council was also unsatisfactory. The duty lay upon county councils to requisition the burghs in their area for a share of each financial year's expenditure on major functions in proportion of rateability and thus, until the town councils were informed, as they had to be by a statutory date in each year, of the extent of their liability, their own plans for the

350

ensuing year had to remain unfinalised so as to ensure the rate that they finally imposed on their ratepayers was not impossibly onerous.

As we move into the mid-1960s and the 1970s, the structure and effectiveness of local authority services came under criticism — described as ineffective, overly expensive, not attracting the highest calibre of staff — and with the view being expressed that larger units would be more efficient and less under the control of central government. These rumblings led to the appointment of a royal commission under the chairmanship of the late Lord Wheatley to examine the existing structure of local government and report with recommendations on its future. The commission's findings led in turn to the passage into law of the Local Government (Scotland) Act 1973 which sounded the death knell of county councils and town councils in Scotland as at 15 May 1975, and to the establishment in their place of regional councils and district councils and also, where desired, community councils.

What then were the implications of these reforms in a local context? Borders Regional Council (basically represented by the four former counties — Peebles, Selkirk, Roxburgh and Berwick) retained the major functions of education, planning, finance, roads and water supply (this latter in succession to shortlived water boards appointed under the Water (Scotland) Act 1949). Services such as Police and Fire continued to be provided on a joint basis with other areas. District councils retained fairly limited jurisdiction over local housing, cleansing, parks, recreation, cemeteries and similar essential local interests.

Noteworthy achievements of the district council in recent years were the provision of a modern swimming baths complex on the site of the central and convenient site of the former Tweedside Mill and the redevelopment of the Cuddyside area with modern municipal housing. Until the introduction of the Community Charge in 1989/90, the rating authority was the region, who having been advised of the district revenue requirements levied a composite rate and accounted to the lesser authority for its share. A new concept was the community council designed to provide a forum for local discussion but without any fund-raising or borrowing powers. Such a council was established in Peebles and in other areas throughout the county.

Regrettably, however, these changes have not proved equal to their early promise — a state of affairs not assisted by the years of excessive inflation which started in 1975. The truth gradually dawned on the population that what had occurred was not a reform of local government but its substitution by a form of regional and district local government remote from the people it existed to serve, just as expensive if not more so than the previous system and even more in day-to-day conflict with central government. The merits and demerits of the Community Charge (Poll Tax) are a subject for discussion outwith the scope of this summary, but all in all, it is true to say that the present structure of local government in Scotland has certainly not found universal approval and is likely to be the subject of further change in the near future, possibly with an emphasis on single-tier authorities, although in fairness it should be recorded that all essential services continue to be provided and the burgh remains a most desirable place of residence.

To end on a personal note, I write these words at the end of a decade when only two ex-provosts of the Royal and Ancient Burgh survive, while I myself remain as the only surviving ex-town clerk.

My recollection is of a friendly and closely-knit town council whose members were also the proud custodians of local tradition, and throughout the Borders there was not only rivalry but lasting friendship and mutual respect between its famous burghs. To typify the spirit which existed, I reproduce in full a letter which I received from the late Provost William Pate of Galashiels on the occasion in 1975 when in its dying days the town council of Peebles unanimously resolved to confer the Honorary Freedom of the Royal Burgh on my wife and myself. It expresses eloquently my own thoughts:

> Lintonbank,
> Galashiels,
> Selkirkshire.
> 22 January 1975.

Dear Mr and Mrs Laverock,

On behalf of my wife and self I write to say how pleased we are to hear that you are to have the Freedom of the Royal Burgh of Peebles which you have served so well, and in whose daily life you have taken such an active and helpful part.

Life is one constant process of change and we must go along with it but in years to come I am sure there will be many backward glances and recollections of more intimate times when local government really was local and its councillors and officers readily available and well known to all, and in that picture in the public mind in Peebles, your names will long be spoken of as part of a system which once was and might still have been.

The decision will give pleasure to all who know you, a compliment which will add lustre to your future activities in the kindly town of Peebles.

Yours sincerely,
(signed) William Pate.

Finally, by way of appendix and for the information of those interested, there is reproduced below a chronological list of those who are known to have served as provosts and town clerks of the burgh throughout the centuries, and also of those who have served as Conveners of the County and County Clerks.

PROVOSTS OF PEEBLES

1555	John, Lord Hay of Yester
1556 – 1562	No record
1562 – 1564	William, Lord Hay of Yester
1565 – 1568	No record
1569 – 1572	William, Lord Hay of Yester
1573 – 1577	No record
1578	William, Lord Hay of Yester
1579 – 1604	No record
1605 – 1606	James, Lord Hay of Yester
1607 – 1609	No record
1609 – 1613	John Dikisoun
1614 – 1619	No record
1620 – 1625	James Williamson
1625 – 1626	Charles Pringil
1626 – 1629	James Williamson
1629 – 1634	John Lowis
1634 – 1636	James Williamson
1636 – 1639	John Lowis
1639 – 1640	James Williamson
1640 – 1641	John Lowis
1641 – 1645	James Williamson
1645 – 1646	John Lowis
1646 – 1648	Patrick Thomson
1648 – 1649	James Williamson

PART IV

1649 – 1650 John Lowes
1650 – 1651 James Williamson
1651 – 1652 John Lowes
1652 – 1655 William Lowes
1655 – 1656 Alexander Williamson
1656 – 1658 John Andrew
1658 – 1660 Alexander Williamson
1660 – 1662 John Plenderleith
1662 – 1664 Alexander Williamson
1664 – 1666 John Plenderleith
1666 – 1669 Alexander Williamson
1669 – 1671 John Plenderleith
1671 – 1675 Alexander Williamson
1675 – 1676 James Horsburgh
1676 – 1680 Gavin Thomson
1680 – 1682 William Plenderleith
1682 – 1684 John Hope
1684 – 1685 William Plenderleith
1685 – 1689 John Govan
1689 – 1691 John Mure
1691 – 1692 Patrick Brotherstanes
1692 – 1694 John Mure
1694 – 1697 Robert Forrester   .
1697 – 1700 Archibald Shiell
1700   Robert Forrester
1700 – 1703 Archibald Shiell
1703 – 1707 John Tueiddy
1707 – 1709 Robert Forrester
1709 – 1711 John Browne
1711 – 1713 John Frier
1713 – 1717 John Jonkiesone
1717 – 1720 Robert Forrester
1720 – 1722 John Stevenson
1722 – 1727 John Ramidge
1727 – 1728 John Williamson
1728 – 1733 Alexander Russell
1733 – 1736 Francis Gibson
1736 – 1741 John Ramidge
1741 – 1747 James Haldine or Haldan
1747 – 1754 John Alexander

1754 – 1760 James Haldan
1760 – 1766 James Ballantyne
1766 – 1771 Francis Russell
1771 – 1773 Walter Ritchie
1773 – 1778 William Ker
1778 – 1783 James Reid
1783 – 1788 Thomas Alexander
1788 – 1803 James Reid
1803 – 1807 James Ker
1807 – 1811 Thomas Smibert
1811 – 1826 James Ker
1826 – 1829 William Turnbull
1829 – 1830 Alexander Renton
1830 – 1836 William Turnbull
1836 – 1838 Walter Thorburn
1838 – 1841 John Paterson
1841 – 1847 Robert Wightman Ker
1847 – 1849 John Stirling
1849   John Paterson (ad interim)
1849 – 1850 Robert Wightman Ker
1850 – 1852 John Paterson
1852 – 1855 William Steuart
1855 – 1864 John Stirling
1864 – 1867 John Paterson
1867 – 1870 John Keddie
1870 – 1875 Robert Todd
1875 – 1877 Robert Veitch
1877 – 1881 Andrew Green
1881 – 1883 Robert Todd
1883 – 1889 William Whitie
1889 – 1892 Robert Mathieson
1892 – 1898 James Paterson Lossock
1898 – 1907 Henry Ballantyne (later Sir Henry Ballantyne)
1907 – 1913 John A. Ballantyne
1913 – 1915 Peter Dalling
1916 – 1921 James Forrester
1921 – 1922 George Wilkie
1922 – 1926 Robert Davidson
1926 – 1933 George Anderson
1933 – 1945 John Fergusson

PART IV

1945 – 1949 William Cleland
1949 – 1954 Arthur Park Daniels
1954 – 1957 John Pace Duthie
1957 – 1967 James Russell Lawrie
1967 – 1970 Alexander William Walker
1970 – 1973 Alexander Melrose
1973 – 1975 Robert Kirkpatrick

TOWN CLERKS

1459 John Donald
1460 Wyl of Balcaske
1462 Thomas Yong
1469 Thomas Yong and William Smayll (joint)
1476 Wullyam Anderson
1483 – 1497 Sir Thomas of Crawfurde
1498 John Bulloc
1500 Sir Patrick of Stanhous
1534 – 1541 John Hay
1542 – 1546 Sir William Newbye
1555 – 1563 Sir John Allane
1563 John Dickeson
1564 David Crychtoun
1565 – 1568 John Dickeson
1571 Sir John Allane
1578 John Hay
1594 – 1623 John Teudie
1623 – 1649 Patrick Veitch
1650 Thomas Crawford
1651 – 1674 Thomas Smyth
1674 – 1704 William Williamson
1704 – 1735 James Brotherstanes
1735 – 1774 John McEwen
1774 – 1781 James Summers
1781 – 1783 John McEwen
1783 – 1793 William Little
1793 – 1833 Alexander Williamson
1833 – 1835 William McIntosh
1835 – 1853 John Fotheringham
1853 – 1863 John Bathgate

356

1863 – 1880 James Duncan Bathgate
1880 – 1906 William Buchan
1906 – 1948 James Walter Buchan
1948 – 1975 Edward Laverock

CONVENERS OF THE COUNTY OF PEEBLES

1890 – 1901 Sir G. Graham-Montgomery of Stanhope, Bart.
1901   Thomas Tweedie Stodart of Oliver
1901 – 1902 Sir Thomas Gibson Carmichael of Skirling, Bart.
1902 – 1932 Sir Michael G. Thorburn of Glenormiston
1932 – 1958 Sir Ronald J. Thomson of Kaimes
1958 – 1967 Sir James D. Dundas of Arniston, Bart., OBE
1967 – 1975 Major Douglas J. Anderson, MC

COUNTY CLERKS

1889 – 1891 William Blackwood
1891 – 1892 William Blackwood and John Ramsay Smith (joint)
1892 – 1926 John Ramsay Smith
1926 – 1936 John Ramsay Smith and William T. Blackwood, MC
                (joint)
1936 – 1941 John Ramsay Smith
1941 – 1955 John Mackie
1955 – 1975 Walter Geddes, MBE

CHAPTER 22

Parliamentary Representation from 1790

PEEBLES DISTRICT OF BURGHS
(Peebles, Selkirk, Linlithgow, Lanark)
Elected: Member:

1790	William Grieve, London
1796	Rt. Hon. Viscount Stopford
1801	Rt. Hon. Viscount Stopford
1802	Lieutenant-Colonel William Dickson of Kilbucho
1806	Lieutenant-General Sir Charles Lockhart-Ross, of Balnagowan, 7th Baronet
1807	William Maxwell, Carriden
1812	Sir John Buchanan Riddell of Riddell, 9th Baronet
1818	Sir John Buchanan Riddell of Riddell, 9th Baronet
1819	John Pringle, London
1820	Henry Monteith, Carstairs
1826	Adam Hay, Banker, Edinburgh
1830	Henry Monteith, Carstairs
1831	William D. Gillon of Wallhouse, Bathgate

THE COUNTY AND BURGH OF PEEBLES

1832	Sir John Hay of Smithfield and Haystoun, 6th Baronet
1835	Sir John Hay of Smithfield and Haystoun, 6th Baronet
1837	William Forbes Mackenzie of Portmore
1841	William Forbes Mackenzie of Portmore
1845	William Forbes Mackenzie of Portmore
1847	William Forbes Mackenzie of Portmore
1852	Sir Graham Graham-Montgomery of Stanhope, 3rd Baronet
1857	Sir Graham Graham-Montgomery of Stanhope, 3rd Baronet
1859	Sir Graham Graham-Montgomery of Stanhope, 3rd Baronet

Elected: Member:

1865   Sir Graham Graham-Montgomery of Stanhope, 3rd Baronet
1866   Sir Graham Graham-Montgomery of Stanhope, 3rd Baronet

THE UNITED COUNTIES OF PEEBLES AND SELKIRK

1868   Sir Graham Graham-Montgomery of Stanhope, 3rd Baronet
1874   Sir Graham Graham-Montgomery of Stanhope, 3rd Baronet
1880   Charles Tennant of Glen
1885   Sir Charles Tennant of Glen, 1st Baronet
1886   Walter Thorburn
1892   Walter Thorburn of Glenbreck
1895   Walter Thorburn of Glenbreck
1902   Sir Walter Thorburn of Glenbreck
1906   Hon A. C. W. O. Murray, Master of Elibank
1910   William Younger of Auchen Castle
1910   Donald Maclean

PEEBLES AND SOUTH MIDLOTHIAN

1918   Sir Donald Maclean
1922   Joseph Westwood
1923   Joseph Westwood
1924   Joseph Westwood
1929   Joseph Westwood
1931   Captain A. H. Maule Ramsay
1935   Captain A. H. Maule Ramsay*
1945   D. J. Pryde

MIDLOTHIAN AND PEEBLESSHIRE

1950   D. J. Pryde
1951   D. J. Pryde

ROXBURGH, SELKIRKSHIRE AND PEEBLESSHIRE

1955   C. E. M. Donaldson
1959   C. E. M. Donaldson

* Captain A. H. Maule Ramsay was detained during the period of the Second World War under the provisions of 18B of the Defence Regulations; the constituency was represented by Mr David Robertson, Member of Parliament for Streatham

PART IV

Elected: Member:

1964	C. E. M. Donaldson
1965	David Steel
1966	David Steel
1970	David Steel
1974*	David Steel
1979	David Steel
1983	David Steel
1987	David Steel (now Sir David Steel, KBE)

* Elections in February and October 1974

Sources: From 1790 to 1935 — *The Tweeddale Shooting Club: A Sesqui-Centennial Memoir 1790–1940.* Edited and compiled by Captain George Wolfe Murray (Edinburgh, 1950) pp 114–15; thereafter from other records.

CHAPTER 23

The Lord-Lieutenants and Sheriffs of Peeblesshire

Year:
1794	Rt. Hon. Alexander Murray, 7th Baron Elibank
1821	Rt. Hon. Francis Charteris, 8th Earl of Wemyss and March
1853	Rt. Hon. Francis Charteris, 9th Earl of Wemyss and March
1880	Colin James Mackenzie of Portmore
1896	Rt. Hon. Montolieu Fox Oliphant Murray, 10th Baron and (1911) 1st Viscount Elibank
1908	Rt. Hon. Edward Priaulx Tennant, 2nd Baronet and (1911) 1st Baron Glenconner of Glen
1921	Rt. Hon. Thomas David Gibson-Carmichael, 11th Baronet and 1st Baron Carmichael of Skirling, GCSI, GCIE, KCMG
1926	Sir (1933) Michael Grieve Thorburn of Glenormiston
1934	Rt. Hon. (Charles) Gideon Murray, 11th Baron and 2nd Viscount Elibank
1945	Lieut.-Colonel William Thorburn of Craigerne, DSO, TD
1956	Captain Sir Ronald Jordan Thomson of Kaimes
1968	Sir Robert Heatlie Scott, GCMG, CBE
1980	Lieut.-Colonel Aidan Mark Sprot, MC, of Haystoun

Sources: From 1794 to 1945 —*The Tweeddale Shooting Club, a Sesqui-Centennial Memoir, 1790 – 1940,* edited and compiled by Captain George Wolfe Murray (Edinburgh, 1950) p113; thereafter updated.

SHERIFFS

Period:
1184	Symon, son of Malbeth, Sheriff of Traquair
1227	John, Sheriff of Peebles
1233-*c.*1259	Sir Gilbert Fraser, Sheriff of Traquair]

PART IV

From which time it seems to have been heritable in the family of Hay, Lords Yester, Marquises of Tweeddale, until 1686, and after that in the family of Douglas, Earls of March, until the abolition of heritable Jurisdiction after the rebellion of 1745; but John, 3rd Lord Hay of Yester, for letting two thieves escape, was deprived of the office on 27 September 1530, and it was given in December of that year to Malcolm, Lord Flemyng. Lord Yester fought the matter in the Court of Session, and the forfeiture of the office was declared null on 28 April 1543.

From 1821 as shown in Buchan ((iii) pp620 – 21), sheriffs who later became known as sheriffs principal

Period:

had sheriff-substitutes carrying out the actual administration of justice in and running the courts.

From the 1920s sheriffdoms were amalgamated and one sheriff principal had two, three or more former sheriffdoms — but the individual sheriff-substitute system remained. Now known simply as 'sheriff' they continued to run the individual courts. One well-known predecessor of the present sheriff in Peebles was Thomas Henderson Orphoot, sheriff-substitute for no less than forty-four years, 1873 – 1917.

Since 1927 the sheriffs (still, for a time, known as sheriff-substitute) were:

1928 – 1937	William Mitchell
1937 – 1942	Kenneth Douglas Cullen
1942 – 1945	Allan Grierson Walker
1945 – 1952	Joseph McCaig Smart
1952 – 1957	James Aikman Smith
1957 – 1967	Donald McLeod
1968 – 1978	Isobel Lilias Sinclair, QC
1979 – 1985	Neil MacVicar, QC
1985	Nigel Ernest Drummond Thomson

In the times above, sheriffs principal of the combined sheriffdoms of Edinburgh, the Lothians and Peebles later extended to the whole Borders as simply 'Lothians and Borders', were Sir John Fenton, Sir James Gilchrist, Sinclair Shaw, Sir Ross McLean, Sir William Brydon and Sir Michael O'Brien—all KC or later QC.

Sources: 1288 to 1927 — *A History of Peeblesshire,* edited by J. Walter Buchan (Glasgow 1925, 1927) Vol III, pp620-21; thereafter up-dated.

THE FALLEN

When you go home, tell them of us,
Say for your to-morrow we gave our today.

THE FIRST WORLD WAR: 1914 to 1918

D. Adam
J. Amos
G. Anderson
T. M. Archibald
J. H. Baillie
J. Bain
W. Baigrie
W. Blaikie
G. Bortfield
James Brockie
J. N. Brockie
J. Brown
J. Bruce
A. E. Buchan
D. Cairncross
R. L. Callan
J. Cavanagh
T. M. Clark
A. Collier
J. W. Craig
J. Davidson
G. Dick
A. J. Dow
W. Drudge
J. H. Duncan
W. Elliot
J. D. Forrester
A. French
J. Foster
R. Freer
F. T. Gillet
J. H. Hamilton
D. Harkness

Sister Ainsworth
D. Anderson
J. Anderson
A. Armstrong
A. Bain
F. Ball
A. Babron
G. Blake
L. Bottomley
James K. Brockie
J. N. K. Brockie
T. A. Brown
J. Brunton
T. Buchan
J. Caldwell
W. H. Campbell
J. M. Cavers
T. G. C. Clark
P. Conlan
C. S. Currie
W. H. Davies
H. W. Dougall
J. Downie
A. N. Duncan
G. A. Dunn
D. C. Ferguson
J. D. Frame
J. French
J. Fraser
G. Gardner
E. C. Gorman
R. H. Hamilton
P. Hart

R. F. Aitchison
E. Anderson
J. D. Anderson
J. H. Arrol
G. Bain
W. Ball
R. Black
A. Bogle
A. C. Boyd
J. C. Brockie
J. Brown
J. Brownlee
T. E. Brydon
C. R. Bush
D. Caldwell
G. D. Carlan
J. R. T. Chalmers
W. H. Clark
E. J. Cook
H. J. Dalling
J. Denholm
J. Dougan
J. Drummond
J. Duncan
R. Elder
T. Ferguson
R. Frame
J. Forbes
W. C. Fraser
J. Gethin
J. W. Gray
J. Hannan
G. Henderson

364

J. Heugh
J. Horsbrugh
N. Hunter
F. Inverarity
C. T. Ker
W. Laidlaw
D. Lawson
J. G. Liddle
J. Lyon
A. R. N. Malcolm
J. Mathison
A. Michie
T. Millar
A. B. Mitchell
C. Moodie
T. Murdie
J. S. Maclaughlan
J M'Donald
R. W. M'Gill
J. M'Lean
W. M'Morran
W. Oldham
G. Philp
J. Ramsay
J. Reid
J. C. Richardson
E. Russell
R. Scott
W. D. Smith
J. Sterrick
W. Stewart
A. R. Struthers
F. G. Taylor
J. Thomson
L. D. Thomson
J. D. Todd
J. N. Turnbull
J. Veitch
A. Walker
W. Weir

J. Hislop
R. C. D. Hume
H. R. Hush
R. N. Jervis
J. Laidlaw
A. V. Lamb
H. Lawson
J. Little
I. Maddison
A. Mason
J. Maule
W. Michie
J. Milne
A. S. Mitchell
A. H. Mowat
C. R. Murray
J. Macnab
A. R. M'Dougal
R. M'Kay
J. A. M'Martin
H. Neilson
W. Pace
R. Pieroni
T. M'L. Ramsay
W. Reid
J. A. Robertson
W. M. Russell
A. Scougall
G. W. Snow
A. R. Stevenson
R. C. Stewart
C. Swindley
T. Taylor
J. L. Thomson
W. E. Thorburn
J. G. Trench
J. Turner
M. Veitch
R. S. Walker
A. Wilson

A. Hogarth
W. S. Hunter
W. Inglis
J. Johnston
R. Laidlaw
R. Lawrie
J. Lawson
J. S. R. Lorraine
A. N. Malcolm
J. Mason
J. Maule
R. Millar
A. Mitchell
J. Moffat
R. P. Mulholland
W. Murray
J M'Cabe
L. C. M'Gill
J. L. B. M'Lean
W. M'Morran
D. D. Nisbet
D. Philp
J. Porteous
R. Rankine
J. T. Rennie
C. L. Russell
J. Scott
R. Scougall
C. R. Steele
C. S. Stevenson
J. Stodart
F. G. Tarry
E. W. Thiem
J. M. Thomson
R. Tod
James Turnbull
A. Veitch
A. F. Veitch
D. Weir
C. E. Wilson

J. S. Wilson	J. A. Wilson	T. A. Wilson
R. Wood	A. Young	A. G. Young

SECOND WORLD WAR: 1939 to 1945

G. O. Anderson	D. Bennet	J. Bogle
T. Buchan	W. Buchan	W. Bye
A. D. Cairncross	J. T. Carruthers	A. M. Cockburn
R. G. Coulthard	A. L. Cowan	Fay Currie
W. Currie	A. J. Davidson	R. Dickson
E. S. Galbraith	J. Gilchrist	R. Gilmour
A. Goggins	A. Harrington	C. M. Harrower
P. Hay	G. C. Jardine	D. M. R. Johnstone
J. W. Johnstone	N. W. Johnstone	F. Kilner
J. Laidlaw	J. C. Lawrie	J. W. Lowrie
R. Macdonald	C. P. H. Maclaren	G. L. M'Cafferty
A. M'Donald	J. M'Lauchlan	T. H. Marshall
A. W. Milne	A. Morris	R. Mowat
J. Muir	A. Murray	J. Murray
W. Murray	W. Porter	J. P. Power
I. Pretswell	D. Pringle	R. Raeburn
J. Ramsay	J. F. Rennie	R. Ryan
R. C. Scott	W. Scott	A. Smith
J. Smith	A. Sterricks	R. Stewart
E. R. Swan	G. Swanson	A. J. Thorburn
M. V. Thorburn	W. I. E. Thorburn	W. S. Thorburn
J. Todd	A. M. Wallace	F. White
P. G. Wilson	J. Wright	R. Wright
A. Young		

BIBLIOGRAPHY

THIS LIST COVERS works relating to Peeblesshire or Tweeddale which are held in the Peebles Area Library, but excludes maps, 'imaginative works' such as poetry and fiction, neither does it contain articles reprinted from journals or periodicals.

The list is arranged sectionally and alphabetically by area and by author/title, beginning with works of a general nature and moving to works on specific places, e.g. Manor, Peebles, Stobo.

Entries are catalogued using a short entry, and where works are both published and written (or edited) by the same person, the name of the printer and the place of printing have generally been given; while not best practice, it does in some cases give an idea of the 'local imprint' and the number of printers who once flourished in Peebles. Where the place of publication is unknown, the abbreviation 's.1' has been used, and where the data concerning the publication is uncertain square brackets [—] have been used.

PEEBLESSHIRE: GENERAL

ANDERSON, D. Brown, *Reminiscences with occasional essays* (Allan Smyth, Peebles, 1906) printed for private circulation

BUCHAN, J. W. (ed), *A History of Peeblesshire* (Jackson, Wylie & Co., Glasgow, 1925 – 7) three vols

CENSUS 1971, *Scotland: County Report, Peebles* (HMSO, Edinburgh, 1973)

CHAMBERS, William, *A History of Peeblesshire* (W. & R. Chambers, Edinburgh, 1864)

DOUGLAS, Sir G., *A History of the Border Counties: Roxburgh, Selkirk and Peebles: with a bibliography of those counties* (Blackwood, Edinburgh, 1899)

FINDLATER, Revd C., *A General View of the Agriculture of the County of Peebles* (Constable, Edinburgh, 1802)

GUIDE TO PEEBLESSHIRE and adjacent County including St Mary's Loch and the Grey Mare's Tail (Watson, Peebles, s.1)

HOPKINS, W. J., *Factors Influencing Land Use in the Southern Uplands of Scotland* ([NATO], s.1)

INSTRUCTIONS TO A CONSTABLE in the County of Peebles (Hay & Co., Edinburgh, 1815)

MEARS, F., and MOTTRAM, A. H., *Report on the Planning of the County of Peebles* (Peeblesshire County Council, 1946)

PATERSON, William (ed), *Peeblesiana — Newspaper Cuttings connected with the County of Peebles* (Vol 1, 1868, Vol 2, [Leith], 1869)

PEEBLEAN SOCIETY, Minutes Book of the Social Peeblean Society 1782 – 1857

PEEBLESSHIRE: An inventory of the ancient monuments (Royal Commission on Ancient and Historic Monuments, Edinburgh, 1967) two vols

PEEBLESSHIRE: Jewel in the Borders, Official Guide (Peeblesshire Tourist Association)

PEEBLESSHIRE REGISTRATION COURT, Fictitious Votes (Peeblesshire Registration Court, Millar & Fairley, Edinburgh, [1847])

PEEBLESSHIRE SOCIETY, Minutes, accounts, cuttings, etc. 1896 – 1934

PEEBLESSHIRE SOCIETY, Proceedings at the 119th Anniversary Meeting (Neidpath Press, Peebles, 1901)

PRINGLE, George C., *The Counties of Peebles and Selkirk* (Cambridge University Press, Cambridge, 1914)

RAY, Gilbert, *Historical Haunts of Peeblesshire* (Oliver & Boyd, London, 1914)

RENWICK, R., *Historical Notes on Peeblesshire Localities* (Watson & Smyth, Peebles, 1897)

SANDERSON, William, *Peeblesshire Official Guide* (Dundee, s.1)

SCOTT, Sheila A., *Monumental Inscriptions (pre-1885) in Peeblesshire* (Scottish Genealogy Society, 1971)

SINCLAIR, Sir J. (ed), *The Statistical Account of Scotland* (Wm. Creech, Edinburgh, 1797 – 9) 21 vols (Vol 12)

THE NEW STATISTICAL ACCOUNT for Scotland, Committee for the Society for the Benefit of the Sons and Daughters of the Clergy (Blackwood, Edinburgh, 1845) 15 vols (Vol 3)

THE THIRD STATISTICAL ACCOUNT of Scotland, Scottish Council of Social Services (Oliver & Boyd, &c, Edinburgh, 1951 – 3) Vol 24

SMITH, Herbert H., *Recollections of a Tweeddale Laddie* (Thomson, Selkirk, 1987)

TOURIST DEVELOPMENT Proposals and Areas of Great Landscape Value (Peeblesshire County Council, [1968])

VEITCH, John, *Border Essays* (Blackwood, Edinburgh, 1896)

VEITCH, John, *The History and Poetry of the Scottish Border* (Maclehose, Glasgow, 1878)

WATSON, James, *Peeblesshire and its Outland Borders* (Allan Smyth, Peebles, 3rd ed, [1906])

[WATSON, Jean L.] *Peeblesshire and its Historical Ruins; Selkirkshire and its Places of Interest; Roxburgh and its History* ([Edinburgh], 1874)

BARNS

BURNETT, Montgomery, *A Genealogical Account of the Family of Burnett* (printed privately, Edinburgh, 1880)

BROUGHTON

BAIRD, Andrew, *The Annals of a Tweeddale Parish: the History of the United Parish of Broughton, Glenholm and Kilbucho* (John Smith, Glasgow, 1924)

FORRESTER, David M., *Broughton Free Kirk and thereabouts, 1843 – 1943 — a Centenary Record of the Congregation's Story* (Neidpath Press, Peebles, 1943)

FOX, Andrew, *The Kirk in the Midst: the Story of the Parish Church of Broughton, Glenholm and Kilbucho* (Kirk Session of Broughton, Glenholm and Kilbucho, [1985])

SCOTT, Sheila A. (ed), *Glimpses of Old Broughton* (Biggar Museum Trust, Biggar, 1985)

CARLOPS

RAMSAY, Allan. *Book of the Carlops Festival* (Scots Secretariat, Carlops, [1978])

DAWYCK

GUNN, C. B., *The Church of Dawyck, AD1571 – 1930* (Neidpath Press, Peebles, 1931)

DRUMELZIER

GUNN, C. B., *The Church at Drumelzier, AD1531 – 1930* (Neidpath Press, Peebles, 1931)

EDDLESTON

MURRAY, A. C., *Blackbarony, Part 1* (R. Clark, Edinburgh, 1978)

MURRAY, A. C., *The Five Sons of Bare Betty* (Murray, London, 1936)

PART IV

ELIBANK

MURRAY, A. C., *The Five Sons of Bare Betty* (Murray, London, 1936)

MURRAY, A. C., *Memorial of Sir Gideon Murray of Elibank* (Orr, Edinburgh, 1932)

GLENORMISTON

CHAMBERS, William, *Glenormiston* (printed for private use, 1849)

INNERLEITHEN

ANDERSON, Harry, *Innerleithen and Traquair, Ancient and Modern* (New Horizon, Bognor Regis, 1984)

ANDERSON, John A., *The Cleikum — being interesting reminiscences of Old Innerleithen* (Galashiels, 1933)

DOBSON, Thomas, *Reminiscences of Innerleithen and Traquair* (R. Smail, Innerleithen, 1896)

INNERLEITHEN GOLF CLUB, 1886 – 1986 (Innerleithen Golf Club, [1986])

PRINCIPAL EXCURSIONS of the Innerleithen Alpine Club (McQueen, Galashiels, 1895)

ST JAMES'S Innerleithen Centenary, 1881 – 1981 [Innerleithen, 1981]

KAILZIE

GUNN, C. B., *The Church of Traquair and the Church of Kailzie AD1170 – 1930* (Neidpath Press, Peebles, 1931)

KIRKURD

IN MEMORY of Revd David Mitchell, Kirkurd (Elliot, Edinburgh, 1897)

MANOR

CHAMBERS, William, *Life of David Ritchie* (William Brown, Edinburgh, 1885). Reprint of *The Life and Anecdotes of the Black Dwarf* (Edinburgh, 1820)

FERGUSON, J., *The Black Dwarf: A Peeblesshire Legend* (author's typescript)

PEEBLES

ARMSTRONG, Captain, *A Companion to the Map of the County of Peeblesshire; a Geographical Description of Peeblesshire* (Edinburgh, 1775)

ARTICLES AND REGULATIONS of the Friendly Society of Masons of the Old Lodge of Peebles, No XXI (Alex Elder, Peebles, 1817)

BRYCE, Mary R. L., *Memoirs of John Veitch, LLD* (Blackwood & Sons, Glasgow, 1896)

CHAMBERS INSTITUTION: *Handbook to the Chambers Institution* (W. & R. Chambers, Edinburgh, 1859)

CHAMBERS INSTITUTION LIBRARY, Catalogue of Books in the Library (W. & R. Chambers, Edinburgh, 1882)

CHAMBERS, Robert, *Peebles and its Neighbourhood, with a Run on the Railway* (W. & R. Chambers, Edinburgh, 1856)

CHAMBERS, William, *Memoir of Robert Chambers, with Autobiographical Reminiscences of William Chambers, LLD* (W. & R. Chambers, Edinburgh, 1880)

CHAMBERS, W. and RENWICK R., *Charters and Documents relating to Peebles, with Extracts from the Records AD1165 – 1710* (Scottish Burgh Records Society, Edinburgh, 1872)

GOURLAY, R. and TURNER, A., *The Archaeological Implications of Development: Historic Peebles* (Scottish Burgh Survey, Glasgow, 1977)

GROSART, James, *Chronicles of Peebles: Chronicles from Peebles Briggate* (Peebles Press, Peebles, 1899)

GUNN, C. B., *The Book of Peebles Church, St Andrew's Collegiate Parish Church AD1195 – 1560* (Peebles, 1908)

GUNN, C. B., *The Ministry of the Presbytery of Peebles, AD296 – 1910* (Neidpath Press, Peebles, 1910)

GUNN, C. B., *The Church and Monastery of the Holy Cross of Peebles, the Abbey of the Trinitie called the Croce Kirk AD1261 – 1560* (George Allan, Peebles, [1909])

GUNN, C. B. *The Book of the Cross Kirk, Peebles, AD1560 – 1690 Presbyterianism versus Episcopacy* (Allan Smyth/Neidpath Press, Peebles, 1912)

GUNN, C. B., *The Book of the Croce Kirk, Peebles, AD1690 – 1784 Secular Presbyterianism* (Allan Smyth/Neidpath Press, Peebles, 1914)

GUNN, C. B., *The Parish Church of Peebles, AD1784 – 1885* (Allan Smyth, Peebles, 1917)

GUNN, C. B., *The Manual of the Cross Kirk, Peebles, AD1261 – 1914* (Allan Smyth, Peebles, 1914)

371

PART IV

[GUNN, C. B. (translator), *Peebles to the Play* (Lewis, Selkirk) *see also* A. M. KINGHORN]

[GUNN, C. B. (translator), *Rait's Raving* (Allan Smyth/Neidpath Press, Peebles, 1918)]

[GUNN, C. B. (translator), *The Three Tales of the Three Priests of Peebles* (Lewis, Selkirk, 1894)]

GUNN, C. B., *Leaves from the Life of a Country Doctor* (ed R. Crockett), (Ettrick Press, Edinburgh, 1935)

JOHNSON, Christopher Yates, *A History of St Peter's Church* (Peebles, s.1)

KINGHORN, A. M. (ed), *Peblis to the Play* (Quarto Press, London, 1974)

MAYLARD, A. E., *Walks in and around Peebles, with Motor Routes,* 2nd ed (1937, s.1)

PEEBLES BELTANE FESTIVAL Jubilee Book, 1899 – 1949 (J. A. Kerr, Peebles, 1949)

PEEBLES DRAFT LOCAL PLAN (Borders Regional Council, Department of Planning and Development, [1982])

PEEBLES MARCH RIDING and Beltane Queen Festival, 1899 – 1974 (Hawick Press, Hawick, 1974)

PEEBLES GUILDRY CORPORATION (Kemp, Dalkeith, 1956)

PEEBLES RUGBY FOOTBALL CLUB, Isle of Man Tour, 26 – 30 March 1987 (Peebles Rugby Football Club, Peebles, 1987)

PEEBLES TOWN WALK: A Short Guided Tour of the Royal Burgh (Peebles Civic Society, Peebles, 1971)

PROCEEDINGS AT PEEBLES on Entertaining and Presenting the Freedom of the Burgh to Messrs W. and R. Chambers of Edinburgh (Edinburgh, 1841)

RENWICK, R., *Aisle and Monastery: St Mary of Geddes Aisle in the Parish Church of Peebles; and the Church and Monastery of the Holy Cross of Peebles* (Carson & Nicol, Glasgow, 1897)

RENWICK, R., *The Burgh of Peebles: Gleanings from its Records, 1604 – 52* (Watson & Smyth, Peebles, 1892); 2nd ed (Smyth, Peebles, 1912)

RENWICK, R., *Extracts from Records of the Burgh of Peebles, 1652 – 1714, with Appendix 1367 – 1665* (Scottish Burgh Records Society, Glasgow, 1910)

RENWICK, R., *Peebles, Burgh and Parish, in Early History, with Appendix, a descriptive list of Old Charters and Documents* (A. Redpath, Peebles, 1903)

RENWICK, R., *Peebles During the Reign of Queen Mary: with Appendix of Historical Notes and Illustrations* (Neidpath Press, Peebles, 1903)

REPORT ON THE PROCEEDINGS of the Ceremony of Handing Over the Fountain . . . Erected in Peebles in Memory of John Veitch (Watson & Smyth, Peebles, 1898)

ROBB, R. B. and STEVENSON, E. R., *Glimpses of Old Peebles* (Royal Burgh of Peebles Callants Club, Peebles, 1987)

SCOTT, S. A., *John Bathgate, a Sketch of His Life and Times in Edinburgh, Peebles and Dunedin* (Selkirk, 1977)

SCOTT, S. A. (ed), *My Dear Cath: the Study of an Army Doctor's Wife in 1818 – 19* (Selkirk, 1976)

SCOTT, S. A., *Chambers Institution, Peebles* (Selkirk, 1978)

SCOTT, S. A. (ed), *Peebles Gutterbluid Club, Extracts of Minutes 1823 – 83* (Peebles 1973)

SCOTT, S. A., *Thomas Young of Rosetta* (Selkirk, 1980)

TURNER, Richard, *A Descriptive Catalogue of the Geological Collection in the Chambers Institution, Peebles* (James Thin, Edinburgh, 1927)

WILLIAMSON, Revd A., *Glimpses of Peebles, or Forgotten Chapters in its History* (Lewis, Selkirk, 1895)

WILSON, G. W., *Photograph Souvenir (of Peebles)* (Aberdeen, [pre-1887])

SKIRLING

CAMERON, A. D., *The man who loved to draw horses, James Howe, 1780 – 1836* (Aberdeen University Press, 1986)

STOBO

GUNN, C. B., *The Book of Stobo Church* (Anderson, Peebles, 1907)

RANDALL, John, *Stobo — An Introduction to a Rural Area* (Stobo Countryside Centre, [1986])

TALLA

TAIT, W. A., *Notes regarding the Old and New Talla Works of the Edinburgh & District Water Trust* (Banks & Co., Edinburgh, 1905)

TRAQUAIR

ANDERSON, Harry, *Innerleithen and Traquair, Ancient and Modern* (New Horizon, Bognor Regis, 1984)

DOBSON, Thomas, *Reminiscences of Innerleithen and Traquair* (R. Smail, Innerleithen, 1896)
GUNN, C. B., *The Church of Traquair and the Church of Kailzie, AD1170–1930* (Neidpath Press, Peebles, 1931)
MURRAY, A. C., *The Five Sons of Bare Betty* (Murray, London, 1936)

TWEED

BURNETT, George, *Companion to Tweed* (Methuen, London, 1938)
MAXWELL, Sir H., *The Story of Tweed* (Nisbet, London, 1909)
RAE, Gilbert, *Tween Clyde and Tweed* (Macdonald, London, 1919)

TWEEDDALE
(See also Peeblesshire/General)

ARTICLES, REGULATIONS AND RESOLUTIONS of the Tweeddale Police Association (A. Elder, Peebles, 1820)
GRANT, Will, *Tweeddale* (Oliver & Boyd, Edinburgh, 1948)
GUNN, C. B., *The Book of Remembrance for Tweeddale, Burgh and Parish, Book I: August 1914 – May 1917* (Allan Smyth/ Neidpath Press, Peebles, 1920)
GUNN, C. B., *The Book of Remembrance for Tweeddale, Burgh and Parish of Peebles, Book II: June 1917 – July 1919* (Allan Smyth/Peebles, 1921)
GUNN, C. B., *The Book of Remembrance for Tweeddale, the Village of West Linton* [Linton Roderick] (Allan Smyth, Peebles, 1923)
GUNN, C. B., *The Book of Remembrance for Tweeddale, Landward Parishes* (J. A. Kerr, Peebles, 1925)
MORRISON, C. M. (ed), *A Checklist of the Birds in Tweeddale (Peeblesshire)* (Scottish Wildlife Trust (Peebles Support Group), 1978)
MURRAY, Captain George Wolfe (ed), *The Tweeddale Shooting Club, a Sesqui-centennial Memoir, 1790–1940* (Oliver & Boyd, Edinburgh, 1950)
P(ENNICUIK), A(lexander), *A Geographical, Historical Description of Tweeddale . . . with Poems* (John Munro, Edinburgh, 1715)
[PENNICUIK, Alexander, *Works in Prose and Verse* (Allardice, Leith, 1815)]
TWEEDDALE GUIDE (Tweeddale District Council, Galashiels, [1977])

TWEEDDALE in the Scottish Borders — Official Guide (Tweeddale District Council, [1981])
TWEEDDALE OFFICIAL GUIDE, (Tweeddale District Council. [1986])
TWEEDDALE SHOOTING CLUB, *A Centenary Memorial, 1790 – 1890* ([Peebles], 1890) *see also* Captain George Wolfe Murray

WALKERBURN

HENRY BALLANTYNE & SONS LTD, Walkerburn (Biographical Publishing Co., London, 1929)
WALKERBURN RUGBY FOOTBALL CLUB, Centenary Official Brochure (Walkerburn Rugby Football Club, 1984)

WEST LINTON

GUNN, C. B., *The Book of Linton Church, Peeblesshire,* AD*1160 – 1912.* (Allan Smyth/Neidpath Press, Peebles, 1912)
GUNN, C. B., *The Book of Remembrance for Tweeddale, the Village of West Linton* [Linton Roderick] (Allan Smyth, Peebles, 1923)
PATERSON, Isabelle, *West Linton; A Brief Historical Guide* (West Linton Antiquaries Association, [1982])

FURTHER SOURCES:

BIBLIOGRAPHY OF SCOTLAND (National Library of Scotland, Edinburgh, 1976/77 — to date)
HANCOCK, P.D., *A Bibliography of Works Relating to Scotland* (Edinburgh University Press, Edinburgh, 1959 – 60) two vols
MITCHELL, A. and CASH, C. G., *A Contribution to a Bibliography of Scottish Topography* (Constable, Edinburgh, 1917) two vols
SINTON, J., *List of Books relating to or published in the Counties of Roxburgh, Selkirk or Peebles,* in Sir G. Douglas's *History of Roxburgh, Selkirk and Peebles* (Edinburgh, 1899), also issued separately

Index

Index

RB